Research Approaches to
PERSONALITY

Research Approaches to
PERSONALITY

Kathleen M. White

Joseph C. Speisman

Boston University

Brooks/Cole Publishing Company

Monterey, California

To B. B. M., E. W. M., and D. B. W. with great affection

Consulting Editor: Lawrence S. Wrightsman, University of Kansas

Brooks/Cole Publishing Company
A Division of Wadsworth, Inc.

Library of Congress Cataloging in Publication Data

White, Kathleen M., date
Research approaches to personality.

Includes bibliographies and index.
1. Personality—Research. I. Speisman,
Joseph Chester, date   . II. Title.
BF698.W456   155.2'072   81–17011
ISBN 0–8185–0497–8   AACR2

Subject Editor: *Claire Verduin*
Manuscript Editor: *Suzanne Lipsett*
Production Editor: *Suzanne Ewing*
Interior Design: *Jamie Sue Brooks*
Cover Design and Photo: *Stan Rice*
Illustrations: *Brenda Booth*
Typesetting: *Typography Systems International, Dallas, Texas*

Preface

Research Approaches to Personality is a combined text, laboratory manual and reader. Designed to introduce undergraduate students to the systematic study of the person, the book has a unique format: a) chapters focusing on research issues and techniques, b) exercises providing direct, personal experience in the research process, and c) original research reports illustrating the designs and methods under consideration in the chapters. Early chapters orient students to such basics as reading scientific articles critically and formulating research questions. Considerable attention is given to the ethics of research as well as to unobtrusive research approaches such as content analyses and observational studies. The text builds gradually to the more technical, methodological problems involved in test construction and the design of experiments.

Throughout the text we provide examples of empirical strategies that are particularly relevant to the study of personality process, human behavior, and human experience. Whenever possible, we have chosen reports that focus on high-interest areas such as identity and authoritarianism. Because one major goal is to guide students in the design and conduct of their own investigations, we include an appendix containing a primer on statistics, a guide to writing research reports, a mini-report on ethics, and several personality measures for student use.

We owe special appreciation to Lawrence Wrightsman for his thoughtful comments on early versions of the manuscript. We are also grateful to the other reviewers: Janet Beavin Bavelas, University of Victoria; Rae Carlson, Livingston College of Rutgers University; Ed Diener, University of Illinois; Lewis R. Goldberg, Institute of Measurement of Personality; B. Kent Houston, University of Kansas; Donald L. Mosher, University of Connecticut; and Jerry Wiggins, University of British Columbia. Students in our experimental personality classes provided helpful feedback on exercises and selections. Finally, our thanks go to Joanie Spitz, Cathy Imbasciati, Shari Weiss, Debbie Schult, Allison Storms, and Alisa Dennis for their assistance with typing, photocopying, and assembling the manuscript; to Tike Voet and Elinor Macy for their feedback on earlier versions of the manuscript; and to Gordan Kuhan for his help on the index.

Kathleen M. White
Joseph C. Speisman

Contents

5   Observing Behavior in Everyday Settings   70

6   Content Analysis   86

7   Interviews and Questionnaires   111

8 Personality Tests   134

9 The Experimental Method   159

10 Where Do We Go from Here?   186

Appendixes

Exercises

1

General Introduction

THE FIELD OF PERSONALITY

Psychology is an extremely broad and diverse field, stretching from the biological/constitutional/genetic domain at one end of the spectrum to that of social and institutional processes at the other. In the middle, so to speak, lies the individual personality. Most psychologists who specialize in the area of personality believe that this construct provides the central and integrating perspective in the study of human behavior. It is true that scholars and scientists with other viewpoints consider their specialties equally crucial to psychology as a whole, but the reasons cited for the centrality of personality by those who specialize in it seem particularly compelling.

Under the skin, behind the eyeballs, and in the belly of every human being originate the feelings, perceptions, knowledge, illusions, and delusions that color the human condition. Whichever element of human perceptual, cognitive, or social/emotional functioning the psychologist selects for study, it is whole organisms, *people*, that do the seeing, thinking, feeling, or acting. Whether they are observed alone or in groups, in the street or in the laboratory, it is *individuals* who behave, not just brains and muscles. And however carefully scientists watch, measure, and assess, they probably tap only a small proportion of a given individual's total functioning at any particular moment. Can we use the scientific method to describe human functioning adequately and to predict behavior accurately? More properly, is it possible for us to study ourselves completely and scientifically?

Our answer, not surprisingly, is yes. Indeed, it is the purpose of this book to demonstrate some of the major ways in which psychologists study individuals and to teach you to use these methods yourself. Through the text and selected readings, we will illustrate the kinds of questions personality psychologists ask and the procedures they use to find their answers. Exercises and study questions supplement the text and readings to help you develop the skills necessary for understanding and evaluating published research reports and for designing and evaluating studies of your own.

Our major concern in this book is with the ordinary person. Humans rather than lower animals, individuals rather than groups, and normally functioning people rather than groups of patients are the concerns of personality psychology. We explain how to formulate and test questions about personality, as opposed to questions about, for example, intelligence, perceptual ability, or memory. However, maintaining our focus on the person and on personality functioning is not always easy, because the field of personality research is in a major period of transition. Psychologists are currently arguing about what personality is and how it can be studied; however, in providing you with models of empirical studies that you can replicate with relative ease, we are limited to using examples of the research performed in the past. Moreover, we have tried to indicate the directions the field appears to be taking for the future.

The study of personality is both simplified and complicated by the fact that many of the psychologist's methods resemble significantly some common activities associated with daily life. For example, suppose we introduced you to a newcomer in your neighborhood and told you that in two weeks we intended to ask you to describe her personality as completely as you could. What kinds of activities would you engage in to help you in your task? You would probably want to observe the woman's behavior not just once but several times and in a number of different circumstances. You might also want to talk with her directly, asking about her experiences, interests, and goals. Furthermore, you might want to talk with others who know her, asking how they'd rate her on a number of personality characteristics—for example, kindness and honesty. Perhaps you'd even like to put the woman to some sort of "test"—for instance, to see whether she would help when you asked for assistance.

Such everyday activities are similar to techniques to be found in the psychologist's tool chest, but there they have labels such as behavioral observation, interviewing and administering questionnaires, rating scales, and tests. However, some important differences distinguish the ways in which psychologists use their measurement tools from those in which people in the street acquire their information. In particular, psychologists try to be objective and systematic to ensure that their views of a particular phenomenon are not idiosyncratic but can be corroborated by others. Furthermore, as professionals, psychologists agree to relinquish convictions that do not fit with data adequately collected. We hope that, in the process of reading this book, you will come to understand the methods and attitudes of research psychologists and to adopt them in your own pursuit of human understanding.

Of course, psychology isn't about other people alone. You can use scientific methods to try to understand yourself too. Thus, we begin with you. Who are you? Why do you do the things you do? How did you come to be the person you are? In what ways are you like all other people? some other people? no other person? On a more general level, these are the questions that interest personality psychologists, or *personologists*[1], as they are sometimes called. The task of

[1]Murray (1938) describes the field of personality as the branch of psychology that is concerned with the scientific study of human lives and the factors that influence them, with a focus on individual differences and personality types. The emphasis in the personological approach is on the wholistic study of individuals, with a recognition of both the complexity of personality and its developmental changes over time.

personologists is exceptionally complex and challenging—to understand people as *total* individuals who develop over time and who act and react within complex and changing environments.

You, like many students of psychology, might be eager to find answers to the question "Who am I?" Before we proceed any further, it will be useful for you to think a little about your answers to that question. Right now, without reading beyond this paragraph, take a sheet of paper and write "Who am I?" at the top. Start 20 lines with the words "I am . . ."; then finish each sentence with your answer to the question "Who am I?"

When your list is complete, consider how many aspects of your total being your responses cover. Did you make reference to any of your basic biological characteristics—for example, your sex, hair color, or age? How about the groups to which you belong, such as family, religion, and political party? Have you described yourself in motivational terms, as hopeful for success, for instance, or eager to have friends? And what about the emotional aspects of your experience—did you describe yourself as, say, happy or worried? Did you note down any cognitive characteristics such as intelligence and curiosity, or any interpersonal characteristics such as friendliness and trustworthiness?

This exercise should help you to see that even in a quick, simple task in which you are asked to describe yourself, you can identify many different levels and aspects of your total personality. But an exploration of personality only begins with the identification of various parts of the whole. Another problem lies in understanding how all these parts fit together, with each other and with other characteristics not identified in the exercise. Yet another problem is discovering how you have come to be the way you are and why you do what you do—which includes accounting for your use of the particular terms you chose to describe yourself. Furthermore, how can you be sure that your

description of yourself is accurate? What if somebody else described you with a very different set of terms?

Clearly, the task of the personologist is a difficult one. Trying to develop a full and clear picture of just one individual at one point in time is challenging. Trying to compare and contrast a number of individuals in all their complexity and as they develop over time is fraught with problems. Given the difficulty of understanding the whole person, it is not surprising that psychologists have tackled the problem from many different directions and in many different ways. In 1938, Henry A. Murray described the field in terms that are still largely true today:

> In psychology there are few generally valued tests, no traits that are always measured, no common guiding concepts. Some psychologists make precise records of their subjects' overt movements, others inquire into sentiments and theories. Some use physiological techniques, others present batteries of questionnaires. Some record dreams and listen for hours to free associations, others note attitudes in social situations. These different methods yield data which, if not incommensurate, are at least, difficult to organize into one construction. There is no agreement as to what traits or variables are significant. A psychologist who embarks upon a study of normal personality feels free to look for anything he pleases [Murray cited in Sahakian, 1974, p. 242.]

Actually, it would be incorrect to assume that over the past 40 years psychologists have simply been "doing their own thing" in the attempt to understand personality, with no common concepts or methods to guide their search. Among the different approaches to personality, a few unifying assumptions exist about the nature of human beings, the determinants of behavior, and the most fruitful ways to study people. These premises permit us to reduce the diversity of theories and methods to a few broad approaches. For example, Murray (cited in Sahakian, 1974) argued that all psychologists could be classed in one of two groups holding opposite conceptual positions. In his view, *peripheralists* were those psychologists emphasizing objectivity and focusing on clearly observable phenomena such as events in the outer environment, bodily changes, and muscular movements. *Centralists*, by contrast, emphasize subjective events such as feelings, desires, and intentions. In Murray's view, centralists were interested both in underlying personality processes that are not necessarily directly observable and in the whole person as he or she develops over time and as a function of experience.

While Murray grouped all theories into one or the other of these two classes, other psychologists see the major theories as falling into three or more basic categories. For example, Nye (1981) identifies three major schools of thought: psychodynamic theory (exemplified by Sigmund Freud), behaviorism (exemplified by B. F. Skinner), and humanism (exemplified by Carl Rogers). An overview of popular textbooks in personality will reveal other ways of classifying theories.

You should not be alarmed by the fact that approaches to personality can be categorized in a number of different ways. It is one of the achievements of human cognitive development that we can classify phenomena in different ways depending on our needs and goals. For example, suppose you were asked to categorize all living things into a few major groups. You might classify everything into two kingdoms, plants and animals; or into three classes, land-based, air-based, and water-based organisms; or into the more highly differentiated categories called phyla. One system is not necessarily better than another; rather, different systems are useful for emphasizing or analyzing different characteristics of living things. Such is true for personality theories as well.

For the purposes of this introduction, we follow the categorizing system of Endler and Magnusson (1976), who identify five major approaches to personality theory and research—trait psychology, psychodynamics, situationism, interactionism, and phenomenology or humanism. In the following paragraphs, in addition to providing a brief overview of each of these perspectives on human personality, we indicate which of the readings in subsequent chapters of this book contain references to or applications of the different perspectives.

Most psychologists would probably agree with Endler and Magnusson (1976) that the *trait approach* has been a dominant force in personality research and theory. Trait theorists such as Cattell (1950, 1965) generally assume that different traits (that is, personality dispositions such as anxiety, aggressiveness, and dependency) differ with respect to strength and organization. Particular constellations of traits, which are seen by trait theorists as the basic units to be studied in personality, are considered responsible for consistencies in behavior across a variety of situations. Typically, proponents of the trait model have used questionnaires, rating scales, and objective tests for the collection of data. Although none of our selections illustrates a direct application of the trait model, in Chapter 8 we provide a brief discussion of some of Cattell's work. Moreover, many of our examples of issues in personality are consistent with the trait approach, which in many ways is most similar of all the approaches to everyday or commonsense conceptions of personality.

Psychologists adhering to a *psychodynamic* (for example, Freudian) perspective conceive of personality as reflecting an ongoing interplay of innate forces that develop in accordance with biological, or constitutional, determinants. Like trait psychologists, psychodynamic theorists assume that underlying personality factors provide a basis for consistency in behavior across a number of situations. Both trait and psychodynamic theorists acknowledge that situational factors can influence behavior, but both also emphasize inner rather than outer determinants of personality. Psychodynamic psychologists are more likely than trait psychologists to assume that anxiety or such unconscious processes as defense mechanisms or both can operate in ways to make the direct assessment of personality difficult. Consequently, the assessment techniques preferred by psychodynamic psychologists are often disguised in their purposes and indirect in approach. Examples of such techniques are the Rorschach Inkblot Test or the Thematic Apperception Test (a test of "imagination" in which subjects tell stories about pictures presented to them). Even neo-Freudians such as Erikson and his followers tend to use interviews and case histories rather than the objective measures used by trait psychologists for data collection.

In this book, we include two selections by James Marcia, a psychologist in the Eriksonian psychodynamic tradition. In the selection in Chapter 2, Marcia describes the development of his Eriksonian interview and scoring system. (See Appendix D for Marcia's interview and an example of his scoring system.) In our text in Chapter 6, on content analysis, we describe the general procedures by which psychodynamic psychologists make more objective and quantitative the qualitative verbal material they prefer. The article by Orlofsky, Marcia, and Lesser in Chapter 7 is a good illustration of the study of research hypotheses derived from Erikson's theory.

In contrast to trait and psychodynamic theorists, proponents of *situationism*—including "radical behaviorists" such as Skinner (1953) and social-learning theorists such as Rotter (1954) and Mischel (1976)—emphasize situational factors as the basic determinants of human behavior. Indeed, Skinner considers "personality" to be merely a convenient fiction, a myth used to explain the "functional unity" of behavior. Behaviors that we generally attribute

to the personality of the individual are seen by behaviorists as responses to external stimuli that endure because they are reinforced—either positively, by leading to rewards, or negatively, by helping them avoid punishment. While social-learning theorists diverge from strict Skinnerians in their consideration of cognitive factors such as expectancy, their emphasis is still on the situational conditions influencing behavior. Not surprisingly, in this tradition situations are the basic unit of analysis, and the types of data collected frequently consist of tallies of behaviors occurring as a function of environmental conditions. The social-learning theorist Rotter has also made use of self-report measures of expectancies—for example, for inner or outer sources of reinforcement and for interpersonal trust. Some of Rotter's work is discussed in Chapter 8, which also contains one of his original papers.

Endler and Magnusson (1976) argue that *interactionism* is the perspective that holds the most promise for advances in personality research and thought. Proponents of the interactional model stress the importance for personality of reciprocal person/situation interactions. In their view, situations can influence the behavior of individuals, but individuals can select the situations in which they behave and can interpret the nature of situations.

Ideally, Endler and Magnusson argue, the unit of analysis in the interactional model should be the person/situation interaction. Considering person/situation interactions as *units*, as discrete, integrated entities that can be studied scientifically, is difficult both conceptually and methodologically. In reality, person variables and situation variables are often treated both as separate and as interacting determinants of responses in the context of a particular kind of research design called an analysis of variance (ANOVA) design. Consider, for instance, James Marcia's examining the achievement responses of individuals categorized as high or low in identity in situations categorized as being highly stressful or unstressful. Such an analysis would be a good example of an interactional approach in which person variables and situation variables were treated both separately and in interaction. A much more complete discussion of this and other types of research design can be found in Chapter 9.

The data collected by interactional psychologists include test and questionnaire responses, rating-scale scores, and experimental data. Indeed, nearly all the methods described in this book can be considered methodological tools appropriate for interactional psychologists. One important predecessor of the interactional psychology movement was Henry A. Murray (see Ekehammar, 1974; Endler & Magnusson, 1976), developer of the famous Thematic Apperception Test, which will be discussed in several subsequent chapters. A study derived from the Murray tradition can be found in the selection by Stewart and Winter in Chapter 6.

The final major approach to personality theory and research is the *phenomenological*, or *humanistic*, school. Humanistic psychologists have been critical of the psychodynamic and situational traditions for failing to focus on normal, "self-actualizing" individuals in all their complexity. Instead, the humanist argues, the psychodynamic and behavioral traditions focus either on universal laws, ignoring the individual (and individual differences), or on the individual as a case study in psychopathology or behavior modification.

According to the humanistic school of thought, people are individuals; they grow, develop, live, hate, learn, and regress each in accordance with their particular circumstances. While much of behavior may be determined by either personal or situational factors, humanists argue, people have the capacity to recognize those determining forces and consequently to free themselves. It is time, according to humanistic psychologists, that we begin seriously to

study people as unique individuals and to emphasize the positive attributes of human personality. The article by Carlson in Chapter 10 elaborates this position further.

Much of the research carried out in the area of personality is derived from theoretical notions about the determinants of human behavior. Other research areas, however, have originated for reasons quite independent of specific theoretical frameworks. Entire research domains can be derived from an effort to understand political or social upheavals, for example. While incorporating a strong psychoanalytic perspective, the now-classic work on authoritarian personality (Adorno, Frenkel-Brunswik, Levinson, & Sanford, 1950) originated from the researchers' desire to comprehend the psychological roots of the political, social, and personal excesses of the dictatorships of the 1930s and 1940s. The emphasis on authoritarianism in this study was later broadened to include ethnocentrism and dogmatism (for example, Rokeach, 1960). All such "isms" are assumed to have correlates in basic personality attributes that could facilitate and encourage arbitrariness and rigidity both in individuals and in social and governmental bodies. Some illustrations of work in this area—which can be considered consistent with the trait approach to personality—are contained in several of our selections, for example, the article by Wrightsman in Chapter 5 and that by Mitchell and Byrne in Chapter 9.

A PREVIEW OF THE BOOK

In succeeding chapters, we describe the ways in which psychologists systematically study human functioning. We also provide a framework to enable you to conduct research projects of your own. Each chapter is designed to introduce a specific research issue (for example, ethics) or technique (for example, interviewing). Following an introduction, relevant literature regarding the issue or technique is presented, along with concrete suggestions and guidelines to help you make use of the ideas under consideration. Each chapter also contains one or more original articles, accompanied by study questions and supplemented by exercises and a list of suggested readings.

Chapter 2 focuses on the basic tactical elements of research: how to locate and use resources and instruments, how to read original works critically and productively, and how to use self-knowledge to benefit your research. The chapter also includes an article by Marcia particularly well-adapted to our purposes. The article describes the development of a research issue from its conception through the hard, detailed work of constructing and "debugging" a research instrument, and finally to the actual study of the research hypothesis. Chapter 3 surveys the basic conceptual tool kit of the researcher. It focuses particularly on how the researcher poses questions that can be answered empirically, questions that can also be asked and answered by other researchers from slightly different perspectives. Chapter 4 provides an in-depth consideration of ethical principles in psychological research. Chapters 5 through 9 present the principal methods (for example, content analyses, observations, interviews, questionnaires, and tests), settings (such as field, laboratory, and the like), and research designs (for instance, correlational or experimental), used by research psychologists. For each topic, illustrative articles and exercises are included. Finally, in Chapter 10, we suggest some directions for research. The articles by Carlson and by Levenson, Gray, and Ingram in this chapter provide both a challenge and a prescription for research that are relevant to all students of personality.

This book is more than a collection of illustrated ideas and methods. It also contains thematic materials meant to provide you with the opportunity to follow an idea through several stages of development and through several studies. Thus, research on the concept of ego identity is presented first in Chapter 2 in the article by Marcia and again in Chapter 7 in that by Orlofsky, Marcia, and Lesser. The selection by Stewart and Winter in Chapter 6 provides another perspective on the issue of identity.

More thematic material, regarding the concept of authoritarianism, is provided in the selection by Wrightsman in Chapter 5 and that by Mitchell and Byrne in Chapter 9. Reference to authoritarianism is also made in the articles by Marcia in Chapter 2 and by Marcia and his associates in Chapter 7. Finally, to assist you in your own studies of these and other concepts, we provide an introduction to statistics and several sample measurement devices in the appendixes.

ANNOTATED BIBLIOGRAPHY

Rotter, J. B., & Hochreich, D. J. *Personality*. Glenview, Ill.: Scott, Foresman, 1975.

This brief paperback text covers dimensions of personality, several personality theories (including those of Freud, Erikson, Adler, Rogers, Maslow, and Rotter), a quick overview of techniques for personality measurement, and a discussion of several empirical approaches to such aspects of personality as anxiety, aggression, interpersonal trust, and internal versus external control of reinforcement.

Sundberg, N. D. *Assessment of persons*. Englewood Cliffs, N.J.: Prentice-Hall, 1977.

Sundberg's text on methods of studying personal differences and individuality includes techniques for life-history assessment, biopsychological assessment, and the assessment of cognitive abilities and competence.

ADDITIONAL SOURCES

Brody, N., & Oppenheim, P. Tensions in psychology between the methods of behaviorism and phenomenology. *Psychological Review*, 1966, *73*, 295–305.

Christy, R., & Jahoda, M. (Eds.). *Studies in the scope and method of "the authoritarian personality."* New York: Free Press, 1954.

Dailey, C. *Assessment of lives.* San Francisco: Jossey-Bass, 1971.

Erikson, E. H. *Identity: Youth and crisis.* New York: Norton, 1968.

Freud, S. *New introductory lectures on psychoanalysis.* New York: Norton, 1965.

Maddi, S. R., & Costa, P. T. *Humanism in personology: Allport, Maslow & Murray.* New York: Aldine-Atherton, 1972.

Norbeck, E., Price-Williams, D., & McCord, W. M. *The study of personality: An interdisciplinary approach.* New York: Holt, Rinehart & Winston, 1968.

Skinner, B. F. *About behaviorism.* New York: Knopf, 1974.

2

How to Begin

When you must create a project for a course, how do you begin? Do you go to the card catalogue in your library and start thumbing through the cards, praying for an inspiration? Do you have anxiety attacks every time you think of the impossibility of producing a finished product when you have no idea where to start? In your psychology courses, do you flirt with the notion of diagnosing the weird behavior of someone you knew in high school, but abandon the idea as blatantly unacceptable? Because getting started can be one of the most difficult steps in the research process, this chapter is designed to introduce the resources available to you in this undertaking. The two basic categories of resources—that is, the tools you will use—are the existing scientific literature and yourself, the researcher. By learning to use these tools properly, you will be a step closer to accomplishing your research aims efficiently and competently.

SCIENTIFIC LITERATURE

The existing scientific literature consists of reports of the work of other scientists and is the means by which researchers keep in touch with one another. This literature describes past and current research and its conclusions. To begin to make the best use of such scientific reports, you need an understanding of the aims and methods of scientific writing. In writing a scientific report, the author's aim is to communicate a set of ideas, the methods for examining these ideas empirically, and the outcome of the effort. Such an article is intended not to delight but to inform. Therefore, the style is usually plain and to the point, with masses of information condensed into tables or graphs.

To prepare yourself to use and judge a scientific report, it will be helpful if you first develop a general background in the field under study. With respect to this field, for example, read the personality chapters in a few introductory psychology texts to get an overview of the subject, the principal points of view, and the areas of disagreement among those in the field. Next, look through several personality textbooks written from different perspectives, noting the issues, ideas and language of each. You might discover, for example, that the definition of *personality* differs greatly for a humanist and a behaviorist.

The amount of reading being recommended for an overall view of the field may seem overwhelming; however, the endeavor will become much easier if you learn to scan and to focus your attention as you read. In scanning a personality text, remember that you are seeking to identify the particular approach to people taken by a particular author. To get an idea of the topics important to the personality theorists in question, you won't have to read each text thoroughly from beginning to end. Rather, read the table of contents to discover what issues and ideas are stressed in the book. Then read chapter headings, summaries, introductions, and conclusions to gain familiarity with the central ideas. Scanning is a learned art and one well worth having. After you have scanned several books and have noted which issues, problems, and methods are covered in them all, you will have a good sense of the ways in which the field is organized and approached. You will also find that when one area is discussed, the author generally provides references to journal articles and other books. If the area is of particular interest to you, these lists of references might serve as the beginning of the bibliography for your own project.

Once you have scanned some texts relevant to the field, you will be ready to read in earnest, either to pursue your own developing interests or to follow course assignments. In college libraries you can find a number of resources. These resources will become useful as you begin more specialized reading. For example, *Psychological Abstracts* provides a brief paragraph summary of most of the major articles, monographs, and research reports, published and unpublished, in psychology and related fields. If you were looking for articles on self-concept, for example, you might look in the abstracts under the general heading of personality, which in turn would lead to more specific headings, such as self-concept or self-esteem. *Psychological Abstracts* contains summaries of doctoral dissertations and other materials that might not be in your library, but often similar materials can be substituted for those that are unavailable. If you must find a particular source not in your library and you have sufficient time, you can use the interlibrary loan system or write to the author directly. Do not hesitate to follow the latter course if necessary. Authors are usually glad to communicate with others about their work, especially if correspondents provide a brief explanation of their own projects.

Another source, the *Annual Review of Psychology,* reviews current research in selected subfields of psychology. Each chapter in the *Annual Review* covers a major topic, such as perception, personality, and behavior modification. Each topic is reviewed annually, biannually, or sometimes less frequently, depending on the current activity in that area. The authors of the chapters try to provide some organization and perspective for the research they are reviewing and make reference to many current articles and other publications. The *Annual Review* thus informs the reader on major conceptual and methodological themes and provides researchers with a comprehensive bibliography from which they can cull articles specific to a particular area of interest. One can usually find in this resource critical comment on issues of contemporary interest in personality.

The goal of library research utilizing these sources is to become familiar with journal articles or other original sources pertinent to the project you are pursuing. You should read these reports of original work carefully and in a manner quite different than you would use for a short story or an article in a popular magazine. If you answer the questions in Table 2-1, you will have gained an excellent introduction to the critical analysis of a journal article.

TABLE 2-1
Questions to Be Answered in Critically Analyzing a Journal Article
Group I. Questions That Force You to Summarize the Content

1. *What kind of article is it?* (theoretical article, report of an experiment, report of a correlational study, review of research, etc.)
2. *What is the central aim of the article?*
3. *What was done to accomplish the aim?* (observation, systematic recording of observations, analysis of published research, thinking about theory, etc.)
4. *What objective evidence, if any, came out of the author's efforts?* (observations, quotations from others, etc.)
5. *How did the author interpret the evidence and/or relate it to the original problem?* (author's view of evidence rather than the objective findings themselves.)

Reprinted from Gerald R. Levin, *A Self-Directing Guide to the Study of Child Psychology*, Brooks/Cole Publishing Co., Monterey, California, 1973, p. 9.

While these questions are useful for the critical review of an article, a second set (see Table 2-2) serves as a companion guide for assessing the positive contributions made by the article.

Although many articles in psychology journals will not stand up well to critical analysis, some will, and these provide a good model for the kinds of research reporting to which you should aspire. The type of "both sides" view these checklists of questions will give should yield an understanding of scientific articles that will help you to remember them and to abstract from them the particular points relevant to your own research.

TABLE 2-2
Questions to be asked about the contribution of an article.

What are the contributions of the article?
What is said that
1. is new?
2. is a new combination of existing ideas?
3. is surprising—shakes a prior belief?
4. is thought provoking?
5. leads the reader to previously unknown areas?
6. makes the reader think of additional research?
7. helps resolve an inconsistency among previous findings?

In learning to read reports of original work, one is often tempted to do one of two things: (1) to read for content and to accept the printed word too easily as truth or (2) to criticize the methods unremittingly and thus to lose the potential value of what is being stated. We suggest you attempt to strike a balance. Keep in mind that journal articles in psychology rarely, if ever, present the crucial experiment that "proves" a hypothesis. There is no ultimate truth in science. Rather, there is a constant search—and "re-search"—for additional evidence on one side or another of an issue and for new avenues to be explored. The methods of science are imperfect and are always subject to criticism. However, once one has perceived the imperfections in a research project by studying the report, one can weigh the contributions of the research judiciously and determine whether the ideas are worth further pursuit.

SELF-KNOWLEDGE AND EXPERIMENTER EFFECTS

The second tool you, as a scientist, must learn to use is yourself. You are the instrument of observation and inquiry, and as such you require understanding. You will be using your senses in focused observation of specific behaviors or interactions. Just as one can learn to use a microscope or telescope, one can learn to use the senses in specialized ways for the systematic observation of behavioral events. Proper techniques exist for making the best use of oneself as a researcher in order to maximize efficiency and to minimize the limitations inherent in everyday modes of observation. The purpose of these techniques is to help researchers behave, like scientific instruments, in an unbiased and objective manner.

Clearly, self-observation and self-knowledge have important roles in any systematic study of personality. While all the varied approaches to the study of personality incorporate, or should incorporate, some component of self-examination, this aspect of technique has been largely implicit in much psychological research. You will do well to make self-observation an explicit part of personality research, particularly as a means of helping you avoid experimenter effects that can bias your research efforts.

The term *experimenter effects* refers to the many intentional and unintentional ways in which investigators can influence their findings. Unless researchers are very sensitive to the pitfalls of *experimenter bias,* it is all too easy for them to conduct studies in ways that guarantee support for the assumptions their research was designed to test. To avoid falling prey to such methodological dangers as the *self-fulfilling prophecy,* which is one form of experimenter bias, investigators must build a number of precautions into their research design.

One set of precautions, for example, deals with the fact that subjects are sentient beings who might be interested in "psyching out" the purposes of a study in order to give, or to withhold, the responses they believe the experimenters are seeking. If the subjects respond to questions or situations on the basis of what they think your expectations are rather than on the basis of what they really think or would do in normal circumstances, you will be unable to learn much about the issues of interest to you. Fortunately, numerous precautions can be used with different research strategies. For

example, to conduct a laboratory experiment properly, you should be aware of the importance of minimizing *demand characteristics,* that is, cues that help subjects guess what you are trying to "prove" (Orne, 1962). When conducting an interview or administering a questionnaire, you should avoid "leading questions" which would increase the likelihood that compliant respondents will say what they believe you want to hear. Such methods for avoiding experimenter effects are discussed in more detail in later chapters where we describe the various research strategies available.

Other procedures, known as *blinds* and *double blinds,* are used to ensure against both subjects and the data collector becoming aware of the purposes of the study. Blinds, or blind controls, are procedures designed to prevent subjects from learning about the expected outcomes or the objectives of experimental procedures of investigations in which they are participating. To keep yourself from "giving away" clues about your expectations, you might rely on someone else to ask interview questions, conduct the experiment, or make the observations. Of course, to make this procedure effective, you would have to make sure the assistant would not commit the very error you are trying to avoid— that is, revealing expected results to subjects. Double-blind procedures are in effect where both the subjects and the experimenter are kept in the dark as to the purposes of the research and the expected findings.

Blind and double-blind controls are not equally important in all types of empirical investigation, and where they are relevant they raise questions of ethics (see Chapter 4, where issues of deception are discussed). Moreover, the possibility of finding many totally "naive" subjects for psychological studies, whatever precautions are taken, is questionable. Nevertheless, it is useful to keep in mind that good scientists are more interested in discovering the truth than in having their expectations fulfilled.

If you are concerned about experimenter effects but do not want to relinquish the experience of asking questions or making observations yourself, you can arrange to include an additional investigator in the data-gathering process. Where your own findings turn out to be more consistent with your expectations than those of your "naive" co-investigator, then it is likely that some sort of experimenter effect is operating. The use of co-investigators also affords you the opportunity to estimate the repeatability of your observations. Statistical procedures such as those described in Appendix A permit you to determine mathematically just how consistent two different observers are in their judgments of a particular performance.

Some experimenter effects have nothing to do with research expectations. On some topics, subjects might give different answers to a male than to a female or to a White than to a Black interviewer. Furthermore, behavior in some situations or performance on some tasks might vary with respect to the sex, race, or age of the investigator. If your reading on a research topic indicates that the sex or age of the investigator could have an effect on the findings, you might decide to use both male and female or younger and older investigators to conduct your study. Then you would be able to use statistical techniques to determine whether such characteristics of your investigators really made a difference. Where following such procedures is impossible, you could mention in the discussion section of your research report that the risk of the experimenter effect in question was unavoidable.

While the need to be sensitive to potential experimenter effects might make a research effort seem complex and difficult, it should not deter you from becoming an investigator of human personality and behavior. Many of the available safeguards are easy to follow. Remember too that you should never disregard findings because they are inconsistent with your expecta-

tions, no matter how easy it might be to rationalize about the unworthiness of recalcitrant data. Have others check on your procedures and observations. While one need not undertake a profound self-examination every time a study is begun, prejudices and fixed ideas affecting the outcome can nevertheless come to light with even a relatively superficial self-confrontation.

Self-observation need not end with a commitment to safeguard against experimenter effects. Indeed, you can use yourself as a research subject, making observations of your own behavior and even undertaking a program for systematically modifying your behavior. Exercise 3, in the exercise section of this chapter, serves as a practical introduction to the process of self-observation. Also, several good books provide guidelines for the self-modification of behavior to help individuals to improve their study or eating habits, for example, or to become more assertive or to stop smoking. A number of such books are listed in the Additional Sources section at the end of this chapter.

A PREVIEW OF THE CHAPTER SELECTION

To become a good scientist, you need to know more than how to seek out reports of work done on an issue you wish to investigate, how to read critically, and how to conduct an interview or observe an event objectively. You also need an understanding of how empirical work is conducted. A report on research is usually presented as though highly trained scientists have had a brilliant idea, have used this or that method, have carried out an elegant study with clockwork precision, and then have neatly related the findings to previous research and to their own hypotheses. In reality, the process is usually quite different.

The article by James Marcia included in this chapter is intended to illustrate the kind of thinking and effort involved in proceeding from a theoretical idea to a point at which research can begin. Marcia describes how a psychologist would think through one of Erikson's theoretical formulations on ego identity in order to formulate a researchable question. He then outlines the tasks involved in designing the research: specifying the variables inherent in the question, putting these variables into testable terms, deciding on "the best" measurement mode, writing the preliminary questions, and deciding on a scoring procedure. Marcia tells how the research plan is tested and revised to protect against experimenter effects and to assure the repeatability of the research by other psychologists.

Even in focusing on the process of creating a research project, Marcia had to abstract and organize to present the ideas and issues smoothly. He provides only an inkling of the "head-scratching" and problem solving that went on at each stage. Is all the effort that goes into empirical research mere drudgery? Not at all! The process catches one up in the same way that crossword puzzles, contract bridge, chess, and mystery stories can.

If the issues illustrated in Marcia's article are unfamiliar to you at this point, take heart. In the balance of the book, we discuss in considerable detail these fundamental issues: the formulation of a researchable question, the nature of variables, methods of operationalizing variables, the construction of a measuring instrument, and so on. By the end of the book, you might be able to write your own "case history of a construct," to use Marcia's phrase.

As you will discover in answering the study questions for this chapter, this article by Marcia is somewhat different from the rest of the selections in the book. Unlike the typical research report, his article fails to specify the real "nuts and bolts" of the methods used. The self-esteem and stress manipulations are not really described and the data are not summarized in tables. Later selections serve as better models for the form a research paper should take. Nevertheless, Marcia's article describes well the development and execution of a project. (See Appendix D for the interview and scoring guidelines described in his article.)

The Case History of a Construct: Ego Identity Status

James E. Marcia

Few psychologists experience the science vs service conflict more than the clinical psychologist. While he espouses the scientific method as the most effective route to knowledge about human behavior he finds that he must sometimes use methods best described as artistic in his search for the wisdom necessary to deal with the human heart. In the latter task, many clinicians find psychoanalytic theory a valuable source of ideas. However, this theory pays a high price, scientifically speaking, for its attempts to deal with the broader and deeper aspects of personality. Just as individual behavior can appear both confusing and contradictory to us, so does psychoanalytic theory involve many vague concepts and ill-defined terms. Perhaps this is because it attempts to account for so much so inclusively. Be that as it may, the clinical psychologist is frequently caught in the bind of using a scientifically nonproven theory when he wears his "clinical hat" and then having to dissociate himself from that theory when wearing his "scientific hat."

One promising way out of this dilemma may be in the ego psychoanalytic theory of Erik Erikson. A major difficulty, from the psychologists' point of view, with the id-oriented approach of traditional psychoanalysts has been their failure to predict specific behaviors from alleged unconscious motives. Frequently, this has been because of a lack of consideration of the ways in which an individual's environment may nurture, use, abuse, and mold the expression of basic drives. Erikson, while accepting the biological emphasis inherent in the Freudian *psychosexual* approach to human development, goes on to outline a *psychosocial*

scheme based on hypothesized stages of ego growth. These stages of ego growth parallel and then extend beyond the psychosexual stages—each psychosocial stage is marked by a specific crisis in ego growth. The content of these crises involves the development of particular attitudes toward oneself, one's world, and one's relationship to his world. For example, at the oral psychosexual stage, the basic psychosocial crisis involves the infant's development of a sense of basic trust vs mistrust. The rapprochement that was suggested earlier between Erikson's ego psychoanalytic theory and the scientific commitment of the clinical psychologist may be initiated by asking the simple question: "If a particular crisis is resolved, what behaviors should one observe?"

Erikson suggests that the human life cycle involves eight crises in ego growth. These crises, their chronological sequence, and parallel psychosexual stages are presented in the accompanying chart.

Age	Psychosexual Stages	Psychosocial Crises
Infancy	Oral	Basic trust vs mistrust
Early childhood	Anal	Autonomy vs shame, doubt
Play age	Phallic	Initiative vs guilt
School age	Latency	Industry vs inferiority
Adolescence	Genital	Ego identity vs identity diffusion (or role confusion)
Young adult		Intimacy vs isolation
Adulthood		Generativity vs stagnation
Maturity		Ego integrity vs despair

Presenting the psychosocial stages in this way suggests a certain independence among them as well as the possibility of a permanent solution. Neither is the case. The solution of each crisis has ramifications for the solution of the next and is prefigured by the solution of the preceding one. For example, the development of predominant mistrust at infancy may lead to a distrust of time (and consequent difficulty in delaying gratifica-

From "Case History of a Construct: Ego Identity Status," by J. E. Marcia. In E. Vinacke (Ed.), *Readings in General Psychology*. Copyright 1968 by American Book Company. Reprinted by permission.

tion) at adolescence, contributing to a sense of identity diffusion. Similarly, failure to make the occupational and ideological commitments at adolescence necessary to achieve a sense of ego identity may lead to difficulty in interpersonal commitments at young adulthood and, hence, contribute to a feeling of isolation.

Not only are crises interdependent, they may also recur. A fairly common example of this is the "adolescent" identity crisis experienced at maturity when the individual contemplates retirement.

While the question may be simple, the means of answering it are not. The work discussed in this paper has been with that stage of ego growth occurring in late adolescence: the identity crisis. At every stage, there is, hopefully, a "cogwheeling" or mutuality between an individual's needs and capabilities and his society's rewards and demands. The individual's conflicting needs at this stage of late adolescence are both for a feeling of belongingness and independence, for sexual expression and control, for responsibility and freedom. His capabilities are loyalty, skill in the society's technology (e.g., reading and writing), procreation, and realistic decision-making. Society's rewards include citizenship, certain adult privileges (e.g., drinking, driving), greater latitude for sexual expression, increased earning power, and recognition by other adults. Society's demands involve occupational selection, choice of a marriage partner, "responsible" behavior, and the beginning of contribution to the life cycles of others.

According to Erikson, one emerges from the identity crisis with some sense of ego identity or of identity diffusion. Stated simply, ego identity refers to the individual's feeling of knowing who he is and where he is going. Identity diffusion (or role confusion) refers to an individual's sense of uncertainty about both his place and his direction in the scheme of things. The best literary description of ego identity and identity diffusion is to be found in Erikson's highly readable works. The problem here was to answer, empirically, the fol-

lowing questions: Can "ego identity" be defined so as to be measured? Can it then be measured? Having measured it, can behavioral predictions be made? Until these questions were answered, the concepts, while appealing and valuable from a therapeutic and philosophical point of view, were scientifically meaningless.

The initial problem was to get ego identity out into the open, which, to a psychologist, usually means into the laboratory. What behaviors should be observed if some degree of ego identity has been achieved? To look solely at an individual's feelings about himself would miss an essential contribution of Erikson's approach: the psycho*social* aspect. Hence, elements of both the individual's needs and capabilities together with his society's rewards and demands had to be taken into account. The two social components or areas chosen were *occupation* and *ideology*. The societal demand that the late adolescent "get a job" has been celebrated both in song and countless stories, many of the latter emanating from vocational counseling centers on college campuses across the country. The demand to develop an ideology (or philosophy of life or *weltanschauung*) while not so obvious, is equally pressing. As the adolescent changes his role from that of a "taker" to a "giver," from one who was cared for to one who is on the threshold of caring for others, he must adopt a way of viewing the world that facilitates and makes meaningful this transition. This revision in world outlook usually takes the form of some sort of personal religious-political-economic theory. Hence, expressed *commitment* to an occupation and an ideology was chosen as one criterion for the presence of ego identity.

However, commitment alone was not enough. Not all occupations are "chosen," nor are all ideologies "developed." The son of a Methodist, Republican physician who becomes a Methodist, Republican physician with little or no thought in the matter cannot be said to have *achieved* an identity. It appears more that he finds himself at the identity crisis accepting the labels pasted on him since childhood, and cheerfully committing himself to being his parents' alter ego. Another variable, then, in addition to mere commitment was needed. "Crisis" was chosen to refer to a period of decision-making when previous choices, beliefs, and identifications were brought up for questioning by the individual. With the establishment of *crisis* as a variable, half of the first task—an operational definition of ego identity—was completed. Two variables, crisis and commitment, in two areas, occupation and ideology, were to define the extent of ego identity or identity diffusion.

At this point, a new outlook on the problem emerged. The various combinations of the criteria yielded something like separate kinds of "ego identities" rather than just "how much" ego identity. It was decided to approach the identity crisis in terms of *ego identity statuses;* that is, a number of ways in which the identity crisis could be dealt with, only one of which was the achievement of ego identity. Four ego identity statuses were defined: identity achievement, moratorium, foreclosure, and identity diffusion. Identity achievement individuals had experienced a crisis and were committed to an occupation and ideology. Moratorium individuals were currently *in* the crisis or decision-making period with only vague commitments to occupation and ideology. Foreclosure subjects, while committed to an occupation and ideology, seemed to have experienced no crisis period, their commitments being largely parentally determined. Identity diffusion individuals might or might not have come to crisis period; regardless, they were strikingly uncommitted to occupation and ideology.

We now had definitions of ego identity status that would permit at least a rudimentary form of measurement: categorization. The next problem was to decide upon which technique to use to assess an individual's particular status. It was decided that a moderately structured interview with a scoring manual would provide both the degree of accuracy and flexibility demanded by the nature of the statuses. Constructing the interview was a fairly straightforward procedure; questions were devised to tap crisis and commitment in the two areas of occupation and ideology, the latter divided into religion and politics. The building of a scoring manual was a considerably more arduous task. First, theoretical criteria for each variable (crisis and commitment) in each area (occupation, religion, and politics) for each of the four identity statuses were spelled out. Then, by means of actual interviews, examples were gathered. The manual was compiled and taped interviews together with the manual were given to other psychologists not connected with the research to see if they could agree on the placing of individuals in statuses. Areas where they disagreed in their judgments, or where the manual was unclear, were revised. A new sample of interviews was then taped and the new tapes were rated again. Finally, the manual was sufficiently clear that judges could agree on an individual's identity status about 70–75% of the time. While far from ideal, this was thought to be adequate for such complex, global judgments. At this point, a more complete description of each of the identity statuses based on their interviews seems in order.

IDENTITY ACHIEVEMENT

Occupation

He has seriously considered several occupational choices or deviated from what his parents had planned for him. He is reluctant to switch fields and seems to think of himself as *a* teacher, engineer, etc. (Being *a* something means the difference between "taking courses in education" and seeing oneself as a "teacher.") Although his ultimate choice may be only a variation of the parental wishes, he seems to have experienced a crisis period and made a resolution on his own terms. *An example:* His father was a farmer and wanted him to be one; his mother and the townspeople wanted him to be a minister; he decided to be a veterinarian. He says: "I would rather have my DVM than a Ph.D. in anything."

Religion

He appears to have gone through a period of doubting either his past belief or unbelief. This has resulted in a re-evaluation of faith and a commitment to some action (church going, religious discussions, etc.). He may end up as religious or not, in the conventional sense; regardless, he seems to have rethought childhood concepts and achieved a resolution that leaves him free to act. *An example:* He went through a period of rejecting his father's religion. A period of atheism followed disillusionment with a God who would permit an evil world. He resolved the dilemma by deciding that the amount of good balanced evil. He is fairly active in church and plans to raise his children in it.

Politics

The presence of a crisis period is more difficult to ascertain here than in the other two areas. He shows some differences from his parents' political opinions; for example, he may see himself as more liberal than they are. Evidence of commitment is usually seen in the vigor of his pronouncements, his tendency to dispute political questions with others, and any political action-taking. *An example:* A period in the Army angered him at being reacted to according to group membership rather than as an individual. He was attracted to the individualism of conservativism and is against social welfare. He sees a relationship between principles of human nature learned in college classes and his political beliefs.

General Comment

The identity achievement seems generally able to "make it." Particularly, he does not appear as if he would be overwhelmed by sudden shifts in environment or by unexpected burdens of responsibility. He also seems to be making some solid

interpersonal commitments—e.g., engagement, marriage, etc.

MORATORIUM

Occupation

He is dealing with issues often described as "adolescent." He is concerned less with preparing for a specific career than with choosing that career. His parents' plans are still important to him, and he seems to be working to achieve a compromise among them, society's demands, and his own capabilities. It is not that he feels totally bewildered and all at sea, but that he is vitally concerned and rather internally preoccupied with resolving what at times seem to be unresolvable questions. *An example:* He says: "Other people think I'm an easygoing clown. Inside, I'm a big knot. I'd just like some peace and quiet. The future does seem better than the past, though: I'm not so concerned now about what people think." He's majoring in speech, wants to work for a degree in either psychology or sociology while in the Army. In general, wants to do something to help people.

Religion

He seems to be dealing with fundamental religious-philosophical questions, not just a mere "shopping around" among denominations. *An example:* He has doubts about the existence of God and wonders whether there is any kind of Supreme Being. It scares him when he thinks about it, but he still does. He has tentatively decided that there is some kind of God.

Politics

Although he is in doubt about political and religious commitment, he seems dissatisfied with the doubt and is trying to effect a resolution. *An example:* He is confused about politics. He is a Democrat, but has heard about conservatism and is questioning it. On the other hand, the current governor is an inept conservative and this disenchants him. He doesn't really know.

General Comment

At his best, a moratorium is enthusiastic, questioning, idealistic, and usually rather verbal. At his worst, he is paralyzed, unable to act decisively in one way or another—not because of a lack of commitment, but more often because of equal and opposite commitments.

FORECLOSURE

Occupation

It is difficult to distinguish where his parents' goals for him leave off and where his begin. He seems to have experienced either no choice period, or only a brief and inconsequential one. He is becoming what others have influenced him or intended him to become since childhood. In addition, all of this seems acceptable to him. *An example:* His father was a farmer and he'll be a farmer. He says: "I plan to go back and help dad farm." He took agriculture at college because "that's all I know." Although he gave cursory consideration to other fields, "farming was always at the top of the list." "I was brought up like my family was; I was with them so long I just stayed that way."

Religion

His faith (or lack of it) is virtually "the faith of his fathers (or mothers, as the case may be) living still." College experiences serve only as confirmation of childhood beliefs. Dissent seems absent. *An example:* His religion is the same as his parents'. He says: "Maybe it's just a habit with me, I don't know. I've thought a lot and you meet all kinds of people here, but I really haven't changed any of my beliefs. I just have more understanding than I did before. I plan to bring up my children in the church, just the way my dad did with me."

Politics

Again, he is what his parents are with little or no personal stamp of his own. *An example:* Referring to him and parents both being Republican: "You still pull that way, Republican, if your parents are that way. You feel like it's where you should be."

General Comment

Because of his commitment and apparent self-assuredness, a foreclosure appears in everyday life like an identity achievement, although he is characterized by a certain rigidity. However, one feels that if he were placed in a situation where parental values were nonfunctional he would soon be greatly at a loss. It may be that only situations of severe stress would differentiate him from identity achievement.

IDENTITY DIFFUSION

There appear to be several varieties of identity diffusion. One is a *pre*crisis lack of commitment. This individual might have been a foreclosure if strong enough parental values had been established. However, it is likely that the parental attitude was one of "it's up to you; we don't care what you do." Under the guise of democratic child-rearing, the parents may have provided no consistent structure which could be a guide for the growing individual, and, later on, an image against which to compare himself. Because he never really *was* anything, it is almost impossible for him to conceive of himself as *being* anything. The problems that are so immediate and self-consuming for the moratorium never really occur to this precrisis diffuse person.

There are probably two kinds of *post*crisis diffuse individuals. The first is the "playboy" who seems committed only to a lack of commitment. This individual actively seeks to avoid entangling alliances; his motto: "Play the field." No areas of potential gratification are really relinquished; all things must be kept within the realm of possibility.

A second type of postcrisis diffuse is the "loner" for whom any investment of himself in either ideas or people is so frightening that he shies away from any deep involvement. His isolation from others may lead to the development of disorganized thought processes. The main element in all these identity diffuse persons remains a lack of commitment.

Occupation

No one occupational choice is decided upon, nor is there much real concern about it, as contrasted with moratoriums. There is frequently little conception of what a person in the stated preferred occupation does in a day-to-day routine. Any occupational choice would be readily disposed of should opportunities arise elsewhere. There is sometimes an "external" orientation, so that what happens to the individual is seen as a result of luck or fate. An example: His major is engineering. In response to a question about his willingness to change he says: "Oh, I can change. I want to travel, want to try a lot of things. I don't want to get stuck behind a drawing board. I want a degree mainly as an 'in' to production or something else. I just don't want to get tied down."

Religion

He is either uninterested in religious matters or takes a smorgasbord approach in which one religious faith is as good as any other and he is not averse to sampling from all. He will sometimes state his beliefs as being the same as his parents', yet show little commitment to them. An example: He says: "I haven't picked one religion. I'm not interested in any, although I guess it's all right for some people. I just don't care a whole lot about it."

Politics

Both political and social interest are low. He has little idea or concern about where he stands vis-à-vis society. It is as if the world went its way and he went his with little intercourse between the two. An example: He has no interest in politics. He never discusses it with his parents. When given an opportunity in the interview to make a choice between Kennedy and Goldwater, he was unable to.

General Comment

A striking feature of the identity diffusions, aside from their defining characteristic of lack of commitment, is the wide range of adjustment within the group. It varies from the playboy who appears fairly carefree to the loner who is pretty miserable much of the time. There may be some value to future investigations in distinguishing among these varieties of identity diffusion.

Having developed and described the ego identity statuses, the final question of their predictive validity remained to be answered. In other words, all that had been done until this time was the invention of categories, based initially on Erikson's theory, but now extended beyond that theory. Their scientific value, aside from the techniques developed to reliably determine them, was no greater than Erikson's concepts. To establish their scientific worth it was necessary to demonstrate that individuals in different categories behave in predictably characteristic ways in an experimental setting. The experimental tasks to be chosen had to have certain features. They had to be fairly independent of the criteria used to establish the statuses, "meaningful" in the sense that they tapped behaviors having adaptive significance, and sufficiently varied to permit differential predictions for different statuses.

The two main tasks chosen were a concept attainment task administered under stressful conditions and a situation allowing for assessment of vulnerability to self-esteem manipulation. The rationale for the stressful concept attainment task went as follows. A main function of the ego, according to psychoanalytic theory, is the mediation between external (environmental) demands and internal (personal) needs. For example, the stronger the ego, the better able a person should be to think effectively even though he is anxious. According to Erikson's theory, the successful resolution of a psychosocial crisis should yield an increment to ego strength. Hence, the nearer an individual's identity status approaches identity achievement, the greater ego strength he should possess, and the better he should perform on a task requiring him to think under pressure.

The rationale for vulnerability to self-esteem manipulation went something like this. Some people fluctuate in their estimate of themselves with almost every comment that others make about them; other people seem relatively impervious to everyday give and take, and maintain a rather consistent view of themselves. Achieving an ego identity involves a process of deciding for oneself who and what one is to be. To the extent that this has been accomplished, one might be expected to have developed an *internal* locus for self-evaluation and, hence, be less likely to change his opinions of himself when given personality-relevant information by an external source.

As predicted, subjects in the identity achievement and moratorium statuses did a better job on the test of thinking under stress; they also changed less in their self-esteem when given either positive or negative feedback about their performance. Foreclosure and identity diffusion subjects did poorly on the stressful concept attainment task (even though they did not differ in intelligence from identity achievement and moratorium) and they also changed their opinions of themselves more when given the personality-relevant feedback. Some other interesting findings were that moratoriums (in crisis) were either much more anxious than the other statuses or more willing to admit to it; foreclosure subjects tended to agree with authoritarian views and also appeared to set unrealistically high goals for themselves.

The operational definition, fairly reliable measurement, and empirical validation of the ego identity statuses may appear to have closed the issue with respect to this particular segment of ego psychoanalytic theory. However, it seems to be in the nature of science that answers only beget more questions. For example: Why does one person appear in one identity status rather than another? Is it related to characteristics of his parents or their modes of child-rearing? Might the basic thought processes of subjects in one status differ from those in another—perhaps in the sense that one group (foreclosures) may view a stimulus situation as having rather few defining characteristics while another (moratorium) may see many possibilities in the same situation? Since movement from one status to another is not only possible but expected, to what status do, say, moratoriums or foreclosures tend to go? Under what conditions do they go there? All of the work has been done with college students. What about noncollege populations, or groups outside of Western culture? Do the statuses apply there? Most of the work thus far has been with men. What about ego identity in women? Why don't identity diffusions emerge experimentally as a more distinct group? Would subdividing them lead to more refined predictions? In short, there is much to be done.

Finally, one might still find himself asking the question: What is ego identity or identity status *really?* Actually, they are words—constructs put on behavior that allow future behaviors to be predicted. Both this work and the business of science, in general, may be seen as the invention and testing of such labels for phenomena in order to determine the labels' utility for prediction. It may be that the phenomena themselves have "underlying principles" waiting to be "discovered," but even if they have, we have no absolute way of apprehending these or knowing when we have found *the* answer. What we can do is to *impose* ordering principles (construct systems or theories) on events and thereby *give* them order. The identity statuses are such ordering devices; so long as they continue to yield predictions, they are useful and will be retained. When they cease to yield further predictions, which at some time they probably will, they will be discarded in favor of other

constructs of labels that will do the job of predicting this area of human behavior more
efficiently.

STUDY QUESTIONS

1. Compare Marcia's "case history" with
other selections in this book. How does
this article differ in terms of organization
and content? Note that the "case history,"
written specifically as a chapter in an introductory psychology book, does not conform to the pattern implied in the questions on page 11. Nevertheless, many of
the questions presented in both lists on
page 11 are relevant to this selection. Try
to answer them. Decide what additional
information would be needed to make this
selection more like a research report.

2. Note the questions raised by Marcia at the
end of his paper. Which ones seem particularly interesting to you? How would you
go about finding research reports by Marcia and others concerning identity and
some of the other notions mentioned in the
concluding section of the paper?

EXERCISES

1 Using the Library: A Scavenger Hunt

A. Psychological Abstracts

1. Find the titles of three interesting journal articles written in 1976 on the topic of *creativity*.
Give the titles, authors, and journal references.
2. Between 1964 and 1968, Irwin Sarason did a
study on test anxiety and hostility. What is the
title of the report? What journal is it in?

B. The Card Catalogue

1. Is B. F. Skinner's *Contingencies of Reinforcement* available to your library? If so, what is
its call number?
2. In comparative psychology there is a book on
behavioral development and evolution. What is
the title? Who is the editor?
3. Give the call numbers of the journals *Psychological Abstracts, Psychological Review*, and
Journal of Personality. Indicate which years

and which volume numbers of these journals
are in your library's collection.

C. Library Services

1. Describe where and how to check out a book
in your library.
2. Describe where and how to obtain an interlibrary loan on a book you are unable to locate
in your university branch.
3. Does your university library have a library reserve service? If so, describe where and how to
check out a book or an article on reserve.

D. Treasure Hunt (items from LeUnes, 1977)

1. Which presidents of the United States were
first-born children?
2. How many children did Sigmund Freud have?

2 Writing an Autobiographical Essay

Writing an autobiographical essay can aid in the self-
observation process. By focusing on your own actions,
reactions, thoughts, and feelings, you can in effect
use yourself as a subject. The following questions are
intended as guidelines. Let yourself go. You will
discover new ways to look at and think about your
own observations as you continue to read this book.

1. Who are you?
2. Who are the important others in your life?
3. What is your place in society, your community,
your group?
4. How do you feel about authorities? your intellectual abilities? your feelings?
5. What frightens you?
6. What bores you?
7. What are your biases?
8. When do you feel "locked in"?
9. When do you feel free and loose?
10. What makes you sad?
11. What makes you happy?
12. What makes you joyful?

3 Self-Observation[1]

Self-observation is a special technique in psychology.
It is a means by which you can study behavior by
recording what you yourself do. The data—your

[1]Our thanks to John Neill of Boston University for
contributing the exercise on self-observation of behavior.
These and all other exercises have been used by Boston University undergraduates enrolled in a course on Experimental
Psychology: Personality.

dreams, thoughts, feelings, and actions—are readily available to you.

A record of a particular behavior gives you a picture of what you have done in a specific area. Grades, checkbooks, parking tickets, baseball cards, and the like are examples of records of behavior. In ordinary life, the reasons for keeping these records are as different as are the records themselves—to discriminate who has excelled and failed, how much money we have spent and how much is left, who has parked illegally and who will be fined, and what an athlete has done to earn the respect of fans and fellow players. Similarly, your reasons for keeping a record of your own behavior might be to meet one or more of a number of diverse needs.

If we set for ourselves the goal of "winning" records in competition with others, we can enjoy the experience of recording a particular behavior. In the case of self-observation, however, the self is the scorekeeper, runner, and fan all rolled into one. Playing all three roles is a formidable task. Therefore, it is best that we keep the task simple. To help simplify the jobs of observing your self and maintaining an accurate record, keep the following questions and guidelines in mind. (A concrete example of how you can proceed with this exercise follows in the next exercise.)

1. What is the behavior?
2. When does it occur?
3. What events precede it?
4. What events follow it?
5. Depict the behavior on a graph.
6. Depict on a graph the events that precede and follow the behavior.
7. Test a hypothesis by testing your data. Do the data support the hypothesis? How do you know?

4 Study Observation

Keep a 3 × 5 notebook with you at all times. Every time you study, record the time, place, material studied, and how you feel. Recording these data will be easy if you use this form:

		3/9/78		
Place	Time	Duration	Material	Feeling
Home	8:00	60 min.	Psych	Enjoyment
School	10:00	30 min.	History	Boredom
Cafe	1:00	60 min.	Math	Confusion

At the end of the week, add up the time you spent studying, either for an individual subject or for all your subjects. You can also add up the amount of time you spent studying in one place. Plot the material on graphs. The "time-spent" graph might look like this:

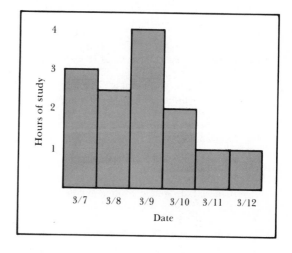

You can make similar graphs for all the different types of data you collected.[2]

To analyze the "time-spent" graph, go back to your notebook. Look for statements about your feelings, where you studied, or other factors you recorded that might indicate what made you study more on one day than on another.

ADDITIONAL SOURCES

I. Getting an Overview
  Borgatta, E. F. & Lambert, W. W. *Handbook of personality theory and research.* Chicago: Rand McNally, 1968.
  Buros, O. K. *Personality tests and reviews.* Highland Park, N.J.: Grypton Press, 1970.
  Norbeck, E., Price-Williams, D., & McCord, W. M. (Eds.) *The study of personality: An interdisciplinary appraisal.* New York: Holt, Rinehart & Winston, 1968.

[2]Chapter 4 provides advice on how to quantify variables such as feelings, which usually are considered to be highly qualitative and subjective. Such quantification techniques will prove very useful in graph construction.

Southwell, E. A., & Merbaum, M. *Personality: Readings in theory and research.* Belmont, Calif.: Wadsworth, 1964.

Wiggins, J. S., Renner, K. E., Clore, G. L., & Rose, R. S. *The psychology of personality.* Reading, Mass.: Addison-Wesley, 1971.

II. Finding References
  A. Standard texts and handbooks (See I above)
  B. Periodicals useful in finding references are *Psychological Abstracts, Child Development Abstracts and Bibliography, The Annual Review of Psychology, Psychological Bulletin*
  C. Periodicals reporting original research are *Journal of Personality and Social Psychology, Personality, Journal of Genetic Psychology, Journal of Orthopsychiatry, Journal of Personality, Journal of Experimental Research in Personality, Journal of Consulting and Clinical Psychology, Journal of Youth and Adolescence, Sex Roles: A Journal of Research*

III. Special-Interest Reading
  A. Identity and Self-Concept
    Bigner, J. J. Sibling position and definition of self. *Journal of Social Psychology,* 1971, *84,* 307–308.
    Constantinople, A. An Eriksonian measure of personality development in college students. *Developmental Psychology,* 1969, *1,* 359–372.
    Hauser, S. T. Adolescent self-image development. *Archives of General Psychiatry,* 1972, *27,* 537–541.
    Heilbrun, A. B. Conformity to masculinity-femininity stereotypes and ego identity in adolescents. *Psychological Reports,* 1964, *14,* 351–357.
    Josselson, R. L. Psychodynamic aspects of identity formation in college women. *Journal of Youth and Adolescence,* 1973, *2,* 3–52.
    Marcia, J. E. Ego identity status: Relationship to change in self-esteem, "general maladjustment," and authoritarianism. *Journal of Personality,* 1967, *35,* 118–134.
    Rosenberg, M. *Society and the adolescent self-image.* Princeton, N. J.: Princeton University Press, 1965.
    Rosenkrantz, P., Vogel, S., Bee, H., Broverman, I., & Broverman, D. M. Sex role stereotypes and self-concepts in college students. *Journal of Consulting and Clinical Psychology,* 1968, *32,* 287–295.

  B. Authoritarianism
    Adorno, T. W., Frenkel-Brunswik, E., Levinson, D. J., & Sanford, R. N. *The authoritarian personality.* New York: Harper, 1950.
    Campbell, D. T., & McCandless, B. R., Ethonocentrism, xenophobia, and personality. *Human Relations,* 1951, *4,* 186–192.
    Chapman, L. J., & Campbell, D. T. Response set in the F scale. *Journal of Abnormal and Social Psychology,* 1957, *54,* 129–132.
    Christie, R., & Jahoda, M. (Eds.) *Studies in the scope and method of "The Authoritarian Personality."* Glencoe, Ill: Free Press, 1954.
    Cohen, T., & Carsch, H. Administration of the *F* Scale to a sample of Germans. *Journal of Abnormal and Social Psychology,* 1954, *49,* 471.
    Frenkel-Brunswik, E. Further explorations by a contributor to "The Authoritarian Personality." In R. Christie and M. Jahoda (Eds.) *Studies in the scope and method of "The Authoritarian Personality,"* Glencoe, Ill.: Free Press, 1954.
    Harvey, O. J. Authoritarianism and conceptual functioning in varied conditions. *Journal of Personality,* 1963, *31,* 462–470.
    Rokeach, M. *The open and closed mind.* New York: Basic Books, 1960.
    Rokeach, M., & Fruchter, B. A factorial study of dogmatism and related concepts, *Journal of Abnormal and Social Psychology.* 1956, *53,* 356–360.
    Scodel, A. & Mussen, P. Social perceptions of authoritarians and non-authoritarians. *Journal of Abnormal and Social Psychology.* 1953, *48,* 181–184.
    Triandis, H. C. A note on Rokeach's theory of prejudice. *Journal of Abnormal and Social Psychology,* 1961, *62,* 184–186.

  C. Self-modification of Behavior
    Berecz, J. Modification of smoking behavior through self-administered punishment of imagined behavior: A new approach to aversive therapy. *Journal of Consulting and Clinical Psychology,* 1972, *38,* 244–250.
    Boyd, H. S., & Sisney, U. V. Immediate self-image confrontation and changes in self-concept. *Journal of Consulting Psychology,* 1967, *31,* 291–294.

Chapman, R. F., Smith, J. W., & Layden, T. A. Elimination of cigarette smoking by punishment and self-management training. *Behavior Research and Therapy*, 1971, *9*, 255–264.

Evans, G., & Oswalt, G. Acceleration of academic progress through the manipulation of peer influence. *Behavior Research and Therapy*, 1967, *5*, 1–7.

Glynn, E. L. Classroom applications of self-determined reinforcement. *Journal of Applied Behavior Analysis*, 1970, *3*, 123–132.

Goldiamond, I. Self-control procedures in personal behavior problems. *Psychological Reports*, 1965, *17*, 851–868.

Hall, S. M. Self-control and therapist control in the behavioral treatment of overweight women. *Behavior Research and Therapy*, 1972, *10*, 59–68.

Jackson, B. Treatment of depression by self-reinforcement. *Behavior Therapy*, 1972, *3*, 298–307.

Kazdin, A. E. Covert self-modeling and the reduction of avoidance behavior. *Journal of Abnormal Psychology*, 1973, *81*, 87–95.

Mahoney, M. J., Moura, N. G. M., & Wade, T. C. The relative efficacy of self-reward, self-punishment, and self-monitoring techniques for weight loss. *Journal of Consulting and Clinical Psychology*, 1973, *40*, 404–407.

Mahoney, M. J., & Thoresen, C. E. *Self-control: Power to the person.* Monterey, CA: Brooks/Cole, 1974.

McNamara, J. R. The use of self-monitoring techniques to treat nail biting. *Behavior Research and Therapy*, 1972, *10*, 193–194.

Meichenbaum, D. Cognitive modification of test anxious college students. *Journal of Consulting and Clinical Psychology*, 1972, *39*, 370–380.

Philip, R. E., Johnson, G. D., & Geyer, A. Self-administered systematic desensitization. *Behavior Research and Therapy*, 1972, *10*, 93–96.

Watson, D. L., & Tharp, R. G. *Self-directed behavior: Self-modification for personal adjustment.* Monterey, CA: Brooks/Cole, 1972.

3

On Asking Questions and Seeking Answers

Where does psychological research begin? Why do psychologists conduct studies? It certainly is not the purpose of psychological researchers simply to collect data. Endless compilations of data per se cannot increase our understanding of human behavior. Percentages of people falling into different categories, frequencies of responses to test items, and types of behavior found in a variety of environments by themselves are all empty data. When used to answer research questions or to test research hypotheses, however, such data can be very important.

Once you have found an issue in psychology that interests you, there are a number of steps to follow to ensure that the data you collect will contribute to psychological knowledge. The following steps must precede any effort to collect actual data, though not necessarily in this order: (1) identifying variables; (2) formulating a research question, or a hypothesis, or both; (3) deciding about the research design; (4) considering reliability and validity issues; (5) selecting a sample; (6) evaluating ethical issues; and (7) choosing measurement procedures. Steps 1 through 5 are described in this chapter. Ethical issues are considered in depth in Chapter 4, and the various procedures for collecting data are reviewed in Chapters 5 through 9.

VARIABLES

Psychological research begins with some sort of question—for example, Why do some people prefer classical music while others prefer popular music? In order to understand how such a general question about human behavior is put into researchable form, you must know what is meant by *variables,* the key components in a research question.

In scientific parlance, the objects of the psychologist's study are variables. A *variable* is any characteristic that exists in all people but that varies from one person to another and sometimes from one situation to another—that is, all characteristics of individuals and environments. In scientific studies, researchers deliberately select or vary what are known as *levels* in the variables of interest to them, while trying to hold all other conditions *constant.* If you as a researcher are interested in sex differences in empathy, for example, obviously only two levels exist to the sex variable—male and female. These two levels are crucial to the investigation of sex differences. That is, it is impossible to conclude that one sex is more empathic than the other if you test the empathy of one sex only. If you are interested in empathy as a function of age, you could decide to select subjects from a number of different age levels—for example, adolescent and adult levels; or adolescent, young-adult, middle-adult, and old-adult levels. Commonly studied individual variables in personality research include anxiety, aggressiveness, dependency, authoritarianism, and self-concept. Commonly studied environmental variables include feedback about test performance, intactness of family, severity of upbringing, and group expectations.

In order to ask questions about how variables are related, we must quantify them. The quantification of psychological variables takes place at several different levels of measurement known as *scales.* The process of scaling, or quantifying, variables ranges from the use of a *nominal scale,* in which different numerals are simply assigned to independent categories of items such as gender, to the use of an *interval scale,* in which an attempt is made to establish relative levels of a particular characteristic, as in the rating of intelligence by means of an IQ test.

Three major types of scales, corresponding to three levels of measurement (nominal, ordinal, and interval), are discussed later in the text in relation to specific kinds of data. Because ratio scales are rarely, if ever, found in psychological investigations, we will not consider them here. Comprehensive descriptions of scaling can be found in many statistics and research methods texts, including Selltiz, Wrightsman, and Cook (1976).

RESEARCH QUESTIONS

While the identification and quantification of variables is crucial to scientific research, they are not the essence of research. Psychological variables are studied in the context of psychological problems—that is, questions that are asked about the relationship between two or more variables. Frequently, the researcher starts out with a broad question—for instance, Is there a relationship between one's personality and one's child-rearing techniques?—and narrows it down to a more researchable problem—say, Are authoritarian parents more likely than democratic parents to discipline their children by physical means?

Questions about the relationship between authoritarianism and punitiveness are easily generalized from the vast empirical literature dealing with the "authoritarian personality" (cf. Adorno, et al., 1950). In addition to building on an integrated body of research, one can derive research questions in other ways. One common type of research problem stems from inconsistencies among previous empirical findings in an area. For example, a great deal of inconsistency is to be found among findings of studies of birth-order effects—that is, the effects on personality of being a first- or only-born versus a later-born. Some studies (for example, Schachter, 1959) have shown first-borns to be higher in dependency (seeking help, approval, and affection from others), while other studies (for example, McGurk & Lewis, 1972) have shown later-borns higher in this need. To find a reason for such inconsistent findings, one could design studies of one's own to isolate and observe the apparently critical variables. This chapter's selection, by Zucker and his colleagues, represents one attempt to test hypotheses drawn from the literature on birth order. In their discussion section, these researchers make a nice effort to reconcile their own findings with some of the inconsistent results of previous investigations.

Research problems can also be derived from an awareness of limitations in previous research—limitations such as single-sex samples or instruments of questionable reliability or validity. Surprisingly, it is not uncommon for studies to involve data from individuals of one sex only. Investigators are frequently unsure whether sex differences exist in the variable they want to study. If the investigators already expect variability on the issue under scrutiny and wish to avoid possible complications resulting from differential responses from males and females, they might choose to study members of just one sex. Before we can generalize from the findings for that sex to people in general, new studies must be done with the other sex.

HYPOTHESES

Generally but not always, research questions are translated into hypotheses, which contain specific predictions about the behaviors expected in particular circumstances or from particular individuals. Hypotheses specify the nature or the direction of the relationship among the variables under consideration. Hypotheses represent both a prediction about the answer to the research question and a narrowing of the question to make possible a precise answer. Moreover, good hypotheses contain within themselves some indication of how the answer to the research question will be sought. The point

of a research project is not to provide full and immediate answers to such questions as "Are males more 'turned on' by sexual stimuli than females?" Rather, we design a number of empirical studies with modest hypotheses such as "More males than females will report feelings of arousal in response to erotic stimuli" (see Abelson, Cohen, Heaton, & Suder, 1971), or "Females respond to erotic stimuli with more negative evaluations than do men" (for example, Byrne, Fisher, Lamberth, & Mitchell, 1974), or "Females are more aroused by affectional themes and males are more aroused by purely libidinous erotica" (Sigusch, Schmidt, Reinfeld, & Wiedemann-Sutor, 1970).

INDEPENDENT AND DEPENDENT VARIABLES

On what kinds of *constructs*—that is, concepts treated as variables in psychological research—do research problems and hypotheses focus? The typical textbook on research design or statistics classifies variables as independent and dependent. The official viewpoint goes something like this: *independent variables* are the causes or determinants of *dependent variables,* which are resultants or effects. Changes in independent variables cause changes in dependent variables. When researchers hypothesize that individuals with poor self-concepts avoid opportunities for meeting new people, they imply that the low self-concept is an independent or causal variable and the avoidance behavior a dependent variable or resultant. Or, consider the hypothesis that authoritarian parents will raise dependent children. What would be the independent variable? What would be the dependent variable?

When we step outside the pages of a textbook and into the real world of research, we find that investigators cannot always justify an assumption that the variables they study are causally related. Many researchers, for example, have looked at behaviors they deemed dependent variables, such as creativity, career goals, and political preference, in relation to characteristics they called independent variables, such as age, sex, or social class, without assuming a simple cause/effect relationship. Let's say we are interested in the relationship between age and attitudes toward parents. We can hypothesize that as children grow older (age being the independent variable), they become more tolerant of parental frailties (level of tolerance being the dependent variable). We would not want to say that age in and of itself causes any attitude or change in attitude. Rather, we might take the position that with increasing age children have many experiences and interactions and undergo many kinds of changes, all of which in some way lead to changes in attitudes. Focusing on the age variable is a simple way of abstracting and representing a multitude of independent variables operating within the environment and within the individual.

In some studies, the investigator has simply explored the relationship among variables, with no speculation about what may be influencing what. Usually, however, investigators imply something about the direction of the relationship among variables, even if they do not treat that relationship in a narrow causal way. In general, the dependent variable can be identified as some sort of behavior (including test responses), while the independent variable can be identified as some feature of the environment or the individual.

One way of avoiding the causal implications of the terms *independent* and *dependent variables* is to use the terms *predictor* and *criterion variables* (Rummell, 1964). This terminology is always acceptable but is particularly appropriate in correlational studies (discussed in a later section). By using this language, researchers make explicit the fact that the choice of independent (predictor) and dependent (criterion) variables is somewhat arbitrary. For example,

we can start with a test of need for achievement and predict performance in school, or we can start with school performance and predict need for achievement. Because the use of *independent* and *dependent* variables is common in the psychological literature, we use these terms in this book; however, you should remember that in many studies, including those concerned with personality, differences in the variables labeled dependent were not necessarily *caused* by differences in the variables labeled independent. Indeed, it is likely that no single cause ever accounts for psychological phenomena and that all behaviors are determined by a number of causes. Personality psychologists can select particular sets of predictor and criterion variables without ever assuming that one causes the other in a simple way.

OPERATIONS AND OPERATIONAL DEFINITIONS

Once we have made a prediction about relationships among variables, what is the next step? We make our hypotheses testable by *operationalizing* the independent and dependent variables. An *operational definition* specifies the activities (or operations) to be used to define (measure, produce) a construct. There are several ways of operationalizing variables. First and most simply, we can *classify,* or categorize, subjects in terms of existing attributes such as age or sex. In such a case, we do nothing to obtain or produce our variable; we merely group people on the basis of prior characteristics.

A second type of operation involves *measuring* a construct. Here we classify or group subjects on the basis of a measurement or test performance. For example, the traits of high- and low-characteristic anxiety might be defined as scores in the top and bottom quartiles of the Taylor Manifest Anxiety Scale (Taylor, 1956). Having thus operationalized anxiety, we might then compare the performances of high- and low-anxious subjects on some type of self-concept task.

A third type of operationalization procedure involves the *manipulation* of an independent or predictor variable (Kerlinger, 1973). For example, suppose you are interested in identifying the predictors of helping behavior. On the basis of your own experience, you might speculate that you are more likely to contribute to a charity when you see others doing so. You might then hypothesize that the experience of observing some people behave charitably is an independent variable that affects the likelihood of other people also behaving charitably (dependent variable). In many investigations, the experimenter *manipulates* the availability of a helpful model, making it either present or absent; the researcher then observes the subjects' behavior to determine whether they are helpful or not helpful as a function of exposure to the model.

The two major types of operational definition, measured and experimental, are associated with two different categories of research, correlational and experimental, to be discussed further in the next section. While independent, or predictor, variables can be either measured or manipulated, dependent variables, by definition, are never manipulated. Regardless of whether the research is correlational or experimental in design, the dependent variables are always measured.

RESEARCH DESIGN

As indicated above, the distinction between variables that are manipulated and those that are categorized or measured relates to the distinction between two basic types of research design—experimental and correlational. The basic *experimental design* consists of a comparison between two treatment conditions—for example, stress versus no stress, or social reinforcement

versus no social reinforcement. In this basic experimental design, the emphasis is on understanding how changes (variability) in the independent variable affect the dependent variables. Subjects are assigned to the experimental and control conditions by means of procedures intended to minimize systematic differences between the two groups on *extraneous variables* (that is, variables that are not under study but that could conceivably affect the results). Experimental and control subjects are then treated identically except for one feature—the experimental manipulation or independent variable. Systematic differences between the groups on the dependent measure are assumed to be due to the experimental manipulation, since all other conditions have been kept equal. (A more comprehensive presentation of experimental design can be found in Chapter 9.)

To make this analysis more concrete, suppose that an experimenter is interested in the concept of aggression. Instead of assuming that aggressive behavior is the result of a relatively stable personality "trait," inhering more in some people than in others, experimentalists are likely to look for environmental determinants of aggression. One can ask (as some psychologists have) whether aggressive behavior increases when individuals are exposed to violence on television. In one experimental investigation of this issue (Feshbach & Singer, 1971), boys living in private residential schools or schools for wards of the state were randomly assigned to a television schedule containing predominantly aggressive programs (experimental conditions) or predominantly nonaggressive programs (control conditions). Measures of aggressiveness were recorded both before and after a six-week experimental period. After the manipulation, experimental subjects displayed significantly *less* verbal and physical aggressiveness towards peers and authority figures than did the control subjects. Feshbach and Singer concluded that the results of their experimental manipulation demonstrate a cathartic effect in detention boys of viewing televised aggression. The cathartic effect refers to the supposition that the boys in the experimental condition were in some way experiencing their aggression while they were watching television and did not need to display as much aggression afterwards.

Not all relationships among variables can be studied with the experimental method. As mentioned earlier, we might be interested in the relationship of certain behaviors to age, sex, or height. These latter variables cannot be manipulated experimentally. We cannot *assign* subjects to age groups, sex groups, or height groups the way we can assign them to treatment conditions. There are also circumstances in which we could manipulate a variable but it would be unethical to do so. For example, we might be interested in the effects of starvation on behavior. It would be possible but not ethical to assign human subjects (randomly) to starvation and control (ample-diet) conditions. True experimental studies of this relationship are indeed conducted with lower animals, but are considered immoral for human subjects. To cite another example, medical experiments conducted in the 1930s and 1940s with syphilis patients who were randomly assigned to treatment and no-treatment conditions are not morally acceptable to most researchers today.

In cases where true experiments are impossible, unethical, or difficult and costly to perform, or where nonexperimental procedures seem intrinsically more appropriate, correlational strategies are employed. In *correlational research,* psychologists look at relationships already existing among variables. In this design, independent variables are not manipulated, but rather consist of measures of existing attributes. Subjects are not assigned randomly to experimental and control conditions; instead, subjects already differing on some presumed independent variable (for example, age, sex, IQ, birth order, need for achievement, or gen-

eral anxiety level) are compared on some presumed dependent variable (for example, academic achievement, passivity, aggressiveness, and so on). Correlational researchers frequently try to make use of "natural experiments" to learn more about the determinants of human behavior. For example, Freud and Dann (1951) attempted to assess the effects of early separation from and loss of parents on the later development of World War II orphans.

Correlational studies are not limited to one statistical procedure. Psychologists using the correlational approach may compute a variety of statistics also available to experimentalists. Regardless of the particular statistic, correlational researchers are able to learn something about the strength and reliability of relationships among variables. However, they are always limited in what they can say confidently about cause/effect relationships. It is well known that a statistically significant relationship exists between smoking and cancer. However, because the data for human subjects are correlational, we cannot be certain whether smoking causes cancer or whether some other variable, perhaps a physiological disposition, causes both smoking and cancer. It is the aim of correlational researchers dealing with such problems to demonstrate that the weight of the evidence favors a particular causal interpretation. With respect to our example, the correlational findings are strong and consistent enough to suggest that one should stop smoking—even though we are not absolutely sure that smoking causes cancer.

RELIABILITY

In designing either a correlational study or an experiment, you will want to take steps to ensure as much reliability and validity for your data as possible. We have already discussed the issue of experimenter bias, which can weaken both the reliability and validity of a set of data, but other issues exist as well.

Generally, *reliability* refers to the consistency or repeatability of one's findings. You can say that your results are reliable when you can demonstrate, within limits defined by scientific convention, that another investigator using the same procedures with a similar sample would obtain similar results. However, the term reliability most often refers to the degree to which the measuring instruments used in the research provide the same results each time they are used.

A number of different methods are used to assess reliability, and these are related to the different data-collecting procedures available. For example, a personality *test* might be considered reliable when successive administrations of the test to the same individual result in scores that are approximately the same. Because scores on even a fairly reliable test, such as an IQ test, can fluctuate somewhat owing to such factors as test-taking practice or fatigue, we use a statistical procedure to indicate whether two or more sets of scores are similar enough—or are sufficiently free of error variation—to justify the conclusion that the test is highly reliable. This statistical procedure involves the calculation of a coefficient of correlation, which is described in Appendix A.

Test scores are not the only kind of data that are beset with problems of reliability. If you are making naturalistic observations of behavior and you see identical actions performed in exactly the same way on two separate occasions but describe the first action as an act of helping and the second as an act of bullying, then you are not a very reliable observer.

Often, observers develop *coding manuals,* which are designed to help them categorize ("code") behaviors reliably. If these manuals are not clear enough or complete enough to allow scorers to code behaviors in a consistent way, then the data that result will be inconsistent or unreliable. If two observers are watching the same events and are categorizing behaviors according to the same coding manual but a coefficient of correlation determined between their two sets of observations is low, then we say that the interscorer reliability for this research is low. The low score might be explained by the fact that one of the observers is unreliable, or that the coding manual is unreliable, or both. If, after reading Chapter 5, you decide to do an observational study, you might have to work out carefully the means of describing objectively the behaviors in question and train another observer to see things the way you do.

As we mentioned earlier, specific problems of reliability are associated with each of the various methods of data collection—for example, testing, interviewing, observing behavior, and manipulating variables. In subsequent chapters, we return to a more complete discussion of the different forms the reliability problem can take, as we consider in detail the various methods of conducting research.

VALIDITY

Validity is essentially a matter of whether your findings mean what you think they mean. In employing the scientific method, are we seeing, recording, and interpreting events correctly? Whichever means of data collection we are using, are we making accurate judgments about the issues under investigation? A measure or procedure is valid if it measures what it was designed and intended to measure. Although findings are usually invalid if they are unreliable, it is possible for them to be reliable but not valid. Two observers might interpret the same behavior the same way, providing good interscorer reliability, but both observers might interpret the behavior wrongly, in which case the findings would have low validity.

When asking questions about the potential validity of the data we wish to collect, as in the case of reliability, we must gear our questions to the types of procedures we are using. For example, when we ask if a test is valid, we are asking if it is measuring what it is supposed to measure. Suppose you develop a test of role-taking ability but scores on your test are determined primarily by the subjects' verbal fluency rather than their ability to adopt the perspective of others. In such a case, your test would not be a valid measure of role-taking ability. Or, if you interview people to determine their attitudes towards war and peace, and they tell you what they think you want to hear rather than what they really believe, your data will not constitute a valid reflection of peoples' attitudes. In subsequent chapters, we discuss some techniques aimed at dealing with such threats to the validity of data.

SAMPLING

When you are designing an empirical study, another basic issue is the *sample* you will need for testing your hypotheses. Research is almost always conducted with samples, which constitute subgroups within populations. As is often true of specific words in psychology, *population* and *sample* have somewhat specialized meanings as scientific terms that are not identical with their meanings in everyday language. A *population* is the total group of cases[1] that conform to some predefined set of specifications. A population is the target group whose characteristics

---

[1]We say *cases* rather than *individuals* because the populations with which we deal are sometimes composed not of a particular kind of person but of, say, written documents such as political speeches or child-rearing manuals, or of other media products, such as films or television shows. This stipulation is true in the case of content analysis, which is discussed in Chapter 6. Generally, however, the populations of interest to psychologists are composed of people or other animals.

and behaviors you as a researcher are trying to understand. Suppose it was your assumption that American women tend to be more intuitive than American men. Two populations would be involved here, defined on the basis of nationality and sex—the populations consisting of all American men and all American women. You could add additional criteria to your specifications so that, for example, all middle-class Protestant American men over age 40 constituted one population, and all middle-class Protestant American women over age 40 constituted the other.

Even when a population is fairly narrowly defined and limited (for example, all college freshmen at a particular university), testing a hypothesis on the entire population is likely to be more expensive and less efficient than is necessary for good research. *Sampling* is the process of selecting a subgroup from a particular population to serve as research subjects. The goal of sampling is to achieve a group of cases that is representative of their populations, so that whatever we learn about our samples will also be true of the populations from which they were drawn. When we analyze data from our samples by means of *inferential statistics,* we are using a set of mathematical procedures developed to help us decide the extent to which we are likely to be correct if we generalize from our samples to the larger populations from which they were drawn.

There are several major types of sampling strategies, sometimes grouped under the headings of probability and nonprobability sampling (for example, by Selltiz, Wrightsman, & Cook, 1976). *Probability samples* involve techniques designed to increase our likelihood of being correct when we infer from our statistical tests that the findings we obtain from our sample do not differ by more than a specifiable amount from the findings we could obtain from the population as a whole.

The most common type of probability sample

is the *simple random sample.* The purpose of simple random sampling is to ensure that every individual case within a population has an equal chance of being included in the sample. The old technique of pulling names out of a hat or fishbowl is a form of simple random sampling, as long as every name that has been pulled from the hat is returned to the initial pool—or population—before the next name is selected. (If the names are not returned, the population becomes a little smaller after each selection, and the likelihood of any particular name being chosen becomes increasingly greater with each successive selection.)

The easiest way to apply the process of simple random selection is to obtain a random-numbers table from any of a number of statistics textbooks. To use a random-numbers table, first number all the cases in the population from which you are drawing your sample. This procedure is rather straightforward if you are working with available documents such as census lists, classroom lists, or voter-registration records. Just assign a number to each individual consecutively: 001, 002, 003, and so on. With this numbered list in front of you, turn to your random-numbers table and enter it at some random starting point—for example, by closing your eyes and putting your finger blindly somewhere on the page. Then move down the columns of numbers, selecting individuals from your list whose numbers are the same as the last two, three, or four digits (depending on how big your population is) of the numbers you are reading off from the random-numbers table. The individuals you choose will constitute your sample.

The assumption behind random sampling is that the procedure increases the probability that the distribution of characteristics in a sample will approximate roughly the distribution of characteristics in the population. Thus, if most but not all the individuals in a population are empathic, self-reliant, and nurturant, then most but not all of the individuals in a sample

selected randomly should also be empathic, self-reliant, and nurturant. Inferential statistics, described in Appendix A, provide a means for determining just how often the average score for such a characteristic as empathy found in a sample is likely to differ by more than a specified amount from the "true" average of the entire population on that characteristic.

In *stratified random sampling,* we divide our population into two or more subgroups on the basis of characteristics that are potentially important to our findings. For example, we might stratify, or subdivide, our population on the basis of sex, age, income, or religion. Once we have stratified the population into these subgroups, we can use the process of simple random sampling to select our final pool of subjects. Often subjects are selected randomly from the different strata in proportions corresponding to the proportions existing in the population under consideration. This latter step is an additional way of ensuring that the sample is truly *representative* of the population.

In reality, few of the studies reported in psychology journals involve true probability sampling—although they *might* involve the random *assignment* of available subjects to experimental and control conditions. Most investigators end up relying on *nonprobability samples,* which are basically composed of whatever subjects are available or can be obtained cheaply. Typically, these investigators simply assume or try to argue that the findings that emerge from their samples are true of some larger population—often not clearly defined. As shown in the selections in Chapter 10, the samples in many studies are composed of college undergraduates (Carlson, 1971; Levenson, Gray, & Ingram, 1976). Whether any particular sample of college students is representative of—and therefore permits generalizations to—all young adults, all college students, all urban college students, or all undergraduates is sometimes a matter of debate and a source of the generation of new research aimed at delimiting the populations to which a set of findings might be relevant.

If you are interested in understanding the logic behind sampling theory, see one of a number of available texts that explain the interconnections among research design, sampling strategies, and statistical analyses (for example, Siegel, 1956; Sheridan, 1976). For practical reasons, your samples, like those of most professional psychologists, are likely to be composed of whatever subjects you can obtain that meet the specifications of interest to you. You might need to rely on volunteers obtained on street corners, in supermarkets, or in college dormitories. Even if you can afford to pay your subjects for their participation, you will be limited to whomever responds to your bulletin board notice, newspaper announcement, or other recruiting device. However you recruit your subjects, try to give some attention to the issue of the larger population they might represent. Where you cannot use mathematical means, use rational ones to build representativeness into your sample. If you are interested in sex differences in a particular characteristic but think age may also be an important variable, make sure you do not confound age and sex by recruiting all your females from one age group and your males from another.

We cover samples again in later chapters where we discuss different types of data-collection methods and research designs. At this point, simply remember that you must be careful to choose a sample that will not bias your results. If you were interested in the average college student's view of adult authority, your sample would be biased if it consisted solely of participants in a sit-in at the university president's office. If you were interested in adolescents' views on marriage, you would limit the validity of your findings by interviewing only children from broken marriages. In both these cases, there would be some rather clear limits on the population to whom you could generalize your findings.

FORM AND SIGNIFICANCE

Two issues are fundamental to the design of your own studies—the form of the research question and its significance. First, while many research problems might have ethical implications, the research problem itself should not take the form of a moral question. "Do authoritarian parents hurt their children's development" is a question of values, not science. "Do a significantly higher percentage of juvenile delinquents have authoritarian than democratic parents" is an empirical question that can be answered with data independently of the researcher's ethical biases. Such words as *should, ought, good,* and *bad* might be appropriate in philosophical debates, but they have no place in research problems.

Research questions should be significant as well as empirical. Carefully printed questionnaires, fancy laboratory space, elaborate equipment, and access to computer programs do not count for much if the research question is trivial or unanswerable by empirical methods. Unfortunately, the distinction between triviality and significance is not always easily discernible.

We have one basic suggestion for the novice researcher: try to make a contribution to the field. Do not simply re-do what you think has been done well already. Instead, look to the sources discussed at the beginning of this chapter for a significant research problem. Fill a gap, resolve an inconsistency, extend findings to a new sample, develop or improve on a measuring instrument, or explore a new area.

A PREVIEW OF THE CHAPTER SELECTION

In this chapter's selection, Zucker, Manosevitz, and Lanyon report on a study that exhibits many elements of a "natural experiment." In the study, Zucker and his colleagues acted quickly to test several hypotheses about the relationship of birth order to feelings of anxiety and the need for affiliation during a real-life crisis—the 1965 power failure in New York City. Besides serving as an interesting illustration of a correlational research design, this study is valuable for its use of two kinds of data that will be discussed in later chapters—questionnaire data and observational data. Also, unlike studies in which the sample consists of one sex only, in this study individuals from both sexes were used. The sex differences found in the study provide clear support for the argument that data from one sex only can never be assumed to represent all individuals.

Birth Order, Anxiety, and Affiliation During a Crisis[2]

Robert A. Zucker, Martin Manosevitz, and Richard I. Lanyon
Rutgers University

The power failure in New York City on November 9–10, 1965, provided an opportunity to test the utility and generality of laboratory-derived notions concerning the relationship of birth order to anxiety and affiliation during an ongoing crisis. It was hypothesized that firstborns would be more anxious and more affiliative than later borns while stranded in this situation. Results tended to support the anxiety hypothesis; the affiliation hypothesis received some confirmation, but only among women. A further hypothesis, that lower anxiety would be reported when affiliative behavior was congruent with the birth order theory of affiliative choice, was also supported. Birth order relationships were complicated by sex differences, suggesting that this parameter needs closer attention in future work.

Comparatively few investigators have been able to carry out a successful in-process crisis investigation in a setting involving large groups of people (e.g., Baker & Chapman, 1962; Nash & Nash, 1965; Walker & Atkinson, 1958). More typically, knowledge of such events is based on data obtained some time after the crisis has passed (Cantril, 1958; Killian, 1956; Raynor, 1957; Veltford & Lee, 1943). Both kinds of studies have focused on two aspects of the response to crisis: (*a*) emotional responses, such as fear arousal or the spread of panic and its modification and eventual subsidence (Cantril, 1958; Janis, 1951; Vernon, 1941; Walker & Atkinson, 1958); and (*b*) the processes employed in coping with the emotional arousal, usually by obtaining or inventing information about the causes of the situation (Cantril, 1958; Killian, 1956; Nash & Nash, 1965; Veltford & Lee, 1943).

[2]The authors are indebted to Martine Zucker for the suggestion that provided the original impetus for this research. The study was in part supported by a grant from the Rutgers University Research Council.

From *Journal of Personality and Social Psychology*, 1968, *8*, 354–359. Copyright 1968 by the American Psychological Association. Reproduced by permission.

These situations all have one element in common; they are concerned with escape behavior and its variants. An unpleasant or fear-arousing social situation occurs that is outside the normal course of events. The situation requires either some instrumental activity to produce a successful escape from the fear-arousing circumstances, or some cognitive and instrumental activity in order to come to terms with them.

Field investigations, although often lacking the appropriate controls of laboratory investigations, have a special value in the behavioral sciences. They can function as pilot studies and may focus the researcher's interest on behavior that has previously been overlooked. In addition, they can test the extent to which relationships established under highly controlled experimental conditions apply to real life situations. Such considerations are particularly important, since laboratory manipulations must be restricted for ethical reasons. The present study was undertaken with the above considerations in mind. The power failure in New York City during the night of November 9–10, 1965, part of the massive blackout of the northeast states, provided a unique opportunity to test the utility of laboratory findings about individual differences in anxiety and affiliative behavior during a crisis situation. This report is based upon data collected that night; its specific focus is on anxiety arousal, anxiety reduction, and affiliative choice as related to birth order.

The hypotheses to be tested have their theoretical basis in an environmental explanation of birth order effects (e.g., Schachter, 1959; Sears, Maccoby, & Levin, 1957). Working within this framework, Schachter (1959) demonstrated that firstborns become more anxious than later borns when exposed to an anxiety-arousing experience. It has also been shown that under laboratory-induced stress conditions firstborns generally express a greater preference than later borns for affiliation (Darley & Aronson, 1966; Gerard & Rabbie, 1961; Sarnoff & Zimbardo, 1961; Schachter, 1959; Zimbardo & Formica, 1963), and they feel more at ease when they are allowed to wait with others (Wrightsman, 1960). In the present situation the stress consisted of being deprived of information and being separated from one's usual affiliative objects (family and friends). In addition, most subjects were physically uncomfortable and uncertain about the outcome.

The hypotheses to be tested were[3]:

1. Firstborn subjects should be more anxious than later borns in a stress situation.
2. Firstborn subjects should be more likely to affiliate than later borns in a stress situation.
3. When people seeking to reduce stress are behaving in a manner congruent with birth order theory, reported anxiety should be lower than it is for people who are not behaving congruently with the theory (cf. Dohrenwend & Dohrenwend, 1966). Thus, firstborn subjects who are affiliating and later borns who are not should report lower levels of anxiety than should firstborn subjects who are not affiliating and later borns who are.

METHOD

Data Collection Setting

The power failure occurred in New York City at about 5:30 P.M., at a time when darkness was falling and the city was at the peak of its evening rush hour. The blackout lasted until the early hours of the next morning. (For a general description of the power failure's effect on individuals, business operations, and the transportation network, see Rosenthal & Gelb, 1965.) The authors arrived in Manhattan shortly before midnight. On the basis of radio information that the major bus terminal for Manhattan had restored some of its operations and thus provided one of the few outlets from the city, it was decided to begin data collection there.

[3]Because of obvious time limitations only the broad outline of the hypotheses was formulated prior to data collection. However, it should be emphasized that they are not ex post facto.

At the terminal there was some dim emergency lighting. A large number of people were standing, sitting, or lying on the floor attempting to rest. The authors identified themselves and requested help in completing a questionnaire about the blackout and their personal experiences of it. Data were obtained from 15 men and 8 women.

At about 1:30 A.M., in an effort to sample another area, we moved toward midtown and discovered that one hotel was operating with adequate illumination from an emergency power plant. The atmosphere here was more lively than it was in the terminal. Data were obtained from 50 men and 27 women at this location. The overall cooperation rate at both sites was approximately 70%.

Sample Characteristics

The total sample consisted of 65 men and 35 women. The mean age for men was 41.9, with a range of 17–70; for women the mean was 37.6, with a range of 18–70. Using Hollingshead's (1957) two-factor index of social position, the social class distribution for Classes 1 (highest) through 5 (lowest) was 14.6, 17.7, 34.4, 2.2, and 4.0%, respectively.

Questionnaire

The main research instrument was a self-administered questionnaire concerned with demographic variables (e.g., age, education, occupation, birth order in family, family size, etc.), and with subjects' feelings about being stranded during the blackout. The following measures were coded:

1. *Birth order.* This measure was simply a score of ordinal position. First and only children were grouped together.

2. *Affiliative preference.* Self-report information was sought concerning subjects' feelings about being stranded alone for a long period of time, if that had been true earlier in the evening, or about having been in the enforced company of others for a long period, if that were true. Subjects who were

with other people for a fairly long period of time were asked to report their preference for affiliation or for being alone on a five-item Likert-type scale. Choices ranged from an extreme affiliative preference ("I very much preferred being together with others"), scored 5, to an extreme preference for isolation ("I very much would have preferred being alone"), scored 1.

A similar scale was given to those who were alone for a long period of time, again with 5 indicating the extreme preference for affiliation and 1 the extreme preference for being alone. Since only 18 subjects answered this item, and their responses to the other questionnaire items were highly similar to those given by subjects who were in the enforced company of others, responses on the two scales were grouped together in the analyses.

3. *Anxiety.* The question used to assess anxiety was: "How nervous or uneasy did you feel during this experience (i.e., the blackout experience over the course of the evening)?" Here also subjects chose their answer from one of the five Likert-type alternatives ranging from "I felt extremely uneasy" (scored 5) to "I felt completely calm" (scored 1).

Overt Affiliative Behavior

In addition to the affiliative preference score, which was a retrospective measure of subjects' experiences earlier in the night, an index was obtained of their actual gregariousness at the time of data collection. Before approaching the prospective subject the researcher noted whether he or she was affiliating (either talking or standing with someone) or was alone. The judgment of whether a subject was affiliating or alone was based on several criteria. Verbal interaction was a sufficient condition for the judgment of "together"; if there was merely spatial closeness, subjects were observed briefly to note if they initiated any talk or showed other signs that they were affiliating. A dichotomous affiliation-nonaffiliation measure was employed.

RESULTS

Since the distributions were not normal all hypotheses were tested using chi-square or Fisher's exact test. Following McNemar (1962, pp. 236–238), Fisher's exact test was used wherever the smallest expected cell values were less than 5. When the smallest expected value was 5–10, chi-square corrected for continuity was used. In all instances firstborn and only child subjects were compared with later-born subjects. Median splits were used to categorize the data. Most analyses are based on reduced Ns since questionnaires were not completely filled out by some subjects. Finally, because of sex differences reported in the literature (Gerard & Rabbie, 1961; Miller & Zimbardo, 1966; Warren, 1966) hypotheses were examined separately for men and women.

Hypothesis 1 stated that firstborns would be more anxious than later borns in the blackout situation. The results for men (Table 1) showed a trend ($p < .10$) in the appropriate direction. The results for women (Table 1) were similar ($p = .08$). Analysis of the total sample showed a significant relationship in the predicted direction

($\chi^2 = 6.57$, $p < .05$). Thus there tends to be overall support for Hypothesis 1.

The second hypothesis stated that firstborn subjects should be more likely to affiliate during the blackout situation, as compared to later borns. It was tested using both the measure of overt affiliative *behavior* at the time of contact and the subjects' reports of affiliative *preferences* earlier in the evening. These results are given in Table 2. For men, on the behavioral measure there were no differences in affiliative condition between first- and later borns. Among women a trend was observed ($p = .06$) in the predicted direction.

TABLE 1
Association Between Birth Order And Anxiety, Men and Women Separately

Anxiety	Birth order	
	Firstborn	Later born
Men[a]		
Low (1)[b]	15	24
High (2–5)	15	9
Women[c]		
Low (1, 2)	4	15
High (3–5)	7	6

Note.—All p values are for two-tailed tests.
[a]$N = 63$; $\chi^2 = 3.44$, $p < .10$.
[b]Figures in parentheses indicate the ranges for the high- and low-anxiety groups.
[c]$N = 32$; exact $p = .08$.

TABLE 2
Association Between Birth Order And Affiliative Measures, Men And Women Separately

Affiliation	Birth order	
	Firstborn	Later born
AFFILIATIVE CONDITION AT TIME OF CONTACT		
Men[a]		
Alone	15	13
Together	10	11
Women[b]		
Alone	0	6
Together	10	12
REPORTED AFFILIATIVE PREFERENCE[c]		
Men[d]		
Low	25	17
High	4	13
Women[e]		
Low	3	12
High	8	9

Note.—All p values are for two-tailed tests.
[a]$N = 49$; $\chi^2 = .17$.
[b]$N = 28$; exact $p = .06$.
[c]The affiliative preference scores were 1–4 for the low group and greater than 4 for the high group, for both men and women.
[d]$N = 59$; $\chi^2 = 4.92$, $p < .05$.
[e]$N = 32$; $\chi^2 = 1.53$, corrected for continuity.

The results on the affiliative preference measure (see Table 2) are somewhat different. Firstborn men expressed a weaker preference for being together than did later borns ($p < .05$). Thus the findings for men contradict the hypothesis. For women the data are in the predicted direction but are not significant. Finally, it should be noted that analyses on the combined sample showed no differences ($\chi^2 = .04$ for the behavioral measure; $\chi^2 = 1.65$ for the preference measure).

Hypothesis 3 was concerned with an interaction effect: when affiliative behavior is congruent with the affiliative choice that would be presupposed as a result of birth-order differences, anxiety level should be lower than when the behavior and expected choice are not congruent. This prediction was tested by chi-square, using Cochran's procedure for evaluating heterogeneity among replicate fourfold tables (Bliss, 1967). The direction of the results (see Table 3)[4] is consistent with the hypothesis. The analyses on men showed a heterogeneity effect; that is, significantly different anxiety-affiliation relationships existed between the two birth-order groups. Examination of the within-birth-order data shows that these relationships were in the expected directions, with anxiety being negatively related to affiliation among firstborns and positively related among later borns. However, only the firstborn men's results were significant ($p = .04$). No main effect relationship of affiliation to anxiety across birth order was noted (the pooled chi-square was 1.34, corrected for continuity).

An overall test of heterogeneity could not be computed on the women's data since all the firstborns in our sample were together at the time they were observed. Among later-born women the relationship was in the predicted direction, although it was not significant.

Finally, analyses on the combined sample of

[4]Differences in N's between Tables 1 and 3 are due to missing data on one or another of the variables jointly needed for Table 3 entries.

TABLE 3
Association Between Anxiety And Affiliative Condition At Time Of Contact, Men And Women Separately

| | Birth order | | | |
| | Firstborn | | Later born | |
Anxiety[a]	Alone	Together	Alone	Together
Men[b]				
High	10	2	5	5
Low	4	8	8	6
	Exact $p = .04$		Exact $p = .98$	
Women[c]				
High	0	6	1	6
Low	0	3	5	5
			Exact $p = .31$	

Note.—All p values are for two-tailed tests.
[a]Anxiety score ranges for men were: low (1); high (2–5); for women: low (1, 2); high (3–5).
[b]$N = 48$; chi-square for heterogeneity effect between firstborn and later-born men $= 4.03$, $df = 1$, $p < .05$.
[c]$N = 26$.

men and women also showed a significant heterogeneity effect ($\chi^2_h = 4.11$, $df = 1$, $p < .05$). Neither of the within-birth-order effects was significant but both were in the appropriate direction. Thus the data from the combined sample indicate an interaction effect that is attributable equally to first- and later borns. No main affiliation-anxiety effect was observed (the pooled chi-square was 0.11).

As hypothesized, the general pattern of these results suggests that when birth-order-affiliation patterns are not congruent with the choice expected from birth-order theory, higher anxiety will be reported.

DISCUSSION

Hypothesis 1 was marginally supported among both men and women. These results are consistent with the earlier findings reported for women by Schachter (1959), using a questionnaire measure of anxiety, and by Gerard and Rabbie (1961), using a physiological measure. Our findings for men run counter to the absence of differences observed by Zimbardo and Formica (1963) in college males. However, the present results are consistent with the more recent observations of Nisbett (1967) and Helmreich and Collins (1967). Data from the latter study suggest that the predicted relationship will manifest itself only under conditions of moderate to high fear arousal. In reconciling our findings with this conflicting literature, we can suggest two possibilities: (*a*) the stress of the blackout was not contrived in the laboratory, and its arousal value was probably of moderate to high intensity at its peak; (*b*) the psychological naiveté of our subjects may have contributed to this effect, as may also have been the case in the Helmreich and Collins study (which utilized a high school population).

The tests of the second hypothesis show the following pattern. In the women's data the relationship reaches the trend level on the affiliative behavior measure; on the preference measure the relationship is in the expected direction but is not significant. However, the data from men do not support the hypothesis on the behavioral measure, and on the preference measure there is a significant association in the direction opposite to expectation.

What can account for these sex differences? Examination of the marginal totals from Table 2 shows that 53% of the women expressed a strong preference for affiliation, while only 29% of the men expressed this preference. Moreover, 79% of the women but only 43% of the men were with others at the time of contact. Thus men, irrespective of birth order, are less affiliative on both verbal report and behavioral indexes. These data are congruent with the expected pattern of sex differences in affiliation (cf. Kagan, 1964). So also are the correlations (r_{pb}) between the two affiliation measures (.59, $p < .05$, for women; .17, for men, *ns*). These results highlight the greater complexity

of affiliative relationships among men.

Within this context the finding that firstborn women are more likely to *actually* be together can be viewed as consistent with the *preference* data typically reported for women (e.g., Darley & Aronson, 1966; Gerard & Rabbie, 1961; Schachter, 1959). The results on our preference measure, although not significant, are in the same direction as those reported in the above studies. It appears that only among women, where culturally determined sex-role expectations are congruent with the birth-order-affiliation relationship expected from the "early experience" theory, will the appropriate relationship be manifested. Conversely, among men factors other than birth order may intervene to a greater extent. The fact that first- and later borns were about equally distributed among the two affiliative conditions suggests that this is the case. However, the significant relationship observed on the preference measure still remains unexplained. The data we have do not allow for further exploration of the sources of this relationship. Laboratory studies suggest this could be attributable to an interaction between birth order and either long-term subject variables (cf. Miller & Zimbardo, 1966; Zimbardo & Formica, 1963) or more immediate situational factors (cf. Helmreich & Collins, 1967; Zimbardo & Formica, 1963).

With respect to Hypothesis 3, affiliative performance and birth order were treated as independent variables and their joint relationship to anxiety was evaluated. The results supported the interaction hypothesis. The men's data suggest that the main contribution to this effect was provided by differences among firstborns. One final cautionary note: although the interaction was in accord with our prediction, it is also possible (as it is for the preference effect among men) that both higher anxiety and the propensity for being alone among some firstborn males may be a consequence of a long-term adaptation, rather than being situationally produced.

REFERENCES

Baker, G. W., & Chapman, D. W. (Eds.) *Man and society in disaster*. New York: Basic Books, 1962.

Bliss, C. I. *Statistics in biology*. Vol. 1. New York: McGraw-Hill, 1967.

Cantril, H. The invasion from Mars. In E. E. Maccoby, T. M. Newcomb, & E. L. Hartley (Eds.), *Readings in social psychology*. (3rd ed.) New York: Holt, 1958.

Darley, J. M., & Aronson, E. Self-evaluation vs. direct anxiety reduction as determinants of the fear-affiliation relationship. *Journal of Experimental Social Psychology*, 1966, Suppl. 1, 66–79.

Dohrenwend, B. S., & Dohrenwend, B. P. Stress situations, birth order, and psychological symptoms. *Journal of Abnormal Psychology*, 1966, *71*, 215–223.

Gerard, H. B., & Rabbie, J. M. Fear and social comparison. *Journal of Abnormal and Social Psychology*, 1961, *62*, 586–592.

Helmreich, R. L. & Collins, B. E. Situational determinants of affiliative preference under stress. *Journal of Personality and Social Psychology*, 1967, *6*, 79–85.

Hollingshead, A. B. Two factor index of social position. New Haven: Private printing, 1957.

Janis, I. L. *Air war and emotional stress: Psychological studies of bombing and civilian defense*. New York: McGraw-Hill, 1951.

Kagan, J. Acquisition and significance of sex typing and sex role identity. In M. L. Hoffman & L. W. Hoffman (Eds.), *Review of child development research*. Vol. 1. New York: Russell Sage Foundation, 1964.

Killian, L. M. *A study of the response to the Houston, Texas, fireworks explosion*. Washington, D. C.: National Academy of Sciences, National Research Council, 1956.

McNemar, Q. *Psychological statistics*. (3rd ed.) New York: Wiley, 1962.

Miller, N., & Zimbardo, P. G. Motives for fear-induced affiliation: Emotional comparison or interpersonal similarity? *Journal of Personality*, 1966, *34*, 481–503.

Nash, G., & Nash, P. Attitudes during the blackout. Bureau of Applied Social Research, Columbia University, 1965. (Mimeo)

Nisbett, R. E. Birth order, pain sensitivity, and participation in dangerous sports. Paper presented at the meeting of the Eastern Psychological Association, Boston, April 1967.

Raynor, J. Studies of disasters and other extreme situations—an annotated bibliography. *Human Organization*, 1957, *16*, 30–40.

Rosenthal, A. M., & Gelb, A. *The night when the lights went out*. New York: Signet, 1965.

Sarnoff, I., & Zimbardo, P. G. Anxiety, fear, and social isolation. *Journal of Abnormal and Social Psychology*, 1961, *62*, 356–363.

Schachter, S. *The psychology of affiliation*. Stanford, Calif.: Stanford University Press, 1959.

Sears, R. R., Maccoby, E., & Levin, H. *Patterns of child rearing*. Evanston, Ill.: Row, Peterson, 1957.

Veltford, H. R., & Lee, S. E. The Coconut Grove fire: A study in scapegoating. *Journal of Abnormal and Social Psychology*, 1943, *38*, 138–154.

Vernon, P. E. Psychological effects of air raids. *Journal of Abnormal and Social Psychology*, 1941, *36*, 457–476.

Walker, E. L., & Atkinson, J. W. The expression of fear-related motivation in thematic apperception as a function of proximity to an atomic explosion. In J. W. Atkinson (Ed.), *Motives in fantasy, action, and society*. Princeton, N. J.: Van Nostrand, 1958.

Warren, J. R. Birth order and social behavior. *Psychological Bulletin*, 1966, *65*, 38–49.

Wrightsman, L. S., Jr. Effects of waiting with others on changes in level of felt anxiety. *Journal of Abnormal and Social Psychology*, 1960, *61*, 216–222.

Zimbardo, P. G., & Formica, R. Emotional comparison and self-esteem as determinants of affiliation. *Journal of Personality*, 1963, *31*, 141–162.

STUDY QUESTIONS

1. What were the major variables in this study? Which variables were treated as independent, or predictor, variables and which were treated as dependent, or criterion, variables?

2. How was each variable operationalized?

3. How did the authors obtain their samples? What might be the characteristics of the populations that these samples represent?

4. What further research problems or hypotheses are suggested by the findings of this study?

EXERCISES

1   *Problems and Hypotheses*

A. Give operational definitions for the following constructs:

aggression

affiliation

racism
dependence

B. Formulate research problems for the following constructs:

authoritarianism
homosexuality
achievement motivation
disclosure

C. Develop a research hypothesis for each of the following problems:

Does anxiety affect interpersonal relationships?
What is the relationship between identity status and political preference?
Does family size affect self-disclosure?
Is there a relationship between sexual behavior and academic achievement?

D. Optional Questions

1. What is wrong with the following hypotheses?
Sinister forces can destroy evidence.
Two-parent homes are better for children than one-parent homes.
Human beings are the only animals that think in images.
Athletes have more unconscious sexual hang-ups than musicians.

2. What is wrong with the following definitions (that is, why are they not operational)?
Intelligence is the ability to think quickly in a difficult situation.
Depression is a low, heavy feeling.
A phobia is an irrational, persistent fear of a particular object.

2 Popular Media

Part 1.   Find a selection in the popular media (for example, a daily or weekly newspaper or a popular magazine) that reports psychological information. Finding an article discussing "what's new" on some psychological issue, such as juvenile delinquency, dating patterns, drug use, new modes of child-rearing, aging, and the like, should be fairly easy.

A. Give the source for the selection in complete bibliographic form, using American Psychological Association (APA) form. (See Appendix B for information on APA style. Note that this book as

well as most of the selections it contains conforms to APA style.)

B. Describe briefly the main point(s) of the selection.

C. What information does the author give about the sample from which the data were derived?

D. What information does the author provide about the *ways* information was obtained—for example, through interviews or questionnaires?

E. In what form—that is, quantitative or qualitative—is the information reported? What kinds of data are given? Are the results of any statistical tests reported?

F. Does the author distinguish clearly between fact and assumption, and between data and inference? Explain.

G. What changes would have to be made to make this selection conform to the requirements of good scientific reporting?

Part 2.   Find a selection from the scientific psychological media that is relevant to the popular-media article you chose for Part 1. Give the source in complete bibliographic form, using APA style.

A. What distinguishes the two reporting styles?

B. Are there differences in the conclusions reached in the two selections? If so, what are they?

Part 3.   Develop a study topic of your own based on the two selections:

A. Formulate a research question or hypothesis, being sure to operationalize your variables.

B. If you were to carry out a study of your hypothesis, what would be the characteristics of your population? How would you obtain your sample? What reliability and validity problems would you have to consider?

C. If you were to carry out a study to test your hypothesis, what contribution would your research make to science as a whole? Refer to the second list on page 11 to help you determine the contribution such a study could make.

3 Further Adventures in the Library[5]

Consider each of the clichés listed below. (Your class might add more items to this list.) Note that each saying relates in some way to behavior. Choose two of the clichés and treat them as hypotheses. Go to the

---

[5]Adapted from Gardner (1977).

library and find empirical evidence that either supports or fails to support the hypothesis derived from the saying. Write an abstract of two relevant studies, indicating how they support or fail to support each saying. Cite your sources fully, using APA reference style.

1. She's a chip off the old block.
2. You can't teach an old dog new tricks.
3. Birds of a feather flock together.
4. Out of sight out of mind.
5. Once a thief, always a thief.
6. Where there's life, there's hope.

ANNOTATED BIBLIOGRAPHY

Bowman, P. C. & Auerbach, S. M. Measuring sex-role attitudes: The problem of the well-meaning liberal male. *Personality and Social Psychology Bulletin*, 1978, *4*, 265–271.

Sixteen "well-meaning" and 16 "sincere" liberal males were identified on the basis of their responses to the Attitudes toward Women Scale and the Bentler Questionnaire for sex-role stereotyping. Well-meaning males described themselves as more feminine and also had significantly higher social desirability scores than liberal males, suggesting that they were more susceptible to the social-desirability-response bias. Methodological problems in this as well as other studies are identified as the source of much confusion and contradictory evidence regarding the measurement of sex-role attitudes.

Fiske, D. W. *Measuring the concepts of personality*. Chicago: Aldine, 1971.

Fiske defines personality as the way individuals interact with the world outside themselves and the world within themselves. In his text, Fiske stresses the necessity for an intensive analysis of the concept a researcher wants to measure and for the links between that concept and the measuring operations used to assess it. Topics covered include the modes of measuring personality, the specification of constructs, the fundamentals of measurement, and the taking of tests.

Huck, S. W., Cormier, W. H., & Bounds, W. G., Jr. *Reading statistics and research*. N.Y.: Harper & Row, 1974.

This valuable little book provides an introduction to statistics and research design as they are generally presented in reports on psychological studies. Using a highly readable style and many examples drawn from published research, the authors make it clear that reading about statistics and designs can be fun and profitable.

Kobasa, S. C. Stressful life events, personality, and health: An inquiry into hardiness. *Journal of Personality and Social Psychology*, 1979, *37*, 1–11.

Statistical analyses were performed on two groups of executives who received similar scores on the Holmes and Rahe schedule of recent life events, the first group retaining their health and the second falling ill after high-stress events. The findings suggest that individuals who value themselves, maintain an attitude of vigorousness toward the environment, and have an internal locus of control are less susceptible to illness after experiencing stressful events than individuals who lack this hardiness.

Rodin, J. Research on eating behavior and obesity: Where does it fit in personality and social psychology? *Personality and Social Psychology Bulletin*, 1977, *3*, 333–355.

In her review of current research in the area of eating and obesity, Rodin argues that eating must be examined at many different levels of analysis and with multiple methodologies. She suggests that research on eating is important to our understanding of such issues as stigmatization and deviance, self-perception, and individual differences.

ADDITIONAL SOURCES

Anderson, B. F. *The psychology experiment* (2nd ed.). Monterey: Brooks/Cole, 1971.

Holt, R. R. *Assessing personality*. New York: Harcourt, Brace, Jovanovich, 1971.

Sundberg, N. D. *Assessment of persons*. Englewood Cliffs, N.J.: Prentice-Hall, 1977.

4

Ethical Issues

You know by now how to formulate a research question and how to develop research hypotheses. You have broadened your library research skills and learned how to use a number of valuable resources. And you have considered using yourself as a research investigator and subject. However, before you embark more fully into the research enterprise, we believe it imperative that you think carefully about the ethical and moral issues involved in all forms of research. A number of issues in particular deserve your thoughtful consideration. All these issues are related to the rights, safety, and comfort of your potential subjects and to the content of your interaction with them.

A manual called *Ethical Principles of Research with Human Participants* prepared by the American Psychological Association (APA) and published in 1973 is a very useful guide for researchers concerned about these issues. The APA Committee on Ethical Stan-

dards in Psychological Research (henceforth called the Ethics Committee) explains in the manual the method it used to develop the principles of ethics as well as the reasoning behind them, elucidating with relevant examples from published research. In addition, the manual details steps that investigators can take to facilitate responsible decisions concerning the ethics of research. The whole manual is easy to read, thought-provoking, and well worth your careful perusal. In this chapter we highlight several interrelated ethical issues of special significance raised in the manual: informed consent, subject protection, and debriefing.

INFORMED CONSENT

The principle of informed consent originates in the idea that subjects should understand fully the nature of the research before they agree to participate in it. A general practice among researchers is to have potential subjects first read and discuss a statement about the intended project and then sign their names if they are willing to participate. It should be emphasized that informed consent involves much more than merely obtaining verbal consent. It is the investigator's responsibility to make sure that subjects truly understand the issues and methods involved before they consent to participate. Thus, consent is not where subjects agree to participate, for example, merely because they trust or respect the investigator or because they want course credit. Rather, consent must be based on subjects' full understanding of the project in which their participation is sought, and obtaining such consent is the researcher's goal.

Related to the principle of informed consent are principles pertaining to the level of honesty in the investigator/participant relationship as well as to the importance of allowing subjects to refrain from or discontinue participation. To give you a flavor of the Ethics Manual, we are including two principles verbatim.

> Principle 4. Openness and honesty are essential characteristics of the relationship between investigator and research participant. When the methodological requirements of a study necessitate concealment or deception, the investigator is required to ensure the participants' understanding of the reasons for this action and to restore the quality of the relationship with the investigator [p. 29].
> Principle 5. Ethical research practice requires the investigator to respect the individual's freedom to decline to participate in research or to discontinue participation at any time [p. 42].

These principles, like the other APA principles, are meant not as moral absolutes but as guidelines to the creation of research decisions. The Ethics Committee has recognized that it is possible to design investigations in which exceptions to these principles are both necessary methodologically and justifiable ethically, but urge investigators to be sensitive in all cases to the welfare and dignity of the participant.

In what kinds of studies might informed consent be considered irrelevant? The clearest cases are *naturalistic observations*—observations of unmanipulated real-life situations—and *content analyses* of available documents, both of which are discussed more fully in the next two chapters. In an observational study, you might stand at a street corner and make note of who is more likely to jaywalk—females or males, children or adults, college students or business people. Most investigators in this situation would not stop all the people arriving at the street corner to ask for a signed agreement to having their street-crossing behavior watched. Such investigators would be likely to argue that their observations could cause no conceivable harm to any of the "subjects," and that attempts to obtain informed consent would preclude the possibility of making valid observations of this particular form of everyday behavior.

Do you agree with this argument? Can you think of a case in which naturalistic observation could have real ethical implications? Consider a scenario in which someone stole your findings and published them in a source that used them to inflame antifemale (or antimale) or antistudent (or antibusinessperson) feelings. Or consider the possibility of someone watching you make notes, asking what you are doing, and becoming incensed by the reply. Is it ethical to anger a hapless stranger? How would you handle a problem of this sort?

In thinking about situations in which the principle of informed consent might not apply, the Ethics Committee devoted considerable attention to the issue of privacy. Privacy has been defined as "the freedom of the individual to pick and choose for himself the time and circumstances under which, and most importantly, the extent to which, his attitudes, beliefs, behavior and opinions are to be shared with or withheld from others" (Ruebhausen & Brim, 1966, p. 426). Most people would probably agree that an individual's privacy would be violated if a psychiatrist, teacher, or priest published transcripts of personal conversations with that individual without the person's permission and without disguising his or her identity. On the other hand, if a student made naturalistic observations of mothers entering a well-baby clinic, noting simply whether each mother held her baby to the right or left side of her body (over her heart), it seems likely that few people would consider the privacy of the mothers violated. But if researchers were observing "pick-up" tactics in a dating bar, do you think the case could be made that the privacy of the patrons was being invaded? The Ethics Committee believes that ensuring subjects' right to privacy is a complex problem involving matters of subject protection, informed consent, and more.

The issue of informed consent has been argued philosophically (for example, by Baumrind, 1971; Gergen, 1973; Smith, 1976) and studied empirically (for example, by Wilson & Donnerstein, 1976). In the Wilson and Donnerstein (1976) study, students of the authors interviewed 174 adults selected randomly in field locations such as parking lots, shopping centers, and parks. The procedure consisted of presenting to subjects descriptions of methods used in eight actual field studies conducted in naturalistic settings. The following is an example of one of the study summaries: "Automobiles, parked on streets, look as if they were abandoned. . . . Experimenters hide in nearby buildings and film people who have any contact with the cars (Zimbardo, 1969)" (Wilson & Donnerstein, 1976, p. 767). Subjects were asked questions about the legal and ethical aspects of each method. Sample questions included "If you discovered that you had been a subject in this experiment would you feel that you had been harrassed or annoyed?" and "Do you feel that such an experiment is unethical or immoral?"

While responses regarding the eight different methods varied, in no case did all respondents

judge a procedure to be ethical or report that they would not object to being subjects in the experiment described. It is still a matter of debate whether a majority opinion, a unanimous opinion, or an opinion drawn from "people in the street" should be used to determine whether a particular study is ethical (for example, Baumrind, 1971; Smith, 1976).

We believe that research in *field settings* is an important part of the psychological endeavor. Moreover, the use of naturalistic observations, unobtrusive techniques, and nonreactive measures is frequently justifiable even though informed consent is not obtained with these methodologies. (These procedures will be discussed in more detail in later chapters. Also, see Webb, Campbell, Schwartz, & Sechrest [1966].) We support the position of the Ethics Committee that risks must be weighed against benefits in deciding the question of informed consent, as well as the other ethical principles. The question to ask is What, if any, are the risks (physical or psychological) of such procedures to subject groups, and what are the benefits of the procedures, for example, in terms of knowledge and understanding? The potential risks and benefits of any proposed research should always be evaluated carefully. In many cases, it will be apparent that the study in question could result in little or no physical or psychological harm to anyone, and that the study could make an important contribution to the science of psychology. In other cases, as illustrated in the selections in this chapter, a particular procedure might engender considerable controversy. Because together the three articles in this chapter represent a relatively detailed and thoughtful dialogue about the complex ethical issues involved in a published empirical study, we describe them in some detail here.

A Special Case: A Study of Personal Space

All three articles in this chapter are concerned with a single controversial field experiment conducted by Middlemist, Knowles, and Matter

(1976). As you will read in the first article, these authors were interested in the construct of *personal space*. The basic notion is that except under rather well-defined circumstances of intimacy, we all have an invisible and personally defined space around us and that generally we do not like others to intrude in this space. If someone stands or sits "too close by," we are likely to feel uncomfortable and to want to move away far enough to set up a more comfortable distance for ourselves.

Studies of personal space, especially of responses to "invasions" of personal space, have been carried out in a number of real-life and laboratory settings. Middlemist, Knowles, and Matter decided to study physiological responses to personal-space invasion in a particular natural setting: a men's lavatory. Their hypothesis was that the closer a man wanting to use a urinal had to stand to someone else, the more uncomfortable he would feel. This stress would have a particular physiological effect identified in other research—a delay in the onset of micturation (urination) followed by a shorter, more rapid period of micturation than under nonstress conditions.

The investigators designed an experiment in which anyone entering the lavatory to urinate had to stand either immediately adjacent to or one urinal removed from a confederate[1] who appeared to be using one of the other urinals. In addition to these two experimental conditions a control condition was introduced in which no confederate was present. Because auditory cues could not be used to time onset and cessation of micturation, an observer in a locked toilet stall used an unobtrusive periscope device to make direct visual sightings of the stream of urine. The authors' hypothesis was supported by the data.

What do you think about the ethics of these procedures? Koocher, in the second chapter

---

[1]In psychology, a confederate is an associate of the experimenter who plays a role in the experiment without the knowledge of subjects.

selection, questions the sensitivity of the authors to the human dignity (stressed strongly by the Ethics Committee) of the subjects. He notes that Middlemist and his colleagues neither address the possible discomfort to the subjects in the "close-distance" condition nor the potential harm to an unstable individual who accidently discovered he was being observed. Koocher concludes that the risk/benefit rationale of the investigators should be made explicit in a study of this sort.

In the third chapter selection, Middlemist, Knowles, and Matter reply to Koocher. They explain that a pilot study was conducted prior to the experiment wherein approximately 50% of the subjects were interviewed following the observational procedure. The investigators argue that none of the men had realized he was being observed and none was bothered upon learning of the observation. All agreed to allow their data to be used. The writers also argue that the situations studied, where a man used a urinal near another man either at the next urinal or farther away or used a urinal in a room alone, were "common and unmemorable." Moreover, a number of safeguards were adopted in conjunction with the periscope procedure: (1) no information as to the identity of the subjects was recorded; (2) the confederate was prepared to signal with a cough if an experimental trial should be aborted; (3) all the investigators were ready to anticipate any concern or suspicion expressed by a participant so he could be informed and debriefed (which never happened); and (4) subjects were not informed about having been observed, so they could not be uncomfortable about it.

In their reply to Koocher, Middlemist, Knowles, and Matter (1977) conclude that his article does raise important questions about how ethical principles are to be implemented. They note the need for clearer norms about ethical decision rules and for standards on reporting how those decisions are made (p. 124). The current absence of guidelines does not, of course, relieve researchers of the responsibility for asking ethical questions and acting on their answers before conducting research.

When you read the chapter selections, you might find it easy to respond emotionally to the notion of research that focuses on urination in a public lavatory. But before you dismiss the Middlemist study as either silly or outrageous, consider the fact that important findings often grow out of apparently insignificant efforts at basic research. The inability of some men to urinate in public restrooms is a serious psychological problem that can interfere with all aspects of a man's personal, social, or occupational life. (See, for example, Wilson, 1973.) While Middlemist and his co-workers did not set out to solve this problem, their findings on the relationship between interpersonal distances and stress reactions in a public lavatory would certainly contribute to a solution. If the cost/benefit ratio is to be given serious consideration in the evaluation of research ethics, then neither potential costs nor potential benefits should be construed too narrowly.

Analyzing Available Materials

The other possibly less controversial, type of research in which informed consent is not obtained as a rule is content analysis of *archival*, or *available, materials*. As discussed in Chapter 6, content analysis is a procedure whereby information is abstracted from some type of human communication. Archival materials are forms of human communication that are generally available to the public. Published songs, books, newspaper articles, marriage and birth announcements, lists of "best sellers" are all available materials. You might choose to do a content analysis of song lyrics from 1975 through 1978 and compare them with lyrics from 1965 through 1968 to determine whether love themes were displaced by explicit sexual themes. What, if any, would be the ethical implications of such an undertaking? Would informed consent be necessary? If you think it

would be, from whom would you obtain it? The Ethics Committee suggests that in such "historical research" where no real human participants are involved the principle of informed consent is irrelevant.

Dealing Ethically with Deception

Finally, a research methodology exists in which subject consent is not truly "informed" although subjects are aware that they are participating in research. Moreover, at the end of their participation subjects are frequently informed, or debriefed, as to the nature of the investigation in which they have been involved. This methodology is used in studies where *deception* is considered necessary for valid tests of the hypotheses. Suppose you choose to examine the notion that frustration interferes with performance on a task. You might believe that the only way to test the hypothesis adequately is through an experimental design in which you manipulate frustration—for example, by presenting the subject with an impossible task—and then observe the effects of the frustration. If you told the subjects in advance what you intended to do, it is unlikely that their responses would be the same as when they were naive regarding your purposes and expectations.

Considerable controversy surrounds the acceptability of deception as a scientific procedure. Some psychologists (for example, Baumrind, 1971, 1972) find it ethically reprehensible, and others (for example, Gergen 1973) argue that it is essential to much psychological research and not necessarily damaging in its effects. The Ethics Committee suggests that under certain conditions the use of deception is ethically acceptable. These conditions are as follows:

a) The research problem is of great importance; *b*) it may be demonstrated that the research objectives cannot be realized without deception; *c*) there is sufficient reason for the concealment or misrepresentation that, on being fully informed later on (Principle 8), the research participant may be expected to find it reasonable, and to suffer no loss of confidence in the integrity of the investigator or of others involved; *d*) the research participant is allowed to withdraw from the study at any time (Principle 5), and is free to withdraw the data when the concealment or misrepresentation is revealed (Principle 8); and *e*) the investigator takes full responsibility for detecting and removing stressful aftereffects (Principle 9) [p. 37].

THE PROTECTION OF SUBJECTS

Implicit in the committee's conditions and in its subsequent discussion is the conviction that deceived subjects, like other subjects, must be protected from *undue* and unjustifiable physical and mental stress. A considerable body of research within the biomedical sciences involves the first factor, physical stress to subjects. For example studies exist of (1) the physiological effects of high levels of heat, noise, altitude, and vibration; (2) the psychological and behavioral effects of drugs, including alcohol and LSD; and (3) reactions to pain stimuli such as electric shock. We presume that none of our readers have the qualifications—or the desire—to carry out personal investigations of this sort. Note, however, that generally in such studies informed consent is considered necessary, and that no risk/benefit ratio justifies stress with potentially irreversible aftereffects. Recent disclosures concerning CIA-sponsored research on the effects of LSD on unsuspecting, undebriefed subjects reveal methodologies that are unacceptable in the current code of ethics of both APA and U.S. government—as well as most other widely accepted codes.

The issue of mental stress is more relevant to your personal research considerations. In some cases, psychological stress is built into the design of a study. Usually, in such cases subjects are deceived about the true purposes of the investigation. For example, in a number of studies self-esteem is manipulated—say, by providing subjects with false positive or negative information about themselves. Subjects given negative feedback (for instance "You are certainly dumb") might experience considerable stress during the course of the experiment. Moreover, both they and the subjects given positive feedback might feel angry and distressed after a debriefing in which they are informed that all feedback was false. What do you think? Is it ethical to impose this kind of stress on research participants? In many cases, probably not.

While ethical issues involved in the deliberate manipulation of stress are complex, the problems are at least more explicit than in cases where stress is inadvertent and unintended. Suppose that you are interested in "modern" responses to pornographic pictures among college students. One person's source of titillation might be another's source of embarrassment and dismay. Or, to cite another example, questions concerning parental child-rearing practices might result in considerable discomfort for individuals with unhappy home lives or those in the throes of guilt over rejecting their parents. As a researcher, it is your responsibility to evaluate the possibility of mental distress to potential subjects and determine how to handle it appropriately if you proceed with your investigation.

Later we discuss some steps to take in evaluating projected research procedures, but first let's return to the issue of deception. According to Baumrind (1971), "My own belief . . . is that subjects are less adversely affected by physical pain or stress than they are by experiences that result in loss of trust in themselves and the investigator and, by extension, in the meaningfulness of life itself" [p.890]. In her view, the risk/benefit approach of the Ethics Committee provides investigators too many opportunities to rationalize their own egocentric interests. Moreover, she believes that an approach in which the risk is to the subject and the benefit is to the investigator is morally indefensible.

Baumrind (1971) also argues that research psychologists violate fundamental moral principles of reciprocity and justice whenever they deceive individuals who trust them. "It is unjust to use naive, that is, trusting subjects, and then exploit their naivete, no matter if the directly resulting harm is small. The harm is cumulative to the individual and society" [p. 890]. Other investigators disagree with Baumrind's position. Indeed, while Baumrind believes that the draft report of the Ethics Committee (which was not altered in major substantive ways in the final published document) did not go far enough to protect the rights of subjects, others fear that the committee went too far. Steiner (1972), for example, holds that in the draft report investigators are considered guilty (of unethical intentions) until proven innocent. He expresses concern that the code may erect so many barriers in the path of research that investigators will be immobilized.

Kerlinger (1972) also expresses the position that the Ethics Committee went too far in its efforts to protect human rights. He argues, for example, that privacy is not invaded when researchers observe individuals interacting in a public or semipublic situation—even if the subjects have no knowledge that they are being observed in the context of a research investigation. Naturalistic observations by scientists are, he believes, different in intent and purpose from the clandestine surveillance perpetrated by certain government agencies. According to Kerlinger (1972, p. 894),

> The Committee has extrapolated from surveillance of citizens by police and intelligence agencies to observation in research. Research observation has the basic purpose of obtaining measures of variables. We observe people's behavior, especially verbal behavior, to measure anxiety, authoritarianism, cohesiveness, cooperativeness, and the like. Police and intelligence agencies, however, observe people to obtain information on the past, present and possible future misbehavior as defined by law or by the agencies.

Gergen (1973) believed that the greatest danger in the preliminary code of ethics, as expressed in the draft, was its appeal to abstract moral principles apart from any knowledge about their precise consequences in particular situations. He argues that a code of ethics of psychological researchers should be grounded in information about the effects on human subjects of, for example, gaining or not gaining their informed consent or of deceiving them. In his view, violations of subjects' rights that occurred before APA tried to develop a code of ethics were inconsequential. By formulating a code to prevent further violation of these principles, the Ethics Committee used, he believes, a very dangerous cannon to shoot a mouse.

Much of the debate over deception and related ethical issues is philosophical. It reflects the differing backgrounds and values of those concerned. Behaviorists, who see all behavior as determined anyway, are less concerned with the manipulative aspects of such methodological techniques as deception. Humanists such as Diana Baumrind see methodologies that treat the subject as object, rather than as collaborator, as violations of human freedom and dignity. While this debate might be distressing to those who want guidance in ethical decision making, it highlights the issues that must be considered by all individuals undertaking psychological research. In this regard, you, the novice investigator, are in the same position as more experienced researchers.

One procedure advocated by many investigators who oppose deception is role playing. In a role-playing design, subjects are informed of the research problem of interest and asked specifically to behave spontaneously "as if" they were involved in a real-life situation. The notion is that investigators and participants can work together in an open, honest relationship to promote scientific knowledge rather than in a situation where investigators treat participants as objects to be manipulated and deceived.

Unfortunately, research on the usefulness of role playing as an alternative to deception is not very encouraging. For example, Holmes and Bennett (1974) compared the responses of role-playing subjects to deceived subjects in an experiment in which the deceived subjects were convinced they were going to receive a painful electric shock and the role-playing subjects knew they were just supposed to act as if they were going to receive such a shock. While the role-playing subjects were able to simulate anxiety comparable to that of the deceived subjects on a paper and pencil test, they did not show any comparable changes on two physiological indexes, pulse and respiration rate.

Miller's (1972) review of the literature confirms the view that role playing introduces a whole additional set of variables into any research procedure. Essentially, asking subjects to role play what they would do under a given set of circumstances amounts to asking them to play a guessing game. Even well-intentioned research participants might not always be very good at predicting their own behavior (for example, Milgram, 1963). Moreover, as Miller (1972) points out, at least three potential preoccupations might influence role-playing subjects in undetermined ways: (1) the behavior they would be likely to perform; (2) the behavior they think they should perform, given their particular upbringing; and (3) the behavior the experimenter wants them to perform.

Miller concludes in his review that the prospects for role playing as an alternative to deception are very poor. Surveys of studies in psychological journals (for example, Levenson, et al. 1976; Menges, 1973) indicate that deception continues to be a rather popular methodological device. However, it is likely that the common use of deception in psychological research also introduces a set of confounding variables into the research process. The sample most commonly used in deception studies consists of lower-division psychology students participating in research to satisfy course requirements. Few such subjects are totally naive. Through their own reading or through word of mouth from other students, they have learned of the likelihood of deception. How do their expectations affect their experimental performance? We have little information about this problem.

As a psychology student, you have probably participated in psychological research at some time. Did you expect to be deceived? If so, how did you feel about it? Did you want to "psyche out" the experimenter? To cooperate? To "louse up" the study? To give the expected performance no matter what? All these responses probably occur in many of our studies (for example, see Cox & Sipprelle, 1971; Resnick & Schwartz, 1973; Schappe, 1972), yet for the most part we lack the tools to identify and analyze the contribution of such response patterns to our psychological findings (Menges, 1973).

DEBRIEFING

In general, the Ethics Committee urges researchers not only to obtain the informed consent of subjects and to protect their rights and safety, but also to ensure that subjects do not experience any undesirable aftereffects from their research participation. Potential undesirable aftereffects are seen as stemming not only from participation in a stressful investigation but also from confusion or misinformation about important aspects of the study. Particularly in studies that have involved some deception, the committee recommends that the "responsible investigator" debrief subjects—that is, provide full information about the problem under investigation. As part of the debriefing, the nature of the participant's contribution should be explained (for example, providing evidence concerning physiological responses to stress).

Can you imagine any cases in which debriefing subjects about their research participation might itself produce rather than alleviate undesirable aftereffects? Suppose you were investigating the hypothesis that individuals with an authoritarian personality, as measured by the California F scale, would be likely to insist on taking over control of an unstructured group? Might some of your subjects become uncomfortable at hearing this information as they think of the role they assumed in the group? What might you do about that possibility? Since you would not want to lie about your purposes, what other alternatives would be available to you?

It is this kind of issue that Tesch (1977) is addressing when he asks whether investigators should or should not release participants from "founded," as opposed to unfounded, perceptions—for example, from the inference that not helping an accident victim reflects insensitivity. In response to this kind of dilemma, Baumrind (1971) asserts that no investigator should undertake research that permits only two possible forms of debriefing—that is, (1) *deceptive debriefing,* where the investigator continues to deceive subjects in order to protect their self-esteem; and (2) *inflicted insight,* where the investigator tells subjects things about themselves that they do not want to hear.

Actually, investigators who believe that they are limited to these two alternatives might be losing their appreciation for the complexity of human behavior. It would be naive to assume that all individuals who fail to help a particular accident victim in a particular situation are insensitive or that everyone who does help that accident victim is sensitive. Similarly, we know better than to assume that high scores on an authoritarianism scale can be explained only by high personal authoritarianism and never by other factors.

Thus, part of a researcher's responsibility to subjects should include restraint in the manner in which a particular psychological instrument or measure is represented. It is frequently helpful to see how groups of individuals who differ on one measure (for example, an authoritarianism scale or an empathy scale) differ on some other measure (say, leading a group or assisting others). Moreover, such comparisons are important to the very process of validating psychological instruments—that is, in determining the success of such instruments in measuring what

they are supposed to measure. (Types of validation procedure are discussed more in later chapters.) However, we need to be very cautious about generalizing about or to individuals on the basis of their performance on a given instrument at a given point in time.

Recognition of such limitations in our ability to generalize about individuals on the basis of one performance should lead to a number of procedures in dealing with data. First, we ordinarily assign numbers to the data we collect rather than retaining individual identifying information such as names. Moreover, we generally make predictions and report information about groups rather than about individuals, both in debriefing participants and in our research reports. Additionally, in debriefing subjects, instead of telling them they have just completed a test to tell us whether or not they have an authoritarian personality, we would be more likely to say that the test is intended to give us a general idea about people's views on several classic social and political issues, and that we are interested in the relationship between those views and some other behavior.

A good debriefing is as difficult to design as it is important—so difficult, in fact, that Mills has devoted an entire article in a major psychological journal to the topic (1976). This article provides a fine model to every investigator who is just beginning to learn the art and science of psychological research, and we recommend that you read it. In fact, Mills' emphasis on sensitivity and responsibility to research participants has relevance for all aspects of the research process, not just for debriefing.

But how are thoughtfulness and sensitivity translated into actual interactions between researcher and participant? It is probable that both role playing of and direct experiences in all aspects of the research process are helpful in this regard. Observing other investigators, both experienced and inexperienced, is also likely to be useful. Finally, movies and videotapes of subject-experimenter interactions can also serve to illustrate both desirable and undesirable actions.

What steps can one take in planning and conducting truly ethical research? Even before designing your research project it would be useful to read one of the books on research ethics—that of Diener and Crandall (1978), for example. The Ethics Committee suggests that investigators discuss research plans with local ethics-review committees, colleagues, students, and others. Wilson and Donnerstein (1976), like Baumrind (1971), encourage pretesting, in which potential subject groups are asked their opinion concerning the ethics of a proposed investigation. While routinely having subjects fill out anonymous ethics-related questionnaires will not help you evaluate the ethics of your procedure in advance, Berscheid, Baron, Dermer, and Libman (1973) recommend this course of action. And Baumrind believes that investigators should invite subjects to discuss and evaluate the ethics and procedures of the studies in which they have participated.

In addition to these recommendations from psychologists we offer a number of suggestions from research subjects themselves. Although subjects do not seem to be as rigorous in their interpretation of ethical issues as psychologists (Sullivan & Deiker, 1973), they do expect investigators to show professionalism (for example, good use of the scientific method and a trained intellect) as well as warmth and attentiveness in interpersonal behavior. A failure of investigators to display these qualities might offend subjects, prejudice them against psychologists and psychology, and affect both their current and subsequent research performance in ways that are difficult to ascertain but that nevertheless result in worthless data.

A PREVIEW OF THE CHAPTER SELECTIONS

We have already described in some detail the three selections for the chapter. The original article by Middlemist, Knowles, and Matter, together with Koocher's criticism and the researchers' reply to Koocher, constitute an interesting case study on the ethics of research. These articles are useful in dramatizing the complexity of the issues involved in making and reporting decisions about the ethics of a set of empirical procedures. They also serve as a reminder that scientific "experts" can disagree on ethical matters. You will do well to think through carefully and obtain the input of a variety of other individuals on the ethics of your own research.

We also recommend that you evaluate the other selections in this book and the research reported in other psychological sources you read for the ethics of their procedures. Are there areas in which any of the studies seem to deviate from the APA Ethics Committee guidelines as discussed in this chapter? What additional kinds of information do you think you need to evaluate fairly the ethics of a given study? In each study, consider whether the psychological health of the subjects seems to have been protected adequately. Consider what steps you might have taken to guarantee more securely the rights and safety of the subjects.

Personal Space Invasions in the Lavatory: Suggestive Evidence for Arousal

R. Dennis Middlemist
Eric S. Knowles
Charles F. Matter
Oklahoma State University
Ohio State University
University of Wisconsin—Green Bay

The hypothesis that personal space invasions produce arousal was investigated in a field experiment. A men's lavatory provided a setting where norms for privacy were salient, where personal space invasions could occur in the case of men urinating, where the opportunity for compensatory responses to invasion were minimal, and where proximity-induced arousal could be measured. Research on micturation indicates that social stressors inhibit relaxation of the external urethral sphincter, which would delay the onset of micturation, and that they increase intravesical pressure, which would shorten the duration of micturation once begun. Sixty lavatory users were randomly assigned to one of three levels of interpersonal distance and their micturation times were recorded. In a three-urinal lavatory, a confederate stood immediately adjacent to a subject, one urinal removed, or was absent. Paralleling the results of a correlational pilot study, close interpersonal distances increased the delay of onset and decreased the persistence of micturation. These findings provide objective evidence that personal space invasions produce physiological changes associated with arousal.

In the study of person-environment relations, the concept of personal space has been postulated as a variable that, in part, determines how people respond to their social and physical environments. Sommer (1969) defined personal space as the "area with invisible boundaries surrounding a person's body into which intruders may not come" (p. 26). Investigations of personal space phenom-

The authors thank Daniel Kasten for serving as the confederate and Anthony G. Greenwald for providing comments on an earlier draft. Portions of this research were presented at the Midwestern Psychological Association Convention, Chicago, May 1975.

ena suggest that individuals seek to maintain psychologically comfortable interpersonal distances. If an invasion of personal space takes place, individuals will move away from others and reestablish the personal space boundaries (Felipe & Sommer, 1966; Sommer, 1969) or engage in compensatory behaviors that minimize the closeness (Patterson, Mullens, & Romano, 1971; Cowan, Note 1). Other findings suggest that individuals will avoid invading the personal space of others (Barefoot, Hoople, & McClay, 1972; Sommer & Becker, 1969) or will engage in submissive gestures or verbalized apologies to minimize the impact of invasion (Efran & Cheyne, 1974; Felipe & Sommer, 1966; Knowles, 1973).

Although these behavioral responses related to personal space invasions have been documented and described, there has been little systematic investigation of the reasons why these responses occur. In a recent review, Evans and Howard (1973) concluded that "we do not as yet thoroughly understand all the variables which are relevant to [personal space] behavior, and we are even further away from being able to explain why and how personal space operates for human beings" (p. 341). The most common explanatory position is that emotional arousal is an important variable intervening between personal space and the behavioral responses to personal space invasion. Evans and Howard (1973) and Sommer (1969) are among those who have suggested that invasions of personal space are interpersonally stressful, increasing arousal and discomfort, and that it is this arousal that produces the behavioral responses. These behavioral responses occur because they reduce the arousal caused by the personal space invasion.

Although there is a clear relationship between personal space invasions and the behavioral responses to invasions, there is little unambiguous evidence that arousal plays any role, much less a mediating role, in this relationship. Findings from animal species other than man that chronic crowding is related to adrenal hypertrophy (Christian & Davis, 1966; Deevey, 1966) suggest prolonged arousal, but do not imply that similar processes operate in humans. Various self-report data suggest negative feelings as a result of personal space invasions (Efran & Cheyne, 1974; Porter, Argyle, & Salter, 1970) or crowded conditions (Dabbs, 1971), but these reports may have been produced by factors other than arousal.

Several authors have attempted to obtain more direct indications of arousal. Efran and Cheyne (1974) attempted to measure changes in cardiovascular activity as a result of invasions, and Dabbs (1971) attempted to obtain measures of palmar sweating under conditions of crowding. In both cases the results were inconclusive. McBride, King, and James (1965) measured subjects' galvanic skin responses when they were approached at various distances from various angles by male and female experimenters. They found greater decreases in skin resistance with closer approaches, with frontal rather than side approaches, and with opposite-sex experimenters. Although this study is often cited as providing the most direct indication that personal space invasions produce arousal, it also is not conclusive, at least by itself. The subjects were instrumented, participating in an experiment, and aware of the dimension being manipulated, all of which may have made their behavior and responses different from disguised or naturally occurring invasions (Knowles & Johnsen, 1974).

As an alternative to the laboratory, a men's lavatory provides a setting where personal space violations can occur in a natural yet sufficiently standardized way. Although Kira (1970) has pointed out that use of the bathroom evokes concerns for privacy among members of the middle class, public facilities do not allow complete privacy, particularly in the case of men urinating. Urinals are open and placed side by side so that, under crowded conditions, men stand shoulder to shoulder, coactively engaging in private elimination. Unlike other settings, including the laboratory, these personal space intrusions in the lavatory are minimally confounded by compensatory responses—moving away, changing body orientation, using hands and arms as an interpersonal buffer, reducing eye contact—that a subject makes to an invasion. If compensatory behaviors occur to reduce the arousal caused by invasions, then it would be impossible to measure the degree of arousal accurately if subjects were free to engage in these compensatory behaviors.

In addition, research on micturation suggests that it is a process sensitive to arousal (Scott, Quesada, & Cardus, 1964; Straub, Ripley, & Wolf, 1950; Tanaeho, 1971). At the onset of micturation, the detrusor muscles of the bladder contract, increasing intravesical pressure and forcing urine out of the bladder. At the same time, the two sphincters of the urethra relax, particularly the external sphincter, allowing urine to flow. Social stressors appear to affect both these mechanisms of micturation. Straub et al. (1950) showed that a stressful interview produced a marked and sustained increase in intravesical pressure. Scott et al. (1964) reported that fright and embarrassment inhibited relaxation of the external sphincter of the urethra.

The relationships between social arousal and micturation suggest that, if an individual intent on micturating were subjected to a stressor, the onset of micturation would be delayed because of a reduction in the degree of relaxation of the external sphincter, while the duration of urine flow, once begun, would be foreshortened because of increased intravesicle pressure. If personal space invasions produce arousal, then subjects standing closest to others at lavatory urinals would show increases in the delay of onset of micturation and decreases in the persistence of micturation. Because of the novelty of these hypotheses, a pilot study was first undertaken to investigate whether any relationship between interpersonal distance and micturation times could be observed.

PILOT STUDY

A field observation conducted at a men's lavatory at a western U.S. university provided evidence for a correlation between interpersonal distance and micturation times. Men entering a restroom to urinate were allowed to choose a urinal under prevailing ecological conditions. Data were recorded for 48 subjects, users of the men's lavatory. A user was included as a subject if the degree of interpersonal distance between him and the next nearest user remained constant throughout the duration of his urination. The restroom contained two banks of five urinals, which were bowl-type receptacles jutting out of the wall and containing about 3 inches (8 cm) of standing water, which the user flushed.

An observer was stationed at the sink facilities and appeared to be grooming himself. When a potential subject entered the room and walked to a urinal, the observer recorded the selected urinal and the placement of the next nearest user. He also noted (with a chronographic wristwatch) and recorded the micturation delay (the time between when a subject unzipped his fly and when urination began) and the micturation persistence (the time between the onset and completion of urination). The onset and cessation of micturation were signaled by the sound of the stream of urine striking the water in the urinal.

Of the 48 subjects recorded, none selected a urinal immediately adjacent to another user, 23 were separated by one urinal from the next nearest user, 16 were separated by two urinals, and 9 were separated by three or more urinals. The fact that no subjects were observed choosing an adjacent urinal may reflect active avoidance of the most proximate interpersonal distance. Even with this restricted range of interpersonal distance, significant correlations were found for both measures. Micturation delay showed a negative correlation with the three levels of interpersonal distance, $r(46) = -.315$, $p < .05$.[2] Subjects standing one urinal away had a mean delay of 7.9 seconds, subjects two space away had a delay of 5.9 seconds, and subjects three or more spaces away had a delay of 5.7 seconds. Micturation persistence showed a positive relationship with the three levels of interpersonal distance, $r(46) = +.562$, $p < .001$. The mean persistence was 19.0 seconds with one space, 24.4 seconds with

two spaces, and 32.0 seconds with three or more spaces.

This pilot study, while lacking controls on subject self-selection and open to various interpretations, did suggest that the hypotheses warranted more controlled investigation. The correlations found were in the direction predicted by the hypotheses. Moreover, the pilot study suggested that the micturation measures could be used as the dependent variables in an experimental study. Thus, the following experiment was conducted to test the hypothesis that decreases in interpersonal distance lead to arousal as evidenced by increases in micturation delay and decreases in micturation persistence.

METHOD

Overview

In a field experiment conducted in a men's lavatory at a midwestern U.S. university, subjects were randomly assigned to one of three levels of interpersonal distance. Men who entered a three-urinal lavatory to urinate were forced to use the leftmost urinal. A confederate was placed immediately adjacent to the subject, one urinal removed, or was absent from the lavatory. An observer stationed in a toilet stall timed the delay and persistence of micturation.

Subjects

Data were gathered on 60 users of the men's lavatory. A user was included as a subject if no other user (besides the confederate) was present during his urination. If someone else was present or entered during urination, the user was not counted. Conditions were randomly assigned and prepared before the subject entered the lavatory. Subjects were not informed that they had participated in an experiment.

Procedure

The observed lavatory was just off a main hallway, adjacent to a large classroom. The observed use rate averaged about one person every 6 min-

[2]Two-tailed probabilities are used throughout.

utes. The restroom contained two toilet stalls and three urinals. The urinals were 18 inches (46 cm) wide with 18 inches of tile between adjacent urinals and extended up from the floor about 4 feet (1.2 m). The urinals were automatically flushed at 10-minute intervals.

The subjects were forced to use the leftmost urinal under one of three levels of interpersonal distance. In the close distance condition, a confederate appearing to urinate was stationed at the middle urinal, and a "Don't use, washing urinal" sign accompanied by a bucket of water and a sponge was placed on the rightmost urinal. This arrangement left a distance of approximately 16 to 18 inches (40 to 46 cm) between the shoulders of the subject and confederate. In the moderate distance condition, the confederate stood at the rightmost urinal and the bucket and sign were placed in the middle urinal. This arrangement left a distance of 52 to 54 inches (132 to 137 cm) between the subject and the confederate. In a control condition, the confederate was not present in the lavatory and both the middle and right urinals had signs on them with the water bucket in between.

An observer was stationed in the toilet stall immediately adjacent to the subjects' urinal. During pilot tests of these procedures it became clear that auditory cues could not be used to signal the initiation and cessation of micturation. The urinals were so silent that even the confederate standing adjacent to the subject could not hear the urine striking the urinal.[3] Instead, visual cues were used. The observer used a periscopic prism imbedded in a stack of books lying on the floor of the toilet stall. An 11-inch (28-cm) space between the floor and the wall of toilet stall provided a view, through the periscope, of the user's lower torso and made possible direct visual sightings of the stream of urine. The observer, however, was

unable to see a subject's face. The observer started two stop watches when a subject stepped up to the urinal, stopped one when urination began, and stopped the other when urination was terminated. These times allowed calculation of the two dependent variables: delay of onset and persistence of micturation.

RESULTS

The hypotheses that decreases in interpersonal distance would lead to increases in the delay of micturation and decreases in the persistence of micturation were tested in a multivariate analysis of variance of the effects of conditions on the two micturation measures. Each measure was heteroscedastic, but square root transformations of the data made the cell variances comparable, and the analysis was performed on these transformed scores. The multivariate analysis indicated a significant difference among distance conditions, $F(4, 112) = 10.38$, $p < .001$. A priori multivariate comparisons among conditions showed that the close distance produced responses significantly different from the moderate distance, $F(2, 56) = 10.04$, $p < .001$, and that the confederate-present conditions produced responses significantly different from the confederate-absent condition, $F(2, 56) = 14.53$, $p < .001$. Figure 1, which presents the mean seconds for micturation delay and persistence in each condition, shows that the effects were in the predicted direction.

A test of the univariate effects of distance on micturation delay revealed significant differences among conditions, $F(2, 57) = 12.44$, $p < .001$. Micturation delay increased from a mean of 4.9 seconds in the control conditions to 6.2 seconds in the moderate distance condition to 8.4 seconds in the close distance condition. The a priori tests indicated that the close condition led to significantly longer delays than the moderate condition, $F(1, 57) = 9.01$, $p < .004$, and that the confederate-present conditions led to significantly longer delays than the confederate-absent condition, $F(1, 57) = 15.86$, $p < .001$.

---

[3]Although the silence of the urinals necessitated a change from the pilot study in the mode of observation, it had the advantage of making the confederate credible. During tests of the experimental procedures, none of the test subjects had any suspicions about the confederate's activity.

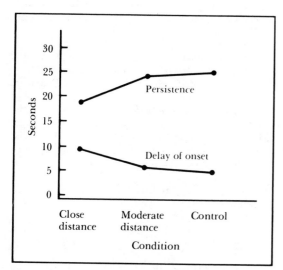

FIGURE 1. *Micturation times.*

Micturation persistence also showed significant differences among conditions, $F(2,57) = 4.41$, $p<.017$. The pattern of means, from 24.8 seconds in the control condition to 23.4 seconds in the moderate distance to 17.4 seconds in the close distance condition, shows the predicted decrease in the persistence of micturation. The close distance produced shorter persistence times than the moderate distance, $F(1,57) = 4.49$, $p<.038$, and the confederate-present conditions produced shorter persistence times than the confederate-absent condition, $F(1,57) = 4.33$, $p<.042$.

The analysis of the effects of interpersonal distance on micturation times supported both hypotheses. Closer distances led to increases in micturation delay and decrease in micturation persistence. Both of these effects, which across conditions produced a negative correlation between cell means, appeared in spite of the fact that the two measures tended to be positively correlated. The within-cell correlation between micturation delay and persistence was $+.349$, which reflected comparable correlations within each condition ($rs = +.308$, $+.304$, and $+.542$ for the control, moderate, and close distance conditions).

DISCUSSION

Variations in interpersonal distance in a lavatory appear to be related in systematic ways to variations in micturation times. The pattern of results supports the hypothesis that arousal increases with decreases in interpersonal distance. The arousal model of personal space invasions proposes that close interpersonal distances are interpersonally stressful, increasing arousal and discomfort, and that it is this arousal that produces behavioral responses to invasions. The purpose of this field study was to investigate the first half of the model, that arousal results from interpersonal closeness, and the findings support this part of the arousal model. What has not been shown by this study or earlier studies is whether the arousal leads to or causes the behavioral responses to personal space violations, as hypothesized in the second half of the model. The arousal indicated in this study may be a concomitant of invasion that has no effect on immediacy behaviors. Subsequent research is needed to investigate the second half of the arousal model.

The results of this experiment reproduced and complemented the results of the pilot study. Both micturation delay and persistence were shown to be related to interpersonal distance, and similar patterns of means were observed. Although neither set of data is precise enough to allow assessment of the form of the relationship between distance and micturation times, it appears that the closest distance had much more of an effect than the next closest distance. This pattern is reminiscent of the nonlinear, exponential relationships observed for much greater distances (Bratfisch, 1969; Ekman & Bratfisch, 1965; Lundberg, Bratfisch, & Ekman, 1972). The present data are not incompatible with Ekman's suggestion that emotional involvement decreases as an inverse power function of distance.

Finally, the present study suggests that the dependent measures may have some utility as unobtrusive measures of social arousal in laboratory as well as field settings. In a laboratory, the effects of intravesical pressure could be more sensitively estimated by using the volume of urine expelled as a covariate to the persistence measure. Presumably, differences in the amount of urine expelled contributed a great deal of variance to the persistence measures in the present study. Yet, both micturation delay and persistence were sensitive to situational differences. Although the parameters of these measures have not been extensively studied, the present study implies that they have some construct validity as indicators of arousal.

REFERENCE NOTE

1. Cowan, R. A. *Invisible walls.* University of California. 16-mm black and white sound film, 1968. (Available from University Extension Media Center, University of California, Berkeley, Berkeley, California 94720.)

REFERENCES

Barefoot, J. C., Hoople, H., & McClay, D. Avoidance of an act which would violate personal space. *Psychonomic Science,* 1972, *28,* 205–206.

Bratfisch, O. A further study of the relation between subjective distance and emotional involvement. *Acta Psychologica,* 1969, *29,* 244–255.

Christian, J. J., & Davis, D. E. Adrenal glands in female voles (*Microtus pennsylvanicus*) as related to reproduction and population size. *Journal of Mammalogy,* 1966, *47,* 1–18.

Dabbs, J. M., Jr. Physical closeness and negative feelings. *Psychonomic Science,* 1971, *23,* 141–143.

Deevey, E. S. The hare and the haruspex. In R. Haber (Ed.), *Current research in motivation.* New York: Holt, Rinehart & Winston, 1966.

Efran, M. G., & Cheyne, J. A. Affective concomitants of the invasion of shared space: Behavioral, physiological, and verbal indicators. *Journal of Personality and Social Psychology,* 1974, *29,* 219–226.

Ekman, G., & Bratfisch, O. Subjective distance and emotional involvement: A psychological mechanism. *Acta Psychologica,* 1965, *24,* 430–437.

Evans, G. W., & Howard, R. B. Personal space. *Psychological Bulletin,* 1973, *80,* 334–344.

Felipe, N., & Sommer, R. Invasions of personal space. *Social Problems,* 1966, *14,* 206–214.

Kira, A. Privacy in the bathroom. In H. M. Proshansky, W. H. Ittelson, & L. G. Rivlin (Eds.) *Environmental psychology: Man and his physical setting.* New York: Holt, Rinehart & Winston, 1970.

Knowles, E. S. Boundaries around group interaction: The effect of group size and member status on boundary permeability. *Journal of Personality and Social Psychology,* 1973, *26,* 327–331.

Knowles, E. S., & Johnsen, P. K. Intrapersonal consistency in interpersonal distance. *JSAS: Catalog of Selected Documents in Psychology,* 1974, *4,* 124.

Lundberg, U., Bratfisch, O., & Ekman, G. Emotional involvement and subjective distance: A summary of investigations. *Journal of Social Psychology,* 1972, *87,* 169–177.

McBride, G., King, M. G., & James, J. W. Social proximity effects on galvanic skin responsiveness in adult humans. *Journal of Psychology,* 1965, *61,* 153–157.

Patterson, M. L., Mullens, S., & Romano, J. Compensatory reactions to spatial intrusion. *Sociometry,* 1971, *34,* 114–121.

Porter, E., Argyle, M., & Salter, V. What is signalled by proximity? *Perceptual and Motor Skills,* 1970, *30,* 39–42.

Scott, F. B., Quesada, E. M., & Cardus, D. Studies of the dynamics of micturation: Observation on healthy men. *Journal of Urology,* 1964, *92,* 455–463.

Sommer, R. *Personal space: The behavioral basis of design.* Englewood Cliffs, N. J.: Prentice-Hall, 1969.

Sommer, R., & Becker, F. D. Territorial defense and the good neighbor. *Journal of Personality and Social Psychology,* 1969, *11,* 85–92.

Straub, L. R., Ripley, H. S., & Wolf, S. Disturbances of bladder function associated with emotional states. *Association for Research in Nervous and Mental Disease: Research Publication,* 1950, *29,* 1019–1029.

Tanaeho, E. A. Interpretation of the physiology of micturation. In F. Hinman, Jr. (Ed.), *Hydrodynamics of micturation.* Springfield, Ill.: Charles C. Thomas, 1971.

STUDY QUESTIONS

1. What is the hypothesis for this study? What are the variables and how are they defined operationally?
2. Is the methodology for this study, including both the sampling and measurement procedure, adequate for testing the hypothesis?
3. Did the procedures involve any possible physical or psychological risk to the subjects?
4. Were the rights of the subjects protected?
5. Is the apparent absence of informed consent and debriefing procedures justified?

6. What is your overall evaluation of the ethics of this investigation? If you were on an ethics-review board, would you have approved the study? Would you have required any steps of the investigators that are not discussed in the article?

Bathroom Behavior and Human Dignity

Gerald P. Koocher
Harvard Medical School

A 1976 article by Middlemist, Knowles, and Matter that appeared in this Journal reported on a study of urinating behavior observed surreptitiously in a men's lavatory. Questions regarding the ethical propriety of the study are raised, along with questions about the role journals play in calling attention to ethical issues or problems in psychological research.

A recent article by Middlemist, Knowles, and Matter (1976) reported on a field experiment in a men's lavatory. Men who entered a "three-urinal lavatory" at a midwestern U.S. university were subjected to one of three conditions: The unknowing subjects either urinated "alone," directly adjacent to a confederate of the experimenter, or into one urinal at a distance removed from a confederate. Another researcher observed this behavior from a toilet stall via a periscope apparatus while using a stopwatch to record the "delay and persistence of micturation" (p. 543). The findings were analyzed and interpreted as offering objective evidence that invasions of personal space may produce physiological changes associated with physical arousal.

The conduct of this research and the publication of it in a major journal raise significant questions about the current state of human dignity as determined by psychological researchers. Although freedom of scientific inquiry and the freedom of the press are supremely important, the judgment of both experimenters and journal editors in this case seems worthy of careful discussion.

Disguised field experiments in public situations have long been considered important areas of inquiry, but they are also subject to important ethical considerations (see APA, 1973). The ethical principles adopted by APA make note of the nar-

Entire article from *Journal of Personality and Social Psychology*, 1977, *35*, 120–121. Copyright 1977 by the American Psychological Association. Reprinted by permission.

row boundary between drawing on everyday experiences and spying. The APA (1973) guidelines clearly state: "The ethical investigator will assume responsibility for undertaking a study employing covert investigation in private situations only after very careful consideration and consultations" (p. 32). The same guidelines stress the importance of maintaining the human dignity of subjects and carefully weighing the costs of the experiment against the anticipated benefits both to the individual subject and to society at large.

Middlemist and his colleagues (1976, p. 544) describe in great detail their selection of a timing device, a periscope apparatus, urinal measurements (complete with metric data), and even the "flushing" arrangements. It is ironic that they use virtually no space in the article discussing the cost versus benefit rationale or otherwise attempting to explain how the projected importance of their research justifies the invasion of their subjects' privacy. Although they note that close interpersonal distance resulted in "micturation delay" and a shortened duration of urination, they do not address the issue of possible discomfort to the subjects nor the reason that this was seemingly thought to be insignificant. Although the subjects were never informed that they had participated in an experiment, the experimenters also seemed oblivious to the potential harm to unsuspecting or unstable individuals who might accidentally discover that they were being observed during the course of the "micturation," or shortly thereafter. At the very least, the design seems laughable and trivial. On the other hand, there appear to be serious ethical questions and potential hazards that are not fully addressed.

If we presume that the investigators did indeed use careful thought and had good justification to expect important scientific gains from their project, one must ask why this was not deemed worthy of at least as much space in the article as descriptions of the urinals and periscope. Though one could claim that a college lavatory is a public place, it is a non sequitur to suggest that one does not expect a degree of privacy there. It is incumbent on the investigator(s) to make the cost/benefit rationale explicit in any case.

One must also consider the role of the journal editors and consultants who reviewed this manuscript. There are those who believe that all journal articles using human subjects ought to include the basis for informed consent as part of the Method section. Indeed, a number of medical journals currently refuse to review manuscripts submitted without such data. I subscribe to the belief that when a potential problem of a subject's rights is at issue, a discussion of the cost/benefit rationale is imperative. Certainly the fact that a study was or was not approved by an institutional or peer review panel ought to be noted. By not insisting on this data, the editors of the journal in question appear to condone the practices, or at the very least tacitly suggest that the methods used represent the acceptable practices of researchers in the field.

When a journal has a rejection rate of 87% (APA Council of Editors, 1976), one must also be concerned about the overall scientific importance and quality in the content of its articles. I cannot help but wonder how the authors of rejected articles felt when they learned that a study of such dubious propriety and theoretical import was deemed worthy of inclusion among the best 13% of what is available in our field. Perhaps that is the most telling comment available on the current status of much psychological research. By placing this article in such a high-visibility position, we may certainly anticipate a veritable flood of bathroom research, to be followed by a book of readings, and ultimately, by a review article.

REFERENCES

American Psychological Association, Committee on Ethical Standards in Psychological Research. *Ethical principles in the conduct of research with human participants.* Washington, D.C.: Author, 1973.

APA Council of Editors. Summary report of journal operations for 1975. *American Psychologist*, 1976, *31,* 468.

Middlemist, D. R., Knowles, E. S., & Matter, C. F. Personal space invasions in the lavatory: Suggestive evidence for arousal. *Journal of Personality and Social Psychology*, 1976, *33*, 541–546.

STUDY QUESTIONS

1. What do you think of the issues raised by Koocher? Were any of your reactions to the article in question similar to his? Did you have criticisms of the study by Middlemist and his colleagues that Koocher did not consider? Are the issues raised by Koocher important or trivial?

2. Consider again question 6 on page 61. Would you change any of your original answers?

What to Do and What to Report: A Reply to Koocher

R. Dennis Middlemist
Eric S. Knowles and Charles F. Matter
Oklahoma State University
University of Wisconsin—Green Bay

A distinction is drawn between the discussion of ethics in an article and the consideration of ethics in designing research. Further information is provided about cost and benefit assessments in the 1976 study by Middlemist, Knowles, and Matter. Concerns for clear reporting standards are echoed.

Gerald Koocher's comment (this issue, pp. 120–121) on our personal space and arousal study conducted in public lavatories (Middlemist, Knowles, & Matter, 1976) appears to criticize what wasn't said more than what was. His major expressed concern is with the lack of a discussion of the ethical and scientific cost/benefit ratio in our article. Our interpretation of the *Ethical Principles in the Conduct of Research with Human Participants* (APA, 1973) was that they deal with issues the investigator must attend to in considering, designing, and executing research. However, they are mute on the issue of what needs to be reported to the scientific community. The *Publication Manual of the American Psychological Association* (APA, 1974) does deal with reporting of research and provides this basic rule: "Include only information essential to comprehend and replicate the study" (p. 17). It was not irony but rather the Publication Manual that led us to emphasize the procedures of the study over the ethical considerations.

ETHICAL CONSIDERATIONS IN PLANNING THE MICTURATION STUDY

Although we find it difficult to respond to the emotionalism of Koocher's comment and to the undocumented dismissal of our study as dubious, trivial, and laughable, we can respond to his request for information about our assessment of the cost/benefit ratio. The pilot study was a field observation; one of the authors stood by a wash basin and recorded micturation times of men using a large public lavatory. The behavior studied was naturally occurring and would have happened in the same way without the observer. The information gathered was available to everyone in the lavatory; the only unusual feature was that the information was being recorded. However, to assess the impact of this feature and of the research, approximately half of the pilot-study participants were interviewed and told of the research. None of the men knew that they had been observed, nor were they bothered when they found out. All of the men gave permission to use their data. These interviews indicated a general low level of concern about the research; the men felt that an invasion of personal space at a urinal was not unusual, had been encountered many times, and was not an experience that caused them any pain or embarrassment. In fact, many of the men related amusing stories or personal experiences relevant to the hypotheses. Part of the subjects' comfort with the study appeared to be related to the fact that it was conducted in a public lavatory at a university. The "clubiness" (cf. Kira, 1976) provided by the university setting and the public nature of the facility seemed to legitimize a wider range of behaviors, such as research.

The problem with the pilot study was that the results were not conclusive; the participants were free to select their own interpersonal distance. In deciding whether to conduct an experimental investigation of the hypotheses, two factors influenced our positive decision. First, the results of the pilot-study interviews, discussions with colleagues, and introspection suggested that men observing other men urinating was not uncommon, at least informally, or stressful. Second, the experimental manipulations, which involved the proximity of another user, were not unusual situations. In contrast to a number of other social psychological field studies in which the experimental situations are unique, powerful, and memorable events (e.g., a medical emergency feigned in a subway, a thief running off with a pocketbook, or even a spatial invasion in a nearly empty library), the situations studied by Middlemist et al. (1976) were common ones that had been encountered by each of the participants many times in the past.

In designing the procedures for the experiment, we considered numerous alternatives for collecting the data. We preferred a repeat of the pilot-study method, in which the observer in a public area of the lavatory would use auditory cues to record the micturation times. However, all of the public lavatories that were accessible to us and that would allow control of the interpersonal distances had floor-standing urinals. The silence of these urinals necessitated the change in method involving the use of a hidden observer with a periscope; others means of visually obtaining the data were not reliable.

We were not pleased with this change in observation method and believed the surreptitious observation to be ethically more costly than the pilot-study procedures. We attempted to minimize the potential cost to the participants in the following ways: First, only the authors served as observers. Second, the apparatus was designed so that the participants could not be identified by the observer. Third, the confederate was informed of the ethical concerns and required (a) not to reveal the identity of any participants to the observer, (b) to signal the observer with a cough and leave the lavatory if for any reason a trial should be aborted or not take place, and (c) to be sensitive to any concern or suspicion expressed by a participant so that he could be informed and debriefed (however, this problem never arose). Fourth, participants were not informed of the observation. If someone were going to be upset by the experiment, debriefing would precipitate rather than ameliorate this upset, since the observations had already been made.

This rather lengthy summary is presented to provide some of the information Koocher requests. It is a historical account of our attempt to assess and deal with the impact and potential harm to the participants. We assessed the general research topic—studying the effects of interpersonal distance on micturation times—to create no hazard for the participants. The situations studied were common and unmemorable. We found that the method of observation used in the pilot study had little impact on the men interviewed. We believed that the method of observation selected for the experimental study was less preferable and that it raised more ethical concerns. We chose to deal with these issues by not precipitating concern, by watching for any signs of suspicion, and by having the authors conduct the experiment and collect the data.

The decision to proceed with research, as Koocher noted, involves an assessment of the cost/benefit ratio. In assessing the benefits, we judged the experiment to have relevance for theories of spatial behavior (discussed in Middlemist et al., 1976) and to add to the literatures on micturation and urinary continence. Although Koocher describes our design as "laughable," we believe, and find no evidence to the contrary, that the pilot observation and the experiment together constitute an example of well-controlled field research, adequate to test the null hypothesis that closeness has no effect on micturation times. We did not "anticipate a veritable flood of bathroom research" (Koocher, 1977, p. 121) to be precipitated by the research, but we did judge it to have sufficient merit to justify its execution.

Standards for Considering and Reporting Research

Current journal policy (APA, 1974, Greenwald, 1976) reaffirms the investigator's responsibility for handling ethical issues and indicates that deviations from current ethical policy need to be discussed explicitly. Koocher is clearly asking for a great deal more, a discussion of what was considered and how the decisions were made. Although investigators should be able to fulfill this kind of request, discussions of cost/benefit considerations do not add much to the scientific value of the research, that is, to an understanding of the

operationalizations and findings, though they may add to the social or ethical value of the research.

At the time we wrote the report of the micturation study, we believed that it conformed to the current publication guidelines of the APA. Although Koocher makes specific denunciations and specific prescriptions, we believe that his comments suggest two general issues on which ethical and publication policy guidelines are ambiguous: (a) What decision rules should researchers and journal editors follow in considering ethics? and (b) What ethical discussions should be presented and required in reports of research? These are important questions as well as logical next questions following the statement of ethical principles. They are questions of how the ethical principles are to be implemented and who is responsible for their implementation. As researchers concerned with their implementation, we hope that discussions of these issues can lead to the emergence of clearer norms about decision rules and reporting standards.

REFERENCES

American Psychological Association, Committee on Ethical Standards in Psychological Research. *Ethical principles in the conduct of research with human participants.* Washington, D. C.: Author, 1973.

American Psychological Association. *Publication manual of the American Psychological Association* (2nd ed.). Washington, D.C.: American Psychological Association, 1974.

Greenwald, A. G. An editorial. *Journal of Personality and Social Psychology*, 1976, *33*, 1–7.

Kira, A. *The bathroom.* New York: Viking Press, 1976.

Koocher, G. P. Bathroom behavior and human dignity. *Journal of Personality and Social Psychology*, 1977, *35*, 120–121.

Middlemist, R. D., Knowles, E. S., & Matter, C. F. Personal space invasions in the lavatory: Suggestive evidence for arousal. *Journal of Personality and Social Psychology*, 1976, *33*, 541–546.

STUDY QUESTIONS

1. Did the authors appear to give adequate consideration to ethical issues in planning the micturation study?

2. Do you think the questions raised by Koocher have been answered adequately in the authors' reply?

3. Consider again your answers to question 6 on page 61. Would you change any of your original answers?

EXERCISE

What follows is the Social Research Practices Opinion Survey developed by Edwin A. Rugg of the George Peabody College for Teachers. Rugg (1975) developed the survey in order to obtain ethical judgments about psychological studies using deception from seven different groups, including social psychologists, undergraduate students, and law professors. For this chapter's exercise, complete the survey yourself, following the survey instructions. It would be useful to compare your responses to those of other students in your class, discussing the differences among your judgments in small groups. When you have finished your discussions and settled on your final set of ratings, compare your responses with those reported by Rugg in the abstract of his study in Appendix C.

Social Research Practices Opinion Survey Description of Procedures

Instructions: Read each of the following descriptions of selected social research procedures, and evaluate them according to the instructions on the Response Form.

Procedure #1: Driver Reactions in Accidents.

Students in a driver education class, unaware that they are being studied in a research experiment, are led to believe that they will be observed by the instructor as usual in normal traffic situations. During the experiment, the instructor and the student driver pass two parked trucks along the curb. At that point, a realistic dummy is pushed from behind the trucks and in front of the car so that the driver cannot avoid hitting it, thus creating the accident situation. Soon afterwards the student discovers that the accident victim was not a real person. The in-

structor quickly dismisses the incident as a prank pulled by a couple of teenagers. Students are never told that the incident was part of a research study conducted by their instructors.

Procedure #2: Homosexual Attitudes.

Men are recruited to participate in an experiment on sexual attitudes, although they are not told that it is actually a study about attitudes toward homosexuality. Participants are led to believe that a "psychogalvanometer" used in the experiment is capable of detecting sexual arousal. They are also told that if the galvanometer registers arousal when an individual looks at slides of nude males, the individual is probably a latent homosexual. The galvanometer is rigged so that all participants are led to believe they are latent homosexuals. Following the experiment, the researcher does not inform the participants that the galvanometer was rigged, nor does he give detailed information about the study and its true purpose.

Procedure #3: The Sales Pitch.

The researcher and his assistants approach used car salesmen, pretending to be interested in buying a used car. The salesmen are unaware that their sales pitches are actually under study. The effects of different customer roles, played by the researcher, are tested. After the experiment, the researcher and his assistants leave without telling the salesmen about the hoax or about the research project.

Procedure #4: Self-Concept and Achievement.

Students at a teacher's college complete a series of placement tests but are not told that the tests are actually part of a psychological experiment. The experiment involves giving half of the students false test results which indicate that they are unfit for a teaching career. The researcher is interested in studying the effects of lowered self-concept on subsequent achievement. Two weeks later the study is completed and the researcher does not tell the students that the test results were falsified, nor are students given any information about the research project.

Procedure #5: Cooperation and Competition.

In a study of cooperation and competition, students, who have agreed to participate in the experiment, play a simple two-person game. The game is conducted such that opponents are physically seated in separate rooms but receive information about each other's "moves" through a loudspeaker. Participants are led to believe that they are playing against another person when, in fact, they are responding to a series of prerecorded moves planned by the experimenter. At the conclusion of the game, the experimenter quickly dismisses the participants without informing them of the nonexistence of their opponents or the details of the study.

Procedure #6: Student Cheating Research.
Without informing his students, a professor uses one of his classes for a research study of cheating behavior. True/False exams are given at various points in the semester. After each test period the exams are collected, copied, and then returned to the students, who are told they will score their own tests. A comparison of student graded exams with ungraded copies will reveal instances where students cheated by changing test answers. At the end of the semester, the professor does not tell his class anything about the research project in which they had participated unknowingly.

Procedure #7: Obedience.
Individuals are recruited to participate in an experiment on memory and learning, although the actual purpose of the experiment is to study obedience. Participants are given the role of "teacher" and told to administer increasingly strong electric shocks to the "learner" whenever the learner makes an error in the memory task. The learner is actually an assistant to the researcher, who receives no actual shocks, and who pretends to experience pain as the shock level becomes more and more severe. The psychological dilemma for the participant involves deciding whether to obey the experimenter, who insists that the participant continue to shock the learner, or to side with the learner, who begs the participant to stop shocking him. When the participant refuses or when the highest shock level is reached, the experiment is over. At that point, the participant is dismissed without being told that the shocks and cries of pain were faked. The true purpose and details of the study are not disclosed.

Procedure #8: Reactions to Fear and Anxiety.
Students, participating in a series of experiments for course credit, are told when they arrive at one of the research laboratories that they will receive an electric shock as part of the experiment. The researcher is interested in the reactions of groups under fear and anxiety. In order to facilitate anxiety arousal, the researcher describes in detail the pain and uncomfortable side-effects that usually accompany the electric shock. Actually, no shocks are ever administered. Following the experiment, the researcher informs the participants that they will not be shocked after all because the shock machine has developed a misfunction. The participants are then dismissed without informing them of the actual experiment that took place.

Procedure #9: Racial Attitude Change.
The purpose of the experiment is to compare the effects of different methods for reducing racial prejudice. Students with strong racial prejudice are recruited for the experiment but are not told the true purpose of the study. Instead they are led to believe that the experiment focuses on a topic unrelated to prejudice. After the experiment is completed, participants are not informed of the true purpose of the study, or of its effects on their personal beliefs. Details of the study are not discussed.

Procedure #10: Curiosity Crowds.
Passersby on a city sidewalk are unaware that they are participating in a study of the conditions under which pedestrians will form curiosity crowds. Various sidewalk disagreements are staged by the researcher and his assistants in order to determine situational characteristics which attract curiosity-seekers. People who stop to watch are never told that the situation was faked nor that they were actually participating in a research study.

Procedure #11: Reward & Performance.
Individuals are promised $2.00 if they participate in an experiment that involves performing a simple but boring task. Some of the participants are later led to believe that they may receive up to $20.00 for their participation even though the researcher has no intention of paying participants more than $2.00 for their time. The researcher is interested in the effects of different anticipated rewards on attitudes toward the task and the quality of task performance. At the end of the experiment, the researcher gives an excuse for not paying participants more than the $2.00 initially agreed upon and quickly dismisses them without explaining the purpose and nature of the research.

Procedure #12: Effects of Combat Stress.
Inexperienced soldiers, unaware thay they are actually involved in a research study of the effects of combat stress, are disoriented, isolated, given false instructions, and led to believe that they have caused artillery to fire on their own troops during final training maneuvers. Since actual ammunition is used in these maneuvers, the soldiers are led to think that real casualties have occurred and that they as individuals are responsible. When the soldiers return to their base of operations, they are told that the incident was staged as part of the training exercise to give them experience with combat stress. The fact that the incident was part of a research study is not disclosed.

Response Form
Social Research Practices Opinion Survey

Please answer questions I, II, and III below by selecting from the statements given the one that best expresses your opinion concerning each research procedure described on the preceding pages. Place the letter (A, B, C, D, E, or F) of the statement you chose in the blank corresponding to the particular procedure you are evaluating.

Opinions of Procedures

I. In your opinion, is the treatment of research participants in this description ethical or unethical?

    A. It seems totally ethical.
    B. It seems mostly ethical.
    C. It seems slightly more ethical than unethical.
    D. It seems slightly more unethical than ethical.
    E. It seems mostly unethical.
    F. It seems totally unethical.

II. Would you classify this procedure as harmful or harmless to research participants based on the information given in the description?

    A. It appears extremely harmful, involving serious irreversible effects.
    B. It appears basically harmful.
    C. It appears slightly more harmful than harmless.
    D. It appears slightly more harmless than harmful.
    E. It appears basically harmless.
    F. It appears completely harmless.

III. How do you feel about the use of this procedure in social research?

    A. I am totally unopposed to its use.
    B. I am basically unopposed to its use.
    C. I am slightly more unopposed than opposed to its use.
    D. I am slightly more opposed than unopposed to its use.
    E. I am basically opposed to its use.
    F. I am opposed to its use under any circumstances.

I	*II*	*III*	*Procedure*	*Comments* (optional)

			#1 Driver Reactions in Accidents	
——	——	——	#2 Homosexual Attitudes	
——	——	——	#3 The Sales Pitch	
——	——	——	#4 Self-Concept & Achievement	
——	——	——	#5 Cooperation & Competition	
——	——	——	#6 Student Cheating Research	
——	——	——	#7 Obedience	
——	——	——	#8 Reactions to Fear & Anxiety	
——	——	——	#9 Racial Attitude Change	
——	——	——	#10 Curiosity Crowds	
——	——	——	#11 Reward & Performance	
——	——	——	#12 Effects of Combat Stress	

ADDITIONAL SOURCES

Argyris, C. Some unintended consequences of rigorous research. *Psychological Bulletin,* 1968, *70,* 185–197.

Baumrind, D. Some thoughts on ethics of research: After reading Milgram's "Behavioral study of obedience." *American Psychologist,* 1964, *19,* 421.

Baumrind, D. Reactions to the May 1972 draft report of the ad hoc Committee on Ethical Standards in Psychological Research. *American Psychologist,* 1972, *27,* 1083–1086.

Bickman, L., & Zarantonello, M. The effects of deception and level of obedience on subjects' ratings of the Milgram study. *Personality and Social Psychology Bulletin,* 1978, *4,* 81–85.

Geller, D. M. Involvement in role-playing simulation: A demonstration with studies on obedience. *Journal of Personality and Social Psychology,* 1978, *36,* 219–235.

Kelman, H. C. Manipulation of human behavior: An ethical dilemma for the social scientist. *Journal of Social Issues,* 1965, *21,* 31–46.

Kelman, H. C. *A time to speak: On human value and social research.* San Francisco: Jossey-Bass, 1968.

Kelman, H. C. The rights of the subject in social research: An analysis in terms of relative power and legitimacy. *American Psychologist,* 1972, *27,* 989–1016.

Milgram, S. Issues in the study of obedience: A reply to Baumrind. *American Psychologist,* 1964, *19,* 848–852.

Rubin, Z. Designing honest experiments. *American Psychologist,* 1973, *28,* 445–448.

Schults, D. P. The human subject in psychological research. *Psychological Bulletin,* 1969, *72,* 214–228.

Shulman, A. D., & Berman, J. H. Role expectations about subjects and experimenters in psychological research. *Journal of Personality and Social Psychology,* 1975, *32,* 368–380.

Willis, R. H., & Willis, Y. A. Role playing versus deception: An experimental comparison. *Journal of Personality and Social Psychology,* 1970, *16,* 472–477.

CHAPTER

5

Observing Behavior in Everyday Settings

In the process of translating ideas into research problems, hypotheses, and variables, it is important to consider what kinds of data can and should be collected from what kinds of individuals and in what settings. One important and very basic means of data collection is *systematic observation*—that is, observations that are planned in advance for research purposes, designed to reduce observer bias, and carried out according to a predefined set of procedures.

Observation is a basic life activity performed by everyone. On the basis of observations everyone also makes inferences that go beyond the observed data and that may or may not be correct. Consider drivers of automobiles. In your experience, does every driver behave exactly in the same way at traffic signals? Or do some drivers "jump the light" while others seem

a million miles away long after the red has changed to green? In all likelihood, you have had many opportunities to observe traffic-light behavior. What have you observed and inferred about the variables affecting that behavior? Some of the variables are likely to be situational—for example, time of day, amount of activity at the intersection, presence or absence of police officers. But what characteristics of drivers themselves seem relevant to traffic-light behavior? This question raises a problem, because it is impossible to observe directly many of the characteristics of drivers that might seem to be important predictors of their behavior—for instance, their moods, attitudes about the law, or desire to reach their destinations.

While observing inner states and motivations directly is impossible, you can observe other driver characteristics, such as age and sex, that might be interesting sources of hypotheses about traffic-light behavior. Even such variables as number and age of passengers, make and year of car, or content of bumper stickers could be considered to be characteristics of drivers rather than of situations. Clearly, these variables do not necessarily *cause* behavior. Being male or female or having a right-to-life sticker on one's car does not directly affect driving behavior—although having a car full of energetic children might. However, growing up as a male or female could result in different experiences that might, in turn, affect driving behaviors. Similarly, social and political attitudes might be related directly or indirectly to a wide variety of behaviors, including conformity to traffic regulations. The selection by Wrightsman is this chapter is a good example of an observational study in which the relationship between attitudes (as reflected by choice of political bumper stickers) and behaviors is considered.

OBSERVATION IN PSYCHOLOGICAL RESEARCH

Most psychological research, whether correlational or experimental, whether in the laboratory or in the field, involves some kind of research. The purpose of this chapter is to teach you how to make unobtrusive and systematic observations in naturalistic, or nonlaboratory, settings. Some of the sources we cite in our discussion of observational methods are actually field experiments, included to indicate the kinds of issues that can be examined in naturalistic settings. The essential difference between a naturalistic study, which is always conducted in a field setting, and an experiment, which can be conducted in either a laboratory or field setting, is that in an experiment the situation is *manipulated* in some way for purposes of the investigation. We consider applications of the experimental method in detail in Chapter 9.

We believe you will find it interesting and enjoyable to heighten the great objectivity you bring to the kinds of observations you make in the everyday world around you. However, by encouraging you to enhance your objectivity we do not mean that all psychological research questions can be examined adequately in naturalistic settings. Two disadvantages of the natural setting are that identifying the exact set of circumstances one wishes to study is often difficult and controlling all irrelevant variables is often impossible. It is also difficult to measure the variables under investigation with as much precision as one might obtain in the laboratory. The great advantage of unobtrusive naturalistic observations, on the other hand, is that they do not distort life as the use of a laboratory setting, personality test, questionnaire, or interview is bound to do. There are a number of reasons why it can be enlightening to observe behavior directly and without interfering with individual or social processes. One reason is that people are often unable accurately to describe and report on their own behaviors. For example, obese and nonobese adolescent girls have reported taking the same amount of interest in active sports, but systematic observations have indicated that obese girls actually are much less active than their nonobese peers (Bullen, Reed & Mayer, 1964).

In other cases, people might be aware of their own behaviors and attitudes but unwilling to report them accurately. If you were interested in determining which kinds of people were willing or unwilling to help individuals of another race or nationality, you would probably get better results observing what they do than studying what they say they do (see Feldman, 1968; Gaertner & Bickman, 1971; Katz, Cohen, & Glass, 1975; Kutner, Wilkins, & Yarrow, 1952). Similarly, if you wondered what factors led ordinary children to steal Halloween candy, you would be most likely to find out if you made concealed systematic observations on Halloween (see Diener, Fraser, Beaman, & Kelem, 1976). Or, if you were interested in the ways in which different people react to a real-life crisis (for example, the power blackout in New

York), you could learn a great deal by observing people in a real-life crisis, as did Zucker, Manosevitz, and Lanyon (1968) in the study reported in our Chapter 3 selection.

While many research questions arise out of everyday experience, some can be answered *only* through observation of everyday behavior. For example, many mothers have insisted that their children are more well behaved away from home than at home. It would be easy enough to test this claim by observing "how well" (operationally defined) children behave at home as compared with how they behave when they are at a neighbor's house or in school.

Naturalistic observations are also appropriate for confirming or invalidating the generality of cause-effect relationships produced in the psychological laboratory. It might be possible to increase aggressive behavior by manipulating the presence of aggressive cues in a laboratory (Berkowitz & LePage, 1967); however, we have no way of knowing whether or not the presence of aggressive weapons (for example, a rifle) increases the likelihood of some kind of aggressive behavior (say, horn honking) in the "real world" until we make the observations outside the laboratory (see the field experiment by Turner, Layton, & Simons, 1975).

THE PURPOSES OF NATURALISTIC STUDIES

Naturalistic settings can be used for a number of purposes in psychological research. Many naturalistic investigations are *exploratory*. To conduct an exploratory study, the investigator tries to become a recording machine, making an objective account of what is going on in an interesting setting or set of circumstances. For example, you might decide to observe the behavior of young boys and girls of different ages when they approach mud puddles (Gelfond, unpublished study). A discovery that three-year-olds regardless of sex tend to go *through* puddles, and that children six and over of both sexes go *around* puddles is serendipitous indeed!

Such an observation could lead to a variety of hypotheses about the early socialization of the sexes.

All of us are surrounded by settings and circumstances that are ripe with possibilities for such exploratory behavioral observations. Try waiting in line for a World Series ticket, going to a sale at a bargain basement, or simply looking around the next time you are caught in a traffic jam. What kinds of people seem to show anxiety (for instance, by biting their fingernails or chain smoking) while waiting in a line? Young people? Males? Females? People who seem "generally nervous"? People who dress in a sophisticated way?

Exploratory observations can lead to a tentative hypothesis about a specific aspect of human functioning in a particular set of circumstances. For example, you might speculate that males become more distressed while waiting in lines than females, or that people with low self-esteem become more anxious than people with high self-esteem. To test out these hypotheses, you might choose to move into a laboratory setting to separate potentially relevant variables (for example, sex or self-esteem) from the irrelevant (time of day, location of observations, or weather). As in laboratory studies, observations in naturalistic settings can have explicit *hypothesis-testing purposes*. In some cases, you might have formulated your hypotheses on the basis of exploratory observations in similar settings. At other times, as already noted, you might be trying to generalize findings from the laboratory to less artificial settings.

OBSERVATION TECHNIQUES

As already noted, we all are observers of human behavior. But consider what might happen if you asked someone to describe what he or she had just observed in the beginning of a quarrel between two people. You probably would get a description similar to this: "Well, Bob came in obviously boiling for a fight. Jim could tell right away that Bob was going to start something, so he decided to get the jump on him. He began yelling angrily at Jim and Jim got scared and realized he'd better 'cool it.' "

Do these remarks constitute an observation? They certainly do not represent a systematic observation. Rather, they are composed of a series of inferences or interpretations. If we wanted to formulate hypotheses about who starts fights or why, this "description" would be of limited use. In fact, it might tell us more about the friendship preferences of the narrator than about Bob's interaction with Jim. As in the reports of parents, teachers, and others who observe children, it is likely to be full of biases and distortions.

How can you avoid such biases and distortions to become reliable observers of human behavior? How can you achieve objectivity in observations of behavior? A variety of techniques are available that vary in their directness and their similarity to everyday activity.

Ideally, you should obtain a full and unbiased *record* of the behavior being observed. Such a record will allow you to examine and reexamine behavior, to analyze and reanalyze it, long after it has occurred. Barker (1963, 1965; Barker & Gump, 1964; Barker & Wright, 1955) favors making a *narrative account*, or specimen record, of all relevant behavior as it occurs. You can make a narrative account by writing fast and furiously or by speaking quietly into a tape recorder. Suprisingly, there are many settings in which either of these procedures can be used without disrupting the flow of events.

Narrative accounts inevitably involve some selectivity and some distortion. No observer can record faithfully, either by hand or voice, every aspect of even relatively simple behavioral events. Moreover, selectivity in perception has been demonstrated repeatedly to be part of the human condition. Since selectivity in memory can only compound the possibilities for bias, it is important that observations be recorded immediately and not at a later time.

To circumvent the sources of bias, known and unknown, that are likely to be built into narra-

tive accounts, many researchers make use of films (for example, Bullen, Reed, & Mayer, 1964) or videotapes (Sternglanz & Serbin, 1974) to preserve behavioral records. However, even films and videotapes are selective—camera holders cannot always anticipate where the action will be or keep the camera focused on all the participants in a behavioral interaction.

Once we have obtained a behavioral record, the data contained within the record must be *coded*—that is, first categorized and then summarized and quantified—in ways that are appropriate to the research question. A total of 1500 observations in a supermarket are only a series of descriptions until coding and statistical analysis allow the investigator to discover, for example, that "women do more shopping than men, but men do enough of it to warrant the marketer's attention," or "Many shoppers of all types inspect packages carefully before they buy. The tactile dimension, therefore, deserves more attention than it usually receives in package research" (Wells and Lo Sciuto, 1966, p. 233).

It is not necessary for you to wait until after behavior has been captured in a narrative record or on film to code it. Rarely, if ever, do we set out to observe an event without some idea of what we expect to find. We are usually guided by a "hunch," a hypothesis, or even a theory, any of which we can use to establish a preliminary *category system* that focuses on particular behaviors. Such a category system can itself become a selective sort of record when it is used during the observational process.

Generally, preformulated category systems are used to sample only one aspect of behavior. Examples of these behaviors are classified discretely and exhaustively into the particular set of categories. Category systems have been developed to score, for example, facial expressions (Leventhal & Sharp, 1965), mutual glances (Exline, 1963), body movements (Ekman, 1965), spatial behavior (Eberts & Lepper, 1975; Edney, 1975; Fisher & Byrne, 1975), extralinguistic behavior (Gallois & Markel, 1975), and sex-role stereotyping in television characters (Sternglanz & Serbin, 1974).

If you were an observer in an experiment where subjects were being exposed to some sort of stress (for example, Darely & Latané, 1968), you might design a category system in which all vocal responses could be assigned to one of several categories—say, (1) a gasp or "oh!" (2) a curse, (3) a description to oneself of the event ("My God, he's having a fit!"), (4) a question or comment to another, (5) a question to oneself ("Oh, no, what shall I do?"), (6) a prayer, and (7) other responses. Such a category system is not completely foolproof, of course. Even if you could hear the tone of voice, you might not be completely sure where to categorize the exclamation "This can't be for real!"

Sign systems are an alternative to category systems as a technique of obtaining a selective behavioral record while coding behaviors. In using this technique, instead of classifying every example of a particular type of behavior in one of a discrete and exhaustive set of categories, observers watch for and record particular signs—that is, examples, or indicators, of the constructs of interest. To develop a system of sign analysis, the researcher prepares a record sheet listing a number of behaviors that occur in an observational period. During the observational period, the observer makes checks or uses symbols to record the behaviors that occur. Sign systems have often been used for recording classroom interactions (Medley & Smith, 1964).

When we observe behavior for psychological (or other) purposes, we never observe every behavior that our subjects exhibit. Rather, we take samples of behavior. Two types of behavior-sampling procedures appear frequently in observational studies: event sampling and time sampling. In *event sampling*, the investigator watches for a specific kind of behavioral interaction and then makes note of a specific set of predetermined features. For example, you could go to a playground to study childrens' quarrels (Dawe, 1934). Or you could study the ways by which freshmen students become acquainted in a college dorm during the first few weeks of school. In this case, after choosing a setting—for example, the dormitory dining room, laundry room, or lounge—you might impose a category system on all verbal behaviors, developing such categories as help seeking, help giving, and "small talk." Or you might make use of a sign system to record all behaviors—verbal, facial, physical—involved in the intiation of a conversation.

Event sampling can be a frustrating procedure if the event of concern occurs only rarely (you could waste a lot of time sitting in that dormitory). If you were interested in acquaintance behavior and you waited for two strangers to start becoming acquainted, you might have a long wait. Only when an extensive behavioral record is already available does event sampling become a relatively easy procedure.

For such reasons, many investigators prefer to use *time-sampling techniques* to test their hypotheses. If you think that ice-hockey matches elicit more aggression than ice follies, you could count the aggressive behaviors occurring within specified segments of time in each setting. For every 30 seconds you could make a 10-second observation of a selected portion of an ice-hockey or ice-follies audience (for example, the row in front of you) and tally the number of spectators who are jumping out of their seats, waving their fists, cursing, and so on. Or you could simply note whether or not any of these behaviors occur within the observed group during each time period. Chances are that if you checked off such "aggressive" behaviors every 30 seconds and totalled their frequencies over a given time period (say, 15 minutes or 30 minutes), you would find significantly more such behaviors occurring during the hockey match than during the follies. You would have to be sure, of course, that your samples employed identical units of time, equivalent time periods (for example, the second 30-minute period after the beginning of the event), relatively comparable (if possible) groups of people, and so on.

Table 5-1 is an example of a time-sampling record sheet. This observational sheet is from an investigation by Maas (1954), who studied the interactions of adolescent members of middle-class and lower-class boys' clubs in England. Each observer noted the number of collaborative, aggressive, or digressive behaviors (operationally defined, of course) that members made toward each other, their president, and their adult leader during 6-minute observational periods. These observations supported Maas' hypothesis about differences in role relationships among middle- and lower-class adolescent boys.

RELIABILITY AND VALIDITY

All data-gathering methods are subject to problems of reliability and validity, and observational techniques are no exception. As you probably remember, reliability can refer to the stability, consistency, or repeatability of the phenomenon being observed. Of most relevance to naturalistic observations is interobserver reliability or agreement. If two observers are observing the same child and using the same list of categories to check off the performance of particular behaviors, do they check the same categories when particular behaviors occur (Eaton & Clore, 1975)? If two observers are judging the interpersonal space between a child and an adult, do their judgments coincide (see Eberts and Lepper, 1975)? To conduct an observational study of your own, it is important that you use another observer to establish the reliability of your own observations. For example, if you and another observer are using the same observational schedule to record behavior in a sample, you can determine the coefficient of correlation between the two sets of data—that

is, your assignment of behaviors to categories or the frequency with which you observed particular behaviors to occur. This coefficient will give you an objective index of the reliability of your observations.

Validity is always more difficult to ensure than reliability. In the case of naturalistic observation, validity refers to the genuineness of your observations and interpretations—are you *really* seeing what you think you are seeing? Certainly if your observations are unreliable— that is, if no one else sees events or codes them as you do—then it is unlikely that your interpretations of your observations are valid. Probably the best way for you to attempt to establish the validity of your observational studies is to cite the relevant empirical and theoretical literature to make a case that the behavior you are studying represents what you think it is measuring. Are you using eye contact as a measure of affiliation? Why? Are you using the avoidance of eye contact as a measure of embarrassment? Why? Generally, if the relationship between a behavior and an underlying feeling or personality characteristic has common-sense support, some psychologists will have studied it. Find that psychologist's work and use it to help make a case for the validity of your own study.

INDIRECT DATA SOURCES

In making unobtrusive observations in naturalistic settings, you need not limit yourself to observing overt behavior. Bumper stickers, restroom graffiti, carvings on classroom desks, cigarette butts, and garbage are all rich sources of data and hypotheses. The article by Wrightsman in this chapter is a good example of a naturalistic observational study using indirect sources of data.

As noted earlier, archives (marriage records, *Who's Who* and the like) are another source from which data can be collected unobtrusively.

TABLE 5-1

A sample observational schedule

Observer _____ Club name _____

Time started _____ Date _____

Time ended _____ No. members _____

Observation no. 1   2   3 (circle) _____ Co-observer _____

	Leader		President		Member(s)			
Toward (collaboration)	P	M	L	M	L	P	M	
1. suggest								
2. ask for								
3. yield								
4. approve								
5. decide								
6. incorporate								
Against (aggression)	P	M	L	M	L	P	M	
1. compel, force								
2. resist								
verbal								
3. attack non-verbal								
Away from (digression)	P	M	L	M	L	P	M	
verbal								
1. non-group relevant interaction non-verbal								
2. silence								

From "The Role of Members in Clubs of Lower-Class and Middle-Class Adolescents," by H. Maas. In *Child Development*, 1954, *25*, 241–251. Copyright © 1954 by The Society for Research in Child Development, Inc. Reprinted by permission.

We discuss archival sources more thoroughly in the following chapter.

A PREVIEW OF THE CHAPTER SELECTION

The selection by Lawrence Wrightsman has a number of attractive features, not the least of which is that the data were collected by, not on, students enrolled in an undergraduate psychology course. This study is not the only one published in which students participated as research investigators rather than subjects but it serves as a good model of the kind of publishable project that can grow out of an undergraduate psychology course.

The methodological strength of the observational study conducted by Wrightsman and his students lies in its reliance on unobtrusive behavioral measures of law obedience (specifically, compliance with a law requiring display of an automobile-tax sticker on all motor vehicles) and political preference (display of a political bumper sticker endorsing one of the candidates for the 1968 presidential election). While many interesting observational studies are more current than Wrightsman's, they generally reflect an assumption that the behavior under investigation is simply a product of situational influence rather than individual characteristics. The Wrightsman study is relatively unique in its use of an unobtrusive measure that might reflect relatively enduring individual tendencies. Moreover, as Wrightsman points out, an unobtrusive measurement of obedience to law is a means of avoiding a problem inherent in self-report measures: the tendency of some individuals to describe themselves in ways that are socially desirable rather than accurate reports of behavior.

Because the Wrightsman study is not as up-to-date as our other selections, we would like to remind you of the historical context in which it was conducted. The 1968 presidential campaign was a three-way race, at least in the South. At the time of Wrightsman's study, George Wallace, running on an American Party ticket, had done well in presidential primaries, even in the North. His platform was implicitly segregationist, although one of the rallying cries of his campaign was for "law and order." The general question tackled by Wrightsman and his students was "Are supporters of Wallace and his law-and-order platform more likely to obey the law then supporters of the other candidates?" The unobtrusive approach to this question, described in our chapter selection, is ingenious indeed. Note the concern that Wrightsman shows in defining his variables operationally and establishing controls in this naturalistic study. Also note the thoughtfulness with which he describes the limitations of the study.

Wallace Supporters and Adherence To "Law and Order"[1]

Lawrence S. Wrightsman

George Peabody College for Teachers

Cars bearing Davidson County, Tennessee, license plates were observed in public parking lots between the period of November 1 to November 5, 1968, in order to determine if they possessed (*a*) a county auto tax sticker, costing $15 and required as of November 1, or (*b*) a bumper sticker supporting any of the three major presidential candidates. Cars without a presidential sticker, parked adjacent to the above cars, served as controls. The results were as follows: 74.8% of 361 Wallace cars displayed the tax sticker; 86.5% of 304 Nixon cars; 86.5% of 178 Humphrey cars; and 81.25% of 843 controls. Differences in percentages were statistically significant. It was concluded that Wallace supporters less frequently obeyed this law. Possible reasons for this were explored; differences in voters' socioeconomic status and observers' candidate preferences do not appear to be explanations.

During the 1968 presidential election campaign, the issue of "law and order" was a salient one. Though it was often unclear as to just what surplus meanings were attached to this provocative phrase, it was more strongly advanced as a campaign issue by George Wallace than by the other two major candidates. The present study was generated by a curiosity as to whether supporters of Wallace were, in fact, more law abiding than were supporters of the other candidates. A

[1]This study was completed as a project by the Psychology 270 class at Peabody College during the fall semester, 1968. The students and the instructor (and assorted spouses) served as the observer-recorders. This study was completed without the expenditure of any funds from the federal government or private foundations; the only cost to Peabody College was for the typing and duplication of this report. The author wishes to thank the following for their useful comments on an earlier draft of this report: G. W. Baxter, F. C. Noble, Anne Smead Fay, P. Schoggen, Laura Weinstein, and M. Buhl. Portions of this paper were presented at the Midwestern Psychological Association convention, Chicago, May 9, 1969.

Entire article from *Journal of Personality and Social Psychology*, 1969, *13*, 17–22. Copyright 1969 by the American Psychological Association. Reprinted by permission.

second reason for doing the study was that locally, a convenient opportunity to measure obedience of law occurred just at the time of the election.

Obedience to the law is a variable, which if measured by a self-report questionnaire or interviews, is clearly classifiable as a "reactive" one (Webb, Campbell, Schwartz, & Sechrest, 1966); that is, a respondent's response might well be colored or altered by his considerations of social desirability, his needs to appear law abiding, etc. Therefore, a behavioral "unobtrusive measure" of law obedience was sought—one which could be assessed without having to ask the subject anything at all.

An excellent unobtrusive measure of obeying one law manifested itself in Nashville and Davidson County, Tennessee, during the pre-election period. Earlier in the fall of 1968 the Metropolitan Council of Nashville-Davidson County (a consolidated government) passed a law requiring all motor vehicles in Davidson County to display a new automobile tax sticker, effective November 1, 1968. The sticker (henceforth to be called "the Metro sticker") went on sale by mail and at the County Courthouse early in October, at a price of $15 per vehicle. It was announced early in October that failure to possess a Metro sticker after November 1 was illegal and subject to a $50 fine. (In actuality, on Thursday, October 31, it was announced that two days of grace—till midnight Saturday, November 2—would be given because of the long lines waiting to buy the sticker.) Abetted by an influential local newspaper, a great deal of public sentiment developed against the sticker, not only because it was an added tax, but also because the present municipal administration had campaigned against an earlier tax sticker established by the previous administration. Shortly after the present administration took office it terminated requirement of the then-current $10 sticker, only to institute its higher priced one in 1968 (6 years later). However, despite grumbling, many Davidson Countians bought the sticker and slapped it on their car's windshield.

Thus, presence of the Metro sticker on the car served as an operational definition of obeying the law. (It is recognized that this refers to obeyance of only one specific law.) Support of a presidential candidate was assessed by observing the car's bumpers and back window to determine the presence of a political sticker. The following classification was used:

Sticker

"Nixon-Agnew," "Nixon," or "Vote Republican"

"Humphrey-Muskie," "Humphrey," or "Vote Democratic"

"Wallace-LeMay," or "Wallace"

Tabulated as:

_____ Nixon supporter

_____ Humphrey supporter

_____ Wallace supporter

Cars bearing stickers for other political candidates (McCarthy, local congressional candidates, Snoopy, etc.) were *not* counted as political supporters *or* as controls. Cars with *no* political bumper stickers of any kind were used as controls. Many of the owners of these cars obviously had political preferences, too, but we feel it is defensible to assume their allegiance to and identification with a candidate was less strong than those displaying bumper stickers. There is a problem in the comparability of the strength of allegiance of Wallace supporters versus those of the other two candidates. During much of the campaign, Wallace stickers were not given away free in this area, but rather were sold for $.50 or $1; in the last week of the campaign they were given away. Humphrey and Nixon stickers were generally available for the asking, although donations were accepted. Thus it is probable that the average Wallace bumper-sticker car reflected its owner's stronger allegiance than did cars belonging to supporters of the other two candidates. The extent of difference, if any, is impossible to assess.

METHOD

Cars were observed during the period from 1 P.M. Friday, November 1, through 6 P.M. Tuesday, November 5 (Election Day). Only cars parked in specified parking areas were used (shopping centers, church parking areas, college campus lots, and parking areas for large companies).

Observer-recorders were instructed to survey a parking lot until they found a car with a presidential bumper sticker. If the car bore a Davidson County tag (Tennessee license plates include the name of the county), the following was recorded: type of presidential sticker, license plate number, presence or absence of Metro sticker, and make and age of car. For the latter a crude designation of "new" (post-1964) or "old" (1964 or pre-1964) was used. Then the observer-recorders were instructed to go to the left of the presidential bumper-sticker car and find a "control car" without any bumper sticker. Usually the adjacent car qualified by being from Davidson County and possessing no political bumper sticker. The information about presence or absence of Metro sticker, license plate, and make and year were recorded for this car, also. Thus, after surveying a given area, the recorder would have a list of *x* number of cars with presidential stickers and the same number without. The recording of the controls was carried out in order to have a comparison on "nonsupporters" (or at least less committed supporters) *who came from the same socioeconomic backgrounds* as the political supporters. It was assumed that if two cars were adjacent in the same lot (church, shopping center, etc.) they came from relatively similar or homogeneous socioeconomic backgrounds.

A total of 46 parking areas were surveyed; these included 14 shopping centers, 13 church and synagogue parking areas, 6 college campuses, 2 voting areas, and 11 lots for large factories and businesses.[2] Coverage of the different predominantly white areas of the county was good, ranging from

[2]An analysis by days indicated that fewer cars had Metro stickers on the first 3 days than on Monday and Tuesday, but this difference had no effect on the candidate differences.

upper class to lower class. Only one predominantly Negro area was surveyed—the parking lots in the Fisk University area.

Observer-recorders usually worked singly, although some, working in pairs, checked each other. It should be recognized that the possibility of recording errors motivated by experimenter expectation (Rosenthal, 1966) exist in this study; that is, after recording the presence of a particular bumper sticker a solitary observer could fail to see a Metro tax sticker that was actually there. Several precautions were taken, however. Observers were instructed to walk to the front of the car, observe the presence or absence of the Metro sticker, record, and observe again. The fact that there were suporters of all three major condidates among the 26 observers is also of relevance to possible recording bias. The tabulation of presidential preferences of the observer-recorders was as follows: Humphrey, 15; Nixon, 8; Wallace, 1; none, 2. An analysis of recording results by observers' presidential preferences will be reported in the Discussion section.

RESULTS

Table 1 presents the results of this study. It is estimated that approximately 180,000 cars are registered in Davidson county. A total number of 1,686 cars were observed and recorded in this study. Of these, 304 had Nixon (or Republican) bumper stickers, 178 had Humphrey (or Democratic) stickers, and 361 had Wallace stickers.[3]

[3]These percentages are as follows: Nixon, 36%; Humphrey, 21%, Wallace, 43%. The unofficial vote in Davidson County on November 5 was the following: Nixon, 44,228, or 32.4%; Humphrey, 44,739, or 32.79%; Wallace, 47,464, or 34.79%. However, these totals include the Negro votes (approximately 15%) and the Negro areas of the county were only minimally included in our survey. The predominantly Negro precincts voted strongly for Humphrey (example: Pearl High School precinct, Humphrey, 1,025; Nixon, 17; Wallace, 0; and Hadley Park precinct, Humphrey, 1,235; Nixon, 23; Wallace, 2). If the all-Negro and predominantly Negro boxes are removed from the voting total, the results are as follows: Nixon, 43,117, or 35.05%; Humphrey, 33,350, or 27.10%; Wallace, 45,562, or 37.84%. These latter percentages are closer to those of the bumper sticker sample.

TABLE 1
Numbers and Percentages of Cars Bearing Metro Tax Stickers

No. cars	Groups	With tax sticker		Without tax sticker	
		n	%	n	%
304	Nixon	263	86.51	41	13.49
304	Nixon controls	245	80.59	59	19.41
178	Humphrey	154	86.52	24	13.48
178	Huphrey controls	137	76.97	41	23.03
361	Wallace	270	74.79	91	25.21
361	Wallace controls	303	83.93	58	16.07
843	Political-sticker	687	81.49	156	18.51
843	Controls	685	81.26	158	18.74

Note.—Tests of statistical significance for the difference in two proportions (Walker & Lev, 1953, p. 76): Wallace versus Wallace controls: $z = -5.31, p < .0001$; Nixon versus Nixon controls: $z = 1.97, p < .05$ (two-tailed); Humphrey versus Humphrey controls: $z = 2.33, p < .02$ (two-tailed); Wallace versus Humphrey controls: $z = -3.12, p < .001$ (two-tailed); Wallace versus Nixon controls: $z = -3.77, p < .0001$ (two-tailed).

The remaining 843 cars, without presidential stickers, served as controls.

As Table 1 indicates, 86.5% of the cars of Nixon suporters displayed the Metro sticker, compared with 80.6% of their adjacent controls. The probability of this difference occurring by chance was $p < .05$ (two-tailed test). The percentage of Humphrey cars with the Metro sticker was 86.5%, the same as the Nixon percentage. As was the case with the Nixon cars, the percentage was significantly greater ($p < .02$) than the percentage for the controls (which for the Humphrey controls was 77.0%).

Of the 361 Wallace cars, 270 or 74.8% had the Metro sticker. This percentage is significantly lower ($p < .0001$) than the percentage (83.9%) for the Wallace controls, and is also significantly lower than the percentages for Nixon cars ($p < .0001$) and Humphrey cars ($p < .001$).

It thus appears clear that committed supporters of Wallace were less frequently law abiding than were other groups, including committed supporters of other candidates or others who were not demonstrably committed to any candidate. This difference is even more impressive when one considers that some of the control cars (no bumper stickers) were no doubt Wallace supporters, too; that is, the "control" group possesses some—albeit less committed—experimentals.

It is interesting to note that the percentages of political-supporters cars and control cars having the Metro stickers were almost exactly the same—81.49% and 81.26%, respectively. This is a difference of only 2 cars out of 843.

DISCUSSION

This section of the paper will deal with possible causes of the less frequent law obeyance by Wallace supporters. Several possible explanations, such as defiance of authority and a rejection of the actions of bureaucrats, are not testable by our data. It may be that Wallace supporters are more often characterized by these feelings, but the investigators did not interview any of the owners of cars in the sample and cannot say. Several car owners told the recorders that they had purchased Metro stickers but were carrying them on their person rather than placing them on their car's windshield. They were waiting for the police to stop them, they said, so that they could show the police they were law abiding. There were not enough cases of this interesting (possibly passive-aggressive) behavior, however, to relate it to presidential preference.

Another possible reason that fewer Wallace supporters displayed a Metro sticker is that they are poorer and are less able to pay the $15. Perhaps Wallace supporters are law abiding except when it costs money. The Gallup Poll (1968) and other polls have shown that a relatively greater percentage of Wallace supporters came from the lower socioeconomic class. Therefore it is important to determine whether a social class difference existed between Wallace supporters and their controls. To determine this, the age distribution of Wallace cars was compared with that of the Wallace controls. A total of 208 of the 361 Wallace cars were classified as "new" or "recent" (1964 or later), compared with 231 of the Wallace con-

trols. These percentages—57.6% versus 64.0%—are not significantly different ($z = 1.83, p < .10$) although in the direction of a greater number of Wallace supporters having older cars. The Wallace supporters do less often have newer cars than do the Nixon supporters (74.3%) or the Humphrey supporters (74.7%). (These percentages are amplified in Table 2.)

Of more direct relevance to the issue of age of car (as a measure of socioeconomic status) and presence of a Metro sticker is the fact that the percentage of *old* Wallace cars with the Metro sticker—74.5%, or 114 of 153 cars—is almost identical with the percentage of *new* Wallace cars with the sticker—75.0% or 156 of 208. Apparently lower socioeconomic-level does not serve as an explanation of the candidate-supporter differences in law obeyance.

Could the differences in sticker percentages be a function of observer-recorder bias? Might observers who are pro-Humphrey, for example, fail to "see" the Metro tax sticker when it was on a pro-Nixon or pro-Wallace car? Table 3 presents data relevant to this question, as it shows the number and percentage of each type of car bearing the Metro tax sticker, separated by presidential preference of the observer-recorder. For example, when tabulating Nixon cars, the 15 pro-Humphrey observers reported that 88.39% of the Nixon cars had the Metro sticker, compared to a report by the 8 pro-Nixon observers of 82.79% of *their* Nixon cars possessing the Metro sticker. Table 3 reports these percentages for each of six types of cars (Nixon, Humphrey, and Wallace cars and controls for each); chi-squares were computed and in none of the six sets were the observed frequencies different from the expected. It may be concluded that in observing cars allied with a particular candidate, the observer's presidential preference was unrelated to the percentage of cars he reported bearing the Metro tax sticker.

The data in Table 3 may be studied in another way. One may ask: Do Humphrey supporters report a greater percentage of law-abiding cars for their candidate? Table 3 indicates that pro-Hum-

TABLE 2
Presence of Metro Sticker in New and Old Cars

Group	Sticker present	%	Sticker absent	%	Total	%
Nixon supporters						
New	195	86.28	31	13.72	226	74.34
Old	68	87.18	10	12.82	78	25.66
Total	263	86.51	41	13.49	304	100.00
Nixon controls						
New	181	80.08	45	19.91	226	74.34
Old	64	82.05	14	17.95	78	25.66
Total	245	80.59	59	19.41	304	100.00
Humphrey supporters						
New	119	89.47	14	10.53	133	74.72
Old	35	77.78	10	22.22	45	25.28
Total	154	86.52	24	13.48	178	100.00
Humphrey controls						
New	98	83.05	20	16.95	118	66.29
Old	39	65.00	21	35.00	60	33.71
Total	137	76.97	41	23.03	178	100.00
Wallace supporters						
New	156	75.00	52	25.00	208	57.62
Old	114	74.50	39	25.49	153	42.38
Total	270	74.79	91	25.21	361	100.00
Wallace controls						
New	200	86.58	31	13.42	231	63.99
Old	103	79.23	27	20.77	130	36.01
Total	303	83.93	58	16.07	361	100.00

phrey observers reported that 88.18% of the Humphrey cars had a Metro sticker, 88.39% of the Nixon cars did, and 77.84% of the Wallace cars did. Pro-Nixon observers reported that 82.79% of the Nixon cars, 85.19% of Humphrey cars, and 70.63% of the Wallace cars had a Metro sticker. Thus both pro-Humphrey and pro-Nixon observers reported a slightly higher percentage for another candidate than for their own. The lone observer who was pro-Wallace reported higher percentages of Nixon and Humphrey cars having the tax sticker (100%) than the Wallace cars (75%, or 3 of 4).

Although the data of Table 3 are not a conclusive test of the possible effects of observer bias, there is nothing in the table which indicates that the observer's presidential preference influenced his recording.

Further evidence for candidate-supporter differences emerges from an independent study by John McCarthy[4] of law-breaking also done in Nashville in the fall of 1968. He stationed observers at a Nashville intersection with a stop sign and recorded the percentage and types of cars failing to stop. A significantly higher percentage of cars with Wallace bumper stickers failed to stop.

It seems that while Wallace has advocated "law and order," his supporters, in their own behavior, subscribe to it to a less frequent degree than do other citizens.

[4] J. McCarthy. Personal communication, December 2, 1968.

TABLE 3
Numbers and Percentages of Cars Bearing Metro Tax Sticker, Separated by Presidential Preference of Observer-Recorder

No. observers	Observers' preference	Nixon cars				Control cars (Nixon)			
		Yes	%	No	%	Yes	%	No	%
15	Humphrey	137	88.39	18	11.61	133	85.81	22	14.19
8	Nixon	101	82.79	21	17.21	90	73.77	32	26.23
1	Wallace	14	100.00	0	0.00	11	78.57	3	21.43
2	None	11	84.62	2	15.38	11	84.62	2	15.38
Total		263	86.51	41	13.49	245	80.59	59	19.41

No. observers	Observers' preference	Humphrey cars				Control cars (Humphrey)			
15	Humphrey	97	88.18	13	11.82	88	80.00	22	20.00
8	Nixon	46	85.19	8	14.81	40	74.07	14	25.92
1	Wallace	5	100.00	0	0.00	3	60.00	2	40.00
2	None	6	66.67	3	33.33	6	66.67	3	33.33
Total		154	86.52	24	13.48	137	76.97	41	23.03

No. observers	Observers' preference	Wallace cars				Control cars (Wallace)			
15	Humphrey	144	77.84	41	22.16	162	87.57	23	12.43
8	Nixon	101	70.63	42	29.37	112	78.32	31	21.68
1	Wallace	3	75.00	1	25.00	3	75.00	1	25.00
2	None	22	75.86	7	24.14	26	89.66	3	10.34
Total		270	74.74	91	25.21	303	83.93	58	16.07

Note.—Chi-square for the differences; Nixon cars: $\chi^2 = 4.11$, $p < .25$; Nixon controls: $\chi^2 = 6.7$, $p < .10$; Humphrey cars: $\chi^2 = 5.27$, $p < .25$; Humphrey controls: $\chi^2 = 2.18$, $p > .50$; Wallace cars: $\chi^2 = 2.24$, $p < .50$; Wallace controls: $\chi^2 = 6.08$, $p < .25$.

REFERENCES

Gallup, G. Voting profile in 1968. *Nashville Tennessean*, December 8, 1968, 5B.

Rosenthal, R. *Experimenter effects in behavioral research*. New York: Appleton-Century-Crofts, 1966.

Walker, H., & Lev, J. *Statistical inference*. New York: Holt, Rinehart & Winston, 1953.

Webb, E. J., Campbell, D. T., Schwartz, R. D., & Sechrest, L. *Unobtrusive measures: Nonreactive research in the social sciences*. Chicago: Rand McNally, 1966.

STUDY QUESTIONS

1. What was Wrightsman's hypothesis?
2. How did he operationalize his variables?
3. Were his procedures ethical? Should he have obtained informed consent from his subjects or debriefed them?
4. What other kinds of observational studies might be done using bumper stickers as a source of data?
5. How do the measures used in the Wrightsman study avoid the issue of social desirability?
6. What controls are employed in the study? What are the issues for which controls are employed?
7. What measures are taken to guard against experimenter bias?
8. What are some of the explicit limitations of the unobtrusive measures as discussed in the article?

EXERCISE

Developing an Observational Study

You should be ready by now to develop your own observational study and complete an independent observational project. The following steps should be helpful to you in this undertaking.

1. Choose a setting of interest—for example, the subway station at rush hour, a bargain basement, a busy street corner, a teen-age hangout.

2. Make some preliminary observations of the kinds of interactions that go on in that setting—for example, friendly, aggressive, avoidant behavior—and select the kind of behavior you want to study.

3. Formulate a hypothesis about the antecedents of that behavior or the other behaviors that may be related to it. Are you suggesting that subway riders are friendlier at noon than during rush hour, that males are more aggressive than females at sales?

4. Use library resources to find other research relevant to your topic. Consider whether you want to revise your hypothesis on the basis of the published literature.

5. Decide whether an event- or time-sampling procedure and a category or sign system will be most likely to provide you with the kind of data you need to test your hypotheses.

6. Develop an observational record sheet with places for the signs, symbols, or other marks you have chosen and with time intervals built in if you plan to use a time-sampling procedure. Remember to include headings for time, place, observer's name, subjects, and so on.

7. Record your observations, if possible with the help of a friend, so that you can obtain some data on interobserver reliability.

8. Analyze your results.

ANNOTATED BIBLIOGRAPHY

Friedman, H. S., D. Matteo, M. R., & Mertz, T. I. Nonverbal communication on television news: The facial expressions of broadcasters during coverage of a Presidential election campaign. *Personality and Social Psychology Bulletin*, 1980, *6*, 427–435.

In a "nonverbal-content analysis," the authors studied the facial expressions of network-television-news anchorpersons while they were uttering names of presidential candidates. Significant differences in the perceived positivity of facial expressions were found as a function of the candidates.

Helsin, R., & Boss, D. Nonverbal intimacy in airport arrival and departure. *Personality and Social Psychology Bulletin*, 1980, *6*, 248–252.

Observers at an airport coded the nonverbal behavior of 103 travelers and their companions. Nonverbal intimacy (for example, shaking hands, hugging, kissing) was related positively to closeness of the relationship. Men tended to initiate touch with women more than vice versa.

Sorrentino, R. M., & Sheppard, B. H. Effects of affiliation-related motives on swimmers in individual vs. group competition: A field experiment. *Journal of Personality and Social Psychology*, 1978, *36*, 704-714.

In this field experiment, 76 male and female intercollegiate swimmers received motivation assessments and were later observed in both individual and group competition. Subject swim speeds were compared in singular and group races and differences were found between approval-oriented and rejection-threatened swimmers, success-oriented and failure-threatened swimmers, as well as between males and females.

Stiles, W. B. Verbal response modes and dimensions of interpersonal votes: A method of discourse analysis. *Journal of Personality and Social Psychology*, 1978, *36*, 693–703.

In this theoretically based analysis of dyadic communication, eight verbal-response modes were defined by the intersection of the speaker's or the other's source of experience, frame of reference, and focus. These verbal response modes were used to define three dimensions of interpersonal roles. Data from this analysis were then compared with Bale's interaction-process analysis.

ADDITIONAL SOURCES

Bales, R. F. *Personality and interpersonal behavior.* New York: Holt, Reinhart & Winston, 1970.

Block, J. *Lives through time.* Berkeley, Calif.: Bancroft, 1971.

Dailey, C. A. *Assessment of lives.* San Francisco: Jossey-Bass, 1971.

Elig, T. W., & Frieze, I. H. A multi-dimensional scheme for coding and interpreting perceived causality for success and failure events: The coding scheme of perceived causality (CSPC). *JSAS: Catalog of Selected Documents in Psychology*, 1975, *5*, 313 (Ms. #1069).

Friedrich, L., & Stein, A. Aggressive and prosocial television programs and the natural behavior of preschool children. *Monographs of the Society for Research in Child Development*, 1973, *38* (4, Serial No. 151).

Hunter, J. E. Images of woman. *Journal of Social Issues*, 1976, *32*, 7–17.

Katz, E. W. A content-analytic method for studying themes of interpersonal behavior. *Psychological Bulletin*, 1966, *66*, 419–422.

Kounin, J. S., & Gump, P. V. The comparative influence of punitive and nonpunitive teachers upon children's concepts of school misconduct. *Journal of Educational Psychology*, 1961, *52*, 44–49.

Lantz, H. R., Britton, M., Schmitt, R., & Snyder, E. C. Pre-industrial patterns in the colonial family in America: A content analysis of colonial magazines. *American Sociological Review*, 1968, *33*, 413–426.

Manheim, L., & Manheim, E. *Hidden patterns: Studies in psychoanalytic literary criticism*. New York: Macmillan, 1966.

May, R. Sex differences in fantasy patterns. *Journal of Projective Techniques*, 1966, *30*, 252–259.

McClelland, D. C. Love and power: The psychological signals of war. *Psychology Today*, 1975, *8*, 44–48.

McGuire, W. J. The yin and yang of progress in social psychology: Seven koan. *Journal of Personality and Social Psychology*, 1973, *26*, 446–456.

Price, R. H., & Bouffard, D. L. Behavioral appropriateness and situation constraint as dimensions of social behavior. *Journal of Personality and Social Psychology*, 1974, *30*, 579–586.

Shneidman, E. S. Plan II. The logic of politics. In L. Arons and M. A. May (Eds.), *Television and human behavior*. New York: Appleton-Century-Crofts, 1963.

Simonton, D. K. Interdisciplinary creativity over historical time: A correlational analysis of generational fluctuations. *Social Behavior and Personality*, 1975, *5*, 181–188.

Simonton, D. K. Biographical determinants of achieved eminence: A multivariate approach to the Cox data. *Journal of Personality and Social Psychology*, 1976, *33*, 218–226. (a)

Simonton, D. K. The sociopolitical context of philosophical beliefs: A transhistorical causal analysis. *Social Forces*, 1976, *54*, 513–523. (b)

Stern G. G. *People in context: Measuring person-environment congruence in education and industry.* New York: Wiley, 1970.

Watson, J., & Potter, R. J. The analytic unit for the study of interaction. *Human Relations*, 1962, *16*, 245–263.

CHAPTER

6

Content Analysis

Content Analysis is closely related to naturalistic observation. As you will see in this chapter, content analysis is similar to observational study in its techniques and many of its purposes and applications. Moreover, like naturalistic observation, content analysis can range from casual and intuitive to highly scientific. However, the material that is categorized and analyzed in a content analysis is not behavior generally but communicative behavior specifically. That is, content analysis is used to study people's oral and written communications, their conversations, speeches, diaries, and recorded fantasies, and even such archival materials as census reports and crime statistics.

Like naturalistic observation, content analysis has the advantage of being unobtrusive. We can conduct content analyses of verbal behavior without intruding on or affecting the individuals in whom we are interested. Moreover, because content analysis can be applied to almost any kind of human communication, we can use it to make inferences from documents that have long since become part of history. Newspapers and periodicals, histories and anthologies, novels and songs, letters and diaries can all be analyzed for their psychological content, either globally and intuitively or systematically and objectively.

CONTENT ANALYSIS IN PSYCHOLOGICAL RESEARCH

To illustrate what this technique involves when it is used for psychological-research purposes, we turn to a concrete example of content analysis. In 1947 Lewin was interested in whether or not American Boy Scouts and Hitler Youth in the late 30s and early 40s were being trained in different goals and values within their respective youth groups. He examined comparable samples of the Boy Scout magazine *Boy's Life* and the Hitler Youth yearbook *Jungen-Eure Welt,* and found that he could identify 18 goals mentioned in one or the other or both magazines. For example, both publications contained statements concerning the allegiance of the individual to the nation and its leaders such as "The Hitler Youth is the youth of the Fuehrer," "Your body belongs to the nation," "Boy Scouts are grass root Americans," and "Scouts in time of emergency will do more than ever dreamed of before." Such statements of allegiance occurred significantly more often in the Hitler Youth yearbook than in the Boy Scout magazine. Lewin found that some goals received equal endorsement in both magazines. However, national loyalty was a more frequent theme in the Hitler Youth magazine, and fair play and reverence for a deity were more frequent themes in the Boy Scout magazine. Altogether, Lewin found differences between the two magazines for 6 out of 18 goals.

Content analysis, like naturalistic observation, is frequently used when investigators believe that people cannot or will not give true or adequate answers to their questions. For example, you might be interested in what motivates individuals to seek high political office and how their motivations will affect what they do in office. Even if you could interview candidates for the presidency of the United States, you might not trust your respondent's ability or willingness to give straightforward and in-depth responses to questions about their underlying motives. It is even more unlikely that you would have the opportunity to administer psychological tests to presidential candidates or other aspiring politicians. However, Winter (1973a, 1973b) has developed a system of content analysis for scoring motives embedded in various types of imaginative verbal material—including announcements of political candidacy, inaugural addresses, and the like.

Consider the following examples of Winter's (1976) motive scoring as applied to the announcement speeches of several 1976 presidential candidates. Senator Frank Church's assertion that "we must strive for better, not bigger government" is scored as reflecting the achievement motive, as is President Carter's comment that "our government can and must represent the best and the highest ideals of those of us who voluntarily submit to its authority." Senator Humphrey's hope that "the young must be full and effective partners. . . . united in friendship, compassion and mutual respect" is scored as indicative of the affiliation motive, while Henry Jackson's warning that "there is a neglected agenda in this country that cries out for leadership and demands something better than stop-gap action when a crisis develops" is scored as reflecting the need for power.

With Winter's system, one can compare candidates for their relative tendency to make statements reflecting each motive (achievement, affiliation, and power). One can also examine the relationship among the motives in the speeches of different candidates. Furthermore, analysis of the speeches of past presidents and an examination of their actual behavior in office allows us to make predictions about the likely behavior of current leaders with similar motive patterns (Winter, 1976).

One of the greatest advantages of content analysis is the potential it affords us for making inferences and testing hypotheses about historical individuals and about the operation of psychological variables across historical time. As another example, suppose you were interested in determining what kinds of changes have taken place in child-rearing advice over the centuries and in how these changes are related to broader social changes or changes in popular literary themes. It would be a fairly straightforward process to score child-rearing manuals for the presence or absence of treatments of such issues as dependence/independence training, sex differentiation, virtues admired and vices condemned in children, and so on (Stewart, Winter, & Jones, 1975). Or you might be interested in whether various types of individual creative accomplishments are related to such social-political variables as political stability or instability, or political unity or fragmentation. Again, answers to such questions can be derived through content analyses of archival sources—for instance, histories, anthologies, and biographical dictionaries (Simonton, 1975).

TYPES OF MATERIALS

As already noted, almost any kind of verbal material can be subjected to content analysis and used in a study of psychological variables. Psychoanalytically oriented critics might examine a fictional character to make inferences about the personality dynamics and unconscious strivings of the author (McCurdy, 1947; also see White, 1947). Anthropologists and sociologists might analyze the rites and reported customs of simple societies to investigate hypotheses about the relationship between child-rearing variables and adult personality characteristics (for example, Whiting & Child, 1953). Biographers frequently examine letters, writings, and archival materials to explain the principal characteristics and the life themes of their subjects (compare to Tozzer, 1948). Similarly, psycho-historical analyses of historical figures ranging from Woodrow Wilson (Freud & Bullitt, 1967) and Mahatma Gandhi (Erikson, 1969) to Richard Nixon (Mazlish, 1972) have relied heavily on analyses of personal documents and archival materials.

In addition to analyses of individual fictional and historical characters, researchers sometimes analyze personal documents such as autobiographical essays to answer very general questions about personality functioning—for example, "How much do social catastrophes disrupt personality integration?" (Allport, Bruner & Jandorf, 1941). Clinicians might use expressive materials such as diaries and artistic pro-

ductions to help in their assessment of clients (Allport, 1965). Moreover, as we discuss later in this chapter, clinicians subject data from many of the personality tests known as *projective tests* to forms of content analysis to make their interpretations of client functioning.

Even data that are already fairly objective can be used for purposes quite different than originally intended when subjected to content analysis. For example, Sales (1972) examined census data and the statistics maintained by churches to investigate the notion that in economic bad times (such as the Great Depression), the rate of religious conversions to authoritarian churches increases. Here, as in most psychological studies, the investigator must make judgments about how the available data are to be categorized and interpreted—for example, judgments about what constitutes an authoritarian church or economic hard times. Census and voter registration lists, school records, and records of voluntary associations are all sources of available data that can be used to answer a variety of research questions once such judgments have been made.

Most often, the verbal material used in content analyses are *coded* in some way for the variables of interest. Thus, picture books for preschool children can be coded to reveal sex-role stereotyping (Weitzman, Eifler, Hokada, & Ross, 1972), as can elementary school readers (Child, Potter, & Levine, 1946). And children's readers, like political speeches, can be coded for the types of motives portrayed. Changes in emphasis in particular motives (for instance, achievement versus affiliation) can be studied across many generations (de Charms & Moeller, 1962). Similarly, popular songs can be coded for common themes, and changes in these common themes can be examined in relation to changes in the youth culture (Keesing, 1974).

In addition to its applications to archival and other available materials, content analysis can be used with verbal responses to a number of psychological tests developed for purposes of personality assessment and research. Content analysis is not needed when subjects must choose among a set of predefined response alternatives (as in a multiple-choice test or questionnaire), give answers that can be scored correct or incorrect (as in IQ, aptitude, or achievement tests), or respond in ways that are intrinsically quantifiable (as in performance tests). However, whenever subjects must respond to a task or situation "in their own words," some sort of content analysis is needed to quantify the qualitative or objectify the subjective responses.

The range of materials in psychological assessment to which content analysis is applicable is enormous. For example, open-ended interviews, in which respondents discuss their self-concepts, crises, commitments, beliefs, values, and the like, must be coded for content in systematic ways to identify major similarities and differences in subjects' responses. The range of possible ways of coding a single interview is also enormous, as illustrated by the great variety of content analyses conducted on psychotherapeutic interviews between therapists and clients (Marsden, 1965). The process of developing, conducting, and analyzing interviews is discussed in more detail in Chapter 7.

A number of verbal tasks have been designed to aid investigators in assessing stages of development in various domains. For example, stories have been constructed to elicit subject's reasoning about ethical issues and role-taking situations. Also, children's and adult's judgments about moral dilemmas (for example, individual versus property rights) and social role taking as it pertains to moral dilemmas can be coded for stage of moral development (Kohlberg & Gilligan, 1971) or role-taking development (Selman & Byrne, 1972). Similarly, an individual's endings to a standard set of incomplete sentences can be coded to yield the subject's stage of ego development (Loevinger, Wessler & Redmore, 1970). Piaget used a classification task (where children were asked to group together things

that belonged together) to illustrate cognitive processes related to developmental stage. And White (1971) showed that the same set of grouping responses could be coded both for cognitive ability (related to stage of development) and cognitive style (related to personality variables).

The whole body of personality-assessment techniques termed *projective* (for example, Pervin, 1975) involves some sort of content analysis for interpretation. The assumption behind projective methods is that subjects will project important aspects of their own personalities into verbal responses to any relatively unstructured or ambiguous task—especially when the assessment situation is disguised in ways to keep subjects from being "on guard" and afraid of revealing themselves. Proponents of projective techniques believe that it is only when individuals express themselves relatively freely and in a personalized fashion that we can begin to get a picture of the "whole person," including unconscious as well as conscious needs, motivations, defenses, and so on. Projective techniques include word-association and sentence-completion tasks, Rorschach and other inkblot tests, and the eliciting of such expressive products as autobiographical essays and figure drawings.

In one popular projective technique, individuals are presented with pictures. For each picture they must tell a story with a beginning, middle, and end. The story is supposed to describe what is going on in the picture, what led up to it, what the people in the picture are thinking and feeling, and how it will all turn out. It is assumed that with this, like other projective techniques, individuals will project a good deal of their own personality into the ambiguous and rather unstructured task. The most commonly used version of this picture-story technique is known as the Thematic Apperception Test, or TAT (Murray, 1938). In the TAT, stories are coded for the types of personal needs (or motives) and types of environmental press (pressures or demands) expressed by the individual. The TAT has given rise to extensive research on the achievement motive in particular, both as it varies as a function of socialization forces within our own society and as it varies cross-culturally (for example, McClelland, 1955b; et al., 1953). Winter's research (1973a & b; 1976) on the motives of political candidates and office holders also arises out of this tradition.

Regardless of whether they are applied to a story, a book, an autobiographical essay or other verbal material, content analyses can vary tremendously with respect to the level of objectivity and systematicity built into them. In psychohistorical studies (for example, Erikson, 1969), self-analyses (for example, Climo, 1975), or case histories (for example, Blos, 1941), the analysis is frequently rather subjective and intuitive. In such instances, emphasis is on studying "whole persons" in all their uniqueness and complexity. Even when used for more narrowly defined research purposes, content analyses reflect varying degrees of commitment to the quantitative (see Marsden, 1965). We believe it is useful for the novice researcher to make the attempt to be as systematic, objective, and quantitatively oriented as possible. It is this more objective form of content analysis that is treated in the remaining sections of this chapter.

THE PROCEDURE

There are approximately four steps to follow in conducting a content analysis: (1) deciding on the communicative material you should analyze to answer your research question; (2) selecting your unit of analysis (for example, a sentence, a paragraph, a whole conversation); (3) categorizing the units of analysis within the selected content according to a category system relevant to your question; and (4) developing an appropriate system for quantifying your categorical data. Each of these steps is summarized

in detail below, along with examples from the available literature.

Choosing Your Material

The first step in a content analysis is to determine the particular type of communication whose content you want to analyze. If you are interested in the motives of politicians, do you want to analyze their pre- or post-election speeches, their letters, or transcripts of their telephone conversations (assuming, as is sometimes the case, that these are available to you)? If you are interested in how children's books contribute to the maintenance of sex-role stereotypes, do you want to look at readers commonly used in elementary schools or at picture books for preschool children?

Selecting The Unit Of Analysis

Once selected, the content in which you are interested must be subdivided into analyzable units. Sometimes the unit is fairly concrete and corresponds to established grammatical categories—for example, the word, the sentence, or the paragraph. In one study that used the sentence as unit of analysis, Henle and Hubbell (1938) were interested in whether adult conversation was less "egocentric" than child conversation. Every sentence in their samples of child and adult conversations was coded as belonging to one of five categories, including ego-related sentences, social sentences, and others. Henle and Hubbell found that the percentages of ego-related remarks (sentences) were similar in the two age groups. The sentence is also the basic unit of analysis in Winter's motive scoring of presidential speeches—with the reservation that two consecutive sentences reflecting the same motive (for example, power) are counted as one sentence (Donley & Winter, 1970).

The paragraph or the word are equally concrete and grammatically defined types of units. In Lewin's (1947) study of goals expressed in Boy Scout and Hitler Youth magazines, the unit of analysis is the paragraph or sometimes, in short stories or autobiographical sketches, the entire article. One of the variables of interest in Stewart and Winter's 1974 study, this chapter's selection, is the ways women deal with causality in TAT stories. In this study, Stewart and Winter assign a positive score for causality to every word or set of words explicitly indicating a causal relationship (for example, *because, therefore, thus, in order to*). Similarly, if you were interested in whether adolescents were more concerned with social values than their parents, it would be relatively easy to code conversations in both groups for the occurrence of social-value words (clearly defined, of course).

The use of the *item*—that is, the entire article, conversation, or television commercial under study—is also fairly common in content analyses. The Stewart, Winter, and Jones (1975) system for coding child-rearing behaviors is designed for use in an item analysis. That is, coders simply note the presence or absence of each of 42 categories of child-rearing behaviors in each of the child-rearing manuals under consideration. In an early study of sex differences in conversation (Carlson, Cook, & Stromberg, 1936), same-sex or mixed-sex conversations were the items analyzed, with each conversation being coded as to principal topic.

Often, the unit of analysis does not correspond to concrete grammatical units. Indeed, the task of establishing the unit of analysis, like that of developing the coding system itself, can call heavily on the researcher's ability to define units creatively and impose a well-articulated structure on verbal material. One type of "created" unit of analysis, which varies in its definition from study to study, is the *thema*. One representative application of the thema can be found in a study of children's readers by Child, Potter, and Levine (1946). Here, the thema was defined as a series of psychological events consisting of (1) a situation or set of circumstances confronting a person, (2) the behavior

(internal and external) with which the person responds, and (3) the consequences of the behavior as felt by the person. Generally, as in this case, the definition of a thema emphasizes psychological events rather than grammatical units.

Categorizing The Units Of Analysis

Selecting a unit of analysis goes hand in hand with the task of developing a system of categorizing units. In some cases, coding schemes take the form of *sign systems,* similar to those used in systematic behavioral observations. Thus, one might note in the unit under analysis, the simple presence or absence of a particular sign—for example, reference to a behavior or issue of interest. The Stewart, Winter, and Jones (1975) system for coding child-rearing behaviors was designed to be used in this way. When the form of communication being analyzed is an ongoing conversation, researchers interested, for example, in sex differences in choice of topics, might rely on a checklist that is comparable to any other sign system used in making systematic observations (see Carlson, Cook, & Stromberg, 1936).

Coding systems designed for categorizing *motive imagery* can be considered a form of sign system. In Winter's research on motives in political leaders (for example, Winter & Stewart, 1977), speeches are scored for frequency of occurrence of images reflecting the specific motives achievement, affiliation, and power. In this scheme, any sentence with a content that involves a concern with standards of excellence, unique accomplishments, long-term involvements, or success in competition is categorized as reflecting achievement imagery, and is scored positively for the achievement motive ($\underline{n}$ Ach). Any sentence reflecting a concern with establishing, maintaining, or restoring warm and friendly relationships or friendly, convivial activity is categorized as showing affiliation imagery and scored positively for the affiliation motive (n Aff). Finally, statements of concern with an impact on others through inherently powerful actions or arousal of strong emotions are scored for the power motive (n Power), as are statements of concern with reputation. (Look back at the earlier examples of scoring from the speeches of Church, Carter, Humphrey, and Jackson. Can you see why they were scored as they were?) This approach can be considered a sign system rather than a category system because not all units are coded.

Other coding schemes are comparable to the category systems of systematic behavioral observation. In these systems, all units are categorized into one of a set of discrete categories. In Lewin's study (1947) of Boy Scout and Hitler Youth magazines, every concept that could be considered a goal was coded into one of 18 categories. In Keesing's (1974) study of trends in popular music, songs were categorized into one of seven different categories on the basis of their themes—love and romance versus "new" values (such as fun), social/political issues, geography, history/biography, fads, novelty tunes, and religion. Songs, for example, that mentioned some sort of response to a chalenge—of a romantic or political nature—were also coded for coping strategy. For the latter, songs were categorized into one of three groups depending on whether they favored active engagement with the problem, passive acceptance, or disengagement.

Most procedures for scoring materials for stage of development also rely on a form of category system. Elaborate scoring manuals are available to guide the investigator in administering and scoring standardized tasks for ego development (Loevinger, Wessler, & Redmore, 1970), identity development (Marcia, 1976), moral-judgment development (Kohlberg, 1977), and role-taking development (Selman & Byrne, 1972). All these manuals follow the same basic format, providing descriptions and examples of responses to be classified into each of the different stage categories.

Quantifying The Data

The final step in an objective and systematic content analysis is the choice of a method of quantification. Common methods for summarizing information about the numbers of units falling into different categories are frequency counts, percentages, mean scores, and modal scores. In their study of motives in political leaders, Donley and Winter (1970) reported the raw frequency of occurrence for achievement and power images in presidential inaugural speeches. However, comparison of the presidents on these raw-frequency scores would have been misleading, since the length of the speeches varied from 970 words to 5,570 words. Donley and Winter dealt with the variation in speech length by dividing each total score by the number of words in the speech and then multiplying by 1000 to get a corrected score for imagery per thousand words.

Anther quantifying method that is sensitive to differences in the length of the documents being compared is to determine the *percentages* of units falling into each category. For example, in their study of the content of adult conversations, Henle and Hubbell (1938) found that approximately 40% of their subjects' remarks could be categorized as ego related, 37% as social, 6% as mixed, 14% as objective, and 2% as yes, no, or equivalent phrases. These percentages were roughly the same as those found in previous studies with children, a finding that allowed the authors to reject the hypothesis that children are more egocentric in their conversations than adults. Lewin (1947) also looked at percentages of goals falling into different categories in his comparison of Boy Scout and Hitler Youth magazines.

Content analyses in which frequencies and percentages are the principal techniques for summarizing data generally involve coding systems corresponding to nominal scales. A *nominal scale* represents the lowest level of measurement, where categories have no quantitative relationship with each other and cannot be ordered or added. Male/female, egocentric/social/mixed, or religion/courage/discipline are examples of categories on a nominal scale. Items in such categories can be counted or computed as percentages and compared, but cannot be analyzed in more sophisticated quantitative ways.

In other cases, the categories into which items are grouped represent a ranking of items with respect to some characteristic. That is, placing an item in one category means that it has more (or less) of the characteristic in question than items placed in another category. Such a group of categories constitutes an *ordinal scale*, in which an order is discernible among the items. All the coding systems for developmental stage are of the ordinal character. Some moral judgments ("Life is always more valuable than property") are considered to show more cognitive maturity than others ("Grab whatever you can and to hell with the other guy"). Classifying such responses into stage categories is not like classifying individuals as male or female, but involves the assumption that a real order exists among the stage assignments. The advantage of an ordinal scale is that it allows more statistical manipulations than a nominal scale. Thus, it is possible to compare individuals or groups for average level of moral-judgment performance, with either the mean or the mode being used to calculate the average.[1]

The selection included in this chapter (Stewart & Winter, 1974) contains a number of simple ordinal scales developed for the coding of items in a content analysis. For example, women's responses to a question concerning their life plans were coded into four (ordered) *categories*, ranging from a lack of any mention of a job or career (low career orientation) to a description of such traditionally "masculine" lifetime careers as law (high career orientation). Because these categories constitute an ordinal scale corresponding to degree of career orienta-

tion, it is possible to compare *average* career-orientation scores in different groups of women.

RELIABILITY AND VALIDITY

The problems of reliability and validity in content analyses are similar to those in systematic behavioral observations. The basic reliability question is one of intercoder reliability: do two coders (scorers) who are categorizing the same content with the same coding system make the same assignments of items to categories? What is the correlation or percentage of agreement among their assignments? If other researchers tried to score presidential inaugural addresses for the occurrence of power and achievement imagery, would they end up with the same results as Donley and Winter (1970)? Or, if you had all the Stewart and Winter (1974) responses to the question on life plans and were using the same four-point scale for degree of career orientation, how consistent would your category assignments be with theirs?

Many questions have been raised about the validity of content analyses, particularly those of the more qualitative variety. Critics often argue that the judgments made in coding for achievement motivation, career orientation, or national-loyalty goals are not only subjective but also highly inferential. That is, the judgments go well beyond the data, attributing, for example, conscious or unconscious motivations to the authors of the content. However, some of the more sophisticated users of content analysis (such as Winter & Stewart, 1974) make a strong case for the empirical validity of their content analyses by providing evidence about relevant related behaviors in the subjects of their analyses. It is desirable here, as in the case of systematic observations, to make a case at least for the content validity (Does the procedure consider an adequate sample?) of content analyses.

Winter and Stewart (1977) propose the use of a number of questions or tests for evaluating

---

[1]See Appendix A for a treatment of these statistical terms.

the usefulness and explanatory power of procedures designed for analyzing the psychological
content of political communications. Many
of these questions are of general significance and
can, with slight modification, be used in the
evaluation of any content analysis. These revised
Winter and Stewart questions are presented
here.

1. Is the sample of documents being analyzed
representative of all the relevant speeches, songs,
magazines, or whatever the material for the
individuals or groups under consideration? This
question refers to *external validity*. It means,
is your sample really representative of the
content about which you will be generalizing?

2. Are the variables assessed through content
analysis explicitly linked to a psychological
theory or well-conceptualized research area?
This question is relevant to the issue of *internal
validity*. It means, is there a strong conceptual
basis for believing that the categories imposed
on the material capture a psychological meaning
that is really there?

3. Are the categories for the analysis of
content described or defined adequately enough
for different people, working independently,
to make the same judgments about the same
material? This question, of course, refers to
reliability.

4. Is the content analysis carried out and
reported in such a way to facilitate comparison
with other subjects or materials?

5. Are the content samples drawn from
comparable documents?

6. Is the behavior that can be predicted by the
psychological variables of strong interest and
relevance?

A PREVIEW OF THE CHAPTER SELECTION

This chapter's selection, by Stewart and
Winter, considers one aspect of identity in
women, self- versus social definition. Stewart
and Winter used content-analytic procedures to
examine both responses to a set of TAT-type
pictures (the independent variable) and responses to several open-ended interview questions (the dependent variable). In the article,
they explain the development of the research
question, the choice of a TAT-type instrument,
and the components of their scoring system.
They also consider issues of reliability and validity, illustrate a simple ordinal scale, and
present many of the correlates of self- and social
definition in women.

Self-Definition and Social Definition in Women[2]

Abigail J. Stewart
David G. Winter
Harvard University
Wesleyan University

This study is designed to identify and measure the patterns of verbal expression (TAT storytelling) that are associated with planning a career versus those associated with planning marriage and a family without a career among women college undergraduates. Further investigation of the behaviors and background characteristics associated with these two verbal patterns suggests that they define the end points of a general personality dimension of self- versus adjustive social definition.

For some time, women were excluded from psychological research and theory, and attention was concentrated on the study of men (see Schultz, 1969). Quite naturally, then, much of the early research on women focussed on the ways in which they differed from men—the study of sex differences, rather than the study of the psychology of women. Researchers readily found some sex differences, and interpreted them as deriving from differences in genital morphology (Freud, 1924; Erikson, 1963, pp. 97–108), hormone differences (Bardwick, 1970), differences in the distribution of muscle (Engels, 1884; Veblen, 1899), and other less specific biological differences (Kagan and Moss, 1962). A second interpretive line was later introduced by some researchers, who proposed that sex differences were due to differential socialization procedures for boys and girls (de Beauvoir, 1949; Horney, 1926; Horner, 1972; Rossi,

1964). Finally, Maccoby (1966) suggested that sex-difference researchers were explaining only a very minor portion of the variance in both male and female behavior. She argued, for example, that the "overlap" of male and female scores on all parts of the IQ tests was far greater than the small, but much discussed, amount of difference. The implicit suggestion was that the amount of intrasex (within) variation was far greater than the traditionally studied intersex (between) variation.

There have been some studies of intrasex differences among women. However, these studies have almost universally assumed a single "normal" pattern of female behavior with minor variations, from which some women "deviate."[3] In the present research, we proposed to assume nothing about a "normal" female personality or behavioral pattern. Rather than describing or identifying a single normative pattern and lumping all deviations from that pattern into a single residual (and unexplained) class, we attempted to study two female personality patterns which may both be coherent and systematic, each with explicable antecedents and consequences.

We decided to use career orientation as our starting point for studying these two separate patterns. Although we feel this is a crude criterion for differentiating women, it has the advantage of being objective and easily measured; moreover, historically it seems to have been the single characteristic which enabled an individual woman to function free of social role ascriptions. If a woman had a career, she was relatively more free of traditional forms of social definition than if she didn't. In terms of simple social reality, we would argue that the source of a career woman's increased freedom is that she is recognized by men and by society as having a legitimate claim to the

[2] This article is based on Stewart (1971). The authors acknowledge financial support from NIMH Fellowship MH-08027 (to the first author), NIMH Research Grant MH-16,687, a Guggenheim Fellowship, and Wesleyan University Faculty Research Grants (to the second author). They further acknowledge the assistance of D. Hamilton, C. Feinstein, and L. Couch in gathering and analyzing data. Entire article from *Journal of Personality*, 1974, *42*(2), 238–259. Copyright © 1974 Duke University Press. Reprinted by permission.

[3] Thus in discussing the career woman, Parsons (1942, p. 96; 1943, p. 193) uses phrases such as "the basic masculine role" [of a career] and "the normal married woman" [does not have a career]. Kagan (1969, p. 477) refers to the existence and learning of "sex-role standards" that are "appropriate." While intended presumably as descriptions, these and similar terms inevitably have prescriptive and pejorative connations.

systematic and autonomous use of time, space, and money; while a woman who does not have a career is far more vulnerable to any specific or general traditional demand from men, from other women, and from children.

In establishing our criterion for career orientation, we decided that only a full-time career—as demanding of time and energy as that of a man—would be readily recognized as legitimating a woman's claim for the autonomy we describe. That is, work before marriage, part-time work, and brief jobs (e.g., part-time librarian while children in school, or a series of rather temporary jobs), were not adequate to free women from traditional role demands. However, careers which have traditionally been acceptable for women (full-time secretary, elementary school teacher), although in some instances leaving individual women vulnerable to the power and definition of men (bosses, school principals), can provide and often have provided the kind of autonomy described. For our purpose, then, the critical definitional issue of "career" is: "Can an unmarried woman, with no other financial means, support herself with this career?" Alternatively, "Can a man, or do some men, support themselves (and possible dependents) with this career?" We hypothesize that the psychological difference reflected in career plans is a difference in the source of the definition of self. Because for us the crucial distinction to be captured is the degree to which the individual woman is free from traditional ascriptive demands, we have called the difference one of self-definition vs. social-definition. The labels are tentative and heuristic; we expect them to be confirmed by the pattern of personality differences between the two groups.

At the time the research reported in this paper was conducted (autumn, 1970), inquiry about future career plans was a usable and potentially valid way to differentiate the two styles of self-definition. Since that time, however, there has been a rapid, marked change in the social norms and pressures about careers and career plans, especially among college women of the sort studied in the present research. In a recent sample tested in the autumn of 1972, virtually all women who report codable career plans say that they plan a "male" career. The fact that career plans may no longer be a usable way to establish criterion groups for self-definition versus social-definition need not jeopardize the measure derived from such criterion groups in the present research, so long as other behavioral correlates of that measure can still be replicated. (See note 7, however, for further evidence about the validity of career plans statements.)

To summarize, we are not interested in career orientation in itself; rather we have used it as an a priori criterion for establishing a direct measure of broader systematic personality differences—differences in patterns of thinking, in behavior, and in background antecedents.

METHOD

We decided to use the Thematic Apperception Test to measure these hypothetical personality differences for three reasons: (1) The TAT provides a richness of response that we felt was necessary for establishing the kind of personality pattern for which we were looking; (2) The TAT provides a range and variety of response that permits a minimum of a priori assumptions about data, as opposed to questionnaires, in which the "right kind" of questions have to be thought up in advance; (3) The TAT is less subject to the effects of social desirability and the influence of norms about what people ought to be and say than are questionnaire measures (see McClelland, 1958; Winter, 1973, chap. 2). While there are several different theoretically-derived methods of scoring the TAT, we decided to use the procedure advocated by McClelland, Atkinson, Clark, and Lowell (1953) and Winter (1973) for the development of empirically-based measures. Briefly, the TAT scoring system is derived from actual empirical comparison of TATs written by two criterion groups (in the present case, career-oriented versus non-career-oriented groups). The system is then cross-validated on further samples of each group, scored blindly. Such a procedure both permits the testing of a priori hypotheses and intuitions about the nature of the scoring system, and also ensures that the system will have empirically-based definition and validity. (See Winter, 1973, chaps. 2 and 3 for a full account of this derivational technique.) The concept of self-definition, as an alternative to the more traditional social definition in interpreting the significance and meaning of the TAT scoring system draws on Sartre's notion of *authenticity* (1946), as that concept has been directly applied to the problems of women (de Beauvoir, 1949). The actual scoring system, however, was derived empirically in advance of our use of the concepts of Sartre and de Beauvoir.

A brief summary of our method will introduce a more detailed presentation: (1) The scoring system, reflecting self versus social definition and differentiating career-oriented from non-career-oriented women, was developed from TATs of a sample of undergraduate women. (2) This scoring system was then cross-validated on TATs of another sample of undergraduate women from a different college. (3) Behavioral correlates of self-definition were studied by means of a questionnaire given to the second sample immediately after they took the TAT.

Deriving the Scoring System

To derive the scoring system, we administered a four-picture TAT and then a brief questionnaire to 49 white undergraduate women at a small New England women's liberal arts college. The four pictures used were: (1) A woman with her arm around a small boy; (2) A couple in a restaurant drinking with a guitarist nearby; (3) A couple sitting on a marble bench; (4) An older man and a younger man in an office. On the basis of answers to the following question in the questionnaire: "What will you do or be after graduating from college?" we selected as criterion groups eight subjects who showed clear career-

commitment ("become a pediatrician"; "go to law school, practice law and have a family") and eight subjects who planned marriage and family without a career, or a brief job before marriage. Through comparison of the TAT stories written by these two groups, we developed a scoring system that captured the differences between the two sets of stories. On the basis of its content, as well as of its behavioral correlates (presented below), this scoring system is conceived as measuring a person's style of self-definition, either relatively self-defining (use of the positive categories) or relatively socially defined (use of the negative categories).

Outline of the Scoring System for Self-Definition[4]

1. *Causality (scored + 1)*. Scored are any word or words which explicitly indicate a causal relationship (because, therefore, thus) or any expression which could be replaced by the phrase "in order to" or the word "because." This causal connection must be explicit, and not merely implicit in the close juxtaposition of two seemingly-related sentences.

2. *Reason-Action Sequence (scored + 1)*. When the events or actions of the story are arranged chronologically, scored if the final event is an action or purposeful plan for action by any character in the story. Not scored if it is unclear whether a plan will lead to action. Stories which end with feelings or "states of being" or which contain only rituals or nonresolving actions are not scored. Actions which are clearly predicted to be futile or hopeless, even if they occur at the end of the story, are not scored, although final actions which have unpleasant consequences may be scored. A calculated refusal to act in the service of some end is scored if it is the final element of the story.

---

[4]This outline is not adequate for scoring purposes. A full version may be obtained from the authors at Wesleyan University, Middletown, Connecticut 06457.

3. *No Causality (No Action) (scored — 1).*
(a) Scored if actions or events "occur" without reasons, or if they are merely habitual or routine actions. *(b)* Scored if no actions occur or are planned in the story, as when the story is entirely conversation or description of a scene, or an account of the thoughts or feelings of a character in the story.

4. *Mental State Ending (scored — 1).* When the sequence of the story is arranged chronologically, scored if the story *ends* with someone's feelings or thoughts, and not with action or purposeful plans for action. Stories are also scored if they end with "states of being" rather than acts (e.g., "they were happy," "they were successful").

5. *Higher Power Intervention (scored — 1).*[5] Scored if a "higher power" takes some action which has an effect on the lives of one or more specific characters, without any subsequent action by that character; or if all actions by one character are circumscribed by a higher power.

6. *Ineffective Actor (scored — 1). (a)* Futility of acting: scored if it is predicted that whatever action will take place or does take place will make no difference or have no effect on the situation; not scored if actions have merely negative consequences. *(b)* Impersonality: scored if the resolving (or only) actions of the story are phrased in the passive voice or in impersonal construction, or if they are described as compulsions rather than chosen, willed actions.

The categories of this scoring system, and their definitions, are as they are because they differentiate career-oriented and non-career-oriented groups in the first sample. While some of these categories might have been expected to occur on theoretical grounds, the final justification for all elements of the scoring system is that they were empirically successful in differentiating the two groups of the first sample and also were cross-validated in the second sample (see below). The question of why these categories, rather than others, should work will be discussed briefly below;

[5]This category was deleted from the final scoring system, after the cross-validation, as described below.

but a complete answer to that question would involve a full account of the development of sex-role related definitions of self in women, which is beyond the scope of this paper. The further question of why these categories of verbal behavior style should predict career orientation will be answered below in terms of discussion of the other behaviors that are associated with self-definition and social definition.

In summary, the self-defining women (those planning careers) tending to tell stories which ended with instrumental action on the part of the characters, as well as having specific causes for specific events (categories 1 and 2); while socially defined women (those planning marriage, without a career) tended to tell stories which lacked the above characteristics, and which typically were about characters full of feelings and thoughts (categories 3–6), but who did not take any actions. These differences suggest that instrumentality and causality are relatively more salient aspects of the world for self-defining women than they are for socially defined women. They further suggest that the two groups perceive (and thus probably experience) the world in systematically different ways.

The self-defining women appear to view the world as relatively more orderly and sequential. Further, they clearly perceive intentionality (purpose, instrumentality) as located in specific persons. The socially defined women perceive a far less orderly world, with intentionality located in vague unspecified forces that suggest fate (e.g., "It will work out. . . ."). Self-defining women seem to see the world as rational and organized, whereas socially defined women seem to see the world and events as irrational and diffuse.

RESULTS

Cross-Validation of the Scoring System Categories

After its derivation from the first sample, the scoring system was then cross-validated with a sample of 68 white undergraduates at another small New England women's liberal arts college. The following TAT pictures were administered: (1) Girl sitting alone, pensive expression, ambiguous background; (2) Man and woman drinking beer in restaurant with a guitarist nearby; (3) Two women scientists in a laboratory; (4) Man and woman standing on a wall, the woman is smoking; (5) Woman with arm around small boy; (6) Man and woman on trapeze. The pictures were selected because they all contained situations with women in them (to facilitate identification or involvement by the subjects), and because they represented a wide range of stimuli—a woman alone, two women with no men, and women with men in a variety of roles. After taking the TAT, subjects filled out a questionnaire asking about activities, plans, descriptions of parents, and containing several open-ended questions.

From answers to the following question: "If your life could go according to your plans, what will you be doing in ten years (1980) and what has led up to this?" subjects were grouped into four categories, rather than two, in order to give a more refined measure of career orientation:

4. Women who describe life-time careers most frequently pursued by men (doctor, lawyer, professor, politician).

3. Women who describe life-time careers, but in fields more socially acceptable for women according to traditional norms (teachers, librarians, social workers).

2. Women who describe a series of brief jobs and marriage (work before marriage, part-time job while married, but *not* life-time careers).

1. Women who describe marriage and family, but who do not mention jobs or careers of any kind.

Categories 3 vs. 4 and 1 vs. 2 were intended as further distinctions within the broad classes of career-orientation and non-career-orientation.

Eleven of the subjects gave responses which were uncodable because they were incomplete, vague, or because the subject refused to state plans

(e.g., "don't know," "live in a commune," "travel around and do what I like," etc.). Hence these eleven subjects are excluded from the cross-validation reported in Tables 1 and 2, although their self-definition scores are of course included in all of the other results presented below.

TATs of all subjects were scored blindly, and the results of the cross-validation of the scoring system, by total score and by category, for the 57 subjects with codable post-college plans are presented in Tables 1 and 2.

As predicted, the four groups are significantly different from each other, and there is a clear directional trend from categories four through one. The correlation of career-orientation with total self-definition score was high and very significant ($r = +.72$, $p < .001$). In almost all cases, each of the subcategories differentiated among all groups in the predicted direction. One-way analyses of variances among the four groups yielded results as follows for each category (mean scores are given in Table 2): *Causality* ($F = 2.47$, $p < .15$), *Reason-Action Sequence* ($F = 19.88$, $p < .001$), *No Causality* ($F = 4.69$, $p < .05$), *Mental State Ending* ($F = 5.76$, $p < .02$), *Higher Power Intervention* ($F = 1.08$), $p =$ n.s.), and *Ineffective Actor* ($F = 5.75$, $p < .02$). Although *Causality* did not differentiate at usual levels of significance, the category was retained because of its conceptual "fit" with the rest of the scoring system and because the significance level may have been an artifact of the particular pictures chosen. The category *Higher Power Intervention* occurred rarely, did not differentiate significantly, and was therefore dropped from the scoring system and not included in the scores reported in subsequent tables. The trends in mean total-score differences were the same for all pictures, although the strongest (or most powerful) differentiators were pictures 2, 4 and 6, all of which depict men and women together. The least powerful differentiator was picture 5, of a woman and child.

Two naive scorers learned the scoring system after some discussion with the first author and a

TABLE 1
Cross-Validation of the Self-Definition Scoring System: Analysis of Variance of Total Score.

	Career-Orientation Categories:			
	4. Male career ($N=12$)	3. Female career ($N=13$)	2. Brief jobs ($N=14$)	1. Marriage without career ($N=18$)
Mean Score	$+6.37$	$+3.69$	$-.71$	-2.06

Variance table					
Source	*SS*	*df*	*MS*	*F*	*p*
Between	614.19	3	204.73	18.21	<.001
Within	595.64	53	11.24		
Total	1209.83	56			

Differences between career categories

Categories	Means		t	p
1 vs. 2	-2.06	$-.71$	1.17	—
2 vs. 3	$-.71$	$+3.69$	3.26	<.005
3 vs. 4	$+3.69$	$+6.37$	2.00	<.05

Note.—Correlation of Career Category with Self-Definition Score $= +.72, p < .001$.

TABLE 2
Mean Category Scores for the Four Career-Orientation Groups.

	Mean Score for:			
Scoring category	4. Male Career ($N=12$)	3. Female Career ($N=13$)	2. Brief jobs ($N=14$)	1. Marriage without Career ($N=18$)
Causality (scored $+1$)	3.83	3.69	2.57	2.56
Reason-Action sequence (scored $+1$)	4.37	3.15	1.85	1.28
No Causality (scored -1)	$-.08$	$-.15$	$-.43$	$-.94$
Mental State Ending (scored -1)	$-.58$	-2.00	-2.50	-2.22
Higher Power Intervention (scored -1)	$-.08$	$.00$	$-.07$	$-.22$
Ineffective Actor (scored -1)	$-.92$	-1.00	-1.86	-2.56

few hours of practice on other stories. Their scoring correlated highly with that of the first author (*rhos* $= +.89$ and .94; Category Agreement ranging from .86 to .96 computed for agreements on presence of the category). Thus the scoring system seems to possess objectivity and interscorer reliability sufficient for research purposes with TAT instruments (see Atkinson, 1958, pp. 239–240).

Ruling Out Alternative Explanations

In order to be certain that the scores obtained were genuinely a function of the scoring system categories and not some other factor such as verbal fluency or intelligence, several correlations with other variables were checked. No complicating relationships between TAT score and age, college class, intelligence (SAT and MAT scores) or verbal fluency (as measured by the total length of TAT protocol) were found. Thus the scoring system reflects a psychological pattern and is not an artifact of other variables. In addition, self-definition was unrelated to several standard measures of "femininity": the M-F scale of the Strong Vocational Interest Blank, the Femininity Scale of the CPI, and measures used by Carlsmith (1964) and May (1966). This is not surprising, since such measures were developed through the study of sex differences, rather than differences among women. Finally, self-definition was unrelated to internal versus external control of reinforcement (Rotter, 1966), and to n Achievement, n Affiliation, and n Power.

Background Characteristics

Information about family background was requested in the questionnaire given to the second sample, and the background characteristics associated with self-definition are presented in Table 3. Several hypotheses about these characteristics were made on the basis of the studies of career women cited below. Self-defining women tended (though not quite significantly) to be eldest or only children ($t = 1.58$, $p = .06$ pd) and, significantly, not to have older brothers ($t = 1.90$, $p < .05$ pd). If eldest and only subjects are excluded, the trend for no older brothers is slightly reduced ($t = 1.58$, $p \sim .06$ pd). This suggests that the absence of an older male sibling assists a woman in defining herself independently of social role prescriptions; also perhaps that the presence of an older brother fosters the traditional female pattern of social definition as a reaction or adjustment to that of the male.

In answer to the question: "Has your mother worked since you were born? When? How long? Job(s)?" self-defining women significantly more often reported that their mothers had worked, continuously, from the period before they themselves were 12 years old, i.e., that their mothers had worked since approximately their own puberty ($t = 1.41$, $p < .10$ pd). Thus they had an early female model for serious involvement in work.

TABLE 3
Background Characteristics Associated with Self-Definition.

Background characteristic	Self-definition	
	Mean	Standard deviation
Eldest or only child ($N=29$)	2.46	5.14
Not ($N=39$)	.67	4.10
No older brother ($N=44$)	2.21	4.74
Older Brother ($N=24$)	.00	4.13
Of those with an older sibling(s):		
No older brother ($N=13$)	2.23	3.72
Older brother ($N=24$)	.00	4.13
Mother worked[a] ($N=15$)	2.93	3.84
Mother did not work ($N=53$)	1.01	4.78
Father autonomous[b] ($N=33$)	1.73	4.67
Father bureaucratic[c] ($N=19$)	.08	4.84

[a] At a continuous job, at least since the daughter was twelve years old.
[b] Professional, executive, entrepreneur, or other self-employed.
[c] Manager or administrator (17 responses uncodable).

(For additional studies finding "masculine" career plans among women with working mothers, see Astin, 1967; Siegel & Curtis, 1963; Almquist & Angrist, 1970. In addition to the "modelling" aspects of career salience for daughters of working women, Gysbers, Johnston, & Gust, 1968, found that working mothers often exert direct pressure on their daughters to have careers.)

Finally, although there was no relationship between self-definition and social class ($r = .04$, using the measure of Hollingshead and Redlich, 1958, although this sample was relatively homogeneous with respect to social class), self-defining women tended, though not significantly, to have fathers who worked "autonomously" (doctors, lawyers, executives), and socially defined women tended to have fathers who worked within a bureaucratic hierarchy ($t = 1.19$, $p = .12$ pd). Fathers who work independently may tend to foster autonomy—self-definition—in their daughters, while men who themselves must be highly responsive to social pressures may foster adjustive social definition in their daughters.

Behavioral Correlates

Instrumental action. The behavioral correlates of self-definition are presented in Table 4. Self-defining women tended significantly more often than socially defined women to hold office in student organizations ($t = 2.52, p < .02$), thus supporting the hypothesis that in their immediate social and political sphere they would behave more instrumentally. Further, they tended more often to have canvassed for candidates for public office or for issues ($t = 1.93, p < .06$). Thus at both levels of politics, they showed a characteristic instrumental style. In the area of social relationships, they reported significantly more often that they had telephoned a man ($t = 2.06, p < .05$). We viewed this behavior both as instrumental and as predicated on a certain freedom from traditional social norms.

Freedom from traditional norm prescriptions. Self-defining women reported significantly more often than socially defined women that they were majoring in fields most usually associated with men and "male" skills—the sciences and the social sciences—while socially defined women tended to major in the arts and humanities, or to be "undecided" (perhaps a traditional norm for women) about their major ($t = 2.41, p < .02$). The choice of more scientific fields by self-defining women may be aided in part by the more causal, orderly view of the world which appears in their TAT stories. In addition, self-defining women report a significantly greater frequency of "loud, vehement arguments" with their friends ($t = 2.03, p < .05$), an activity that prevailing social stereotypes should negatively sanction for women. They also report a greater swearing frequency, as well as a larger number of "favorite" swearing expressions. All of these findings support our prediction that self-defining women are willing to

TABLE 4
Behavioral Correlates of Self-Definition.

	Self-Definition	
Variable	*Mean*	*Standard Deviation*
Held office in college ($N=25$)	3.24	4.32
Did not hold office ($N=43$)	.38	4.52
Canvassed for a candidate or issue ($N=52$)	1.93	4.63
Did not canvass ($N=15$)	−.67	4.08
Telephoned a man[a] ($N=28$)	2.80	4.50
Did not telephone a man ($N=40$)	.48	4.52
Majoring in social science, science[b] ($N=28$)	3.02	4.44
Majoring in humanities, arts, or undecided[c] ($N=40$)	.33	4.48
Had loud arguments ($N=35$)	2.36	4.58
Did not have loud arguments ($N=31$)	.07	4.40
Correlations with self-definition:		
Reported frequency of daily swearing ($N=67$)	.26*	
Number of different favorite swearing expressions ($N=68$)	.26*	

*$p < .05$.
[a]More than once or twice.
[b]Including Latin American studies, urban affairs, and human ecology.
[c]Including history and child development.

report activities which are incongruent with traditional social prescriptions for the female role.

Social and sexual behavior. Perhaps most interestingly, the prediction that many social behaviors thought to be related to "liberation" in women were not related to self-definition was fully supported by the data. There was no relationship between self-definition and reported drinking behavior, drug use, smoking, heterosexual experience, dating frequency, or masturbation. These nonrelationships suggest rather strongly that the popular conceptions of the women liberated from traditional sex-role definition as either wild and unconstrained, or naive, withdrawn, and unattractive, are inaccurate and do not capture the essential differences between women who accept social definition and women who reject it.

Open-Ended Questions

In an attempt to gain insight into the more profound psychological characteristics of these two kinds of women, we asked several open-ended questions about rather private and potentially affect-laden issues.[6] The results of the coded responses are reported in Table 5.

Pleasures. Self-defining and socially defined women give different answers to the question, "What are the three things that please you most?" Self-defining women report significantly more often that they are pleased by achievement ($t = 2.49$, $p < .02$) and active hobbies ($t = 1.96$, $p < .06$), again confirming the importance of instrumentality to them. In addition, they are pleased by involvement in a serious love relationship (i.e., with a single specified person) ($t =$

[6] We coded the responses to these questions only partially blindly; that is, we attempted to clarify the coding categories post hoc in order to gain a sharper and more accurate picture of the psychological issues among these women. Thus these codes are tentative and need to be cross-validated. They are included here because they expand the nomological network and theoretical portraits of the self-defining and socially defined woman.

4.07, $p < .001$), and by inner feelings which are asocial or independent of a social context, such as "peace of mind," "serenity," and "feelings of accomplishment" ($t = 2.40$, $p < .02$). These two findings suggest that self-defining women are not antisocial or unpopular but rather that they are not so strongly dependent upon others for a definition of themselves. They appear to be more concerned about love relationships.

In contrast, socially defined women report pleasure in "variety" ("new places, new things") ($t = 1.83$, $p \sim .07$). This variety appears not to be a consequence of their activity, but rather a quality of the environment which may or may not be present, since they also are more likely to report pleasure in natural settings (e.g., "sunsets," "snowflakes falling," not including their own activity in a natural setting ($t = 1.72$, $p \sim .09$). Rather than pleasure in a single committed relationship, they report pleasure in "friends" ($t = 2.63$, $p < .02$). Finally, rather than feelings independent of social context, they are pleased by a kind of global, unconditional acceptance by others ($t = 2.63$, $p < .02$). These findings again suggest an intense responsiveness to social or external cues, and a dependence upon them which contrasts sharply with the inner resources and preoccupation with an individual other person of the self-defining woman.

Fears. There were striking differences in answers to the question, "What are the three things you fear the most?" First, while self-defining women report fears of social problems (e.g., wars, race riots) ($t = 2.37$, $p = .02$), adjustive women report fears of death ($t = 1.83$, $p < .08$) and of violence to themselves ($t = 1.73$, $p < .10$). This suggests that the self-defining woman may be relatively less impeded by traditional cultural views of women as vulnerable and helpless, and is thus freer to be seriously concerned about broader social issues, a concern that is expressed in her relatively greater political action.

Second, self-defining women are afraid of failure when it is the result of a miscarried instru-

TABLE 5
Open-Ended Question Responses Associated with Self-Definition.

	Mention			Do not Mention		
	N	Mean	SD	N	Mean	SD
PLEASURES						
Self-defining						
Involvement in a love relationship	9	6.78	2.66		0.62	4.35
Asocial feelings	6	5.67	2.56	62	1.02	4.61
Achievement	15	4.00	3.46	53	0.71	4.69
Active hobby or activity	9	4.22	3.68	59	1.01	4.64
Socially defined						
Friends	8	−2.50	1.58	60	1.96	4.68
Global acceptance	8	−2.50	2.87	60	1.96	4.60
Natural settings	6	−1.67	1.80	62	1.73	4.74
Variety	5	−2.20	2.56	63	1.72	4.67
FEARS						
Self-defining						
Social problems	8	5.00	3.64	60	0.96	4.57
Failure, seen as a miscarried instrumental act	14	4.00	5.02	53	0.55	4.17
Loneliness, social isolation	11	4.40	5.10	57	0.86	4.34
Socially defined						
Death	23	0.00	4.03	45	2.17	4.78
Violence to self	12	−0.67	3.09	56	1.88	4.81
Failure, seen as an unelicited, imposed social definition	9	−2.44	2.51	58	1.84	4.53
Unelicited external things done to the self	14	−1.29	3.62	53	1.94	4.55
SECRETS[a]						
Self-defining						
Inferiority	5	5.00	3.03	44	1.26	4.59
Dependency needs	8	6.18	2.76	41	0.76	4.36
Appearance-reality conflict	7	4.71	2.25	41	0.88	4.46
Socially defined						
Hostility	9	−0.62	5.48	40	2.15	4.22
Tabooed feelings	4	−4.00	1.23	45	2.14	4.45

[a] Excluding those who listed no secrets, answered "I won't tell," and so forth.

mental act (e.g., "that I won't live up to my potential") ($t = 2.63, p < .02$), whereas socially defined women fear the definition of themselves as a failure by external persons and institutions (e.g., "flunking out of school") ($t = 2.76, p < .01$). Again, this points up the self-defining woman's tendency to view herself as an agent in her own life, and as capable and responsible for action. The socially defined woman, on the other hand, tends to view herself as acted-upon by a potentially hostile environment.

Finally, self-defining women report a fear of loneliness and social isolation ($t = 2.37, p = .02$), which may be the result of a realistic assessment of the social consequences of self-definition for women—i.e., isolation from those parts of the society that are based on traditional norms. Socially defined women, on the other hand, fear unelicited actions by others which will hurt them (e.g., "that my boyfriend will leave me") ($t = 2.45, p = .02$). Thus the self-defining woman sees herself as risking rejection, but not, as the socially defined woman sees herself, as the passive object of actions of others.

Secrets. The last open-ended question was, "Most people have at least a few things about themselves that they haven't told anyone; what are three things about yourself that you have never or would be very reluctant to tell anyone?" Nineteen women did not answer the question, either by leaving it blank or by saying something such as "If I wouldn't tell anyone else, I wouldn't write it on a questionnaire." These subjects were excluded from the analysis of "secrets" which follows; they did not differ from the rest of the sample on self-definition. Among those subjects listing secrets, then, self-defining women report that they conceal (and, therefore, presumably feel guilty about) their dependency needs ($t = 3.32$, $p < .01$). This finding was clarified by a further "secret" typical of self-defining women, i.e., a conflict which they feel and which they hide, between the way they appear to others and what they "really are" ($t = 2.18, p < .05$). In other words, they feel guilty about appearing to be more competent, friendly, etc. than they feel they genuinely are. Similarly, we assume that their guilt about dependency needs is caused by their apparent independence, along with their desire to be free of (female) dependency on men. The self-defining woman's other typical secret is "inferiority" ($t = 1.74, p < .10$). The overall issue for self-defining women seems to be a felt disjunction between apparent independence and competence and possibly real, but concealed, weakness.

On the other hand, socially defined women tend to report that they conceal hostility ($t = 1.64, p = .11$) and tabooed feelings (e.g., "murderous jealousy of my brother") ($t = 2.69, p = .01$), suggesting that they are most anxious or guilty

about wishes or feelings which are incongruent with the traditional female role stereotype (hostility), as well as more broadly negatively-sanctioned feelings (tabooed ones). Self-defining women thus report concealment of feelings which are incongruent with those qualities for which they are striving—*against* the current of social norms—while socially defined women conceal feelings which are themselves incongruent with the current of social norms.

Parental Descriptions

Subjects were asked to describe their parents as follows: (1) "In the space below, write a brief description of your father, using whatever words, sentences, form and content, which seem to you to be most meaningful and appropriate." (2) "In the space below, write a brief description of your mother." Self-defining and socially defined women described both of their parents in characteristic and different ways.[7] The results of the coding of the descriptions are presented in Table 6. Self-defining women typically describe their fathers with a favorable adjective, followed by (qualified by) a negative adjective (e.g., "intelligent, but stern")—or "positive-but-negative" ($t = 3.09, p = .01$). This style of description shows concern for an objective, accurate and complete statement of the characteristics of the father. In contrast, the socially defined women strongly tend to describe their fathers not in terms of qualities that inhere in him, but rather in terms of his affective relationship to them, or vis-à-vis them (e.g., "he loves me," "I hate him") ($t = 2.49, p < .02$). Either they are less concerned about his objective characteristics, or else there is interference with such a concern by an affective tie which takes precedence over it. This may indicate that socially defined women are more strongly bound, emotionally, to their fathers, so that they are less able to achieve analytic distance. Perhaps this

[7]These codes were developed by empirical comparison of the five highest and the five lowest scorers' descriptions. The rest of the descriptions were coded blindly.

TABLE 6
Characteristics of Parental Descriptions Associated with Self-Definition

	Mention			Do not Mention		
	N	Mean	SD	N	Mean	SD
Father						
Self-defining						
Father as positive-but-negative	18	4.19	5.09	50	0.44	4.06
Socially defined						
Father as vis-a-vis self	15	−1.13	3.34	53	2.16	4.72
Mother						
Self-defining						
Mother seen analytically	13	5.49	4.39	55	0.47	4.18
Mother as unhappy	10	4.34	5.14	58	0.93	4.38
Socially defined						
Mother as emotional	25	0.12	4.42	43	2.20	4.62
Either parent as having traditional views on sexual morality	9	−1.56	3.62	59	1.89	4.63

Note.—Correlations with self-definition score:
    Length of description of father: .04;
    Length of description of mother: .22;
    Length of description of mother minus length of description of father: .27, $p < .05$.

emotional bond is the original source for their subsequent lack of causal perceptions.

Similarly, self-defining women describe their mothers in terms which analyze her personality structure (e.g., "she's an obsessive-compulsive") or describe the consequences of the mother for the whole family rather than vis-à-vis the individual daughter ("she's the backbone of the family"), while socially defined women do not ($t = 3.80$, $p < .001$). Self-defining women also describe their mothers as unhappy, unfulfilled, etc. ($t = 2.18$, $p < .05$), while socially defined women describe theirs as "emotional" ($t = 1.79$, $p < .08$). We do not necessarily assume that the mothers of the two kinds of women actually differ, though they may well do so, but rather that the aspects of the mother which are attended to, or the categories of thought applied to them by their daughters differ. Thus what is simply coded as "emotional" behavior by a socially defined daughter might be more causally described as "unhappy" or "compulsively driven" behavior by the self-defining daughter. The self-defining daughter appears to distance herself from her mother by using analytic descriptive tools, while the socially defined daughter reacts to her mother in an inchoate, unanalyzed way.

Finally, socially defined women report significantly more often that either or both parents expressed traditional or conservative attitudes about sexual morality ($t = 2.10$, $p < .05$). This suggests that for the socially defined woman there is either greater pressure for social conformity or else greater attention to such pressures.

A final objective index of these hypothesized differences in self-defining and socially defined women's attitudes about their parents is reflected in the significant positive correlation between self-defining self-definition and the length of the description of mother minus length of the description of father. In short, self-defining women use more words to describe their mothers than do socially defined women. One possible explanation is that they are more intensely concerned about their positive (and negative) identifications with their mother, and thus more detailed in their description.

DISCUSSION

The present research suggests that it is possible to articulate two patterns of female behavior—patterns which appear to ramify in systematic ways from verbal expression through social and political behavior, and which seem to have some specifiable, different antecedents. Having discovered that women who differ in their aspirations (or plans) differ in the style in which they tell a story, we further discovered that there were systematic antecedents and consequences of that storytelling style which, we suggest, may reflect self- versus social-definition. The two patterns are not merely patterns of career choice or career salience; rather, they appear to be coherent personality patterns or styles. Labelling the two patterns in this way, rather than merely as differences in career plans, has the advantage of suggesting broad alternative patterns of female personality, rather than the traditional notion of "deviation from" or "exceptions to" a single presumed pattern.

The advantages to assessing these two patterns through the use of thematic apperception are twofold. First, any question about career plans as such is, by now, so saturated and distorted by the effects of changing social norms and the mass media that the answers tend to have very little variance, and hence validity.[8] Second, the use of the TAT permits measurement of the two patterns

among women for whom a question about careers simply does not pose realistic alternatives (e.g., older women, working-class women, institutionalized women).

Our results suggest, first, that women who planned full-time careers (in this particular sample, in the autumn of 1970) showed a distinctive style of storytelling, or verbal production. They organize their perception in terms of causality, purpose, and instrumentality, as opposed to irrational diffusion. We have labelled these two patterns self-definition and social definition respectively, and have investigated some of their antecedents in family background and consequences in behavior and attitudes.

Self-defining women tend to have fathers who are autonomous in their work, mothers who work, and no older brothers. Socially defined women tend to have fathers who work within bureaucratic structures, mothers who are housewives, and older brothers. This finding supports the notion that at least formal socialization, modelling, and expressed values in the nuclear family are factors in determining the pattern any particular woman later follows, whatever the importance of biological factors. In addition, self-defining women tend to engage in instrumental behavior more often than do socially defined women, and to engage in (or admit to) behavior which is negatively sanctioned for women in contemporary American culture. The two groups indicate pleasure in, fear of, and guilt over, different kinds of things. This supports strongly our contention that the patterns are broad-ranging, ramify differently, and are indicative of "deeper" personality differences. Finally, the two groups write of their parents in very different ways. Two alternative explanations of this finding are possible: (1) their parents differ, or (2) their intellectual and emotional organization of their perception and experience of their parents differ. In the absence of more data, the second is the more parsimonious interpretation, and the one tentatively proposed here.

The self-definition and social definition patterns may also have importance as moderator var-

[8]For example, in a study of freshmen women at Wesleyan University in 1972, the question about plans for ten years hence elicited either uncodable responses or else "male" careers (category 4 in Tables 1 and 2). Nevertheless, self-definition was significantly correlated with the salience of career as measured by the number of words in the response that referred to career aspects of plans ($rho = .54$, $N = 21$, $p < .01$). Using this measure of career salience in the second sample described in this paper yielded a rho of .49, $p < .001$. Thus there is reason to believe that the self-definition measure continues to possess validity, and is less subject to the influence of norms and social desirability than are so-called objective questions or scales.

iables that increase the predictive value of other personality measures. For example, French and Lesser (1964) found that dividing women into those who had "intellectual" versus "traditional" conceptions of women's role increased the significance and intelligibility of the behavioral correlates of *n* Achievement. Their moderator variable of role conception, associated with the type of college attended, probably overlaps to a considerable extent the present measure of style of self-definition as assessed directly from TAT stories. Pilot studies of power motivation among women (see Winter & Stewart, 1972) suggest that self-definition does have a similar moderating effect.

Our findings support the strategy of studying differences among women as an alternative to research on the differences between the sexes in order to arrive at some correct and complete understanding of the importance of sex as such for understanding personality and behavior. If, as we have found in this research, there are great variations in verbal organization, personality, and behavior among women—variations attributable to factors of treatment or training—then perhaps further research in the paradigm of intrasex differences is an important and urgent priority in the psychological investigation of women.

SUMMARY

Differences in the TAT stories written by college women who plan full-time careers (with or without marriage) and those written by college women who plan marriage (without a career) were developed into a scoring system that is hypothesized to measure self-definition versus social definition, respectively. The measure is uncorrelated with intelligence, social class, and many traditional measures of sex-role or sex differences. Self-defining women have a characteristic background (working mother, no older brothers), report a variety of instrumental actions, and report pleasures, fears, and secrets that all suggest a pattern of thought, feeling and behavior no less coherent than the pattern shown by the more "traditional" socially defined women. The advantage of the TAT over questionnaire procedures for measuring this dimension is discussed.

REFERENCES

Almquist, E., & Angrist, S. S. Career salience and atypicality of occupational choice among college women. *Journal of Marriage and the Family*, 1970, *32*, 242–250.

Astin, H. S. Patterns of career choices over time. *Personnel and Guidance Journal*, 1967, *45*, 541–546.

Atkinson, J. W. (Ed.) *Motives in fantasy, action and society*. Princeton, N.J.: D. Van Nostrand Co., 1958.

Bardwick, J. *The psychology of women*. New York: Harper & Row, 1971.

de Beauvoir, S. *The second sex*. 1949. New York: Knopf, 1953.

Carlsmith, L. K. Effect of early father absence on scholastic aptitude. *Harvard Educational Review*, 1964, *34*, 4–21.

Engels, F. The origin of the family, private property, and the state. 1884. In *Karl Marx and Friedrich Engels—selected works*, Vol. 2. Moscow: Foreign Languages Press, 1962.

Erikson, E. H. *Childhood and society*, second edition. New York: W. W. Norton & Co., Inc., 1963.

French, E., & Lesser, G. S. Some characteristics of the achievement motive in women. *Journal of Abnormal and Social Psychology*, 1964, *68*, 119–128.

Freud, S. Some psychological consequences of the anatomical distinction between the sexes. 1924. *Collected Papers*. London: Hogarth Press, 1950. Vol. 5, pp. 186–194.

Gysbers, N. C., Johnston, J. A., & Gust, T. Characteristics of homemaker and career-oriented women. *Journal of Consulting Psychology*, 1968, *15*, 541–546.

Hollingshead, A. B., & Redlich, F. C. *Social class and mental illness*. New York: John Wiley & Sons, Inc., 1958.

Horner, M. S. Toward an understanding of achievement-related conflicts in women. *Journal of Social Issues*, 1972, *28*, 2, 157–175.

Horney, K. The flight from womanhood. *International Journal of Psychoanalysis*, 1926, *7*, 324–339.

Kagan, J. Personality development. In I. L. Janis, G. F. Mahl, J. Kagan, & R. R. Holt. *Personality dynamics, development and assessment*. New York: Harcourt, Brace & World, Inc., 1969. Pp. 403–572.

Kagan, J. & Moss, H. M. *Birth to maturity*. New York: John Wiley & Sons, Inc., 1962.

McClelland, D. C. Methods of measuring human motivation. In J. W. Atkinson (Ed.), *Motives in fantasy, action and society.* Princeton, N.J.: D. Van Nostrand Co., 1958. Pp. 7–42.

McClelland, D. C., Atkinson, J. W., Clark, R. A. & Lowell, E. L. *The achievement motive.* New York: Appleton-Century-Crofts, 1953.

Maccoby, E. *The development of sex differences.* Stanford, Calif.: Stanford Univ. Press, 1966.

May, R. Sex differences in fantasy patterns. *Journal of Projective Techniques and Personality Assessment,* 1966, *30*, 576–586.

Parsons, T. Age and sex in the social structure of the United States. 1942. In *Essays in sociological theory.* Revised edition. New York: The Free Press, 1954. Pp. 89–103.

Parsons, T. The kinship system of the contemporary United States. 1943. In *Essays in sociological theory.* Revised edition. New York: The Free Press, 1954. Pp. 177–196.

Rossi, A. Equality between the sexes: an immodest proposal. In R. Lifton (Ed.), *The woman in America.* Boston: Houghton Mifflin, 1964. Pp. 98–143.

Rotter, J. B. Generalized expectancies for internal versus external control of reinforcement. *Psychological Monographs,* 1966, *80,* 1 (Whole number 609).

Sartre, J. P. *Anti-Semite and Jew.* 1946. New York: Schocken Books, Inc., 1965.

Schultz, D. P. The human subject in psychological research. *Psychological Bulletin,* 1969, *72,* 214–228.

Siegel, A. E., & Curtis, E. A. Familial correlates of orientation toward future employment among college women. *Journal of Educational Psychology,* 1963, *54,* 33–57.

Stewart, A. J. The nature of woman: a study of female responses to male definition. Unpublished honors thesis, Wesleyan University, 1971.

Veblen, T. *The theory of the leisure class.* New York: Funk & Wagnalls, 1899.

Winter, D. G. *The power motive.* New York: The Free Press, 1973.

Winter, D. G., & Stewart, A. J. Self-definition and the power motives in women. Unpublished paper, Wesleyan University, 1972.

STUDY QUESTIONS

1. Look again at the modified questions by Winter and Stewart (1977) for evaluating a content analysis. How does the selection by Stewart and Winter (1974) deal with each question?

2. If you could make systematic observations of all the Stewart and Winter subjects, what observations would you choose to make? What would your research hypothesis be?

3. This study was conducted with white undergraduate women from a small New England women's liberal arts college. To determine the generalizability (external validity) of the Stewart and Winter findings, where might you replicate the study? What other kinds of research projects would be a next logical step derived from the study?

EXERCISES

Although content analyses can be done by individual students, we recommend that you work on the following exercises either in pairs or small groups. To do these exercises you will need a set of first-hand accounts of the adolescent experience (for example, Goethals & Klos, 1976) or short stories on adolescence (for instance, Gregory, 1978).

1 Identity-Status Scoring

A. Use Marcia's scoring system in Appendix D as a guide for scoring the protagonist of each story or essay for identity status.

B. Compare your identity-status scores with those of a teammate who has scored the same material by the same system. Calculate a percentage of agreement between your scores as follows:

$$\frac{\text{total number of items } - \text{ items on which you agree}}{\text{total number of items}}$$

Alternatively, you can determine the correlation coefficient for your two sets of scores by following the steps in Appendix A.

C. Use your scores to examine a number of questions, whose nature will depend on the nature of the material you have analyzed. Some sample questions are: Which status occurs most frequently across the different stories or essays? And are older protagonists portrayed as identity achievers more often than younger subjects? Ideally, of course, you should formulate your research question in advance of the actual data coding.

2 *Other Coding Systems*

A. Working in small groups, develop your own coding system for the essays or stories. Follow the steps adapted from Winter and Stewart that are presented at the end of this chapter.

B. You may want your class to work in small groups to analyze the same set of materials using both the Marcia system and a different system developed within the class. Compare the kinds of information and insights you can gain about the same protagonists using the different systems.

ANNOTATED BIBLIOGRAPHY

Diener, E., & DeFour, D. Does television violence enhance program popularity? *Journal of Personality and Social Psychology*, 1978, *36*, 333-341.

In the first of two studies, very low and nonsignificant relationships emerged when Nielson popularity percentages, subjective ratings, and objective scores for episodes of fictional television violence were correlated. Subjects in the second study rated either a violence-deleted or uncut version of an adventure program. Uncut episodes were perceived as significantly more violent but ratings for overall enjoyment were not significantly higher.

Gillis, J. S., & Avis, W. E. The male-taller norm in mate selection, *Personality and Social Psychology Bulletin*, 1980, *6*, 396-401.

Height data collected from the bank-account application form of 720 couples were consistent with the notion that an important factor influencing human mate selection is the social norm that the male be taller.

Hermann, M. G. Assessing the personalities of Soviet Politburo members. *Personality and Social Psychology Bulletin*, 1980, *6*, 332-352.

The author performed a content analysis of speeches and interviews of Soviet Politburo members to assess such personal characteristics as ethnocentrism, need for power, and need for affiliation. She also reported interrelations among personal characteristics, background data, and position on detente.

Jemmott, J. B. III, & Tebbets, R. Applying social cognition: A content analysis of the Bakke case.

Personality and Social Psychology Bulletin, 1980, *6*, 30-36.

Analyzing a sample of 12 newspapers from a social-psychological perspective, two raters scored all the articles and editorials about the Bakke Supreme Court case on reverse discrimination. Content analysis indicated disproportionate amounts of case-history information favorable to Bakke and of anchoring information (information about the abstract, moral, or legal context to which an issue is linked) unfavorable to his position.

ADDITIONAL SOURCES

Borgatta, E. F., & Crowther, B. *A workbook for the study of social interaction processes*. Chicago: Rand-McNally, 1965.

Carlson, R. Sex differences in ego functioning: Exploratory studies of agency and communion. *Journal of Consulting and Clinical Psychology*, 1971, *37*, 267-277.

Colby, B. N. Cultural patterns in narrative. *Science*, 1966, *151*, 793-798.

Dailey, C. A. *Assessment of lives*. San Francisco: Jossey-Bass, 1971.

Elig, T. W., & Frieze, I. H. A multi-dimensional scheme for coding and interpreting perceived causality for success and failure events: The coding scheme of perceived causality (CSPC). *JSAS: Catalog of Selected Documents in Psychology*, 1975, *5*, 313 (MS. #1069).

Friedrich, L., & Stein, A. Aggressive and prosocial television programs and the natural behavior of preschool children. *Monographs of the Society for Research in Child Development*, 1973, *38* (4, Serial No. 151).

Gottsschalk, L. A., Goldine, C. G., & Springer, K. J. Three hostility scales applicable to verbal samples. *Archives of General Psychology*, 1963, *9*, 254-279.

Harrison, A. A., & Saeed, L. Let's make a deal: An analysis of revelations and stipulations in lonely hearts advertisements. *Journal of Personality and Social Psychology*, 1977, *35*, 257-264.

Hunter, J. E. Images of woman. *Journal of Social Issues*, 1976, *32*, 7-17.

Katz, E. W. A content-analytic method for studying themes of interpersonal behavior. *Psychological Bulletin*, 1966, *66*, 419-422.

CHAPTER

7

Interviews and Questionnaires

We have seen that one way to learn about individuals is to watch what they do (to make behavioral observations). Another way is to analyze the nature of their communications (to do content analyses). In both activities there is a real distance between investigator and subject and an absence of any relationship between them. Indeed, in naturalistic observations and content analyses, subjects are generally unaware that they are objects of psychological research. The situation is quite different when it comes to a third way of learning about individuals—that is, by asking them about themselves in personal interviews.

DEFINITIONS

Interviews are probably the most commonly used of all assessment procedures. Whereas you might never have been the subject of a na-

turalistic observation or a content analysis, it is likely that you have been interviewed—by a physician, potential employer, school official, voter registration agent, and so on. Moreover, you might easily have taken part in interviews designed specifically for research purposes—for example, a political poll or a door-to-door survey on a consumer product. Finally, you might even have been engaged in interviews designed to gain data relevant to individual psychological attributes, including attitudes, values, needs, interests, and more fundamental personality characteristics. It is with this type of interview, and particularly with the design and use of such interviews to test psychological hypotheses, that we are most concerned in this chapter.

An *interview* can be defined as a direct interpersonal communication process between a respondent and an interviewer whose purpose is obtaining information from the respondent. Ordinarily, such communications take place face to face, but interviews are sometimes conducted over the telephone as well. While questionnaires are also a means of gathering informaton from respondents, they are not used within the context of an interpersonal relationship. Thus, in our definition, a *questionnaire* is a self-administered instrument, which can be completed by a respondent without any personal interaction with an investigator. Both interviews and questionnaires can vary in their directness or indirectness, both have advantages and disadvantages, and, like other measuring instruments, both involve particular problems of reliability and validity.

When is it appropriate to use an interview to investigate a research question? (We will return to the use of questionnaires later in this chapter.) Interviews are probably most useful when we are interested in learning about private psychological processes such as thoughts, feelings, or people's own views of who they are and how they came to be that way. As an example, in making behaviorial observations, you might note that many people give money to Salvation Army street volunteers at Christmas time. While this behavior is interesting by itself, you might also suspect that different people give money for different reasons. If you want to determine what those reasons are, the tactic most likely to be successful is to ask people. Of course, it is possible that the individuals you question will refuse to be interviewed, might lie to you, or might not even be sure of their own motivations. To have any confidence in the answers you receive, you must have confidence in the questions you have developed and in your own skill at interviewing, a subtle art.

INTERVIEWS

The Marcia article in Chapter 2 provides a good illustration of the kinds of steps a researcher goes through in developing an inter-

view procedure. It might be helpful to think of this process as consisting of the following steps: (1) formulating objectives; (2) deciding on a format; (3) developing questions; (4) conducting pilot tests with the preliminary instrument; and (5) revising and refining the instrument on the basis of pilot data. (See Kahn & Cannell, 1957, for a full exposition of the steps involved in developing and conducting interviews.)

Formulating Objectives

The first step, formulating objectives, refers to the usual process of specifying the particular kinds of information you must collect to answer your research question. For example, to identify different forms of adolescent identity predictable from Erikson's theory, Marcia decided that he would need data concerning the experiences of crisis and commitment in the areas of occupation and ideology. To achieve these objectives, he still needed to decide what kinds of questions to ask, in what order, with what wording, and so on. Once the objectives have been formulated, the investigation is ready to proceed with the development of the actual interview.

Developing the Format

Interviews tend to be based on one or both of two basic question formats: fixed-alternative questions and open-ended questions. *Fixed-alternative* (or *closed* or *restricted*) *questions* require subjects to select one alternative from a predetermined set of categories that best applies to them. Examples of this type of question are "Do you consider yourself to be liberal, moderate, or conservative?" and "Would you describe your present relationship with your family as largely conflictual or largely cordial?" In *open-ended*, or *unrestricted*, *questions*, respondents are expected to reply in their own words. Examples of this type of item are. "Tell me about your basic political philosophy" and "describe your relationships with your parents right now."

Most interviews contain some fixed-alternative items designed to elicit basic classifying information about respondents—for example, their sex, marital status, level of education, and occupational status. Other interview questions are designed to elicit problem information, and these may be either open or fixed in form. Open questions have the advantages of allowing interviewers to respond to expressions of uncertainty on the part of the subject for the purposes of clarifying what is being sought, requesting additional information, and eliciting a fuller, more individualized statement of the respondent's thoughts or feelings.

Everyone who has ever taken a multiple-choice exam or has filled out information forms has probably faced the problem that none of the fixed alternatives seem quite correct. Asking open questions is a way of avoiding that difficulty. On the other hand, as we shall see, open questions require a content-analysis approach to scoring, which can be much more subjective than the scoring of fixed-alternative items. Indeed, fixed-alternative questions are not only easier to score than open questions but also ensure a standardization of response alternatives, as each respondent must consider the same alternatives and decide which is most correct.

The creation of the interview format also involves decisions as to how questions should be organized. We seldom begin an interview with point-blank problem questions aimed at eliciting complete answers immediately. Thus, it is unlikely that we would begin an interview by asking respondents to describe family relations, their views on religion, or their thoughts on sex. Generally, our opening questions are designed to reassure subjects that they are not being faced with too difficult or embarrassing a task and to lead them gradually and comfortably into the issues of concern.

Frequently, the questions in an interview follow a *funnel sequence*. In this format, we begin with rather general and unrestricted questions and gradually narrow our focus to more specific and restricted items. Thus, if our ultimate objective were to analyze young men's views of possible authoritarian traits in their fathers, we might start out by asking about family relationships or even interpersonal relationships in general. In a logical and smooth set of steps, we would lead into the more specific issue of concern. The funnel sequence, from general to specific, has several purposes: (1) to provide an opportunity for investigator and respondents to establish a comfortable interaction; (2) to prevent respondents from developing a premature mental "set" concerning the issue under investigation; and (3) to allow respondents to "sort through" thoughts and feelings that they may not have articulated before.

Developing Specific Questions

Developing specific questions to achieve your research objectives is not as easy as it might appear, even after you have settled on an appropriate interview format. There are a number of considerations to keep in mind when you are composing items for an interview: (1) make questions clear and unambiguous, (2) keep the vocabulary appropriate to the educational level and experience of your respondents; (3) make sure questions do not demand information your respondents might not have; (4) be prepared to specify a clear frame of reference for the questions—that is, a means of interpreting the questions—or elicit from your respondents the frame of reference they are employing; and (5) focus each item on a single idea rather than touching on separate problems that might or might not evoke similar responses.

Let us create a hypothetical situation in which a team of investigators is interested in self-esteem. They decide, for better or worse, to use an open-ended interview format, and begin on the wrong foot by composing a number of questions that do not meet the criteria for good question writing outlined in the preceding paragraph. We can analyze each question and modify it to increase both its clarity and usefulness.

1. What kind of person are you?

In addition to being vague and overly general, this question is ambiguous because it lacks a specified frame of reference. The investigators might know that the kind of response they seek is "self-confident," "insecure", or "shy and nervous." The respondent, however, will not know whether the desired answer is "Democrat, Catholic, of Irish extraction," "well-educated, middle class, and upwardly mobile," or something else entirely. Rather than putting respondents in this dilemma, waiting for them to interpret the question or provide their own frame of reference, and then correcting them if necessary, the investigators should reword the item entirely or specify the frame of reference. A much better question would be "We are interested in people's self concepts—whether they feel good or bad about themselves, whether they see themselves as competent or incompetent, that sort of thing. What kind of person are you?"

2. Does your level of self-esteem exhibit temporal and cross-situational consistency?

While respondents would have no trouble with the language of this question if they were all psychologists, the question is nevertheless full of jargon. All respondents, psychologists and laypeople alike, would find a clearer, less ambiguous question easier to answer—for example, "You say that you have a lot of self-respect and self-confidence. Has that always been true? Are you equally self-confident in all situations, or do you feel better about yourself at some times and in some situations than others?"

A few more questions follow that could be improved for interviews with the general public. What is wrong with each question and how would you go about reformulating it?

3. What is the ontogenetic history of your self-concept?

4. Tell me a little about yourself.

5. Do you think that you have a positive self-concept and a level of self-esteem similar to your father's?

Good interview questions meet a number of other criteria. For example, make each question relevant to your research objectives. Extraneous questions could confuse your subjects and put them "off the track." Also avoid asking "leading questions." No matter who your respondents are, you could be pretty sure how they would answer such questions as "You're in favor of peace as much as the next guy, right?" or "You probably haven't thought through all the ramifications of your early childhood experience, have you?" Furthermore, avoid phrasing questions so that they have only one socially desirable response—for example, "Are you narrow-minded, intellectually rigid, and a bigot?" or "Are you basically a decent human being?"

Pilot Testing and Revising

There is only one way to be sure that your questions are well worded, well organized, and useful for meeting your research objectives—that is, to try them out. Pilot testing is an important part of any research endeavor and is certainly indispensable to the development of an interview study. You might want to begin by testing your questions on some of your friends, but it will still be important to try them out on others who are representative of the population you intend to study. Be prepared to discover that some of your questions will have to be reworded or abandoned altogether. This happens to the most experienced of question writers!

Interviewer/Respondent Relationships

As mentioned earlier, the value of responses to an interview depends not only on the questions asked but also on the roles played by the interviewer and respondent. That is, an interview is, or should be, a dialogue between two people, and the content of any dialogue depends on the characteristics of both participants.

All of us have acquired skills in the art of communication, and these skills include concealing as well as revealing and distorting as well as clarifying. There will always be respondents who simply will not answer some of your questions fully and honestly no matter how skillful an interviewer you are. Nevertheless, most potential subjects will prove responsive if you keep the following points in mind. Your goal in conducting an interview study is to learn something about the respondents. You are asking people to take the time to talk to you and to answer questions as honestly as they can. You are seeking some degree of self-disclosure on the part of your respondents, whether the topic be as impersonal as views on the state of the world or as personal as the nature of their relationships with the opposite sex.

From the respondents point of view, the question is What's in it for me? Why should I bother? Part of the answer may be obvious. Talking with an interested, sympathetic listener can be a rewarding experience. Indeed, one of the principal ways that some acquaintances become friends is through conversations in which views and experiences are shared. Ordinarily, an interview is more one-sided than a developing friendship, but interviewers can be interested and sympathetic, and interviews can become conversations that benefit the respondent as well as the investigator.

Interviewing Techniques

How do you begin the process that leads to a successful interview? Whether you are interviewing people in the street or college freshmen who are required to participate in research as part of their introductory psychology course, you will probably begin by explaining the purpose of your study. Generally, you will want to obtain the informed consent of your potential subjects. To do this you need not discuss your hypotheses in detail, but you should describe the general areas to be covered in your questions so that subjects will be prepared for any sensitive issues that might arise. If your research objectives include obtaining such information as details on family relationships, sexual attitudes, or opinions about different national groups, your subjects have the right to know in advance—and to refuse to participate if they wish.

Your introductory statement will probably briefly describe your sample and explain how the subject fits in. Are you trying to obtain responses from " the man on the street?" Are you interested in talking to women too? Are you stopping passers-by who seem to be between the ages of 50 and 70? Are you trying to talk to as many people as possible in different communities within a metropolitan area? Are you limiting your study to college freshman? Why? Are you conducting the interview as part of an assignment for a psychology course, or for a thesis, or for part-time work sponsored by an agency? If so, say so. Again, you need not go into extensive detail, but neither do you want your respondents to start an interview worrying "Why me? What's going on?"

Remember that one of your major concerns must be to motivate people to participate and to continue participating in your project. To this end, reassure your subject that you will treat the information you collect anonymously or confidentially where this is the case. Also, be prepared to handle with respect and sympathy whatever the subject says. You could hardly expect an interview to continue if you belittled the respondent or acted shocked at something you were told.

If your questions are open ended rather than restricted, one of your concerns will be to ensure that you obtain comparable data from all your respondents—that is, data that can be coded for the information you need to satisfy your research objectives. Obtaining such data can be challenging because not all respondents will answer the same question with equal detail and clarity. Frequently, you will need to supplement your initial queries on a topic with probing questions, or *probes,* to obtain a sufficient response. Be sure that your probes are not leading questions and that they do not suggest that the respondent's earlier reply showed stupidity, a lack of understanding, or an uncooperative spirit.

If you are dealing with issues that are very personal or possibly embarrassing or threatening to some subjects, you might have to explain the relevance or importance of your questions and remind subjects that their responses will be treated as anonymous. Also, it is often helpful to lead in to potentially threatening questions with the reassurance that whatever a respondent's response is it is bound to fall within the range of normality and acceptability. One such reassurance might be, "All families fight among themselves on occasion. What kinds of issues are most likely to create a controversy between you and your parents?" Remember, however, that whatever probes or lead-in statements you use, it is important to maintain some standardization, or consistency, of approach across respondents. If you use probes with male subjects only and not with females you may find interesting sex differences in your data that have nothing to do with the personal characteristics or views of your male and female subjects.

Maintaining consistency in your approach to all subjects is a means of avoiding two common sources of bias in an interview study. Besides poorly constructed interview questions, both interviewers and respondents are potential sources of bias. Subjects can produce biased and thus unreliable responses by being unwilling to give open and honest answers to questions, by being concerned primarily with presenting themselves in a socially desirable way, or by lacking information or insight on the issues under investigation. Interviewers can introduce bias into the data by using unsystematic or ineffective probes, leading questions, selective reinforcement of certain types of response, and inappropriate behaviors toward respondents.

In addition to being aware of these potential sources of bias, interviewers need to be conscientious about the process of recording responses. It is generally difficult to write down every word a respondent utters. Moreover, the use of a tape recorder can create more problems than it solves. Some respondents will be less sure of their anonymity and more guarded in their responses if you use a tape recorder, and even where responses are adequate, the process of making verbatim transcriptions of tapes is enormously tedious. The best procedure is to develop a fast and accurate "shorthand" system of your own and to write down as much as possible of what each subject says, being careful not to translate the subject's responses into your own words.

One of the best ways to become a good interviewer is through practice, particularly practice that provides direct feedback on your methods. You will gain some experience in conducting an interview when collecting pilot data. Role playing an interview with friends can be particularly useful. It is helpful to have a number of trial runs before you begin collecting interview data for analysis. If you conduct several interviews and then decide to "throw out" the data because your procedures or styles have been changing, the cost in time can be enormous.

Advantages and Disadvantages

Interviews have the advantage of putting investigators in direct touch with their subjects. Unlike systematic observations, interviews make it possible for researchers to obtain information on how and what individuals think about themselves and the world around them. Unlike questionnaires and objective tests, interviews provide investigators with an opportunity to clarify questions and answers, to develop an intrinsic motivation for self-disclosure, and to recognize and deal with subject resistance, embarrassment and defensiveness.

The disadvantage of interviews is that they are costly. Multiply a 1-hour interview by, say, 30 subjects and you have a minimum time commitment of 30 hours just for data collection. If you decided to compare forms of heterosexual relationships in 30 young men classifiable as identity achievers with 30 classifiable as identity foreclosures, you would have to spend more than 120 hours interviewing people (two 1-hour interviews for each subject). Add to that the time involved in transcribing and coding the data, and you have a massive project indeed!

QUESTIONNAIRES

One way to avoid the expense of interview studies is to put questions into a self-administered questionnaire format. Once an adequate questionnaire has been developed, one can obtain data from 60, 120, or an indefinite number of respondents at once—in a classroom, a lecture hall, an auditorium, or even through the mail. While items on a questionnaire can be either open ended or closed, generally they tend to be of the latter type—characterized by fixed-alternative responses. Questionnaires of this variety are both easy to score and easy to administer.

Questionnaires have a number of advantages over interviews. When totally anonymous, they can elicit a far greater degree of honesty and frankness than is likely in the face-to-face interview situation. Moreover, because they can be administered rather easily to large numbers of respondents, they are much less expensive to use than individual interviews. However, like any form of measurement, questionnaires also have drawbacks. Questionnaires are subject to various kinds of *response bias*—for example, tendencies of subjects to agree or disagree with items regardless of their content. That is, there are yea-sayers as well as nay-sayers among questionnaire respondents, and both types fail to provide useful problem information on the questions they answer. Also, on questionnaires, as in interviews, some respondents will be more concerned with presenting themselves in a socially desirable way than in revealing how

they actually think about issues. Moreover, on the same questionnaire items might be interpreted in different ways by different people, and with no interviewer available to recognize differences in interpretation or other kinds of confusion, misinterpretations could go uncorrected. Despite these limitations, however, it is likely that questionnaires will continue to be popular because they are easy and inexpensive to use.

Direct and Indirect Approaches to Interviews and Questionnaires

As already noted, both interviews and questionnaires can vary in the directness with which they approach the information investigators need to attain their research objectives. In a direct approach to individual motive patterns, we might ask our respondents, "What is most important to you, the need to achieve—that is, the need to gain success through your own efforts,—or the need for affiliation—that is, the need for close relationships with others?" While the format for this direct question is already relatively closed, it could be restricted even further to the fixed-alternative pattern. For example, one might ask the following questions with these choices in a questionnaire:

1. How important is it to you to achieve success through your own efforts?
   a. extremely important
   b. fairly important
   c. sometimes important, sometimes not
   d. fairly unimportant
   e. extremely unimportant
2. How important is it to you to enjoy close relationships with others?
   a. extremely important
   b. fairly important
   c. sometimes important, sometimes not
   d. fairly unimportant
   e. extremely unimportant
3. If you are in a situation where you have to choose between achieving success through your own efforts and achieving a close re-

lationship with someone, how likely is it
that you will act to achieve success?

a. extremely likely
b. somewhat likely
c. a toss-up
d. somewhat unlikely
e. extremely unlikely

Direct questions concerning motive patterns
can also be presented in an open-ended form.
For example, you might say "Tell me a little
about the relative importance for you of achieving success through your own efforts. I am
particularly interested in how that goal com-
pares in importance with the goal of achieving
close relationships with other people."

Direct questions often prove quite successful
in eliciting the kind of information we want.
Frequently, however, an indirect approach,
which avoids directly confronting the issues under consideration, can be more useful for attaining research objectives. Indirect approaches
are particularly helpful when subjects are unwilling or unable to provide the desired information because it is too threatening, too
embarrassing, or not directly available to their
own conscious awareness. No matter how highly
motivated and cooperative respondents might
be, it is possible that they simply do not know
whether their need for achievement is stronger
than their need for affiliation.

When the indirect approach is combined with
an open-ended interview format, the resulting
instrument overlaps with the area of psychological measurement known as *projective testing.*
Basic to a projective test is the presentation to
subjects of an external stimulus, such as a set of
pictures, stories, or descriptions of imaginary
characters. Rather than asking respondents
what they themselves would think or do in a
particular set of circumstances, we ask them to
make up stories about the the pictures (as in
the Thematic Apperception Test), to complete incomplete stories, or to speculate about
what an imaginary person would do in a given
situation.

As explained in Chapter 6, the assumption
underlying projective tests is that respondents
will project their own thoughts and feelings into
any relatively unstructured or ambiguous task.
Projective tests are similar to open-ended interviews in relying on subjects' responses as the
principal data for personality study. Projective
tests differ from interviews precisely in their indirectness, in providing subjects with an ambiguous stimulus or situation to discuss rather
than posing direct questions. Projective tests
such as the TAT, the Rorschach Inkblot Test,
or a sentence-completion task frequently form
part of the clinical assessment process. As such,
they are used primarily to provide insight into a
client's unconscious needs, strivings, and defensive processes. In this context, projective tests
might form the core of both a diagnosis and a
plan for psychotherapy. However, these tests are
used in personality research to identify individual differences in personality structure or process and as a basis for predictions about various
forms of behavior.

Clearly, it is the use of projective techniques
in personality research that is most relevant
to our purposes. Of all the projective devices,
the Thematic Apperception Test and its deriva-
tives are probably the most popular as research
instruments. In Chapter 6, we mentioned some
of the research uses of thematic apperception
tasks—for example, in the analysis of self-
versus other orientation in women (Stewart &
Winter, 1974) and in the study of the need
for achievement and its correlates in a number
of societies (Atkinson, 1958; McClelland, 1955,
1961). Thematic apperception tests have also
been used in the identification of major themes
in the life of a single individual (Keniston,
1963) and the analysis of sex differences in the
fantasy patterns of men and women (May,
1966). Incomplete stories, or "verbal TAT
cues," were the major assessment instrument in
studies of the fear of success as a motive interfering with the achievement of success through
one's own efforts (Horner, 1970; Weston &
Mednick, 1970). Reports of any of these studies

rich source of ideas for the research applications of open-ended indirect approaches to personality as exemplified by projective techniques.

Indirect approaches can also be combined with fixed-alternative questionnaire formats. Such questionnaires overlap in form and purpose with so-called *objective* (multiple-choice), or **psychometric tests**—including personality inventories and attitudes, interests, and values scales. Since we discuss objective tests in detail in the next chapter, we limit ourselves here to an example of the objective measurement of a single trait—that is, internal versus external locus of control.

Suppose you were interested in identifying groups of individuals who see their major reinforcements in life as falling either inside or outside their own control. You could ask them directly to identify the source of their major reinforcements. Alternatively, you could take the indirect approach used by Rotter (1966) and provide a series of statements seemingly relevant to the locus of control, internal versus external. (In Rotter's questionnaire, respondents must choose which item in a series of item pairs is most true of themselves. Item pairs are of the following variety: a. I have control over my own destiny; b. it doesn't matter much what people do—their fate is in the stars.) Then you could simply ask respondents to indicate whether they agree or disagree with each statement. The total number of extrinsic-locus statements they endorsed would be considered a total score for the scale. This score would be presumed to correspond with an underlying trait or dimension of which the respondents might not be directly aware but that could have a number of predictable behavioral correlates. For example, it has been found (Baron, Cowan, Ganz, & McDonald, 1974) that individuals with an internal locus of control do better on a task when they can discover for themselves whether their performance is right or wrong. By contrast, individuals with an external locus of control do better when an experimenter praises their correct responses.

DATA ANALYSIS

Basically, the purpose of an interview or questionnaire, direct or indirect, is to *measure* some characteristic of the individual—for example, a personality trait, an interest, or an attitude. At the simplest level, interviews and questionnaires are scored in a way that allows us to *categorize* people. At this *nominal* level of measurement,—where we arbitrarily assign numerals to classes of people—we categorize people on the basis of their responses, for example, as Republican or Democrat; fully employed, partly employed or unemployed; inner directed or outer directed; and so on.

In a nominal scale, the numerals assigned to groups do not have any quantitative meaning. If we assign a *1* to all males, and a *2* to all females, we are not implying that females have more gender than males. On the other hand, in an *ordinal* scale, the categories to which numerals are assigned do stand in quantitative relationship to each other. For example, if we have a 5-point ordinal scale representing achievement motivation, we could use a *1* to represent subjects with very low achievement motivation, a *3* to represent average motivation, and a *5* for very high motivation.

With the closed, fixed-alternative type of instrument, the scoring is objective—that is, it is built into the form of the questions and requires no judgment on the part of the investigator. Investigators impose categories with such an instrument, but they do so before rather than after data are collected. Typically, subjects simply check off or circle the categories offered that apply best to them—for example, in favor of or opposed to a constitutional amendment; very hopeful, moderately hopeful, or not at all hopeful about the future.

With open-ended items, on the other hand, the researcher must use a system of content analysis to code the data collected for the categories of interest. As noted in the last chapter, content analysis requires *judgments* on the part of the scorer, although every effort is made to ensure that these judgments are as objective as possible. Suppose you were interested in categorizing respondents as politically liberal or conservative on the basis of their responses to such an open-ended request as "Please tell me a little about your basic political philosophy." If a young woman replied that she was in favor of immediate disarmament, international peace, the dismantling of the Pentagon and the total military establishment, approval of the Equal Rights Amendment, a full pardon for all military deserters, legalization of marijuana, free abortion on demand, and an end to all attempts to legislate morality, you would probably be on safe grounds if you classified her as a liberal —or even a radical if that were part of your category system. Nevertheless, such categorization reflects *your* judgment and thus is one step removed from the more objective approach of asking the subject to classify herself as a liberal or conservative.

When we code open-ended interview data into nominal categories, we generally begin with some sort of category system in mind. Frequently, however, we add to or modify our coding system in the process of analyzing data. For example, in coding responses to a question about political philosophy, you might begin with the intention of using just two categories, liberal and conservative. After looking carefully at a set of responses, however, you might decide you need two additional categories, radical and moderate, to do justice to the kinds of "natural" groupings that appear in the data.

Sometimes investigators are not even sure what kinds of categories will emerge in answers to open-ended questions. For example, Troll (1972) has administered a 12-item, open-ended interview that included the items "Think of a man" and "Think of a woman." While she might have assumed in advance that responses would include family members as well as unrelated individuals, there was no way of knowing in advance of data collection that such groups as

in-laws, cousins, and grandparents would occur with sufficient frequency to prove useful categories. This is what happened.

As is true in content analysis in general, we can code interview and questionnaire data at the ordinal level of measurement. For example, Troll (1975) scored responses to several open-ended interview questions for achievement motivation. Statements concerning orientation toward task mastery, creativity, achievement as recognized by others, and achievement through influence over others were all scored as indicative of achievement motivation and summed to provide a total score. The assumption was that the more types of achievement orientation the respondents showed in their statements, the stronger was the achievement motive.

An ordinal level of measurement can also be built into fixed-alternative questionnaires. In this case, instead of just presenting the respondent with nominal categories such as male/female or single/married/divorced/widowed, we present a number of items all presumed to be representative of the same trait, attitude, or characteristic. Thus, we might ask respondents to agree or disagree with a number of items designed to represent empathy: "I enjoy helping others", "I'd go out of my way to do a favor for someone less fortunate than myself", "I cry easily when I see other people experiencing strong emotions." If Woman A agreed with more items than Woman B, A would receive a higher score on the questionnaire (because of the additive nature of ordinal data) and might be presumed to be a more empathic person. The scoring is objective because the investigator simply adds together the number of agreements rather than making judgments about a trait on the basis of a free response. While such objective instruments are easy and inexpensive to use and present no problems of interscorer reliability, they have their own particular advantages and disadvantages, as discussed in the next chapter.

A PREVIEW OF THE CHAPTER SELECTION

This chapter's selection, by Orlofsky, Marcia, and Lesser, provides a further look at ego-identity status and its correlates. In this study, all subjects completed two interviews and three questionnaires. Responses to the interviews allowed the investigators to determine both the ego-identity status of the subjects and their *intimacy* statuses—another construct derived from Erikson's theory. The investigators examined relationships between identity and intimacy statuses as determined from the interviews, and attempted to provide validating evidence for the intimacy status and a new identity status through the questionnaires. Thus, the total set of instruments used comprised both open-ended and restricted formats and fairly direct as well as rather indirect approaches to constructs.

Ego Identity Status and the Intimacy versus Isolation Crisis of Young Adulthood

Jacob L. Orlofsky, James E. Marcia,[1]
and Ira M. Lesser
State University of New York at Buffalo

Ego identity status and intimacy status were determined for 53 college men and related to each other and to measures of intimacy, isolation, social desirability, autonomy, affiliation, and heterosexuality. Subjects in the identity achievement status and the alienated achievement status, a new identity status, appeared to have the greatest capacity for engaging in intimate interpersonal relationships. The interpersonal relationships of foreclosure and identity diffusion subjects were stereotyped and superficial. Moratorium subjects were the most variable. Identity diffusion individuals were least intimate and most isolated, while alienated achievement subjects were least isolated. The latter were also highest in autonomy and affiliation. Foreclosure subjects obtained the lowest autonomy and the highest social desirability scores. The results were interpreted as supporting the hypothesis that favorable resolution of the intimacy-isolation crisis is related to successful resolution of the identity crisis.

Three goals of this study were (*a*) the description and partial validation of a new ego identity status—"alienated achievement"; (*b*) the description and partial validation of intimacy statuses—styles of coping with Erikson's (1959) intimacy versus isolation psychosocial crisis; and finally, (*c*) the investigation of the relationship between the ego identity statuses and the new intimacy statuses.

Marcia's (1964) experimental approach to Erikson's concept of ego identity used the following psychosocial criteria: the presence of commitment to an occupation and an ideology preceded by

[1] The authors express their appreciation to Judy Finer, Ronnie Mahler, Diana Easton, Harold Brown, and Barbara Fisher for their assistance in conducting interviews, and to Jacyra Mahoney, for her assistance in rating interviews.

"crisis," the experience of decision making. Using these criteria, four identity statuses were conceptualized.

Identity Achievement

Identity achievement subjects express a strong degree of commitment to occupational and ideological choices. These choices are arrived at usually after a fairly extensive period of searching among alternatives. Identity achievement subjects appear fairly stable, able to establish and pursue realistic goals, and able to cope with sudden shifts in the environment. Their self-concept has been found to be based on an internal as opposed to an external frame of reference (Marcia, 1967; Waterman, Beubel, & Waterman, 1970).

Moratorium

Moratorium subjects are currently in the identity crisis, and their commitments are vague. In males, their performance on many measures resembles that of identity achievement subjects. They have contradictory needs for both rebellion and guidance manifested in their somewhat ambivalent views toward authority (Podd, Marcia, & Rubin, 1968). They appear the most verbal and most variable of the statuses. At their best, moratorium subjects are active, engaging, and creative; at their worst, they are paralyzed by an inner turmoil of indecisiveness.

Foreclosure

Foreclosure individuals are committed to an occupation and ideology, but this commitment is not one that has been achieved by them. Rather, they have simply accepted whatever identity their parents or parent surrogates had planned for them. They are the most authoritarian of the statuses (Marcia, 1967) and generally impress one with their rigidity. So long as they remain in the type of situation in which their identity was given to them, they operate quite adequately; however, when the situation changes, they give the impression that they would soon be greatly at a loss. In spite of their apparent commitment, foreclosure individuals have not experienced an identity crisis.

Identity Diffusion

Identity diffusion individuals may or may not have had the crisis experience. Regardless, they are not committed. This lack of commitment may be manifested in a "playboy" life style, in which the individual actively seeks noncommitment, shunning any really demanding situations, or it may take the form of a schizoid personality, in which the individual seems aimless, aloof, drifting, and empty. Identity diffusion subjects are notable in the interview for their confusion of goals and the ease with which the interviewer can push them from one seeming "choice" to another. Construct validity for the identity statuses has been established in several studies besides the ones cited above (Cross & Allen, 1969; Marcia & Friedman, 1970; Waterman & Waterman, in press).

Recent work by Bob (1968) and Orlofsky (1970) suggested a fifth identity status—alienated achievement. This grew out of a dissatisfaction with the classification of a certain type of individual as identity diffusion. Although these individuals express a lack of occupational commitment, they seem to have a consistent rationale for it, to which they are strongly committed—almost as if they have formed an ideological commitment that precluded an occupational one. Bob (1968) described these individuals as "the very students who do the most thinking or philosophizing at some point and, hence, become diffuse out of cynical refusal to make commitments [p. 88]." This study attempts to provide some validational evidence for this new status.

According to the developmental scheme proposed by Erikson (1956, 1959, 1963), the achievement of an identity is both the precursor to and partial prerequisite for the establishment of an intimate mode of interpersonal relationships.

> True "engagement" with others is the result and the test of firm self delineation. Where this is still missing, the young individual, when seeking tentative forms of playful intimacy in friendship and competition, in sex play and love, . . . is apt to experience a peculiar strain, as if such tentative engagement might turn into an interpersonal fusion amounting to loss of identity. [Further] it is only after a reasonable sense of identity has been

established that real intimacy with the other sex (or, for that matter, with any other person . . .) is possible [Erikson, 1959, p. 95].

Although a number of theorists have written about intimacy (e.g., Dreyfus, 1967; Fromm, 1956), Yufit (1956) has done the only systematic study within the Eriksonian framework. Using an activities index checklist with college freshmen, Yufit found that the intimate individual was characterized by stability, sociability, and warmth. The isolate, on the other hand, was self-centered, self-doubting, mistrustful, and "at best his relationships with others are formal and stereotyped, lacking in warmth and spontaneity [Yufit, 1956, p. 69]." With especial reference to the present study, Yufit also found that successful resolution of the intimacy versus isolation crisis was most dependent on favorable resolution of three of five previous psychosocial crises: trust, autonomy, and identity. With respect to identity, the isolate was less certain of his vocation than was the intimate. A similar finding—that subjects high in ego identity scored higher on a pencil-and-paper measure of intimacy than subjects low in ego identity—was reported by Simmons (1969).

While Yufit's study provided valuable descriptions of intimates and isolates, it had several shortcomings. First, only those individuals at the extremes of the continuum were studied; the great majority of those with less striking "resolutions" were ignored. Second, his sample was drawn from a very young population—college freshmen. Few, if any, of his subjects could be expected to have resolved the intimacy crisis which Erikson described as occurring during early adulthood. Third, the dependent measures used were nearly identical to the questionnaire criteria that Yufit used to define intimacy and isolation. Finally, the study failed to demonstrate any behavioral differences between these two types of individuals; that is, no predictive validity was established for the two constructs.

In the present study, a semistructured interview covering extent and depth of relationships with men and women, as well as attitudes toward in-terpersonal issues, was constructed. A rating manual using criteria drawn from Erikson's theory (e.g., mutuality, responsibility, commitments to others, and genital maturity) was used to determine the intimacy status, descriptions of which follow.

Intimate

The intimate individual works at developing mutual personal relationships and has several close friends with whom he discusses both his and their personal matters. He has an intimate relationship with one or more girlfriends. The sexual relationship is mutually satisfactory, usually involving intercourse. He shares private worries and problems with his girlfriend and expresses both affectionate and angry feelings toward her. He may or may not have made a lasting commitment, such as marriage, to one woman as of yet. Chances are that he has lived with his girlfriend for a period of time. The intimate subject is generally characterized by a good deal of self-awareness, a genuine interest in others, and the absence of significant defensiveness.

Preintimate

The individual in this status, while he has had some dating experience, has not had an intimate love relationship with a woman. He is aware of the possibilities of relating intimately with women. He has close relationships with other men and often with women friends. The values of the preintimate subject are such as to predispose him to intimacy—respect for the integrity of others, openness, responsibility, and mutuality. He is conflicted about commitment; his relationships are marked by some ambivalence about the risk involved in intimate sexuality. He is somewhat internally preoccupied, and, like the intimate individual, has a good deal of self-awareness, genuine interest in others, and a lack of significant defensiveness.

Stereotyped Relationships

The individual in this status ranges from the moderately constricted and immature type of individual who has yet to get beyond superficial dating relationships to the "Joe College" and playboy types. Generally he has several friends whom he likes, enjoys being with, and sees regularly; however, these relationships lack any significant depth. He dates regularly, sometimes sees the same girl for several months, but becomes no further involved. He enjoys sex and tends to be constantly "on the make," going from one conquest to the next. He treats others more or less as objects, interested more in what he can get from them than in establishing mutually satisfying close relationships. He is characterized by moderate constriction, shallowness, and paucity of self-awareness.

A subtype of this status is pseudointimacy. Generally, the same pattern exists with respect to same-sex peers as in stereotyped relationships; however, the main difference is that the pseudointimate individual has made a more or less lasting commitment to one woman and, in this sense, resembles the intimate individual. However, rather than being truly intimate, he seems only to be going through some of the motions. The relationship remains superficial; he has little sense of responsibility and takes a stance of openness only when it is to his advantage. Both he and his partner treat each other as conveniences, although they may appear to be quite close. The relationship is, as Erikson put it, a "folie á deux," a mutual isolation in the guise of intimacy.

Isolate

The isolate subject is characterized by marked constriction of life space, with the absence of any enduring personal relationships. Though he may have a few peer acquaintances he sees infrequently, rarely does he initiate social contacts. He may date infrequently but usually less than once per month; it is unlikely for him to see the same girl more than two or three times. Any investment of himself in other people seems to threaten the isolate individual with ego "dissolution." The anxiety accompanying close personal contact forces him to withdraw and isolate himself from others. He tends to be anxious and immature and

generally lacking in assertiveness and social skills. He may present himself as bitter and mistrustful or smug and self-satisfied.

Several measures were administered to establish some concurrent and construct validity for the new identity status and for the intimacy statuses. These were (a) three scales from the Edwards Personal Preference Schedule (Edwards, 1954)—Autonomy, Affiliation, and Heterosexuality; (b) an abbreviated version of Yufit's (1956) intimacy–isolation activities checklist; and (c) Ford's Social Desirability scale (1964).

Predictions for the ego identity statuses were as follows: Foreclosure subjects were expected to receive the highest social desirability scores, following Marcia and Friedman's (1970) suggestion that they were unusually sensitive to the social implications of their behavior. Foreclosure subjects, in view of their previously suggested dependence on authority (Marcia, 1966, 1967; Podd, Marcia, & Rubin, 1968), were also expected to obtain the lowest autonomy scores. Identity achievement and moratorium subjects were expected to score high on the intimacy–isolation scale, with identity diffusion subjects scoring the lowest. It was expected that proximity to, or achievement of, an identity would both free the individual and enable him to become intimate. Alienated achievement individuals were also hypothesized to score high on this measure, because of their identity achievement and the apparent importance of interpersonal relationships to them found in interviews described by Bob (1968). No predictions were made for foreclosure subjects on this measure. Alienated achievement subjects were expected to obtain the highest scores on the Affiliation scale, again by virtue of the importance of relationships to them.

Predictions for the intimacy statuses were that intimate and preintimate subjects would score highest on the intimacy scale and lowest on the isolation scale, while the opposite relation would hold for isolate subjects. It was hypothesized that intimate and preintimate individuals would score highest on the intimacy–isolation scale (total score), followed by pseudointimate and stereo-typed relationships subjects, with isolate subjects scoring lowest. In addition, isolate subjects were expected to score lowest on the Edwards Affiliation and Heterosexuality scales. Consistent with Pam's (1970) finding that people in love score lowest on a measure of social desirability, it was predicted that intimate plus pseudointimate subjects would score lower than the other three statuses on the Ford Social Desirability Scale.

The major hypothesis of the current study was that those subjects closest to identity achievement would also be establishing relationships coming closest to fulfilling the criteria for intimacy. Hence, a correspondence between identity statuses and intimacy statuses was predicted.

METHOD

Subjects

Subjects were 53 junior and senior male students at the State University of New York at Buffalo who had volunteered to participate. Each subject was paid $3 for his 2 hours (approximately) of participation.

Ego identity status. This was determined by the standard interview described previously and rated according to Marcia's manual (1964). Interviews and ratings were done by five senior undergraduates enrolled in an ego identity seminar at the State University of New York at Buffalo. The first and third authors each listened to approximately half of the tape-recorded interviews and made independent ratings. Interjudge reliability (between the two independent raters across 47 interviews) was 83%. If there were disagreements between the two judges, the first author acted as referee. No subjects were dropped.

In addition to the standard four-status classification, identity diffusion subjects were rated as either identity diffusion or alienated achievement. Interviewers differentiated between these two sta-

tuses on the basis of the following criteria: At the conclusion of an interview with a subject rated identity diffusion, the subject was questioned about his feelings regarding his apparent lack of commitment. If he did not seem to care one way or the other, or if he became generally anxious and self-demeaning, he was kept in the identity diffusion category. However, if his reaction to this line of questioning included disgust or disillusionment with the "system," the society and its values, etc., and if this seemed part of a consistent world outlook, he was rated as alienated achievment. Frequently, the alienated achievement individual wanted to learn some handicrafts, "get back to the land," or join a commune rather than choose a steady occupation. Generally, he was more engaging and interesting to talk with than the identity diffusion subject. Interjudge reliability for differentiating the alienated achievement from the identity diffusion subject was 86% across 14 interviews.

Intimacy status. This was determined by means of a 20–30-minute semistructured interview evaluating presence or absence of close interpersonal relationships with peers and extent of openness, responsibility, closeness, mutuality and commitment in the subject's most significant relationships. The first part of the interview consisted of questions concerning the following: how close he felt with his male friends; whether he could share personal problems and worries with them, whether he had insight into his friends and himself; if his relationships with friends were enduring; if he had lived with the same friends for several years or if he had constantly changed roommates; what friendship meant to him. The second part, dealing with relationships with girlfriends, was along the same basic lines but more involved. The interview centered around the extent of the subject's dating experience: if he was dating, or if he had ever dated one girl steadily, exclusively. Questions about the specific relationships dealt with feelings of openness, closeness, jealousy, possessiveness, degree of commitment, sexual activity, ability to express and resolve angry feelings, and insight into his own needs, his girlfriend's needs, problems in the relationship, etc.

Three major intimacy statuses were defined with respect to the above criteria: intimacy, stereotyped relationships, and isolation. In addition, two other substatuses were defined: preintimacy, a substatus of the intimacy status, and pseudointimacy, a substatus of the stereotyped relationships status. Subjects were assigned two ratings—one for relationships with men, the other for relationships with women—and also a combined rating. If the two ratings were different, greater emphasis was placed on the second rating.

Interviews were done by the first and third authors. Interjudge reliability between the two independent raters for 32 randomly selected interviews was computed. For the three major statuses (intimacy plus preintimacy, stereotyped relationships plus pseudointimacy, and isolation), the percentage of agreement was 94%. For the five statuses, reliability was 81%. In addition, a third rater (a psychology student), unfamiliar with the identity statuses, was trained to rate intimacy interviews. On 20 randomly selected interviews, her percentage of agreement for the three major statuses was 85% with one of the raters and 80% with the other rater. For the five statuses, the percentage of agreement was 85% with one rater and 70% with the other.

Intimacy–isolation scale. This measure was an abridged version of Yufit's activities index checklist (1956). There were 20 intimacy items (e.g., leading an active social life, talking with people about their innermost problems and difficulties, being constant in the subject's affections) and 20 isolation items (e.g., avoiding excitement or emotional tension, remaining unnoticed in a group, picking someone else's argument to pieces) embedded in 30 filler items. Three scores were derived for each subject; intimacy score, isolation score, and total score, computed by the formula: Intimacy + ([20 − Isolation]).

Edwards Personal Preference Schedule scales. (Edwards, 1954). Items from the Autonomy, Affiliation, and Heterosexuality scales were administered. All 28 items from each scale were used, but since the items of the 15 Edwards subscales are placed against each other in a forced-choice format, there were 75 two-choice items in all.

Social desirability. Subjects were administered a 40-item forced-choice social desirability questionnaire developed by Ford (1964). The items from this scale were embedded in the items from the Edwards scales.

Procedure

On the first of two sessions, subjects were administered the pencil-and-paper questionnaires in groups of about 20. They were given the intimacy–isolation scale first, followed by the combined Social Desirability and Autonomy, Affiliation, and Heterosexuality scales. Subjects were then scheduled for the second session, occurring from 3 days to 2 weeks after the initial session. Here, each was given two interviews, the first for identity, the second for intimacy, by two different experimenters.

RESULTS

Ego Identity Status and Edwards Subscales

Significant differences among the statuses were obtained on the Autonomy scale ($F = 3.19$, $df = 4/48$, $p < .02$). Foreclosure subjects obtained the lowest scores as predicted ($t = 2.14$, $df = 51$, $p < .025$, one-tailed).[2] An additional finding was that alienated achievement subjects scored higher than subjects in the other statuses ($t = 3.08$, $df = 51$, $p < .01$, two-tailed). A one-way analysis of variance on the Affiliation scale was not significant, although t tests suggested that some differences might exist among the statuses. Alienated

---

[2]Where specifically predicted, the significance levels for t are one-tailed; all other significance levels are two-tailed.

achievement subjects obtained higher scores than subjects in the other statuses combined, as predicted ($t = 1.78$, $df = 51$, $p < .05$, one-tailed). Scores for this status were also higher than for the identity achievement status ($t = 1.90$, $df = 17$, $p < .05$, one-tailed). No significant differences among the statuses were obtained on the Heterosexuality scale.

Ego Identity Status and Social Desirability

Significant differences were found among the statuses ($F = 2.80$, $df = 4/48$, $p < .05$). As predicted, foreclosure subjects obtained higher scores than subjects in the other statuses ($t = 2.99$, $df = 51$, $p < .005$, one-tailed). In addition there was a nonsignificant tendency for the alienated achievement status to score lower than the other statuses ($t = 1.75$, $df = 51$, $p < .10$, two-tailed).

Ego Identity Status and the Intimacy–Isolation Scale

Mean scores of the identity statuses on the intimacy–isolation scale are presented in Table 1. Statuses differed significantly on the total score of this scale (Intimacy + [20 − Isolation]) ($F = 2.66$, $df = 4/48$, $p < .05$). The hypothesis that identity diffusion subjects would score lowest on this measure was supported ($t = 3.22$, $df = 51$,

TABLE 1
Mean Scores of the Identity Statuses on the Intimacy–Isolation Scale

Status	n	Intimacy scale mean	Isolation scale mean	Intimacy-isolation scale M	SD
Identity achievement	11	12.73	6.18	26.55	4.97
Alienated achievement	8	12.13	4.75	27.38	2.06
Moratorium	11	12.82	6.73	26.09	3.42
Foreclosure	11	13.64	7.73	26.82	4.49
Identity diffusion	12	9.83	8.17	21.67	6.62

Note. For the intimacy–isolation scale, the total score = (Intimacy + [20 − Isolation]). $F = 2.66$, $df = 4/48$, $p < .05$ (total score).

$p < .005$, one-tailed). The findings on the isolation subscale parallel these with the additional finding that alienated achievement subjects scored lower than subjects in the other statuses combined ($t = 2.33$, $df = 51$, $p < .05$, two-tailed). These results suggest that identity diffusion subjects are least intimate and most isolated from others, while alienated achievement subjects are least isolated.

Intimacy Status and the Intimacy-Isolation Scale

Mean scores for the intimacy statuses on the intimacy–isolation scale are presented in Table 2. Statuses differed significantly on the total score of this scale ($F = 4.50$, $df = 4/48$, $p < .005$). All hypotheses with respect to this measure were supported. Intimate plus preintimate subjects scored significantly higher than pseudointimate and stereotyped relationships subjects ($t = 2.58$, $df = 44$, $p < .01$, one-tailed), who in turn scored higher than isolate subjects ($t = 2.06$, $df = 26$, $p < .025$, one-tailed). Intimate plus preintimate statuses obtained higher scores than did the isolate status ($t = 3.93$, $df = 30$, $p < .001$, one-tailed), and higher than the other statuses combined ($t = 3.28$, $df = 51$, $p < .005$, one-tailed). Isolate subjects scored lowest on this scale ($t = 3.32$, $df = 51$, $p < .005$, one-tailed) and highest on the isolation subscale ($t = 2.88$, $df = 51$, $p < .005$, one-tailed).

Intimacy Status and Social Desirability

No significant differences were found among the statuses on this measure. The hypothesis that intimate plus pseudointimate subjects would score lowest was not supported ($t = 1.25$, $df = 51$, $p < .15$, one-tailed), although the means were in the predicted direction.

Intimacy Status and Edwards Subscales

Statuses differed significantly on the Heterosexuality scale ($F = 2.67$, $df = 4/48$, $p < .05$). As predicted, isolate subjects obtained the lowest scores ($t = 1.92$, $df = 51$, $p < .05$, one-tailed).

TABLE 2
Mean Scores of the Intimacy Statuses on the Intimacy–Isolation Scale

Status	n	Intimacy scale mean	Isolation scale mean	Intimacy–Isolation scale	
				M	SD
Intimate	14	12.93	6.07	27.57 27.76	4.13 3.38
Preintimate	11	13.91	5.91	28.00	2.28
Pseudointimate	12	12.42	7.25	25.17 24.71	5.39 4.42
Stereotyped relationships	9	10.67	6.56	24.11	2.85
Isolate	7	9.57	9.57	20.00	7.07

Note. For the intimacy isolation scale, the total score = (Intimacy + [20 − Isolation]); $F = 4.50$, $df = 4/48$, $p < .005$ (total score).

In addition, pseudointimate plus stereotyped relationships subjects were found to score higher than subjects in the other statuses combined ($t = 2.94$, $df = 51$, $p < .01$, two-tailed). A one-way analysis of variance on the Autonomy scale was not significant ($F = 1.83$, $df = 4/48$, $p < .14$). However, t tests suggested some differences among the statuses. Intimate plus preintimate subjects obtained higher scores than isolate subjects ($t = 2.16$, $df = 30$, $p < .05$, two-tailed) and higher scores than subjects in the other statuses combined ($t = 2.35$, $df = 51$, $p < .05$, two-tailed). No significant differences were found among the statuses on the Affiliation scale.

Ego Identity Statuses and Intimacy Statuses

Frequencies and proportions of each identity status in the intimacy statuses are presented in Table 3. Inspection of these frequencies suggests that the identity and intimacy statuses were related. In order to perform a test of significance, the intimacy statuses were divided roughly between high intimacy (intimate plus preintimate) and low intimacy (pseudointimate, stereotyped relationships, and isolate). An overall chi-square analysis was significant ($x^2 = 26.62$, $df = 4$, $p < .001$). Individual comparisons revealed that identity achievement, moratorium, and alienated achievement subjects (high-identity statuses) were each significantly higher in intimacy status than foreclosure or identity diffusion subjects (low-identity statuses).

Fisher exact probability tests revealed no significant differences between identity achievement and alienated achievement subjects in intimacy status. However, identity achievement and moratorium subjects differed somewhat, in that achievement individuals were predominantly in the intimate status and moratorium individuals were predominantly in the preintimate status ($p < .07$). No significant differences were found between foreclosure and identity diffusion subjects. The diffusion status did have a higher proportion of isolate subjects than the other statuses combined ($p < .05$). Noteworthy were the differences between the alienated achievement and the identity diffusion statuses. Nearly 90% of the alienated

TABLE 3
Frequencies and Proportion of Identity Statuses in Intimacy Statuses

Identity	Intimate (intimate + preintimate)	Stereotyped relationships (pseudointimate + stereotyped relationships)	Isolate
Identity achievement	(7) .82 (2)	(2) .18 (0)	(0) .00
Alienated achievement	(4) .88 (3)	(0) .12 (1)	(0) .00
Moratorium	(2) .64 (5)	(0) .27 (3)	(1) .09
Foreclosure	(1) .18 (1)	(4) .64 (3)	(2) .18
Identity diffusion	(0) .00 (0)	(6) .67 (2)	(4) .33

Note. Frequencies are in parentheses.

achievement subjects were in either the intimate or preintimate status. In contrast, none of the identity diffusion subjects were in intimate or preintimate statuses; 100% of these subjects were in either the pseudointimate, stereotyped relationships, or isolate statuses.

DISCUSSION

The new identity status, alienated achievement, stood out as a distinct group on several measures. The low social desirability scores of this status suggest a lack of significant defensiveness and a low need for approval. In addition, these subjects scored highest on need for autonomy. These findings are consistent with a picture of individuals who are self-reliant and defiant toward the social order and conventional ways of doing things. At the same time, they seem least isolated from others and tend to have the strongest needs for affiliation of all the statuses. The positive findings for this status suggest that the alienated achievement individual probably equals the identity achievement individual in ego strength and, in a sense, in degree of identity resolution. The main difference seems to lie in the areas in which these two types of individuals resolve the identity crisis. It is suggested here that the alienated achievement individual bases his identity more on his style of relating to other people than on matters of occupational and ideological choice. His ideology consists largely of his attitudes and values concerning intimate interpersonal involvement. It is as if he chooses to forgo the identity crisis in favor of the intimacy crisis, his stance toward the latter becoming the basis of his identity.

Identity diffusion subjects were least intimate and most isolated in their interests. Clearly, the alienated achievement status and the identity diffusion status comprise two distinct groups.

As predicted, foreclosure subjects had the highest need for social approval with the defensiveness which this betokens. This finding lends some support to Marcia and Friedman's (1970) suggestion of "plus-getting" on personality tests by foreclosure subjects. In addition, foreclosure individuals were also least autonomous, consistent with their not having broken parental ties.

The positive findings obtained for the intimacy statuses support the validity of these constructs. Most noteworthy were the findings on the Yufit intimacy–isolation scale. The criteria used for determining intimacy status were somewhat different from Yufit's intimacy–isolation criteria.[3] Despite these differences, there was close agreement between the two measures. Intimate plus preintimate subjects scored highest on Yufit's scale, isolate subjects scored lowest. However, the interview goes beyond Yufit's definition of the two poles, intimates and isolates, and defines a middle range of intimacy crisis resolution comprising the pseudointimate and stereotyped relationships statuses described previously. Subjects in these latter two statuses scored highest on the Heterosexuality scale.

Whereas subjects in the stereotyped relationships and pseudointimate statuses had high need for heterosexuality, the isolate subjects seemed retarded in the development of heterosexual interest. This is consistent with the marked constriction of life space and inhibition of impulses characteristic of the isolate individual.

Intimate and preintimate subjects were the most intimate, the least isolated, the most autonomy seeking, and tended to have the highest (though nonsignificant) need for affiliation. These findings are seen as consistent with the rationale underlying the constructs. In much the same way as achieving an identity makes intimate engagement with others possible, a sense of oneself as autonomous is a prerequisite for authentic intimacy. Hence, those who were most intimate were also most autonomous.

The intimacy statuses appear to be reliably observable, valid constructs. Differences among the three major statuses (intimate plus preintimate,

---

[3]The latter are concerned with assessing the degree of impulse expression and the tendency of the subject to be outgoing and friendly or aloof, hostile, and brooding in relation to other people.

stereotyped relationships plus pseudointimate, and isolate) were found on several of the pencil-and-paper measures. Missing were significant differences within these statuses. That is, intimate subjects could not be distinguished from preintimate subjects, nor could pseudointimate subjects be distinguished from stereotyped relationships subjects on the dependent measures.

The failure to find intrastatus differences might well indicate that the preintimate status should not be conceptually separated from the intimate, and that the pseudointimate status should not be distinguished from the stereotyped relationships status. However, the lack of significant differences may be a function of the type of dependent measures used, that is, pencil-and-paper questionnaires. These scales measure attitudes and interests more than anything else. It is in precisely these areas that intrastatus differences are unlikely to emerge. For example, the values of the preintimate individual mirror those of the intimate; little wonder that his responses on pencil-and-paper tests mirror those of the intimate. In order for differences between these two statuses to become apparent, behavioral measures are probably necessary.

The hypotheses concerning the relationship between the psychosocial states of identity and intimacy were confirmed. Identity achievement subjects were generally found to have successful, mature, intimate relationships. Moratorium subjects, for the most part, were found to be similar to achievement subjects and were predominant in the preintimate status. Most of them had intimate relationships with male friends; however, only a few of them had yet ventured into enduring heterosexual love relationships. The findings for both identity achievement and moratorium subjects relate to a basic premise of the study, that genuine intimacy generally occurs only after a reasonable sense of identity has been established.

Foreclosure subjects were stereotyped in their relationships. Many had yet to get beyond formal dating relationships, although there were some who were involved in enduring heterosexual relationships. However, their relationships usually lacked the depth and genuine closeness characteristic of the achievement individual's relationships. The same was true for the identity diffusion status. These individuals were either stereotyped or pseudointimate in their relationships, or else they were isolate, with no close friends and no dating experience.

In contrast were the alienated achievement subjects who most closely resembled individuals in the other high-identity statuses. Like identity achievement and many of the moratorium subjects, their relationships with friends and girlfriends were generally characterized by openness and genuine, noncontrolling closeness.

This study was a beginning. It defined a new identity status. It also operationalized the intimacy–isolation crisis and attempted to study the relationship between this stage and the identity crisis stage which precedes it. While a positive relationship was found, there remain a number of loose ends. The criteria for defining the intimacy status constructs can be made more explicit and involve less "clinical judgment" in categorization of subjects. More systematic study of the interpersonal attitudes characteristic of the various identity and intimacy statuses is needed. Finally, the intimacy statuses must be compared on behavioral measures in order to properly assess and extend their validity.

REFERENCES

Bob, S. R. An investigation of the relationship between identity status, cognitive style and stress. Unpublished doctoral dissertation, State University of New York at Buffalo, 1968.

Cross, H. J., & Allen, J. G. Antecedents of developmental changes in ego identity status. Paper presented at the meeting of the Eastern Psychological Association, Philadelphia, April 1969.

Dreyfus, E. A. The search for intimacy. *Adolescence*, 1967, *2*, (5), 25–40.

Edwards, A. L. *Edwards Personal Preference Schedule*. New York: Psychological Corporation, 1954.

Erikson, E. H. The problem of ego identity. *Journal of the American Psychoanalytic Association*, 1956, *4*, 56–121.

Erikson, E. H. *Identity and the life cycle*. (*Psychological issues*, No. 1) New York: International Universities Press, 1959.

Erikson, E. H. *Childhood and society*. (2nd ed.) New York: Norton, 1963.

Ford, L. H. A forced-choice, acquiescence-free, social desirability (defensiveness) scale. *Journal of Consulting Psychology*, 1964, *28*, 475.

Fromm, E. *The art of loving*. New York: Harper & Row, 1956.

Marcia, J. E. Determination and construct validity of ego identity status. Unpublished doctoral dissertation, Ohio State University, 1964.

Marcia, J. E. Development and validation of ego-identity status. *Journal of Personality and Social Psychology*, 1966, *3*, 551–558.

Marcia, J. E. Ego identity status: Relationship to change in self-esteem, "general maladjustment" and authoritarianism. *Journal of Personality*, 1967, *35*, 118–133.

Marcia, J. E., & Friedman, M. L. Ego identity status in college women. *Journal of Personality*, 1970, *2*, 249–263.

Orlofsky, J. L. The development of a methodology for the study of ego identity. Unpublished manuscript, State University of New York at Buffalo, 1970.

Pam, A. A field study: Psychological factors in college courtship. Unpublished doctoral dissertation, State University of New York at Buffalo, 1970.

Podd, M., Marcia, J. E., & Rubin, R. The effects of ego identity status and partner perception on a prisoner's dilemma game. *Journal of Social Psychology*, 1968, *82*, 117–126.

Rasmussen, J. E. Relationship of ego identity to psychosocial effectiveness. *Psychological Reports*, 1964, *15*, 815–825.

Simmons, D. Development of an objective measure of identity achievement status. Paper presented at the meeting of the Western Psychological Association, Vancouver, British Columbia, June 1969.

Waterman, C. K., Beubel, M. E., & Waterman, A. S. Relationship between resolution of the identity crisis and outcomes of previous psychosocial crises. *Proceedings of the 78th Annual Convention of the American Psychological Association*, 1970, *5*, 467–468. (Summary)

Waterman, A., & Waterman, C. The relationship between ego identity and satisfaction with college. *Journal of Educational Research*, in press.

Yufit, R. Intimacy and isolation: Some behavioral and psychodynamic correlates (Doctoral dissertation, University of Chicago, 1956). Ann Arbor, Mich.: University Microfilms, BF698, 9 S6Y8.

STUDY QUESTIONS

1. Of the instruments used in this study, which ones seem most open ended and which seem most restricted?

2. The decision to code interview data for a new identity status, alienated achievement, grew out of dissatisfaction with the results of a previous interview-scoring system. Could a fixed-alternative questionnaire format have led to the same decision? What does your answer suggest about the relative strengths and weaknesses of open-ended and closed-response formats?

3. The investigators mention a number of different kinds of reliability and validity. Which forms of reliability and validity seem applicable to both the open-ended and the fixed-alternative instruments? Which are more relevant to just one type of instrument?

4. Now that Marcia and his associates have accomplished some preliminary work on identity and intimacy, what would be the advantages and disadvantages at this point in time of trying to formulate fixed-alternative questionnaires (objective tests) to measure identity and intimacy statuses?

5. How would you go about trying to validate a questionnaire measure of these statuses?

EXERCISE

Developing an Interview or a Questionnaire

As is true with most procedures, one of the best ways of learning how to develop an interview or questionnaire is to try it. Although each student can tackle the job of constructing questions individually, the shared critical judgment of colleagues is probably the best context in which to develop an instrument. For this exercise, we recommend that the class be divided into at least three or four research teams that can then proceed according to the following steps.

1. All groups should formulate a common objective. A good issue might be the concept of intimacy as discussed in the article by Orlofsky and his colleagues. The advantage of using this issue is that the article provides definitions for categories of intimacy.

2. Each group should select a different format for the construction of questions from the following possibilities: (1) fixed-alternative interview questions, (2) open-ended interview questions plus preliminary categories for coding responses, (3) fixed-alternative questionnaire items of the multiple-choice variety, and (4) yes/no or true/false fixed-alternative questionnaire questions. Each group should develop at least ten questions.

3. Each group should review the questions prepared by another group, with, for example, the groups developing interview items exchanging their sets of questions and the groups developing questionnaires exchanging their sets. At this stage, groups should review each other's work with respect to three considerations: (1) relevance to the objective, (2) clarity and avoidance of jargon, and (3) social desirability and response bias. Next, a discussion of each set of questions by the whole class might be useful as a means of helping the groups revise and modify their original sets of questions.

4. If feasible, the different sets of questions should be administered to a number of groups of subjects and the different responses compared for similarity or discrepancy.

5. As a class, replicate a portion of the Orlofsky study by administering both one set of questions and a simple social-desirability scale, either the one developed by Ford and administered by Orlofsky and his colleagues or the Crowne-Marlowe (1964) scale. Compare the class' findings with those reported in the article.

ANNOTATED BIBLIOGRAPHY

Babad, E. Y. Personality correlates of susceptibility to biasing information. *Journal of Personality and Social Psychology*, 1979, *37*, 195–202.

Subjects were divided into high-bias and no-bias groups based on their scores for two pictures allegedly drawn by one high-status child and one disadvantaged child. Self-descriptions from high-bias individuals seemed to reflect a need system suggestive of dogmatic personality types. In a second study supporting this notion that high-bias individuals are more dogmatic than no-bias individuals, high-bias subjects responded more extremely to questions concerning their political ideology.

Barnett, M. A., Howard, J. A., King, L. M., & Dino, G. A. Antecendents of empathy: Retrospective accounts of early socialization. *Personality and Social Psychology Bulletin*, 1980, *6*, 361–365.

Undergraduates scoring at the extremes on an empathy scale completed a questionnaire tapping their early socialization experiences. A number of differences were found between the high- and low-empathy groups, as well as between males and females.

Holahan, C. K., & Holahan, C. J. The relationship of psychological masculinity and feminity and gender to personalization and social emphasis in environmental schematization. *Personality and Social Psychology Bulletin*, 1979, *5*, 231–235.

In this study, men and women scoring as masculine, feminine, androgynous, and undifferentiated were asked to describe their current and childhood environments. Androgynous subjects tended to personalize their environments and emphasize social dimensions (for example, friendships) more than other subjects.

Rubin, Z. Self-disclosure in dating couples: Sex roles and the ethic of openness. *Journal of Marriage and the Family*, 1980, *42*, 305–317.

In this questionnaire study of 231 college student dating couples, it was found that women revealed more than men about their greatest fears and that women in general were more likely to be identified as the more highly disclosing partner. Both men and women in couples with egalitarian sex-role attitudes disclosed more to each other than those in couples with traditional sex-role attitudes.

Sadd, S., Miller, F. D., & Zeitz, B. Sex roles and achievement conflicts. *Personality and Social Psychology Bulletin*, 1979, *5*, 352–355.

Male and female subjects completed questionnaires concerning their sex-role orientation, fear of success, and self-deprecation and insecurity. Statistical analyses indicated that feminity scores were not related to fear of success or to self-deprecation and insecurity. Masculinity scores were negatively related to fear of success in both men and women.

Steil, J., Tuchman, B., & Deutsch, M. An exploratory study of the meanings of injustice and frustration. *Personality and Social Psychology Bulletin*, 1978, *4*, 393–398.

High school students responded to a variety of measures—including word associations, incident descriptions, and drawings—that were designed to assess differences in the experience of justice and frustration. The data indicated that the sense of injustice to another—as compared to frustration to another—was personally experienced by subjects as more painful, more immoral, and more harmful to security as well as making them feel uglier, angrier, and more motivated to do something about it.

ADDITIONAL SOURCES

Brickman, P., Coates, D., & Janoff-Bulman, R. Lottery winners and accident victims: Is happiness relative? *Journal of Personality and Social Psychology*, 1978, *36*, 917–927.

Campos, F., & Thurow, C. Attributions of moods and symptoms to the menstrual cycle. *Personality and Social Psychology Bulletin*, 1978, *4*, 272–276.

Dion, K. K., & Dion, K. L. Self esteem and romantic love. *Journal of Personality*, 1975, *43*, 39–57.

Feild, H. S. Attitudes toward rape: A comparative analysis of police, rapists, crisis counselors and citizens. *Journal of Personality and Social Psychology*, 1978, *36*, 156–179.

Haan, N. Two moralities in action contexts: Relationships to thought, ego regulation, and development. *Journal of Personality and Social Psychology*, 1978, *36*, 286–305.

Hoyt, M. F., & Raven, B. H. Birth order and the 1971 Los Angeles earthquake. *Journal of Personality and Social Psychology*, 1973, *28*, 123–128.

Martin, D. G. *Personality: Effective and ineffective.* Monterey, Calif: Brooks/Cole, 1976.

Mehrabian, A. Affiliation as a function of attitude discrepancy with another and arousal-seeking tendency. *Journal of Personality*, 1975, *43*, 582–590.

Parmellee, P., & Werner, C. Lonely losers: Stereotypes of single dwellers. *Personality and Social Psychology Bulletin*, 1978, *4*, 292–295.

CHAPTER

8

Personality Tests

How do psychologists study personality? If you had been asked that question before you began reading this book, your guess might very well have been "with personality tests." Tests are probably the measurement devices most commonly associated with the study of personality, and they can be useful devices indeed. Taking a test can be scary, aggravating, or fun, depending on the difficulty of the test and the intended uses of the results. Developing and administering your own test and interpreting responses to it can also be scary, aggravating, or fun, depending on how much you know about test construction and how difficult is the construct you are attempting to assess. There is nothing magical about personality tests, either as they are developed by "experts" or as they may be developed by you, the fledgling researcher. Like other psychological research techniques, tests require an under-standing of measurement principles and careful attention to such classic concerns as reliability and validity.

To begin, we ask that you take the test in Box 8-1. Find a piece of paper, write the numbers 1 to 5 in a column, and then consider each statement in Box 8-1 to determine the extent to which you agree with it. As indicated in the instructions, you should rate items according to the following scale: 1=strongly agree; 2=mildly agree; 3=agree and disagree equally; 4= mildly disagree; and 5=strongly disagree. Much of the material in this chapter will be directed at an analysis of this test and at the chapter selection by Rotter, which describes its development and validation. We believe that your completion of the test before reading the rest of the chapter will help make our discussion of personality tests in general clearer and more meaningful.

BOX 8-1 General-Opinion Survey

This is a questionnaire to determine the attitudes and beliefs of different people on a variety of statements. Please answer the statements by giving as true a picture of your own beliefs as possible. Be sure to read each item carefully and show your beliefs by marking the appropriate number on your answer card (or answer sheet).

If you strongly agree with an item, fill in the space numbered 1. Mark the space numbered 2 if you mildly agree with the item. That is, mark 2 if you think the item is generally more true than untrue according to your beliefs. *Fill in the space numbered 3 if you feel the item is about equally true as untrue. Fill in the space numbered 4 if you mildly disagree with the item.* That is, mark 4 if you feel the item is more untrue than true. *If you strongly disagree with an item, fill in the space numbered 5.*

1. Strongly agree
2. Mildly agree
3. Agree and disagree equally
4. Mildly disagree
5. Strongly disagree

Please be sure to fill in the spaces completely and to erase completely any marks to be changed. Make no extra marks on either the answer card or the questionnaire.

1. In dealing with strangers one is better off to be cautious until they have provided evidence that they are trustworthy.
2. Parents can usually be relied upon to keep their promises.
3. Parents and teachers are likely to say what they believe themselves and not just what they think is good for the child to hear.
4. Most elected public officials are sincere in their campaign promises.
5. Even though we have reports in newspapers, radio, and television, it is hard to get objective accounts of public events.

Taken from Interpersonal Test Scale *by Julian Rotter. Reprinted by permission.*

The items to which you responded were selected from Rotter's test of interpersonal trust. In contrast to the open-ended projective measures described in Chapter 6 and discussed again later in this chapter, Rotter's measure is an *objective test,*—that is, the test is highly structured and provides a limited set of response choices. Other types of objective tests with which you are familiar include true/false and multiple-choice instruments. Whereas projective tests tend to be much less structured and to elicit responses in subjects' own words, objective tests direct subjects to choose among a limited set of response choices. The scoring of projective tests such as the Rorschach test generally requires training to ensure the validity of the qualitative evaluation or subjective interpretation of results. By contrast, objective tests are characterized by standardized and predefined scoring systems that make the process of scoring

responses and arriving at a total score essentially mechanical.

While objective tests pose few problems of interscorer agreement, it should be noted that no test is completely objective—that is, no test is totally free of interpretative, and thus potentially biasing, activity on the part of test developers and users. One of the most widely used clinical and research tests is the Minnesota Multiphasic Personality Inventory (MMPI). Items on this inventory constitute 14 standard scales (for example, depression and paranoia scales), although researchers frequently use MMPI items to develop and validate new scales. In order to interpret the responses of any single subject or client, the researcher or clinician must examine patterns of scores. In the effort to determine the meaning of the subject's performance, the test developer or test user imposes his or her preconceptions on the subject's total test results.

Moreover, as you will see later in this chapter, the objective-response format does not free objective tests from their own particular problems of reliability and validity.

The choice of one particular type of test—for example, objective—over another type of test—say, projective—is influenced by the investigator's prior theoretical assumptions. Frequently, objective tests are associated with the perspective known as *trait psychology*, discussed briefly in Chapter 1. This perspective incorporates one of the traditional assumptions of personality theory: that the individual's characteristics are relatively enduring and that they do not change in significant ways from one set of circumstances to another. In other words, it is assumed that people "carry around" a consistent personal style and a set of relatively stable characteristics. Trait psychologists generally assume that while all human beings might possess the same basic characteristics, individuals differ in the degree or amount of the various characteristics (traits) they exhibit. Aggressiveness, for example, might be a fundamental human trait, but some people seem consistently more aggressive than others. If we can measure the amount of a particular trait such as aggressiveness or anxiety that is typical of a particular individual, we should then be able to predict with considerable accuracy how that individual will behave in a variety of circumstances.

Many psychologists—most notably Mischel (1968; 1973)—argue that the assumption of enduring traits or consistency across situations has not been supported by empirical evidence. Others (for example, Block, 1961; Epstein, 1976) maintain that when research is carefully done and the data are analyzed appropriately, there is indeed good evidence of individual consistency. The continuing controversy as to whether the person or the situation is the major source of individual behavior has led to the interactionist formulations mentioned in Chapter 1 and later in this chapter.

Objective tests are not only related to trait-theory approaches to human functioning. Social-learning theorists such as Julian Rotter argue that much of the consistency of human behavior stems from the role of *expectancies* in human behavior—that is, from the tendency of people to behave in ways that reflect their past experience in obtaining reinforcements. Rotter developed a scale for measuring internal versus external locus of control of reinforcements in order to assess expectations about the extent to which control over reinforcements is a function of one's own efforts or of events that are beyond one's influence. Rotter's interpersonal-trust scale, sampled in Box 8-1 and described in the chapter selection, was developed to assess the extent to which individuals expect that others will behave in trustworthy ways.

CONSTRUCTING OBJECTIVE TESTS

The steps to be followed in constructing an objective test are reasonably straightforward. Since typically the purpose of the test is to measure particular characteristics of the individual (for example, traits, attitudes, or expectancies), the first and possibly most important step is to define carefully the characteristics to be measured. The definition, once it is satisfactory, leads to the next step, which is the formulation of a series of questions or statements, usually called *items,* that represent the defined properties of the trait. This procedure is known as an *a priori approach* to test construction because the investigator begins with items assumed to assess the characteristic in question and only later gathers the data necessary to determine whether the items are really valid representations of the characteristic. The first step in test construction is illustrated in the Rotter article included in this chapter.

Part of the process of item development involves deciding what kind of numerical scale should be built into the response alternatives.

Rotter's interpersonal-trust measure is a fairly typical objective measure in its use of a Likert scale—that is, a continuous ordinal scale for assessing attitudes ranging from the negative through the positive (or vice versa). In the case of the interpersonal-trust test, we have a five-point Likert scale, ranging from agree strongly to disagree strongly. It would have been equally possible to have a three-point scale (1 = agree, 2 = unsure, 3 = disagree) or a seven-point scale (1 = disagree strongly, 2 = disagree moderately, 3 = disagree a little, 4 = neither agree nor disagree, 5 = agree a little, 6 = agree moderately, 7 = agree strongly). The measure is also fairly typical in its *additive* nature. That is, scores expressing trust in somewhat different institutions (for instance, family, government, society) are added together to form a total score representing a generalized tendency to trust. This additive component of the interpersonal-trust scale has been a source of criticism from researchers who argue that trust in governmental institutions represents a separate attitude or tendency from trust in one's friends and family (for example, Mirels, 1970.)

Typically, the preliminary items used in scale development are somewhat rough and are only a first approximation of the final set of items. One might think of the next several stages as analogous to the steps taken by a blacksmith who has forged the separate pieces of a machine and now must refine and test them to ensure that they fit together and regularly do the job for which they were intended. In order to refine preliminary test items, one might ask several people not associated with the project to be "judges"—that is, to read the items, eliminate poor or confusing sentence structure, and cull out redundant or duplicate items.

These steps can result in a scale that is both consistent and comprehensible. Yet unless additional procedures are applied, whether the items are actually relevant to the trait being measured remains unclear. At the beginning of the discussion on the derivation of scale items, we suggested that the most important step might be careful definition of the trait. For research purposes, one of the most important uses of assessment is to examine a theoretical issue; indeed, the care with which the element of theory is defined is crucial. Yet, even with the most tightly reasoned theoretical principle, one must still translate the elements of the theory into test items. To write items that seem to represent the trait or theory being examined is chancy at best. In fact, this step is usually the only one taken by popular-magazine writers who construct tests purporting to answer such questions as "How strong is your marriage?" or, "Are you a dominant person?" To assess the theoretical relevance of the items that have been written, one might again call upon judges who are expert in the theory being tested, asking them to indicate the degree to which the items represent the theory. In this judgmental, or *rational*, method, agreement among experts is at least a step toward confirmation that the items are actually relevant to the trait.

The remaining item pool can now be administered to a group of subjects. This step leads to the technical but simple procedure called *item analysis*. After the responses have been collected, one can determine the contribution that each item makes to the scale by correlating the scores on each item with the total. (The word *scale* here simply means the total group of items that are intended to measure the trait.) Those items that make a low or a negative contribution (have a low correlation) to the total are dropped. After following these steps, the test constructor has a group of items that are clearly stated, judged to be theoretically relevant, and make a contribution to the total scale. Also by these means, he or she has presumably reduced the original item pool, a step that is important for efficiency and ease of administration. As you will read in the chapter selection, Rotter used a sample of 547 introductory psychology students to help him in the revision of his original a priori form of the interpersonal-trust scale. Correlations of item scores with a total-scale score and with social-desirability scores resulted in the dropping of three items.

Another procedure that can be used to derive scale items is often called the *criterion method*. This procedure is used to ascertain whether or not items discriminate among groups who are known to differ on some important attribute. The clearest illustration of this method can be found in the steps used to validate the Strong Vocational Interest Blank (Strong, 1943). Strong compared professional and other occupational groups (for example, physicians, lawyers, morticians, and so on), called *criterion groups*, with people in general on a pool of items that represented interests or likes and dislikes. The items did not necessarily have a logical connection with the occupations, but the procedure was based on the assumption that people in particular occupations will have similar interests even beyond those of work and career. In this method, those items that discriminate the criterion group from people in general are formed into a scale. The Strong Inventory has recently been revised by David Campbell (Campbell, 1971) largely to account for the changing roles, lifestyles, and occupations of American women.

Finally, the method of *factor analysis*, in which each item is correlated with all other items, can be used to determine whether the scales of an existing test are internally consistent. Factor analysis is used to derive scales by locating those items that have high intercorrelations with each other (called factors or clusters) and that have low intercorrelations with other items. Cattell (1965), Eysenck (1953), and Guilford (1959) have probably done the most extensive work with this method.

Even with all or most of these steps completed, we are still not assured that the scale will function in the same way each time (reliability); nor do we have much empirical evidence

to indicate that the scale measures what we have undertaken to measure (validity). Objective tests, like all the other procedures used to collect data about human functioning, have their own particular problems of reliability and validity. As with the other procedures, we must consider these problems carefully if we are to have any confidence in our findings.

RELIABILITY

The most common approaches to assessing the reliability of objective tests are the test-retest, split-half, and equivalent-forms methods. Each of these approaches to reliability provides somewhat different information about the scale or test. Whenever you read an article describing the use of a new measure, check to see what kinds of information about reliability are provided. If you are developing a measure of your own, determine which kinds of information about reliability you can obtain.

The split-half and equivalent-forms approaches to reliability provide information about the consistency among items or the content of the scale. If two *equivalent forms* of a particular measure are available, the reliability question is: Do the two forms yield essentially the same scores for the same person? If Rotter had developed two alternative forms of his interpersonal-trust test, would a person scoring high on one score high on the other? If scores on the two forms correlated very highly in a sample of subjects, we would say that there was evidence of good reliability across the two forms of the test.

With the split-half reliability method, the question becomes Do people taking the test achieve essentially the same score on one half of the test (for example, on the even-numbered items) as they do on the other half (on the odd-numbered items)? In general, the more homogeneous the content of the domain being measured, the less error is to be expected from item to item. In discussing the somewhat low split-half reliability coefficients for his interpersonal-trust measure, Rotter reminds us that his test is additive, consisting of items sampling a variety of trust domains rather than one homogeneous area.

While the information obtained about the interpersonal consistency (or content reliability) of a measure is very important, test-retest information about the reliability of a measure over time is essential. The basic assumption of trait theory is that traits are enduring characteristics; thus, the test-retest measure is a relatively direct assessment of this assumption.

It is extremely rare for an identical test score to be achieved time after time by the same individual. Many factors, such as degree of fatigue or mood, and different conditions of test administration, such as time of day, temperature, and so on, conspire to produce a shift in a person's response (static or error) at any given time. Most students of measurement conceive of a person's scores over time—even on attributes such as typing skills, which are much less complex than personality traits—to vary within a range. The narrower the range of scores achieved, the more reliable we can consider each score to be.

Reliability Coefficients

An estimate of the reliability of a scale can be expresses by means of a coefficient of correlation (usually a Pearson Product-Moment Correlation, described in Appendix A). A correlation of +1.0 (symbolized as $r = 1.0$) expresses an error-free or a perfect positive relationship between two sets of scores or two variables. (The plus sign [+] is omitted when the relationship is positive.) A correlation of 0.00 indicates no relationship, and a correlation of −1.0 indicates a perfect negative, or inverse, relationship among the scores. All the fractional coefficients (for example, .78 and −.30) ranging from 1.00 through 0.00 to −1.00 indicate the degree to which the variables or scales vary together. The calculation of a reliability coefficient is

a statistical means of expressing the degree of relationship or agreement between two sets of independently derived scores on the scale. For example, if the person who scores highest on a scale at one time also scores highest at another time, and the second highest person does the same, and if their pattern continues so that the lowest scoring person scores lowest both times, the correlation would be perfect and would have a value of 1.00. It is perhaps easier to understand why test-retest scores on psychological scales or tests almost never achieve a perfect relationship: If only one person scores at a different level over time the value of the correlation will be something less than 1.00.

The purpose of estimating reliability is to determine the proportion of variation in test scores that is due to actual variation among people, or individual differences on the trait being measured (true variance), and the proportion of variation that might be attributable to "static," or error of measurement. Thus, the correlation coefficient that is calculated as an estimate of reliability tells us two things simultaneously: the degree of relationship between scores and the error of measurement. For example, if we calculate a correlation of $r = .90$ between two sets of scale scores obtained six months apart from the same people, we know that the test-retest reliability over six months is .90. If the obtained correlation is subtracted from what would be a perfect correlation (1.00), we know that the error of measurment is .10. Or, 1.00 (perfect relationship) −.90 (actual correlation) = .10 (error). In addition, if we calculate a split-half reliability on one administration that also turns out to be .90, we have an additional source of error of .10. Since these two sources are independent of one another, they can be added together; thus, we estimate that there is 20% error in the measure. Two reliability coefficients of .90 tell us that the actual reliability of the scale is only .80. That is, 1.00 (perfect relationship) −.10 (test-retest error) −.10 (split-half error) =.80.

This discussion of reliability covers only the minimum necessary for understanding the concept. For a more comprehensive treatment of reliability and test-construction problems, refer to such sources as Wiggins, 1973; Cronbach, 1970; and Anastasi, 1976.

VALIDITY

One can develop a highly reliable instrument and still be unsure whether it is valid for the intended purpose. It is true that when we are measuring traits assumed to be enduring dispositions, we cannot really assess validity unless we have ascertained a high degree of reliability. Yet, once we have established reliability, we must demonstrate validity separately and empirically. The three most commonly used ways of demonstrating test validity are known as the methods of content validity, criterion validity, and construct validity.

Content validity refers to the degree to which the scale or test covers the area being studied and is not confounded with other materials. As students, you might recall declaring a test invalid. If you were studying Shakespeare's plays and found that your next quiz covered the sonnets, you would have a legitimate complaint on the grounds of content validity. Similarly, if the final examination in your Shakespeare course focused almost exclusively on *King Lear* and ignored the other plays, the examination obviously did not cover enough of the relevant course material to be considered a valid test of your knowledge of Shakespeare's plays. Similarly, we must examine all tests logically and knowledgeably to ascertain that the appropriate material is receiving adequate coverage. Often, tests are evaluated by someone other than the test developer so that a relatively detached and unbiased judgment of content validity can be obtained. Determining content validity is often a first step in the development of a new test, but this form of validity is considered rather weak compared with the criterion and construct approaches.

Criterion validity is established by procedures designed to determine the relationship of test responses to criteria external to the test. This process is usually undertaken in one of two time frames. For example, scores obtained from a scale measuring affiliation might be correlated with current reports of social relationships established among dormitory residents. This approach is *concurrent validation*, because both sets of the measures are taken during the same time period. To determine *predictive validity*, one seeks to establish the degree to which scores on the scale will predict performance on some future criterion. Tests measuring intellectual performance are familiar examples of measures intended to be predictors of success in school. If there is a high positive correlation between scores on an IQ test taken in elementary school and grades achieved in junior high, we say the IQ test has good predictive validity.

Construct validity is probably the most important approach to theoretically based research; it is also the most complex and comprehensive approach to validity. The concept of construct validity, introduced by Cronbach and Meehl (1955), provides a rationale for understanding the relationships among constructs (for example, anxiety or extroversion) within a theoretical system and the methods (for instance, observations, tests, or scales) that are used to measure the constructs.

All our theories about personality are abstractions about human beings and their behavior. In effect, a theory is a system of interrelated ideas or intellectual "constructions" by the theorist about how and why people feel, think, and act as they do. Because we cannot immediately observe the hows and whys of people's thoughts and feelings, the constructs themselves cannot be tested directly. Nevertheless, a theory involving trait anxiety or extroversion should provide us with not only insights about the relationships among the constructs of the theory but also a basis for hypotheses about the kinds of observable characteristics and behaviors associated with the trait. Using a particular theory about extroversion, we might expect an extrovert to have relatively many acquaintances and to prefer sociable rather than solitary work. Therefore, construct validity of a scale measuring extroversion might be indicated by the degree of relationship between test scores, indexes of work preferences, and observations of friendship patterns. When you obtain positive results in testing such hypotheses, you are learning simultaneously about the construct and the theory from which it is derived, as well as about the measuring instruments.

Many hypotheses should be tested in order to confirm the construct validity of a scale. In fact, you should think of construct validation not as a one-time technique but as a relatively continuous research process. Think of this process as locating a point on a multidimensional grid (for example, a topological map), with the understanding that the more directions are ascertained the more precisely the location of the point can be identified. When the point is surrounded from several directions, you will know where it is.

In order to begin to understand the construct validity of a scale in a theoretical matrix, you would want to ensure that results on the scale are positively related to results from different methods of measuring the same or similar traits or constructs—that is, to ensure the *convergent validity*. At the same time, you would also want to be sure that scores on the scale are unrelated to scores on measures of constructs considered to be theoretically different, ensuring the test's *discriminant validity*.

In the chapter selection, Rotter describes the testing of a series of hypotheses designed to provide an approximation of the construct validity of his new scale for the measurement of interpersonal trust. In addition to developing the interpersonal-trust scale, Rotter employed several different methods to measure trust and several other traits. His choice of measures allowed him to obtain evidence for both the convergent and discriminant validity of his trust scale.

As part of his construct-validation program, Rotter used measures of humor, popularity and friendships, self-ratings of trust, and sociometric ratings of trustworthiness, interpersonal trust, dependency, and gullibility. *Sociometric rating* is a technique that employs members of groups who are well known to each other (such as fraternity and sorority members) and requires that each member rank all other members of the group on the traits being measured (for instance, trustworthiness). In the studies represented in the article, Rotter also includes several status variables such as ordinal position in the family (birth order), religious affiliation (or nonaffiliation), socioeconomic status of the subject's family, and Scholastic Aptitude Test (SAT) scores.

Each of the different traits or attributes and the different types of measurement were used to form the basis for hypothetical relationships with the trait of interpersonal trust as Rotter defined the variable. For example, in assessing convergent validity, you would expect high positive correlations between trust as measured by the new scale and trust as measured by sociometric ratings and/or by self-report. In one study reported in the article, these correlations are .38 and .29 respectively, both of which are statistically significant. Are these coefficients satisfactory reflections of convergent validity? How does the investigator discuss the levels of these relationships?

Discriminant validity requires that there should be virtually no correlation between measures of constructs considered to be theoretically distinct. Rotter found that the correlations between a measure of general scholastic ability (SAT) and the interpersonal-trust scale was −.16 for females and −.06 for males, which would seem to support the discriminant validity of the scale. The findings that reflect the relationship between interpersonal trust and social desirability (that is, the effort to make oneself "look good") are not as clear cut as are the findings with the SAT measure. What should be the relationship with social desirability? It is obvious that the theoretical definitions of the various constructs must be fully understood before any meaningful interpretation of the correlations can be made.

It is often necessary to discriminate a new scale from such general characteristics as scholastic ability (for example, as a reflection of "intelligence") and social desirability. After all, Rotter does not intend to create another measure of intelligence nor a measure that subjects can "fake" in order to score in a direction that appears to be "good" or socially desirable.

While these general discriminations are necessary, it is at least equally important to demonstrate distinctions between the construct that is being measured—in this case, interpersonal trust—and other constructs that are embedded within the general theory from which the constructs are derived. A paraphrase of Rotter's theoretical statement might read as follows: "People who score high on the interpersonal-trust scale hold a generalized expectancy that the word or statements of other people can be relied upon." Does he mean then that people who score high on a measure of interpersonal trust are simply gullible? that they believe almost anything they hear or read? The answer is no. Especially in later conceptualizations (see Rotter, 1980), Rotter theoretically discriminates between people high on interpersonal trust from people who see all the world as a benign place or all people as essentially "good." Those who are seen as generally trusting should also respond with skepticism when there is evidence indicating that their trust in a particular set of circumstances is unwarranted. Thus, the finding that the interpersonal-trust scale correlates −.03 with the sociometric measurement of gullibility is an additional bit of evidence for discriminant validity.

One final comment is necessary about a research program that seeks to establish construct validity: the various modes of establishing validity should be evaluated with respect to the reliability of the instrument. In general, we expect that an index of reliability should be quite high (that is, that measurement error should be low); we should also expect that correlations reflecting reliabilities should be higher than those reflecting either convergent or discriminant validity. Rotter provides conceptual reasons for what appear to be somewhat disappointing indices of content reliability (split half) and especially the correlations reflecting reliability over time (test-retest). You will be well rewarded by a careful examination of these date presented in Rotter's article. In fact, to go beyond this presentation of construct validity, you should review a systematic procedure, called the multitrait, multimethod design (Campbell & Fiske, 1959), which permits a simultaneous evaluation of the validity and reliability of different measures of several traits.

NORMATIVE GROUPS

Another important source of information about a test is contained in the description of the group or groups to which the test has been administered. For some tests that purport to assess characteristics of a specific group of people, such as children under ten years of age, the description of the normative group is crucial. A *normative group* in this instance is intended to represent the population for which a test is designed to be used. The user of a test designed to assess intelligence of children under ten in the United States must know that the normative sample includes all the socioeconomic, geographic, and other relevant dimensions in proportion to the population of the country. A test that is intended for a more limited population, such as college-bound high school seniors, would provide information relevant to that group. Normative information enables the tester to evaluate an individual's score by comparing it to the scores of the population in question.

For ease of interpretation, the raw scores obtained from the normative group are usually transformed into a percentile score or a standard score. Other transformations can be made, but these are the most commonly used. A *percentile score* obtained by an individual indicates the proportion of scores in the normative group that were lower than the obtained score. Thus, a percentile score of 80 indicates that 80 out of every 100 persons taking the test had scores that were lower.

The *standard score* is a transformation of the raw score that uses the mean and standard deviation of the distribution of scores. Because normative groups are generally very large, they usually produce scores such as those for height or weight, with few scores at either end and increasing numbers toward the middle—that provide a normal or bell-shaped distribution or curve, especially when tests are designed to produce such a distribution. Since a normal distribution is symmetrical on both sides of the mean score, the standard deviation of the raw-score distribution can be used to indicate the position of an individual's score compared to the population of scores. Most often, the standard deviation is transformed into a simple scale known as a z score. In this instance, a raw score falling 1 standard deviation above the mean will be indicated by a z score of 1; a score falling 1.5 standard deviations below the mean will receive a z score of -1.5.

RESPONSE STYLES

Up to this point in the chapter, we have outlined the essential steps in the construction and evaluation of objective tests. We now turn to an additional set of issues, usually categorized as *response style*, to give you a more complete perspective on objective tests.

An experimenter or interviewer always has some uncertainty about the degree to which the information obtained is an accurate reflection of the thoughts, feelings, or opinions of the respondent. Most of us have experienced the temptation to make ourselves "look better" in the eyes of others, and this tendency becomes a major methodological issue in any serious study that utilizes objective tests or other self-examination and self-report techniques. Several of the inquiry systems we have mentioned—interviews, questionnaires, and psychological testing procedures—employ one means or another of detecting the very human tendency among subjects to misrepresent facts about themselves insofar as they know these "facts." Indeed, whole areas of research focus almost exclusively on the attempt to detect the subject's intentional or unintentional response distortion.

A good illustration of an inquiry into *response styles,* or "sets"—tendencies to answer questions in certain ways—is the area called social desirability (see Crowne & Marlowe, 1964). As we have noted previously, some subjects seem to be concerned with presenting themselves in the best possible light. Their responses to an interview, questionnaire, or test might be determined much more strongly by what they think is good, right, or socially desirable than by what they actually think about the issue under consideration. Crowne and Marlowe's (1964) objective test assessing concern with social desirability is frequently used along with questionnaires or tests designed to tap the area of interest to the investigator. Scores on the Crowne-Marlowe scale provide the researcher with a means of assessing the degree to which any particular subject is likely to give responses that cannot be trusted to reflect anything more than the subject's view of what is socially acceptable. Sometimes, (for example, Bem, 1974), investigators build their own test of social desirability into an instrument designed primarily to assess another trait. Also, tests that have been in use for many years have approached the problem of untrustworthy responses somewhat differently by including indicators of unusual test-taking behaviors. For example, the Minnesota Multiphasic Personality Inventory (MMPI) F (frequency) scale and the commonality scale of the California Psychological Inventory (CPI) indicate the degree to which the subject's answers to a specific set of questions are unusual or infrequent responses compared to norms. If the score on social desirability or similar items is excessively high, the investigator might conclude that the entire protocol (test) is untrustworthy as a reflection of the subject's "true" beliefs.

Rather than assessing social desirability, investigators can design tests or questionnaires to make them less susceptible to the impact of social desirability. For example, in a *forced-choice* format, subjects must select one response from two or more alternatives that have been matched for social desirability. One widely used personality test employing this method is Rotter's internal/external locus of control scale, mentioned earlier.

In addition to being influenced by social desirability, some people learn response styles that distort their answers. One such tendency is to answer questions by using the midpoint of a scale and avoiding the extremes (known as "hugging the middle"). The forced-choice format, which is also employed in the *Q*-sort technique described in the next section, is helpful in discouraging such response styles as "hugging the middle."

Another response style is *acquiescence* , the tendency to answer "yes" or "true" indiscriminately to all questions that seem ambiguous or about which one is unsure, regardless of the content (used by "yea-sayers"). Another is the negative tendency to answer "no" or "false" to ambiguous items regardless of their content (used by "nay-sayers"). One way to identify individuals with such response styles is to include some items in both a positive and a negative form, so that the subject, to be consistent, must agree with one item and disagree with the other. If the subject says "yes" to the item "Do you frequently find it necessary to be dishonest?" as well as to the item "Are you always honest?" then it is likely that a response style is at work that invalidates that subject's protocol.

Most of us on occasion have probably performed in a way that reveals the operation of a response style. On timed objective tests, some people work for speed rather than accuracy, and others work for accuracy rather than speed. If you were being questioned by someone you liked, you probably tried at least sometimes to tell them what you thought they wanted to hear. If you were being questioned by someone you dislike, the opposite tendency might have prevailed. And if, when using a rating scale ranging from 1 (very true) to 7 (never true), you found it difficult to give the "unmodest" answer of 1 to items such as "intelligent," "creative," "empathic" and "sensitive," then you might have responded by "hugging the middle." Response style is largely a technical problem of test construction and test interpretation. While there still remains some controversy about the biasing effects of style, the solutions we described appear to be adequate for most purposes.

SUBJECTIVE AND PROJECTIVE TECHNIQUES

In this section, we describe briefly two other major categories of tests known as subjective and projective techniques (Pervin, 1975). Used for both clinical and research purposes, these techniques are most appropriately administered to individuals rather than groups, and the rationale for their use is quite different from that of objective tests. Subjective assessment techniques are usually more structured than projective techniques and are more similar to objective tests.

Subjective Assessment Techniques

Subjective assessment techniques are endorsed by humanistic and many trait psychologists, both of whom are interested, as noted in Chapter 1, in the intensive study of individuals rather than of group responses. Humanistic psychologists generally believe that if we really want to understand people, we should ask them about themselves. Psychoanalytically oriented psychologists believe that the important determinants of personality are not available to consciousness, and behavioristic psychologists believe that it is behavior and not personality that should concern us, but humanistic psychologists believe that humans are introspective beings whose thoughts about themselves have important effects on their behavior and the overall functioning of their personalities.

Among the most popular techniques used to assess and compare the individual responses of people, especially for research purposes, are the Adjective Check List (ACL) proposed by Gough and Heilbrun (1965) and the Q sort introduced by Stephenson (1953). The *ACL* is composed of 300 adjectives. Individuals respond by indicating those adjectives that are descriptive of themselves. The ACL can be scored for traits that indicate dominance, acheivement, self-confidence, and so on.

Other than the projective tests to be described in the next section, the technique that has been most extensively used in subjective assessment is the Q sort. This technique has been used by Carl Rogers and his associates (Rogers and Dymond 1954) to assess response to therapy and by Block (1961) in his longitudinal research on developmental issues. The Q sort consists of a number of adjectives or statements typed on separate cards. Depending on the exact instructions of the investigator, subjects place specified numbers of cards (usually 7 or 9) into different piles according to, for example, how well the statements describe them, or someone they know, or the person they would like to be. Typically, subjects are told exactly how many cards to put in each pile, on a continuum from least characteristic to most characteristic. This predetermined, forced distribution of items into piles approximates a normal distribution. Thus, a Q sort could consist of 48 cards descriptive of personality characteristics (for example, "funny," "intelligent," "moody," "indepen-

dent") that subjects are asked to sort into nine piles providing a descriptive range from least to most true of themselves. A typical distribution for such a task is illustrated in Table 8-1.

TABLE 8-1
A *Q*-Sort Distribution

Pile Number	Instruction (Degree of Similarity)	Number of Cards in each pile
1	Definitely like me	2
2	Strongly like me	4
3	Moderately like me	6
4	Slightly like me	7
5	Neutral or ambivalent	10
6	Slightly unlike me	7
7	Moderately unlike me	6
8	Strongly unlike me	4
9	Definitely unlike me	2

The Q sort is a general technique rather than a specific test. Q sorts have been used as means for having subjects describe themselves, their ideal selves, their best friends, their parents' child-rearing practices, their view of a patient, their view of what their parents would like them to be, and so on (for example, Haan, 1974; Rogers and Dymond, 1954; Stephenson, 1953; Thompson and Nishimura, 1952). The forced normal distribution permits simple statistical computations—for example, the degree of correlation between one's ideal self and one's view of one's best friend (Thompson and Nishimura, 1952). The forced distribution format also helps prevent such response sets as yea-saying and nay-saying on true/false items or "hugging the middle" on rating scales.

The Q sort is considered a useful means for determining how individuals feel about themselves. In general, for example, the greater the discrepancy between a self sort and an ideal-self sort, the lower would be the statistical correlation, and the worse, one presumes, would be the self-concept and the level of the person's happiness. This subjective test is more structured than common projective techniques such as the Rorschach inkblots and the Thematic Apperception Test (see Chapter 7), and less structured than the typical multiple-choice objective test. Both number of piles and the number of cards to be put in each pile are predetermined by the investigator, which imposes a certain degree of structure on the task, but subjects still have considerable choice in deciding which items should go where to best describe themselves. An exercise on Q technique to give you a first-hand experience in constructing and using this procedure has been included in the exercises section of this chapter.

Projective Tests

Projective tests constitute the final major category of tests used to assess personality. As we noted earlier, one of the basic assumptions underlying projective tests is that individuals are simply unable or unwilling to tell you about important aspects of their own personality and motivation. Another assumption is that if such individuals are faced in a relaxed setting with an ambiguous stimulus such as a TAT or Rorschach card or an incomplete sentence and are asked to describe the card or complete the sentence, they will unconsciously project their own needs and characteristics into their responses.

The most common use of projective tests is clinical diagnosis and assessment. A valid interpretation of responses is considered to require considerable training; consequently, many projective tests are not supposed to be sold to individuals who are not professionally trained. A major exception to this clinical emphasis is the Thematic Apperception Test, which has been used widely for research purposes. Investigators using the TAT for research on motivational processes analyze responses according to the principles of content analysis described in Chapter 6. If you are interested in using tests of this sort, refer back to Chapter 6.

PUTTING PERSONALITY TESTS INTO PERSPECTIVE

A final comment is essential to your understanding of some of the social, political, and ethical problems associated with tests and the procedures of testing. Over the past several years, many objections have been raised regarding the indiscriminant use of objective tests (for example, American Psychological Association, 1965). These objections, and the controversies they provoke, appear at times to be paradoxical. That is, tests that purport to assess, for example, the readiness of a high school student to undertake college work (SAT and ACT) have been attacked on the grounds that they are arbitrary and ineffective. Similarly, the practice of intelligence testing in elementary schools has been attacked on the grounds that the common IQ tests are inappropriate for many groups. Conversely, popularized warnings have appeared against mind controlling and brainwashing (for example, Gross, 1962; Whyte, 1956) that imply that tests are so powerful that they must be banned. Serious objections have also been raised to testing practices as invasions of privacy.

There is undoubtedly some truth to all these objections. If used as the exclusive measure of a student's ability and performance, any test will prove to be inadequate. Moreover, if students from a particular background are assessed by means of tests that were developed without reference to these groups in the derivation of items and establishment of norms, the assessment will almost certainly be inadequate. If adherence to ethical procedures is lax, invasion of privacy and other problems of this kind might well occur. The discussion of ethical practices in Chapter 4, of course, applies here in providing a framework for a consideration of such problems. The problems are not intrinsic to the tests themselves, but rather are reflections of the misuse of tests and of abuses in the interpretation of test results. The most flagrant abuses are probably due to the indiscriminant use of tests and ignorance of the principles of test construction as outlined in this chapter and elsewhere in the book. It is the responsibility of all of us—student, professional psychologist, and teacher, especially as test users—to understand the psychometric properties of a test and to use a test only for appropriate purposes under ethical conditions.

A PREVIEW OF THE CHAPTER SELECTION

This chapter's selection describes the development and validation of Rotter's measure of interpersonal trust. In discussing the derivation of his scale, Rotter begins with a brief presentation of the perspective provided by social-learning theory. His discussion of the role of expectancy in affecting behavior is equally relevant to his test of interpersonal trust and his scale of internal-external locus of control. Rotter's selection is useful in illustrating the steps involved in the construction of an additive scale from an a priori approach. It exemplifies the test constructor's concern with minimizing problems related to social desirability and response bias while maximizing various forms of reliability. Finally, the selection describes the steps taken by the investigators to establish the construct validity of their measures. A careful reading of the article in conjunction with this chapter should provide you with a good foundation for developing objective tests of your own.

A New Scale for the Measurement of Interpersonal Trust[1]

Julian B. Rotter
University of Connecticut

Interpersonal trust, defined as a generalized expectancy that the verbal statements of others can be relied upon, appears potentially to be a fruitful variable for investigation in several fields of psychology. A new, Likert-type scale was developed and refined on the basis of item analysis of internal consistency, relative independence of social desirability and item spread. Overall internal consistency and test-retest reliability appear satisfactory. Demographic data were examined for 547 college students. Trust scale scores are related significantly to position in the family, socioeconomic level, religion, and religious differences between parents. A first assessment of construct and discriminant validity was attempted by a sociometric study of two fraternities and two sororities. Results indicate both good construct and discriminant validity for the Interpersonal Trust Scale.

One of the most salient factors in the effectiveness of our present complex social organization is the willingness of one or more individuals in a social unit to trust others. The efficiency, adjustment and even survival of any social group depends upon the presence or absence of such trust.

Interpersonal trust is defined here as an expectancy held by an individual or a group that the word, promise, verbal or written statement of another individual or group can be relied upon. This definition clearly departs significantly from Erikson's (1953) broad use of the concept of *basic trust* which Erikson describes as a central ingredient in "the healthy personality".

Various writers have already indicated that a high expectancy that others can be relied upon is an important variable in the development of adequate family relationships and of healthy per-

[1]This investigation was supported by a grant from the National Institute of Mental Health (MH 11455).

Entire article from *Journal of Personality*, 1967, *35*, 651-665. Copyright 1967 by Duke University Press. Reprinted by permission.

sonalities in children. The failure to trust others, particularly representatives of society, such as parents, teachers, and powerful community leaders, has frequently been cited as an important determinant in delinquency (Redl & Wineman, 1951). Difficulties in race relationships and in minority group-majority group relationships have, likewise, been frequently related to expectancies of one group that the verbal statements of the other cannot be accepted. Many pschotherapists believe interpersonal trust is a major determinant in the success of psychotherapy. In fact, an expectancy that others can be believed must be an important variable in human learning in general. Much of the both formal and informal learning that humans acquire is based on the verbal and written statements of others and what they learn must be significantly affected by the degree to which they believe their informants without independent evidence.

It seems evident that an adequate measure of individual differences in interpersonal trust would be of great value for research in the areas of social psychology, personality and clinical psychology. Social scientists have investigated some of the conditions relating to interpersonal trust using game theory (Rapaport & Orwant, 1962; Deutsch, 1958, 1960; and Scodel, 1962). For the most part these investigations have shown that a typical reaction of two strangers in a two-person non-zero-sum game situation involving trust produces behavior usually indicative of competitive rather than cooperative attitudes. One might conclude that Americans at least are a highly suspicious and extremely competitive group who would give up many benefits rather than cooperate with someone else. The results of these studies, however, do not seem consistent with a common sense analysis of our own society. From the family unit to big business, cooperation seems to mark the everyday behavior of individuals and organizations to a far greater degree than would be anticipated from the study of two game situations. Perhaps this is the result of special reactions to these laboratory situations which are highly competitive in nature and are specific to these situa-

tions, or at least have limited generality. The writer has previously published an analysis of some of the factors involving specificity of reaction to test and experimental laboratory situations which may be applicable here (Rotter, 1955, 1960).

Studies involving the communication of information (Mellinger, 1956; Loomis, 1959; Kelley & Ring, 1961) have several characteristics in common with game approaches but present situations somewhat closer to the present study. These investigations indicate that people who trust others more are also more trustworthy, or cooperative.

Similar findings were obtained by Deutsch (1960) using the "game" paradigm.

Other recent literature has dealt with trust indirectly. Discussions of Machiavellianism, i.e., the tendency to manipulate others to gain one's own ends (Christie & Merton, 1958) and anomie (Merton, 1949) suggest that, at least in part, distrust of others is dependent upon normlessness in the social organization.

The problem of trust in the present research is being viewed from the perspective of social learning theory (Rotter, 1954). From this orientation, choice behavior in specific situations depends upon the expectancy that a given behavior will lead to a particular outcome or reinforcement in that situation and the preference value of that reinforcement for the individual in that situation.

It is a natural implication of social learning theory that experiences of promised negative or positive reinforcements occurring would vary for different individuals and that, consequently, people would develop different expectancies that such reinforcements would occur when promised by other people. It is also natural to expect, to some degree, that such expectancies that promises of other social agents will be kept would generalize from one social agent to another. That is, individuals would differ in a *generalized expectancy* that the oral or written statements of other people can be relied upon. The development of such a generalized attitude may be learned directly from the behavior of parents, teachers, peers, etc. and also from verbal statements regarding others made by significant people or trusted sources of communication such as newspapers and television. It is ironic that we can learn to distrust large groups of peoples without personal experience validating such distrust, because people who are themselves trusted teach distrust.

Previous work on the choice of a smaller immediate reward versus a more highly valued, delayed reward by Mahrer (1956) & Mischel (1961a, 1961b) is related to the concept of trust as defined here. These studies strongly suggest that children who have experienced a higher proportion of promises kept by parents and authority figures in the past have a higher generalized expectancy for interpersonal trust from other authority figures.

CONSTRUCTION OF THE INTERPERSONAL TRUST SCALE

As a first step in the construction of the scale a number of items was written using a Likert format. An attempt was made to sample a wide variety of social objects so that a subject would be called upon to express his trust of parents, teachers, physicians, politicians, classmates, friends, etc. In other words the scale was constructed as an *additive* scale in which a high score would show trust for a great variety of social objects. In addition to the specific items, a few items were stated in broader terms presumed to measure a more general optimism regarding the society. Finally, a number of filler items, intended to partially disguise the purpose of the scale, was written and included in the first experimental form.

The experimental form was group administered to two large classes of students in the introductory psychology course. The sample was comprised of 248 male and 299 female subjects. Along with this scale the Marlowe-Crowne Social Desirability Scale (1964) of "need for social approval" was administered.

Three criteria were used for inclusion of an item in the final scale: (1) the item had to have a significant correlation with the total of the other trust items with that item removed; (2) the item had to have a relatively low correlation with the Marlowe-Crowne Social Desirability Scale score; and (3) endorsement of the item showed reasonable spread over the five Likert categories of (1) strongly agree, (2) mildly agree, (3) agree and disagree equally, (4) mildly disagree and (5) strongly disagree. A final form of the scale was determined by dropping three items from the *a priori* scale.

In the experimental form of the test half of the crucial items were written so that an agree response would indicate trust and half so that a disagree response would indicate trust. In the final form of this scale the items selected were similarly balanced so that 13 indicated trust for agreeing and 12 distrust for agreeing. Filler items did not show significant relationships to the trust items but helped partially obscure the purpose of the test. The final form of the test included 25 items measuring trust and 15 filler items. Some sample items are presented below:

In dealing with strangers one is better off to be cautious until they have provided evidence that they are trustworthy.

Parents usually can be relied upon to keep their promises.

Parents and teachers are likely to say what they believe themselves and not just what they think is good for the child to hear.

Most elected public officials are really sincere in their campaign promises.

In addition to the Marlowe-Crowne Social Desirability Scale, the 547 subjects completed a personal information questionnaire which included information on age, class level, father's occupation, father's and mother's religion and place of birth, and siblings, so that position in the family and family size could be determined. College aptitude scores were also available on these subjects and were obtained directly from the students' admission records. At later dates several of the students were subjects in other studies involving the administration of the same trust scale. It was therefore possible to obtain test-retest reliabilities for long periods of time, where the testing conditions were different for the two administrations. An analysis of this data is presented below.

TEST CHARACTERISTICS

Internal Consistency and Test-Retest Reliability

Table 1 . . . provides means and standard deviations of the 248 male and 299 female college student subjects. Internal consistency based on split-half reliability, corrected by the Spearman-Brown formula, are also provided. While these consistencies are not high for objective type tests, it should be remembered that these are *additive* scales sampling a variety of different social objects rather than a measure of intensity limited to a narrow area of behavior. Regarded in this light these internal consistencies are reasonably high. The difference in mean scores for males and females is not statistically significant and distributions of scores for both sexes are similar.

Two estimates of test-retest reliability are available. The first of these involves 24 subjects, 10 male and 14 female, who took the test originally in a large group testing situation and repeated the test as part of a sociometric study to be described later. The average length of time between first and second tests was approximately seven months. The correlation was .56, (p = < .01). The second measure of test-retest reliability was obtained on students who had also taken the test originally in a large group situation. Their second test was part of an experiment in which the trust scale was given in groups of between 2 and 13 with two other tests appearing equally often in first, second and third positions in order of administration. There were 34 males and 8 females in this group and the approximate average time between tests was 3 months. The correlation was .68, (p = < .01). Considering the important differences in administration procedures and the relatively long periods of time these test-retest coefficients indicate surprising stability of test scores.

TABLE 1
Test Data for the Interpersonal Trust Scale

Group	N	Mean	S.D.
Males	248	73.01	10.23
Females	299	71.91	9.95
Total	547	72.41	10.90

Split-Half Reliability*

		r	p
Males	248	.77	<.001
Females	299	.75	<.001
Total	547	.76	<.001

*Corrected by the Spearman-Brown Prophecy Formula

For the 248 male subjects the correlation with the Marlowe-Crowne S-D Scale was .21, for the 299 females .38; the overall correlation was .29. All correlations were statistically significant. These results suggest that trust is regarded as a socially desirable trait but that the total amount of variance in the trust scale accounted for by the social approval motive is relatively small. To determine the relationship, if any, with general ability 100 male and 100 female subjects were selected at random and their trust scores correlated with the college entrance (SAT) scores. The correlation for 100 females was −.16 and for the 100 males −.06. At least for this sample of college students, ability has no significant influence on trust scale scores.

Demographic Characteristics of High and Low Trust Individuals

From the personal information sheet filled out by all of the 547 students who took the Interpersonal Trust Scale, analyses of variance were computed for the variables of ordinal position, family size, religion, socioeconomic status, age and number of semesters in college. In addition, the subjects were grouped into two categories based on whether or not the reported religions for both parents were the same or different. Since male and female subjects were essentially similar throughout this analysis, data was combined for the sexes.

There were no significant differences in test scores for subjects of different ages or for the number of semesters of college attended. However, the range for both of these variables was extremely narrow. The data of family size were dichotomized into three children or less, or more than three children. Students from larger families did not show significantly different trust scores from those with three or less children. Significant differences were obtained on all the other variables.

Table 2 presents mean scores for the various breakdowns of subjects for the variables of ordinal position, religion, religious differences and socioeconomic status. A multiple comparisons test for a single degree of freedom contrast (Myers, 1966) was made to determine differences among means. It should be noted that in many cases there are significant differences because of the large number of subjects in the sample, but actual mean differences are relatively small.

Inspection of the findings for birth order reveals one significant difference but the actual mean differences are sufficiently small to suggest no important psychological variability in this group. However, in a separate smaller sample, Geller (1966) also found youngest children to be the least trusting and significantly different from all other ordinal positions. While this finding cannot be interpreted without additional data, it is possible that the youngest child has less interaction with his parents and has the least acceptance of the adult interpretation of the verities of our society.

The data on religion are more clearcut. Students who fill out the blank by stating any religion

TABLE 2
Demographic Data for the Interpersonal Trust Scale

Variable and Group	N	Mean	Significant Diff. between groups $p = < .05$
Ordinal Position			
Only	52	73.08	
Oldest	195	72.21	
Middle	129	73.02	Youngest
Youngest	171	71.97	Middle
ANOV Overall $F = 3.71, p = < .05$			
Religion			
Left Blank	12	71.50	Jewish, None
Jewish	85	74.65	All groups except Misc.
Protestant	197	73.31	Jewish, Catholic, None
Catholic	203	71.33	Jewish, Protestant, None, Misc.
Miscellaneous	17	73.82	Catholic, None
None, Agnostic, Atheist	33	67.48	All groups
ANOV Overall $F = 46.78, p = < .001$			
Religious Differences			
No information	13	72.38	
Parents Same	434	73.13	
Parents Different	100	69.29	Parents same & No information
ANOV Overall $F = 75.06, p = < .001$			
Socioeconomic Level			
No information	25	73.48	V
Warner Group I	117	73.45	III, V
Warner Group II	150	72.70	V
Warner Group III	91	71.81	I
Warner Grop IV	64	72.48	
Warner Group V	100	70.97	No information, I, II
ANOV Overall $F = 8.63, p = < .01$			

tend to be more trusting than those who state they are agnostics, atheists, or write "none". Since it is clear that such students are already expressing less faith in one currently accepted institution it is not surprising that they show a generalized lower trust in others.

Perhaps most interesting is the lower trust scores for subjects with religious differences between parents. In any case where the student indicated a religious difference for the two parents, including one parent being atheistic and the other not, the subject was put into the religious difference category. This group includes all subjects who listed different religions for the parents, regardless of the religion stated for the subject himself. Only nine of the 100 subjects so classified gave their own religion as "none", "atheist", or "agnostic" so that this group of subjects has only a minimum overlap with the students who were classified as non-religious in the previous analysis. It seems reasonable that a child subjected to two different kinds of adult interpretations in such an important area as religion would grow up to be more cynical of the verbal communications of authority figures.

Finally, the data on socioeconomic status more or less follows the expected progression for more trust at the highest economic level to less trust at the lowest economic level. For this analysis, subjects were classified according to Warner's system based upon father's occupation. The interpretation again seems to be consistent with the general notion that those students who had least reason to accept the status quo as defined and defended by the authorities in the social system, tended to show the least trust of those authorities. It should be reiterated here, though, that the differences are again small and the overlap among groups very great.

VALIDITY

In order to assess the validity of the Interpersonal Trust Scale it would be optimal to obtain one or more natural life criterion situations. The two-person non-zero-sum game seems like a face valid procedure to investigate interpersonal trust. However, the results of these studies suggest that the situation is reacted to by many if not all subjects as a competitive game, often regardless of special instructions. For the reasons cited earlier it was decided to test the validity of the scale against observations of everyday behavior by a sociometric technique. Two fraternities (N = 35, N = 38) and two sororities (N = 41, N = 42) on the University of Connecticut campus were asked to cooperate in the study. Lump sum payments were provided to each of the four organizations if they could promise that all members would be available for a single evening and all would agree to take the sociometric and two brief tests. However, members would only be used in the study if they had lived in the house for a period of at least six months prior to the date of testing. The data was collected by the author and, in each case, a research assistant of the same sex as the subjects[2]. In addition to asking the subjects to nominate members of the group who were the highest and lowest in interpersonal trust, subjects were also asked to nominate others high and low on dependency, gullibility and trustworthiness. As control variables, scales were also included for humor, popularity and friendship. Finally the subjects were asked to make a self-rating of trust on a four point scale of: (1) much more than the average college student, (2) more than the average college student, (3) less than the average college student and (4) much less than the average college student.

To avoid halo effect elaborate instructions were given asking each subject to pay special attention to the different characteristics required for each sociometric description. Confidentiality was assured as well as the fact that we were not interested in individuals and that we would eliminate the use of names as soon as the data were obtained, substituting numbers for each individual. To

[2]Grateful acknowledgment is made to Mr. Ray Mulry and Miss Linda Yuccas who assisted in this research.

avoid stereotyping no labels were used for the sociometric scales but rather descriptions of typical behaviors. In each group the order of presentation was first the trust scale, second the sociometric scales and last the Marlowe-Crowne Social Desirability Scale. However, the Marlowe-Crowne S-D Scale was not given to the first group.

One other difference occurred in the procedure for the first of the four groups. In this group, a sorority, each subject was asked to nominate the five highest and five lowest on each sociometric scale. These data were analyzed using four methods of scoring. In method one the highest was weighted 5, the next highest 4, the next 3 and so on and the negative nominations were similarly weighted −5, −4, −3, etc. The second was also a weighting method, but using only the first three nominations for the negative and positive ends of each scale. The third method involved no weighting but gave a score of 1 for each mention, utilizing all 5 nominations. The last method gave a score of 1 only for the top 3 and the bottom 3 nominations. Intercorrelations of the four methods indicated no substantial differences among them. Since subjects found difficulty in finding 5 names for the top and bottom of each scale subsequent groups were asked to nominate only the top 3 and bottom 3. Each mention was then scored either 1 or −1 to give an overall score on that scale. Instructions for the sociometric are given below as are the descriptions for the trust variable. The order of presentation was (1) dependency, (2) trust, (3) humor, (4) gullibility, (5) trustworthiness, (6) popularity, (7) friendship and (8) self-rating of trust. During the administration of the sociometric a strong attempt was made to keep a serious atmosphere which was more or less successful. However, the success was greater in the sororities than in the fraternities.

SOCIOMETRIC INSTRUCTIONS

On the following pages you will be asked to nominate some people in your group who fit various descriptions. Please do so as thoughtfully as possible, paying special attention to the *different characteristics* called for in each description. Again let me assure you the results are confidential and we have no interest in you as individuals. The data from these questionnaires will be placed on IBM cards identified only by numbers, not names.

On the next seven pages various kinds of people will be described. Place the name of the person who most closely fits the description after the (1), next most closely after the (2), and so on until you have listed the three people in the group who most closely fit the description. *List only the names of people who are here in the group now. Do not list any members who are not present.*

Do each page in order. Do not look at the page ahead until you have finished the one you are working on. You may wish as you go along to use some of the same names on different descriptions.

You may find the task difficult but we hope you will take it seriously and do the best you can. We feel we are doing important research and hope you will cooperate with us to the fullest.

DESCRIPTION OF TRUST VARIABLE

This person expects others to be honest. She is not suspicious of other people's intentions, she expects others to be open and that they can be relied upon to do what they say they will do.

This person is cynical. She thinks other people are out to get as much as they can for themselves. She has little faith in human nature and in the promises or statements of other people.

The correlations to be reported below are combined for the four groups. They were obtained by calculating separate correlations for each group, transforming to z scores, finding the average z score and then transforming to an r for the entire group. Before testing the validity of the trust scale against the sociometric it was necessary to determine whether or not the sociometric was reliable. This was done by dividing each group into random, equivalent halves and obtaining the sociometric score on each variable for each person in the two sub-groups. The resulting correlations shown in Table 3 indicate the degree to which the members of the group are likely to see each other in a similar way. It can be seen that the correlations are unusually high, suggesting not only good cooperation but also that the members of the groups were basing their ratings on a common core of observations.

The intercorrelations for the 10 variables are presented in Table 4. This includes the Trust Scale, the seven sociometric ratings, the self-rating of trust and the Social Desirability Scale. It can be seen from Table 4 that the Interpersonal Trust Scale was significantly related to the sociometric trust score. Individual correlations in the four groups range from .23 to .55. The overall correlation of .38 is significantly higher than that for the control variables of humor, popularity and friendship indicating that the sociometric rating for trust was measuring an independent variable and was not merely the result of "halo" effect. Both the trust scale and the sociometric rating of trust correlated significantly with trustworthiness, providing strong support for the belief that people who trust others are regarded themselves as being dependable.

It is of considerable interest that no significant relationship was found between gullibility which was defined on the sociometric scale as . . . naive and easily fooled in contrast to sophisticated, experienced, etc. . . . and trust as measured by the sociometric or the Interpersonal Trust Scale. While it is somewhat difficult conceptually to en-

tirely separate gullibility from interpersonal trust it is clear that in practice the individuals in our sample made such separation and saw the two traits as independent.

The other significant relationships with the trust scale were for the self-rating of trust and the negative relationship with dependency. The trusting individual is seen as less dependent on others (making decisions, seeking advice and help) than the individual rated as low in trust. But dependency is seen as a clearly negative trait correlating $-.46$ with popularity and $-.53$ with friendship. Some of this relationship may be negative halo since it is clear that there is a significant although quite low positive relationship between trust and friendship and popularity. The correlation between self-rating of trust and the sociometric rating of trust (.39) is also indicative of the cooperation and seriousness with which the subjects completed the sociometric task. It may be surprising to some that the self-rating showed a relatively high relationship (.39) with the rating of trust made by others. It should be remembered, however, that the self-rating came at the end of the sociometric and all of the subjects knew that they were being rated on the same trait by others providing pressure on them towards honesty. Similarly, the relationship between the trust scale and the self-rating of trust (.29) might not have been so high if the knowledge that others had just rated them were not influencing the self-rating.

The insignificant correlation between the Trust Scale and the S-D Scale may appear surprising in light of the correlation of .29 found in the large sample. However, the S-D Scale was given in this case after a sociometric in which each subject knew he was being rated by others on a number of variables. As a result mean scores for the S-D test were significantly depressed in the direction of greater honesty. The mean S-D score for the sociometric study was 12.4, for the earlier study it was 14.3.

While trust and trustworthiness showed a significant relationship some evidence that they are also regarded somewhat differently can be found

TABLE 3
Split-Half Reliabilities of Sociometric Scores,
Combined Groups ($N = 156$)

Variable	r
Dependency	.88
Trust	.87
Humor	.93
Gullibility	.93
Trustworthiness	.89
Popularity	.95
Friendship	.82

$r = .21$ for $p = < .01$

TABLE 4
Combined Intercorrelations of Sociometric and Test Scores
Combined Groups ($N = 156$)

Variable	2	3	4	5	6	7	8	9	10*
1. Interpersonal Trust Scale	−.23	.38	.09	−.03	.31	.20	.19	.29	.13
2. Sociometric Dependency		−.07	−.36	.78	−.45	−.46	−.53	−.06	−.05
3. Sociometric Trust			.34	.13	.62	.43	.42	.39	.02
4. Sociometric Humor				−.33	.26	.61	.66	.14	−.08
5. Sociometric Gullibility					−.24	−.43	−.60	.01	.01
6. Sociometric Trustworthiness						.57	.50	.24	.01
7. Sociometric Popularity							.83	.05	−.11
8. Sociometric Friendship								.09	−.15
9. Self-Rating of Trust									.31
10. Marlowe-Crowne S-D Scale*									

*$N = 114$ for all correlations involving the S-D Scale

$r = .21$ for $p = <.01$ (N = 156)
$r = .16$ for $p = <.05$ (N = 156)
$r = .18$ for $p = <.05$ (N = 114)

in the correlations of both variables, measured sociometrically, with popularity and friendship. Trustworthiness is clearly seen as the more desirable trait with the significantly higher relationship to popularity.

In summary, sociometric analysis reveals relatively good construct and discriminant validity for the Interpersonal Trust Scale as against observed behavior in groups who have had ample opportunity and a long time to observe each other. Trust as measured sociometrically was negatively related to dependency, not significantly related to gullibility, and positively related to humor, friendship, popularity and especially trustworthiness.

REFERENCES

Christie, R., & Merton, R. K. Procedures for the sociological study of the values climate of medical schools. *Journal of Medical Education*, 1958, *33*, 125–133.

Crowne, D. P., & Marlowe, D. *The approval motive: studies in evaluative dependence.* New York: John Wiley & Sons, Inc., 1964.

Deutsch, M. Trust and suspicion. *Journal of Conflict Resolution*, 1958, *2*, 265–279.

Deutsch, M. Trust, trustworthiness, and the F scale. *Journal of Abnormal and Social Psychology*, 1960, *61*, 138–140.

Erikson, E. H. Growth and crises of the "Healthy personality". In C. Kluckhohn and H. Murray (Eds.), *Personality in nature, society, and culture*, 2nd ed., New York: Knopf, 1953.

Geller, J. D. Some personal and situational determinants of interpersonal trust. Unpublished doctoral dissertation, Univer. of Connecticut, 1966.

Kelley, H., & Ring, K. Some effects of "suspiciousness" versus "trusting" training schedules. *Journal of Abnormal and Social Psychology*, 1961, *63*, 294–301.

Loomis, J. L. Communication, the development of trust, and cooperative behavior. *Human Relations*, 1959, *12*, 305–315.

Mahrer, R. R. The role of expectancy in delayed reinforcement. *Journal of Experimental Psychology*, 1956, *52*, 101–105.

Mellinger, G. D. Interpersonal trust as a factor in communication. *Journal of Abnormal and Social Psychology*, 1956, *52*, 304–309.

Merton, R. *Social theory and social structure.* Glencoe, Ill.: Free Press, 1949.

Mischel W. Father-absence and delay of gratification. Cross-cultural comparisons. *Journal of Abnormal and Social Psychology*, 1961, *63*, 116–124. (a)

Mischel, W. Preference for delayed reinforcement and social responsibility. *Journal of Abnormal and Social Psychology*, 1961, *62*, 1–7. (b)

Rapaport, A., & Orwant, Carol. Experimental games: a review. *Behavioral Science*, 1962, *7*, 1–37.

Redl, F., & Wineman, A. *Children who hate.* Glencoe, Ill.: Free Press, 1951.

Rotter, J. B. *Social learning and clinical psychology.* Englewood Cliffs, N. J.: Prentice-Hall, 1954.

Rotter, J. B. The role of the psychological situation in determining the direction of human behavior. In M. R. Jones (Ed.), *Nebraska symposium on motivation.* Lincoln: Univer. of Nebraska Press, 1955.

Rotter, J. B. Some implications of a social learning theory for the prediction of goal directed behavior from testing procedures. *Psychological Review,* 1960, *67*, 301–316.

Scodel, A. Induced collaboration in some non-zero-sum games. *Journal of Conflict Resolution,* 1962, *6*, 335–340.

STUDY QUESTIONS

1. What are the theoretical distinctions discussed in the article?
2. How were the problems of social desirability addressed?
3. How were the items derived and how were they refined?
4. What steps were involved in the assessment of construct validity?
5. Do you think the article achieves a multitrait, multimethod solution to issues of validity?

EXERCISES

1   Evaluating Tests

Select three tests.[3] Using the following questions as guides, evaluate the psychometric properties of each of the tests. Judge the appropriateness of the tests for particular populations and comment on any ethical issues that arise.

1. What is the degree of reliability and what are the means of determining it?
2. What is the degree of validity and what are the means of determining it?

[3]If you do not have a test library available, a good source is Buros, 1970. Also, refer to the recommendations in Chapter 2 for searching the literature and follow these practices in seeking out newly developed tests or scales reported in the literature. Another source is your professor, who undoubtedly receives distributions in the mail from commercial test publishers.

3. Identify the normative groups.
4. How is response style dealt with?
5. Is the test appropriate for use with college students? males? females? children? minority groups?
6. Do questions of ethics arise?

2   Q Sorts

To understand the procedures involved in the *Q* sort, it is probably a good idea actually to perform several sorts. For items to use in these *Q*-sorts, see Block's 1966 book or the article by Sundberg, Rohila, Tyler (1970). It would probably be easiest to do just two self-descriptive sorts. For example, one sort might be "myself as I am" and another "as I would like to be" or "as my mother sees me." Compare the two sorts by using a simple rank-order correlation achieved by following these steps:

Write out the items on 3 by 5 cards or on a blank sheet leaving sufficient space to cut out, in approximately equal sizes, the pieces of paper on which they are written. You now have a *Q*-sort "deck" of 16 items.

Number additional cards or slips from 1 to 7. On each card write one of the seven instructions listed in Table 8-2. You should have seven cards and on each card you should have written one instruction. Place each of the seven instruction cards on a table in numerical order, thereby forming a seven-point numerical scale. The number of cards to go into each pile and the rank assigned to cards in each pile are specified in Table 8-2.

Now you are ready to do the actual *Q* sort. Place the required number of cards below each of the categories— for example, the one card that best fits in

TABLE 8-2
Illustration of a Q-Sort Distribution

Pile No.	Instruction (Degree of Similarity)	Number of Cards in each pile	Rank
1	Definitely like me	1	1
2	Moderately like me	2	2.5
3	Slightly like me	3	5
4	Neutral or ambivalent	4	8.5
5	Slightly unlike me	3	12
6	Moderately unlike me	2	14.5
7	Definitely unlike me	1	16

the "definitely like me" pile, the two cards that best fit the "moderately like me" pile, and so on until the distribution is complete.

Record on the data sheet, illustrated in Table 8-3, the actual rank (given in Table 8-2) that is achieved for each item or card. If the item falls into pile 1 it gets a rank of 1, the two items that are placed in pile 2 both get a rank of 2.5, the 3 items in pile 5 each get a rank of 12, and so on. If you have a larger scale (for example, a 9-point scale) or more items, the ranks will change.

Compare the two sorts by calculating a rank-order correlation coefficient, sometimes called rho (Siegel 1956), using the following steps:

1. For each sort, calculate the difference between ranks by subtracting the smaller rank from the larger. Record the difference on the data sheet.
2. Square the differences and record these on the data sheet.
3. Add the squared differences in step 2 (Σd^2).
4. Multiply by 6 the sum obtained ($6\Sigma d^2$).
5. Divide by 4080 the product obtained in step 4 ($N^3 - N$).

The working formula for rho (Siegel 1056) is

$$\rho_s = 1 - \frac{6 \Sigma d^2}{N^3 - N}.$$

TABLE 8-3
Data Sheet for a Q-Sort

Item Number	1st Sort Rank	2nd Sort Rank	Difference	Difference Squared
1				
2				
3				
4				
5				
6				
7				
8				
9				
10				
11				
12				
13				
14				
15				
16				
		Sum of differences squared:		_____

If the rho is positive, then a similarity exists between the Q sorts, and the way you see yourself now is similar to the way you would like to be. If the rho is negative, then you see yourself as dissimilar to your ideal self. The closer the rho is to 1 or -1 the greater the degree of convergence or divergence of your two views of yourself.

ANNOTATED BIBLIOGRAPHY

Biaggio, M. K. Anger arousal and personality characteristics. *Journal of Personality and Social Psychology*, 1980, *39*, 352–356.

College students selected on the basis of anger-self-report and anger-inventory scores completed the California Psychological Inventory. As hypothesized, high-anger-arousal subjects scored lower on socialization, self-control, tolerance, psychological-mindedness, and flexibility than low-anger-arousal subjects, who scored higher on responsibility, socialization, and good impression.

DeGregorio, E., & Carver, C. S. Type A behavior pattern, sex role orientation and psychological adjustment. *Journal of Personality and Social Psychology*, 1980, *39*, 286–293.

College students completed a number of personality tests designed to measure Type A ("coronary-prone") behavioral style, sex-role orientation, self-esteem, social anxiety, and depression. Subjects who were characterized by both the Type A pattern and low masculinity also showed low self-esteem (true of both sexes), social anxiety, and depression (true of the women only).

Friedman, H. S., Prince, L. M., Riggio, R. E., & DiMatteo, M. R. Understanding and assessing nonverbal expressiveness: The affective communication test. *Journal of Personality and Social Psychology*, 1980, *39*, 333–351.

This article describes the development of a 13-item self-report affective-communication test (included in the article), and reports data showing the test to be a reliable and valid measure of individual differences in expressiveness ("charisma").

Russell, D., Peplau, L. A., & Cutrona, C. E. The revised UCLA Loneliness Scale: Concurrent and discriminant validity evidence. *Journal of Personality and Social Psychology*, 1980, *39*, 472–480.

The authors report two studies contributing to the validation of their revised loneliness scale (included in the article).

Strickland, B. R., & Haley, W. E. Sex differences on the Rotter I-E Scale. *Journal of Personality and Social Psychology*, 1980, *39*, 930–939.

This study involved a factor analysis and item analysis of the scores of male and female college students who completed Rotter's I-E scale according to the usual instructions. Results indicated that both total scores and some of the scale factors might have different meanings for males and females. The authors discuss the implications of their findings for test construction and validation.

Woll, S. B., & Cozby, P. C. Category of moral judgment and attitudes towards amnesty and the Nixon pardon. *PSPB*, 1976, *2*, 183–186.

Scores on Hogan's survey of ethical attitudes (SEA) correlated with positive attitudes towards the pardon of Nixon and negative attitudes towards amnesty for draft evaders. The authors argue that these results support their notion that the SEA is primarily a measure of political and social preferences rather than a scale of moral judgment.

ADDITIONAL SOURCES

Horner, M. The motive to avoid success and changing aspirations of college women. In J. H. Bardwick (Ed.), *Readings on the psychology of women.* New York: Harper & Row, 1972. (Reprinted from *Women on Campus: 1970, a symposium.* Center for the Continuing Education of Women, Ann Arbor, Michigan.)

Kahn, R. L., & Cannell, C. F. *The dynamics of interviewing: Theory, technique, and cases.* New York: Wiley, 1957.

Keniston, K. Inburn: An American Ishmael. In R. W. White (Ed.), *The study of lives.* New York: Atherton, 1963.

May, R. Sex differences in fantasy patterns. *Journal of Projective Techniques.* 1966, *30*, 252–259.

McClelland, D. C. *Studies in motivation.* New York: Appleton-Century-Crofts, 1955.

McClelland, D. C. *The achieving society.* Princeton, N. J.: Van Nostrand, 1961.

Orlofsky, J. L., Marcia, J. E., & Lesser, I. M. Ego identity status and the intimacy vs. isolation crisis of young adulthood. *Journal of Personality and Social Psychology*, 1973, *27*, 211–219.

Rotter, J. B. Generalized expectancies for internal versus external control of reinforcement. *Psychological Monographs*, 1966, *30* (Whole No. 609).

Stewart, A. S., & Winter, D. G. Self-definition and social definition in women. *Journal of Personality*, 1974, *42*, 238–259.

Troll, L. E. The salience of members of 3-generation families for one another. Paper presented at The American Psychological Association meeting, Honolulu, 1972.

Troll, L. E. Generational change in women's cognitive and achievement orientation. Paper presented at the Symposium on Future of Aging Women, International Gerontological Society, Jerusalem, 1975.

Weston, P. J., & Mednick, M. T. Race, social class, and the motive to avoid success in women. *Journal of Cross-Cultural Psychology*, 1970, *1*, 284–291.

CHAPTER

9

The Experimental Method

As you have learned, psychological research strategies reflect two major scientific traditions, the correlational and the experimental. Thus far, we have devoted little attention to experimental designs; however, they are the research strategies of choice for many psychologists. Helmreich (1975) notes that many social psychologists, for example, have adopted a philosophical orientation in which the laboratory/experimental methodology is viewed as the true path to knowledge. Such an approach is particularly characteristic of researchers known as behaviorists, or experimental psychologists. Social and experimental psychologists are two more groups of scientists who share an interest in identifying environmental determinants of behavior and a disinterest in examining individual differences. They see *situation variables* rather than *person variables* as crucial to the process of specifying laws of behavior.

We would argue that in psychology, as in most forms of inquiry, no single method is crucial or correct. Rather, different forms of systematic approach are appropriate at different stages of scientific development and under different circumstances. Both the correlational and experimental strategies can be used in ways that yield either meaningful and enlightening or trivial and misleading data. The thoughtfulness and care with which an investigator develops a research question are probably the most important ingredients in any investigation. The choice of a research strategy for investigating the question is vital but nevertheless subsidiary. No methodology is so robust that it can replace the need for significant and well-conceptualized questions.

For many questions and in many settings, as we shall see, the experimental method is a most powerful tool indeed. Like the other methodological tools with which it is frequently combined, the experimental method proves its usefulness in a variety of settings. Usually, one thinks of experiments taking place in a specially designed laboratory. However, experimentation can be done in any number of different locations depending on the circumstances, the question being asked, and the opportunity for data collection. As you will see, one of the basic characteristics of the experiment is control of the conditions under which information is derived. It is true that the laboratory is usually well designed to permit control of conditions. Nevertheless, if researchers limited themselves to laboratory settings alone, much useful information and evidence would be lost. For example, many naturally occurring events and many issues of personality are extremely difficult, if not impossible, to reproduce adequately in the laboratory. If one wished to study, say, the effects on people of disasters or even of less dramatic events such as elections, it might be much more useful to initiate such studies under natural conditions than to try to fit them into a laboratory setting. The power blackout described in the Zucker, Manosevitz and Lanyon study in Chapter 3 is a good example of conditions that would be exceedingly difficult to reproduce fully.

Most investigators today recognize that a balance can be struck between the more complete control provided in the laboratory and the potentially more realistic outcome that occurs in the field. Optimally, the personality researcher should be able to explore naturally occurring events in the field, enter the laboratory with the results of such explorations, and then perhaps return to the field with more precisely specified questions.

THE EXPERIMENT

The goal of experimental research is to establish the existence of causal relationships among variables, generally by showing that a change in one variable (the independent variable) produces change in another variable (the dependent variable). One of the key requirements of the experimental method is *control*—over levels of the independent variable and all other conditions that could affect the dependent variable.

Let's say that you have a favorite charity and that you would like to see an increase in donations to that charity. In addition to writing your own check, you could conduct an experiment in which the dependent variable would be the number or size of donations made to charity. What could you do to produce an increase in donations? To use experimental language, what variables could you "manipulate"? What "treatments" could you apply? What aspects of the charity drive could you "control" in a way that could have a positive effect on the level of donations? That is, what would be the independent variable in your experiment? You might decide, as Cialdini and Schroeder (1976) did, that an effective way of influencing people's donations to a charity is to provide an assurance that a contribution of any size is acceptable— "even a penny will help." In the Cialdini and Schroeder (1976) field experiment on donations to the American Cancer Society, legitimization of paltry contributions ("even a penny will help") was the independent variable and subject contributions was the dependent variable.

If you were designing the experiment on donations to charity, how would you test the experimental hypothesis that donations can be increased by legitimizing even very small contributions? Perhaps you would spend an afternoon going door to door around your neighborhood saying "I'm collecting for the American Cancer Society. Please give. Even a penny will help." If you followed that procedure and only that procedure, you would be committing the error of the one-shot case study (for example, Huck, Cormier, & Bounds, 1974) rather than conducting a true experiment. Because you would be following the same procdures with every subject, you would have no way of knowing what features of the request—for example, your appearance, the familiarity of your face, the closeness of the request to payday—were affecting the response (that is, people's contributions).

Suppose, in your one-shot case study, you collected $25 from 20 households. How could you be sure that it was the particular nature of your request ("even a penny will help") that led people to make donations? How would you rule out alternative explanations for why you received the donations you did? It is not enough to say that "last year American Cancer Society volunteers collected less money on this block" or that "my friend received fewer donations from 20 families in a neighboring district." Last year a lot of circumstances might have been different and even this year your friend might have been approaching a group of people who differed in important ways—for example, in income, interpersonal trust, family size—from members of your sample. You would not be able to rule out alternative explanations for the particular set of results you received, because you had not included *controls* in your investigation.

What do we mean by *controls*? Controls are the steps we take or the procedures we follow to make sure the results we achieve with our dependent variable—donations in our example—really are produced by our independent variable—"even a penny will help"—and not by some other variable, such as income level of subject or attractiveness of solicitor. At the very least, we need to be able to *compare* results achieved when the independent variable is present (experimental condition) with results achieved when the independent variable is absent (control condition). In the Cialdini and Schroeder (1976) experiment, all subjects (residents of a middle-income suburban housing area) were treated identically by solicitors except that with half the subjects (the experimental group) the plea "Even a penny will help" was added to the standard request "Would you be willing to help by giving a donation?" and with the other half of the sample (the

control group) the plea was not added. Because these were two comparable groups treated identically except for the independent variable, legitimation of small contributions in the experimental group, differences between groups in amount of giving could be attributed to the independent variable.

If we are to be confident that differences on the dependent variable between experimental and control groups are caused by the independent variable and not by some other, *extraneous* variable, we must take steps to ensure that the experimental and control groups do not differ in any important way except in exposure to the independent variable. In laboratory experiments, initial equivalence of groups is usually sought by randomly[1] assigning available subjects to the experimental and control conditions. When subjects are assigned to groups randomly, initial differences among them should balance or cancel each other out, so that subjects in the experimental group are not systematically different from those in the control group in characteristics that could be related to outcome on the dependent variable.

In field experiments, investigators frequently select subjects or assign subjects to conditions by procedures that are not random but are nevertheless used systematically to avoid bias. Cialdini and Schroeder (1976) do not report how they determined which residents within their sample would receive the experimental treatment ("even a penny will help") and which residents would be in the control group. It is possible that before canvassing began, they assigned every household a number and then used a random-numbers table to determine

---

[1]In scientific terminology, *random* does not mean haphazard. *Random selection* of subjects from a population means following procedures that are designed to avoid bias and ensure that every individual in the population has an equal chance of being selected for the sample. *Random assignment* of available subjects to experimental and control conditions means following procedures designed to ensure that every subject has an equal chance of being assigned to a particular group.

which households would be in the experimental condition and which would be controls. It is also possible that solicitors systematically alternated between the experimental and control versions of their request as they went from household to household, taking special steps to ensure that an equal number of corner houses were included in the experimental and control conditions. Such a precaution is important because corner lots are generally more expensive than property in the middle of a block and consequently might be owned by individuals with somewhat higher incomes than their neighbors. In all likelihood, Cialdini and Schroeder did not alternate the experimental and control requests by entire blocks or by side of street. Consider the kinds of bias that might be introduced if all residents on the north side of a street were put into the experimental condition and all residents on the south side were put into the control condition.

The need to develop and establish controls for the effects of extraneous influences in an experiment stems from an important reality about human behavior: that it is complex and has multiple determinants. Consider a behavior such as eating. How we eat, what we eat, and when we eat all depend on a multitude of determinants—for example, internal states (such as hunger), external cues (such as where we are and what other people are doing), the customs of the society into which we were born, our own prior experience, the availability of food, and so on. Moreover, not only can a single behavior have many different causes, but a single cause can have many different effects. If something frustrates you, you might yell, refuse to speak, light a cigarette, go for a walk, eat a candy bar, or respond in any number of other ways.

Extraneous influences, then, are factors other than those selected for manipulation that can have an impact on the dependent variable in an experiment. In real life, the influence of such extraneous variables can be just as real and just as important as that of the independent variable under consideration. Indeed, one investigator's

extraneous variable may be another's independent variable. For an investigator interested in the relationship between self-esteem and aggression, for example, frustration might be an extraneous variable, whereas for an investigator interested in the effects of frustration on aggression, self-esteem might be an extraneous variable. Both of these hypothetical investigators would have to design experiments allowing them to isolate the effects on aggression of the particular variable in which they are interested while minimizing the effects of other potential variables on their measure of aggression.

UNWANTED VARIANCE IN COMPLEX DESIGNS

The Cialdini and Schroeder (1976) fund-raising experiment is simple in its design, focusing as it does on the effect of one independent variable ("even a penny will help") on one dependent variable (donations). There is no attempt in this experiment to consider the possible sources of individual differences in charitable donations within the experimental and control groups. Cialdini and Schroeder do not examine person variables at all in their study of donating behavior. They consider only one situation variable, manipulated in their request for contributions.

While recognizing that situation variables influence behavior, personality psychologists are particularly interested in individual differences in behavior that reflect characteristics of the person rather than characteristics of the situation. Experiments that are designed to test the impact of both person variables and situation variables are more complex than those testing a single situation variable. The former require careful attention to numerous sources of potential *static*[2]—unwanted variance—in the dependent variable. Below, we consider an ex-

[2]We are using the term *static* to refer to variability (in statistical language, *variance*) in scores on the dependent variable that is due to unwanted influences rather than to the operation of the independent variable.

ample (Greene, 1976) of a quasi-experimental[3] investigation in which both person and situation variables were analyzed. Then we review the potential sources of static that a researcher must confront when designing a well-controlled investigation.

A Case Study in Complex Design

Like Cialdini and Schroeder (1976), Greene (1976) conducted his investigation in a naturalistic setting, in this case, a weight-reduction clinic. The dependent variable of interest to Green was weight loss. Green hypothesizes that specific behaviors of the weight-clinic personnel acted as situational variables affecting clients' feelings about their initial clinic interviews as well as affecting their compliance in a weight-reduction program. However, Greene also believed that personality characteristics of the client would operate to affect both clients' feelings about the interview and their compliance in weight-reduction programs.

The personality variable Greene selected for study was field independence/field dependence. Derived from the work of Witkin (e.g., Witkin, Dyk, Faterson, Goodenough, & Karp, 1962), the dimension of field independence/dependence refers to the extent to which individuals are independent of environmental cues in interpreting experience. Some people are much more likely than others to isolate their experiences and activities from the surrounding context. The personal tendencies of people to be more or less field independent have been shown to have implications for a variety of social interactions (Witkin, Goodenough, & Oltman, 1979). For example, field-dependent individuals tend to have an interpersonal orientation expressed in preferences such as wanting to be physically close to others, whereas field-independent individuals have a more autonomous and impersonal orientation.

In his weight-reduction study, Greene (1976) hypothesized that because of their interpersonal orientation, field-dependent clients would have more positive feelings toward a counselor who sat close and provided positive feedback than toward a counselor remaining distant and providing neutral feedback. Conversely, he expected that field-independent clients would express more positive feelings toward counselors who maintained a greater distance and offered neutral rather than positive feedback. Because field-dependent people appear to have the greater need for emotional support from others, Greene also hypothesized that they would be less successful than field-independent people in actually complying in a self-monitored 5-week weight-reduction program in which there was no further interaction with a counselor.

To test these hypotheses, Greene developed a complex design with three major independent variables: client's classification as field independent or dependent (a person variable), amount of interpersonal space between counselor and client (a situation variable), and type of feedback (positive or neutral) given to the client by the counselor (a situation variable). Such a design, which incorporates more than one independent variable, is called *factorial design*. Each of the independent variables is a *factor* that might have some effect on the dependent variable—either alone or in combination with the other independent variable(s). One could describe Greene's design as a 2 by 2 by 2 factorial, each number referring to the number of levels present in each independent variable. In Greene's 2 by 2 by 2 factorial, there were two levels of the personality variable (field independent and field dependent), two levels of evaluative feedback (positive and neutral), and two levels of physical proximity (2 feet and 5 feet).[4]

---

[3]When a research design incorporates some but not all the features of a "true" experiment, it is called *quasi experimental*.

[4]In reality, because he used *two* trained interviewers as "clinic counselors," Greene treated each counselor as a "level" of a fourth independent variable in a 2 by 2 by 2 factorial design. That is, he used statistical techniques to determine whether any results on the dependent variables

Greene assessed the impact of his independent variables on a variety of dependent variables, including (1) the client's nonverbal behaviors during the interview with the counselor, (2) an unobtrusive measure of speech disturbance designed to assess client discomfort during the interview, (3) a postinterview questionnaire designed to assess clients' feelings about the counselor, and (4) a behavioral measure of long-term compliance with the weight-reduction program (success or failure in returning to the clinic with a weight loss of at least 5 pounds after 5 weeks).

In this experiment, as in every experiment, it was important for the investigator to establish controls, to ensure that differences between groups on the dependent measure were due to the operation of the independent variables and not some other influence. In the following section, we discuss major sources of static (again, influences other than the independent variables that might have an impact on the dependent variables) that investigators must consider in designing experiments and illustrate how Greene controlled for these sources of static in his experiment.

Static Due to Conditions

In any experimental investigation, it is important that, apart from the experimental treatment, the conditions under which subjects are observed or interviewed or tested be kept constant across treatment groups. If you were observing interpersonal behavior as a function of an independent variable and you were fairly sure that noise or temperature levels could affect interpersonal behavior, you would not observe the interpersonal behavior of some subjects in a hot, noisy room and of other subjects in a

cold, quiet room. You would not want to *confound* effects due to the extraneous influences of noise and heat with the effects of your independent variables—for example, as in Greene's study, the physical proximity and verbal feedback of an interviewer. Thus, in experiments we control for the effects of many potential influences—for example, time of day, weather, temperature, lighting, noise—by holding them constant across experimental conditions. Whenever there is evidence that a particular feature of a situation in addition to our independent variables can influence the dependent variables, we must provide controls for these influences.

In addition to the relatively simple problems of controlling such factors as time and experiment location, investigators must deal with the more difficult problem of controlling experimenter bias. As mentioned in earlier chapters, it has been demonstrated repeatedly (for example, Rosenthal, 1976) that the expectations of the experimenter can influence the collection of data in favor of the hypotheses under study. Barber and Silver (1968) have argued that there are eleven possible sources of experimenter activity that can influence the results of an experiment. These activities include giving voice cues, body-language cues, and verbal reinforcement of desired responses, as well as misjudging subject responses and misrecording responses.

Unlike temperature, noise, or location, experimenter bias cannot be controlled adequately by an attempt to keep it constant across experimental conditions. As we've mentioned before, the simplest way to control for many types of experimenter bias is to ask an assistant to collect the data. This person should be uninformed about the experimental hypotheses—that is, he or she should be "blind" as to the intentions behind the experiment. The assumption underlying this particular use of blinds is that an experimenter who does not know the hypotheses being tested cannot unintentionally (or intentionally!) influence the outcome in a systematic way.

---

could be attributed to the particular counselor the client saw. This kind of *statistical control* allowed Greene to conclude that it was not which of the two counselors the client saw but more particular behaviors of counselors (proximity, feedback) that made a difference for the field-dependent and -independent clients.

A procedure used as an alternative or in addition to this form of control consists of employing two or more experimenters as data collectors. Where there are several experimenters, statistical procedures can be used to determine interexperimenter reliability by calculating the degree of consistency in results across experimenters—just as Greene used statistical techniques to determine whether systematically different results were being obtained across his two interviewers. If consistency across experimenters is low, it is possible that some sort of unintentional bias is operating to influence the results.

Static Due to Sampling

Usually, it is impossible to test all the members of the population to which you wish to generalize. Consequently, as noted earlier, you are likely to select from the population of interest a sample that you intend to be representative of that larger population. However, we know that the impact of almost any experimental condition will differ from one subject to another and for a variety of reasons that have nothing to do with your independent variable. Consequently, the manner in which you obtain your sample from the population is very important in minimizing the effect of irrelevant influences on your dependent measures.

If, in his study of weight reduction, Greene had used college students participating in research in order to complete a course requirement, the outcome of his study might have been affected by static due to sampling. For example, such students might not be motivated to lose weight at all, although they might go through the motions of an initial interview and subsequent follow-up visit to receive their course credit. It is also possible that college students fulfilling a course requirement differ systematically from the ordinary clientele of weight-reduction clinics in their tendency to comply with programs of instruction of any sort. In either case, the outcome of the study might have

indicated that neither field independence nor counselor behavior had an effect on client attitudes or compliance. However, such findings would have occurred only because of particular characteristics of the student sample and not because field independence and counselor behavior have no "real-life effects" on attitudes and compliance. To avoid such sampling influences, Greene by-passed the common strategy of working with readily available college students and used newspaper advertisements to recruit women interested in the services of a weight-reduction clinic. Moreover, rather than paying subjects, Greene offered a weight-reduction program free of charge in exchange for participation in the research project. What kinds of problems could have occurred if Greene's sample consisted of paid subjects?

Greene imposed two further controls on his sampling procedures: he restricted the sample to women and he accepted only those women who were no more than 45 pounds overweight. As we indicated in Chapter 3, it is not unusual for investigators to limit their samples to one sex only. Investigators often use single-sex designs to avoid static in a dependent variable as a function of sex when sex differences are not of interest. However, by eliminating one sex from an experiment, an investigator is also limiting the applicability of the results of the experiment. In Greene's case, he cannot generalize his findings to the total population of volunteers for weight-reduction programs but only to female volunteers who are no more than 45 pounds overweight. Consider for a moment the kind of unwanted static that might have occurred if Greene had not set some limits on the extent to which potential subjects were overweight.

Static Due to Subject Assignment

In assigning subjects to treatment conditions, you will want to ensure that no preexisting differences exist between members of different conditions that can account for ultimate differences between the groups on the dependent variables. For example, it would have been silly for Greene to assign all the field-dependent women to an experimental condition in which the counselor sat close and provided positive feedback and all the field-independent women to a condition where the counselor sat farther away and provided neutral feedback. Had he followed such a procedure and obtained statistically significant differences between treatment groups in evaluation of counselor and compliance in weight-reduction program, he would not have known whether these results were due to field independence/dependence, counselor proximity, counselor feedback, or some combination of these variables.

The recommended control procedure for avoiding static due to faulty subject assignment is to assign subjects randomly to experimental and control conditions—for example, through such techniques as coin tossing or use of a random-number table. Greene reports that in his experiment assignment of the first 60 clients to the particular verbal-feedback and physical-proximity conditions was randomized and assignment of the last 20 clients interviewed was made on the basis of ensuring equal numbers of clients across the experimental conditions. To form the field-independence and -dependence groups within these conditions, scores on Witkin's Embedded Figures Test (Witkin, Oltman, Raskin, & Karp, 1971) were dichotomized at the median score.

There are times when a more precise form of control than simple randomization is needed to minimize error that might occur because of preexisting characteristics of the subjects. Consider the unlikely possibility that success in weight loss was so strongly related to IQ that it masked any impact on weight loss stemming from different counselor behaviors interacting with field independence. In such a case, Greene would have been well advised to employ a procedure known as *matched random assignment*. This matching procedure requires three

steps: (1) information is obtained on the variable to be matched (in our example, scores on an IQ test); (2) the subjects are paired on the variable so that the two subjects scoring highest on the IQ test form one pair, the next two scores will provide a second pair, and so on; (3) each pair member is randomly assigned to the different conditions of the experiment. This matched random assignment would have been extremely difficult to perform in Greene's experiment, where a personality variable and two experimental manipulations were already built into the design.

In addition to using the procedural control of random assignment, Greene used statistical controls to determine whether initial biasing differences existed between treatment groups on extraneous variables. By *statistical controls*, we mean that the investigator performs statistical tests to determine whether any statistically significant differences exist among treatment groups (the experimental and control groups, groups exposed to different levels of independent variables) on extraneous variables that could affect the experimental outcome. A quotation from the method section of Greene's report (1976, p. 571) illustrates his use of statistical controls:

> Subjects were 80 residents of the New Haven area whose ages ranged from 19 to 67 years, with a mean of 39.7 years. All clients expressed an interest in losing between 15 and 45 pounds. No differences across experimental conditions on these variables were obtained. An intelligence index . . . also yielded no significant differences across conditions.

Thus, by comparing his groups statistically, Greene was reasonably sure that neither age nor desired amount of weight loss nor intelligence (as he measured it) had any systematic effects on the outcome of the study.

Static Due to Unreliability

Investigators from all scientific disciplines have to deal with the problem of unreliability in measuring instruments. If 20 individuals had their heights measured with 20 different measuring tapes or with the same tape 20 times in succession, small differences in the heights would be recorded in successive measurements. Similarly, if a sample of subjects took the same psychological test several different times, it is unlikely that each subject would obtain the identical score every time. You will recall from our discussion of reliability and validity in Chapter 8 that psychological tests are not perfectly reliable, and that the degree of unreliability of tests can contribute to static in the findings. While there is no complete control for this form of static (known as error variance), it is obvious that tests or other instruments with demonstrably high reliability and validity will contribute less error than will measures with questionable degrees of reliability and validity. In his weight-loss study, Greene avoided the temptation to develop his own original measure of field independence/dependence, and relied on an established measure (the Embedded Figures Test), which has been used in numerous other studies and which is supported by a substantial body of reliability and validity data.

When the measuring instrument is a person—that is, an observer—other types of static can affect one's findings. For example, an observer might consistently favor one group of subjects over another. Or an observer might gradually become fatigued, and be steadily less and less sensitive to the events under observation. Conversely, an observer's skill might improve over time, so that more of the relevant events are recorded in later experimental sessions than in earlier sessions. Thus, personal bias, progressive fatigue, or progressive skill can produce systematic differences between groups of scores quite apart from the effects of independent variables.

Such systematic influences on test scores are not the only sources of static having an impact on experimental results. Chance differences in the subjects themselves (for example, energy level, sense of confidence, health) can contribute to static in each subject's scores over time. This kind of static (or error variance) is unsystematic in its impact, and affects the reliability of any individual's scores on any given measure. For example, a subject with an initial score of 11 on an affiliation test might later receive a score of 9 and still later one of 12 on the very same test. These unsystematic influences on the measurement process reflect the operation of different factors at different times. The experimental controls already discussed (control of conditions, assignment, and sampling) are intended to reduce systematic error to a minimum. If these controls are employed properly in experimental design, it is also expected that unsystematic or random error will balance out across conditions.

Minimizing Static: A Summary

A review of the previous sections on sources of static (extraneous or error variance) in experimental designs will reveal that there are three principal techniques for minimizing unwanted influences on the data. First, one tries to hold conditions constant across experimental groups. Second, one randomly assigns subjects to conditions, under the assumption that potentially biasing individual differences among subjects will balance themselves out across groups. The effectiveness of this type of *methodological control* can be checked through *statistical-control procedures*—that is, statistical tests designed to determine whether initial differences exist among groups on relevant extraneous variables —for example, IQ. Third, one can build an extraneous variable into the design as an additional independent variable, the effects of which can be determined through statistical tests. For example, investigators often build sex of subject into their designs as an additional variable when the possibility of sex differences is not of substantive interest but the investigator wants to discover whether sex differences occur on the dependent variable under consideration.

In his study, Greene treated his interviewers as an independent variable to establish whether or not one interviewer received systematically different evaluations and results than the other.

TIME OF MEASUREMENT

We have been discussing influences on dependent variables and ways of controlling for unwanted influences in an experimental design. Another important issue for the experimental researcher is deciding when measurements on the dependent variable should be taken. Although there are many variants, the two most basic strategies are (1) taking measurements on the dependent variable both before and after introduction of the independent variable (the *pretest/post-test design*, also known as the *before-after design*), and (2) taking measurements on the dependent variable only after the experimental group has been exposed to the independent variable (the *post-test–only design*). As you will see, Greene used the pretest/post-test strategy with one of his dependent variables (weight) and the post-test–only strategy with his other dependent variables. Cialdini and Schroeder (1976) used the post-test–only strategy to determine the impact of minimizing paltry contributions ("even a penny will help").

When the pretest/post-test design is used with an experimental and a control group, subjects are assigned randomly to groups and then pretested on the dependent variable to establish their baseline scores on that measure—for example, weight. After a period in which the groups are treated identically except for presentation of the independent variable to the experimental group and not to the control group, all subjects are post-tested on the dependent measure. In a variant on this basic design, all groups receive a different form of the independent variable—as in Greene's investigation, where all groups received either positive or neutral feedback from a counselor sitting either 2 feet or 5 feet away. Generally, statistical analyses are done to show whether changes from pretest to post-test are greater (to an extent that is statistically significant) for the experimental group than for the control group, or for one experimental condition as compared with others. This before-after design, with random assignment of subjects to conditions, incorporates controls for unwanted influences occurring during the pretest and post-test as well as for the mere passage of time—since such influences should affect the different conditions equally.

In Greene's weight-clinic study, subject weight was determined both before the initial counseling interview and after the 5 week weight-reduction program. Although it is not altogether clear precisely how Greene analyzed the weight variable, it is clear that differences among groups in "post-test weight" would have to be adjusted by statistical means (for example, by analysis of covariance) for initial differences in " pretest weight" scores. Stated simply, Greene could not determine whether weight loss was affected by field independence/dependence, counselor feedback, and counselor proximity without knowing how much each client weighed before as well as after the treatment program.

While the pretest/post-test strategy has many useful applications, in some situations the very fact of taking a pretest will have an effect on a subject's post-test results. Tests and other forms of verbal report can be *reactive* measures—that is, they can inadvertently cause a reaction in subjects that influences the data the experimenter is collecting. The very fact of taking a test, experiencing some sort of intervention, and then taking the test again can affect the second set of scores. If you gave college students an empathy test, showed them a film illustrating the positive aspects of one person's empathy for another, and then gave them the empathy test again, many of them would figure out what your assumptions were. In such a case, where the *experimental blinds* were inadequate, the post-test scores of some subjects might reflect their desire to please or distress you more than the malleability of their tendency to show empathy. Even when the subjects make no deliberate attempt to manipulate their own test results, their scores may be affected by practice or familiarity.

Both the Greene and the Cialdini and Schroeder experiments illustrate other kinds of limitations than can beset before-after designs. It would have been possible for Greene to ask clients to evaluate counselor characteristics before as well as after they had interacted with their counselors, but it certainly would have been difficult to interpret the meaning of the preliminary evaluations and of changes in the evaluations. Similarly, Cialdini and Schroeder could have canvassed the same neighborhood twice, comparing donations both before and after they added the plea "even a penny will help" to their request for contributions. What problems would such a strategy have created?

To avoid the *experimental contamination* (that is, effects on the dependent variable stemming from the data-collecting process) built into some pretest/post-test designs, experimenters often use a *post-test-only* design. In this experimental design, subjects are assigned randomly to experimental and control groups or to different forms of the experimental treatment. The experimental group is then exposed to the independent variable—for example, some sort of counselor behavior—and both groups are measured on the dependent variable—such as the willingness to comply with counselor recommendations. It is assumed that random assignment of subjects results in the samples being initially equivalent on the dependent variable as well as on extraneous variables, so that any statistically significant differences emerging between the groups after the experimental treatment are due to the experimental treatment— that is, to the independent variable. While random assignment cannot eliminate the possi-

bility of important preliminary differences among treatment groups, this possibility is significantly reduced through the randomization process.

Greene (1976) made use of a post-test–only type of design for several of his dependent variables—psychological involvement with the interviewer, attraction for the interviewer, and intention to adhere to dieting recommendations. Data on these variables were collected just once, during or after the counseling interviews. Using a statistical technique called a factorial analysis of variance (to be discussed in more detail later), Greene examined the scores on these different dependent measures in each of his treatment groups. The factorial analysis of variance confirmed a number of predicted *interactions* among the independent variables. For example, *field-dependent clients* showed *more* attraction and responsiveness to counselors who provided positive feedback, whereas field-independent clients were not influenced by the feedback variable at all.

FACTORIAL DESIGNS

Greene's investigation is a good example of the use of a factorial design to examine the way a personality characteristic can serve as a *mediating variable* (or *moderator variable*) that intervenes between environmental events and individual behavior. We are reminded again that not everyone responds to the same events in the same way. Greene's investigation indicated that particular counselor behaviors can affect different clients differently, depending on whether the clients are characteristically field independent or -dependent.

Given the personality psychologist's emphasis on the complexity of person/situation transactions and on multiple causation in human behavior, the factorial design is often the design of choice for personologists wanting to gain the precision and control of the experimental method. In our discussion of the advantages of factorial experiments, we will rely heavily on this chapter's selection by Mitchell and Byrne as a case study in factorial design.

One of the major advantages of factorial designs is that they allow us to examine the effects of two or more independent variables both separately (as *main effects*) and in combination with each other (as *interactions*). It is not essential that one of these independent variables be a manipulated situational variable and that one be a measured person variable, although such a combination might be of particular interest to personality psychologists. The design can involve two or more independent variables, all of which are treated experimentally or all of which are correlational. For example, Greene could have used a 2 by 2 factorial design to determine the effects on weight loss of two levels of counselor feedback and two levels of counselor proximity. Or he could have divided his subjects into three age groups and used a 2 by 3 factorial design to determine the effects of two levels of field independence and three levels of age status on weight loss. If he had administered another personality test to his subjects as an additional independent variable in a factorial design, it would have been necessary to choose a personality test that was not highly correlated with field independence. That is, if subjects who scored high on field independence also tended to score high on the second personality measure, the effects of the independent variables on the dependent variable would be spuriously inflated because the independent variables were operating in the same fashion.

How does one select the appropriate variables for a factorial design? Often in psychology, a number of investigators will be studying the same behavior (a dependent variable) but focusing on different determinants or predictors (independent variables) of that behavior. In a factorial design, several independent variables that have been identified as predictors of a particular behavior can be brought together in a

single investigation. For example, in their review of 65 years of research on the psychology of law, reported in the chapter selection, Mitchell and Byrne noted that investigators had found three major classes of variables to influence juror decisions in simulated trial situations: characteristics of the defendant, procedural characteristics of the trial, and characteristics of the jurors themselves. What Mitchell and Byrne wondered was how do all these variables fit together?

In their investigation of influences on juror's decision making, Mitchell and Byrne simulated a court trial. College students were asked to consider themselves members of a jury hearing the case of a man charged with negligent homicide. Subjects read a transcript of an actual court trial, except that the transcript was adapted to incorporate two manipulated independent variables, reflecting the defendant's character and the judge's instructions. A third independent variable was subject authoritarianism. These three independent variables were operationalized as follows:

1. *Subject authoritarianism.* An initial group of 143 male and female college students took a test for authoritarianism. Those individuals ($n = 92$) scoring in the top third and bottom third on this test constituted the final sample of high- and low-authoritarian subjects. Thus, the authoritarianism variable had two levels— high and low scores, called high authoritarians and low authoritarians.

2. *Defendant's character.* Half of the subjects read a positive statement about the defendant describing him as a warm, sincere, friendly person. The other half of the subjects read a negative statement describing the defendant as cold, unreliable, and unfriendly. Thus, this variable also had two levels—a positive and a negative character description.

3. *Judge's instructions.* The final independent variable consisted of three levels of instructions from the judge to the subject/jurors. In one

condition, subjects were instructed to ignore the testimony that described the defendant's character; in a second condition, subjects were told to give special attention to this testimony; and in the third condition, subjects were given no instruction at all about testimony concerning the defendant's character.

In summary, Mitchell and Byrne used a 2 by 2 by 3 factorial design that contained two levels of subject authoritarianism, two levels of defendant's-character description, and three levels of judicial instruction. The effects of each of these independent variables was tested on four dependent variables: (1) the subject's degree of certainty as to the defendant's guilt; (2) the subject's decision as to the length of prison time; (3) the subject's recommendation on length of time before the defendant might be paroled; and (4) the subject's description of the defendant using a set of adjectives. A 2 by 2 by 3 factorial analysis of variance was computed for each of these dependent measures. It might be useful for you to compare Mitchell and Byrne's procedures and findings with those of one of the simpler investigations they review to see just how rich and complex a picture investigators can achieve by using the factorial design.

If you undertake a factorial experiment of your own, a statistics text will guide you through the steps of a factorial analysis of variance—or a computer can do all the hard work for you with just a few instructions. To help you understand the logic that underlies both the factorial design and the factorial analysis of variance, we will analyze the Mitchell and Byrne experiment a bit more fully.

Figure 9-1 shows how Mitchell and Byrne's factorial design might look.[5] This design matrix tells you that eight high- and eight low-authori-

tarian subjects are to be exposed to a positive description of the defendant and told to ignore that testimony. Equal numbers of high- and low-authoritarian subjects are to be exposed to the other combinations of the defendant description and judge's instructions, except that only seven high- and seven low-authoritarian subjects are assigned to the control condition where the judge issued no instructions. In general, researchers attempt to assign equal numbers of subjects to each of the experimental conditions (represented by cells in the matrix) in a factorial design, but it is not unusual for investigators to use slightly fewer subjects in the control condition.

If the factorial design requires you to assign subjects to every possible combination of the levels of the independent variables, how can you tell whether either independent variable has an effect of its own on the dependent variable? The statistical test called the (factorial) *analysis of variance* allows you to compare mean scores on your dependent variable as a function of each independent variable separately (as main effects) as well as in combination (as interactions). Let's see how this is possible. Figure 9-2, containing fictitious data, is intended to illustrate the operation of several independent variables in a factorial design modeled after the design used by Mitchell and Byrne. The numbers in the cells of the matrix are average scores on the dependent variable (in this case, number of years recommended as punishment for the defendant) for each of the treatment groups— that is, for each group of high-authoritarian and low-authoritarian subjects exposed to a positive or negative description of the defendant and to instructions from the judge to ignore or pay special attention to that description (or to no instructions from the judge at all). To determine whether biasing testimony (that is, a positive or negative description of the defendant) operates separately (as a main effect) on recommended punishment, we can simply compare the average number of years recommended by all subjects

---

[5]Mitchell and Byrne do not specify the exact distribution of their 92 subjects among the "cells" of their factorial matrix, but our Figure 9-1 represents a reasonable distribution of 92 subjects into the 12 cells of the 2 by 2 by 3 design.

FIGURE 9-1
A Hypothetical Version of Mitchell and Byrne's Factorial Design

Judge's Instructions	Description of Defendant Positive	Negative
Ignore Biasing Testimony	8 Hi Authoritarian Ss* 8 Lo Authoritarian Ss	8 Hi Authoritarian Ss 8 Lo Authoritarian Ss
Heed Biasing Testimony	8 Hi Authoritarian Ss 8 Lo Authoritarian Ss	8 Hi Authoritarian Ss 8 Lo Authoritarian Ss
No Instructions	7 Hi Authoritarian Ss 7 Lo Authoritarian Ss	7 Lo Authoritarian Ss 7 Lo Authoritarian Ss

*Ss means subjects

FIGURE 9-2
Years of Punishment Recommended as a Function of Description of Defendant's Character, Judicial Instructions, and Authoritarianism (Hypothetical Data)*

Judge's Instruction	Description of Defendant Positive	Negative	
Ignore Biasing Testimony	$\overline{X}_{HiA}$ = 3.6 years $\overline{X}_{LoA}$ = 3.5 years	$\overline{X}_{HiA}$ = 7.3 years $\overline{X}_{LoA}$ = 1.8 years	$\overline{X}_{ignore}$ = $\dfrac{16.2}{4}$ = 4.05
Attend to Biasing Testimony	$\overline{X}_{HiA}$ = 3.5 years $\overline{X}_{LoA}$ = 1.8 years	$\overline{X}_{HiA}$ = 5.6 years $\overline{X}_{LoA}$ = 5.5 years	$\overline{X}_{attend}$ = $\dfrac{16.4}{4}$ = 4.10
No Instructions	$\overline{X}_{HiA}$ = 4.7 years $\overline{X}_{LoA}$ = 2.8 years	$\overline{X}_{HiA}$ = 10.0 years $\overline{X}_{LoA}$ = 3.9 years	$\overline{X}_{none}$ = $\dfrac{21.4}{4}$ = 5.35

$$\overline{X}_{pos} = \frac{19.9}{6} = 3.32 \quad \overline{X}_{neg} = \frac{34.6}{6} = 5.68$$

$$\overline{X}_{HiA} = \frac{34.7}{6} = 5.78 \quad \overline{X}_{LoA} = \frac{19.3}{6} = 3.22$$

*Numbers in cells of matrix refer to numbers of years recommended by high-authoritarian and low-authoritarian subjects in each set of conditions defined by description of defendant and judicial instructions.

exposed to positive testimony with the average number of years recommended by all subjects exposed to negative testimony—disregarding judge's instructions. By looking below the two columns of the matrix, you can see that, on the average, subjects reading the negative description recommended more years (5.68) of punishment than did subjects reading the positive testimony (3.22 years). In their experiment, Mitchell and Byrne found a statistically significant main effect for description of defendant.

To determine whether judge's instructions operates separately on recommended punishment, we calculate the average number of years recommended by all subjects told to ignore biasing testimony with the average number of years recommended by subjects told to pay special attention to this testimony or given no instructions at all. At the right of each row in Figure 9-2, you can see the average number of years recommended by subjects at each "level" of judicial instructions concerning biasing testimony. Ranging from 4.05 years to 5.35 years, these average scores do not differ widely from each other, a fact consistent with Mitchell and Byrne's findings of no main effect due to judge's instructions.

Does this mean that judge's instructions have no effect on subject/juror recommendations? No. As you can see in the figure, the judge's instructions affect high- and low-authoritarian subjects differently. First, note that, on the average, high-authoritarian subjects recommend more years of punishment (5.78) than do low-authoritarian subjects (3.22 years). Now look at the average scores within each cell of matrix. You can see that when exposed to a positive description of the defendant, high-authoritarian subjects tend to recommend approximately the same amount of punishment (3.6 versus 3.5 years) regardless of whether they're told to ignore or attend to the biasing testimony. Low-authoritarian subjects, on the other hand, recommend considerably less punishment (1.8 years) when told to pay attention to positive testimony than when told to ignore it (3.5 years). The obverse pattern holds when the biasing testimony is negative. This pattern in our fictitious data is similar to the finding by Mitchell and Byrne of a statistically significant interaction effect between judge's instructions and subject authoritarianism.

USING EXPERIMENTAL DESIGNS

To gain experience in using experimental manipulations in the study of personality, we suggest that you develop a study using some sort of person/situation interaction design. Look at current issues of *Journal of Personality and Social Psychology* or *Personality and Social Psychology Bulletin*. Investigations in these journals still tend to fall into the category that Carlson, in our Chapter 10 selection, calls *generalist*. That is, in reporting the results of experimental manipulations, investigators generally discuss differences between experimental and control groups without making an effort to deal with individual differences. Find a generalist study where you have some ideas about the kinds of personality variables—for example, need for achievement, empathy, authoritarianism—that could account for some of the differences in responses to the experimental manipulation. Then design your own experiment that contains one or more personality variables.

You will have to make a number of interrelated decisions in formulating your research design. Let's say you've decided to look at helping behavior as a function of characteristics of a victim (a typical social-psychological variable) and interpersonal trust in the subject. For your victim, you decide to have a confederate drop a pile of books. Your manipulated independent variable might be physical appearance of the confederate, defined in terms of clothing, grooming, and so on. Your dependent variable might be number of people helping to pick up the books. You must still decide who your subjects will be, where the experimental manipulation will take place (lab or field setting), at what point the experimental manipulation will begin (for example, when a pedestrian approaches within ten feet of the confederate), and when and how you will administer your measured independent variable (the test of interpersonal trust). Moreover, how will you deal with issues of informed consent and debriefing? How many subjects will you need in your two conditions to allow a comparison of these conditions? How will you determine high and low trust—by splitting the sample at the median score? How many high- and low-trust subjects will you need in each condition to examine the interaction of your independent variables?

These questions are not meant to frighten you, but to alert you to the complexities of a well-designed experimental study. In experimental investigations, as in other types of psychological research, it is important to plan your design in advance, thinking through questions about subjects, settings, and measures as well as the kinds of data you will be obtaining and the appropriate statistical tests you will use for analyzing that data. The brief overview of basic statistics in Appendix A should help you not only in analyzing data you've already collected, but in designing studies that will yield the data you need to perform an adequate and appropriate statistical test.

A PREVIEW OF THE CHAPTER SELECTION

As already indicated, this chapter's selection provides a relatively comprehensive example of an interaction experiment combining situational and person variables. In their simulated-trial experiment, Mitchell and Byrne examined the hypothesis that a measured independent variable, authoritarianism, is a personality characteristic that mediates between a trial judge's instructions (a manipulated independent variable) and the subject/juror's responses to those instructions (the dependent variables). In their review of the literature, the investigators use both field and laboratory studies to provide a foundation for their own rather sophisticated factorial design. The method and results sections illustrate well how a factorial design is put into action and how the data from such a design are analyzed in an analysis of variance. The paper thus provides a useful model for your own design of an interaction study.

Minimizing the Influence of Irrelevant Factors in the Courtroom: The Defendant's Character, Judge's Instructions and Authoritarianism[1]

Herman E. Mitchell and Donn Byrne
Purdue University

Shortly after the turn of this century, Hugo Münsterberg made a strong plea to his fellow psychologists to apply their wealth of knowledge to pressing social problems. He conceded that psychology had already assumed an important role in education, medicine, art, and economics. However, he admonished his colleagues for their lack of influence in the field of law. His book, *On the Witness Stand* (Münsterberg, 1907), describes now classic studies examining the influence of psychological phenomena on the testimony of witnesses. Münsterberg stated that his purpose was "to turn the attention of serious men to an absurdly neglected field." The attention of psychologists is still being sought, as evidenced by the recent observation in the *American Psychologist* that "law is much too serious a matter to be entrusted to the lawyers" (Kolasa, 1972, p. 503).

During this 65-year span, experimental social psychologists have indeed turned their attention to the "psychology of law." Often employing a simulated trial technique, these behavioral studies have consistently corroborated the courtroom analyses of legal researchers (Kalven & Zeisel, 1966; Nagel, 1969). Such research has identified three major classes of variables which seem to influence judicial decision-making. First, characteristics of the defendant have been found to have

[1]This research was supported in part by Research Grant 710-0259 from the Ford Foundation to the first author, while he held Graduate Fellowship NI 71-083-GF7 from the National Institute of Law Enforcement and Criminal Justice, Department of Justice, and also supported in part by Research Grant GS-2752 from the National Science Foundation, Donn Byrne, Principal Investigator. The authors wish to thank Frances Cherry and Kerry Deardorf for their assistance.

Portions of this paper were presented at the annual meeting of the Midwestern Psychological Association, Cleveland, May, 1972. Reprinted by permission.

strong and consistent effects on jurors' verdicts and recommended punishments. Character descriptions of the defendant (Landy & Aronson, 1969), the defendant's attitudes (Mitchell & Byrne, in press), and physical appearance[2] have been shown to affect juror decisions. Additionally, the effects of such variables as sex, race, age, family status, and income of the defendant have been documented (Broeder, 1965; Bullock, 1961; Nagel, 1969).

A second important category of factors related to juror decisions concerns procedural characteristics of the trial such as order or presentation of arguments (Lawson, 1967, 1969; Weld & Rolf, 1938) or witnesses (Weld & Danzig, 1940), novelty of arguments (Sears & Freedman, 1965), and the nature of the law violated (Berkowitz & Walker, 1967; Kalven & Zeisel, 1966). Vidmar (1972a) has found that trial outcomes are affected by the jurors' knowledge of punishments accompanying possible verdicts.

A third source of variance in judicial decisions is associated with characteristics of the jurors themselves. Personality variables such as authoritarianism (Boehm, 1968; Crosson, 1968; Jurow, 1971; Mitchell & Byrne, in press) and dogmatism (Vidmar, 1972b) are found to be associated with the conviction-proneness of jurors. Also, jurors' attitudes toward capital punishment (Goldberg, 1970; Jurow, 1971) and the status, education, and sex of jurors play a role in jury decisions (James, 1959; Strodtbeck, James, & Hawkins, 1957).

As Winick (1961, p. 107) has pointed out, "It is logical to expect that Juror X will perceive the world very much as he did when he was Mr. X, and he will not overnight become a judicious evaluator of evidence merely because he is sworn in." Winick's expectation seems to be borne out by the the data. Even though this review of some of the factors which have been identified as potential biasing influences on juror decision-making is by

no means exhaustive, it does indicate the magnitude of such sources of bias and the importance of searching for some method of controlling these extra-legal influences in the courtroom. Behavioral researchers have been quite successful in identifying variables which prejudice juror decisions, yet little attention has been focused on examining procedures which might be effective in minimizing these irrelevant factors.

The responsibility and means by which extraneous factors in a trial may be controlled rest solely with the trial judge (Winick, Gerver, & Blumberg, 1961). His authority to decide upon the admissibility of evidence, relevance of testimony, and, in some states, even to comment on the credibility of witnesses in his instructions to the jury makes him responsible for a fair and impartial trial. When potentially biasing information is presented during a trial, the judge (usually in response to the objections of an attorney) rules upon the admissibility of such testimony. If the judge finds the testimony to be irrelevant, immaterial, and prejudicial, he orders the statement(s) stricken from the record, admonishes the jury to disregard the objectionable testimony and not to consider it in determining the disposition of the case. This, then, is the most common method of procedural control over biasing influences during a trial.

In light of the earlier discussion, it might be expected that a personality variable such as authoritarianism may mediate response to the judge's instructions and hence their effectiveness. Individuals scoring high on the F-Scale are described as being rigid and intolerant, and as having a tendency to reject, condemn, and punish those who violate conventional values (Adorno, Frenkel-Brunswick, Levinson, & Sanford, 1950). The prejudicial aggression and punitiveness of authoritarians has been well documented in a variety of situations (Epstein, 1965, 1966; Roberts & Jessor, 1958; Sherwood, 1966; Thibaut & Riecken, 1955). In a simulated trial situation this punitiveness has been repeatedly observed for authoritarians (Boehm, 1968; Crosson, 1968; Ju-

[2]Michael G. Efran. "The effect of physical appearance on the judgment of guilt, interpersonal attraction, and severity of recommended punishment in a simulated jury task." Unpublished manuscript, 1972 (Mimeo).

row, 1971; Mitchell & Byrne, in press). Additionally, Mitchell and Byrne (in press) found that high authoritarian jurors yield a strong correlation between evaluative judgments of the defendant (e.g., attractiveness and morality) and their legal-judicial decisions (guilt and recommended punishment). Low authoritarians, to the contrary, do not appear to allow their evaluative judgments to affect their legal decisions. On the basis of those findings, it would be hypothesized that low authoritarians ignore biasing information when requested to do so; high authoritarians are hypothesized to have more difficulty in separating their affective feelings toward the defendant from their legal decisions, despite the judge's instructions.

A second, equally tenable possibility exists, which would predict precisely the opposite results from those just hypothesized. Rubin and Moore (1971) have recently reported that high authoritarian subjects are more likely to respond to perceived experimental demands than are low authoritarians who react negatively to demand characteristics. If the judge's instructions can be conceptually equated to an experimental "demand" in this situation, it could be predicted that high authoritarian subject-jurors are more likely to acquiesce to the judge's rulings. Additionally, while there exists some evidence to the contrary (e.g., Gorfein, 1961; Mischel & Schopler, 1959), a number of investigators have found high authoritarians submissive to those of high status or authority (Adorno et al., 1950; Harvey & Beverly, 1961) and more amenable to influence than low authoritarians (Crutchfield, 1955; Johnson & Steiner, 1967; Nadler, 1959; Steiner & Johnson, 1963; Wells, Weinert, & Rubel, 1956). Thus, considering the evidence relating authoritarianism to experimental demands and influenceability, it would be hypothesized that high authoritarian subject-jurors would follow the instructions of the judge, while low authoritarians would not.

The present study was designed to assess the effectiveness of judicial instructions in minimizing the effects of irrelevant information about the de-

fendant and to test the two alternative hypotheses concerning the role of authoritarianism in responding to such instructions. A simulated trial was prepared containing biasing testimony (positive or negative character descriptions of the defendant) followed by the judge's instructions to high and low authoritarian subject-jurors either to ignore or pay special attention[3] to this testimony.

METHOD

Subjects for the experiment were 143 male and female introductory psychology students at Purdue University. Experimental sessions were conducted in groups of 12 to 15 subjects. Each student was given a ten-page booklet containing instructions, a summarized trial transcript, and a questionnaire dealing with the subject-jurors' opinions concerning the case and the defendant involved. The cover page of the booklet contained the following introduction and instructions to the subject.

In recent years there has been a growing interest in the systematic study of judicial decision-making. The study in which you are about to participate is just such an investigation. On the following pages you will find a summary of an actual trial taken from the records of the New York Criminal Court, Manhattan, September 8, 1970 (Dkt. No. B5683/70). The defendant in this case is John S. who has been charged with negligent homicide. On the following pages you will find the summaries of the testimony and legal briefs presented to the New York Criminal Court. Please read this in-

---

[3]The judge's instructions to give special attention to testimony in this experiment not only serves as a conceptual balance for subjects in the condition requested to ignore irrelevant testimony, but also has very real import within the legal system. While it is a less common occurrence, the judge in some states, in his instructions to the jury before deliberation, may review testimony and evidence presented during the trial and recommend that the jury give special consideration and weight to witnesses or evidence which he feels to be especially important. The well-publicized "Harrisburg" trial, at the time of this writing, is being appealed, in part due to just these sort of instructions by the trial judge.

formation carefully and in the order in which it is presented. Following the trial summary are a number of questions soliciting your reactions and recommendations regarding this case.

The subjects then read the description of the violation (negligent homicide) which was a modified version of a case used by Landy and Aronson (1969). The violation was described as follows.

John S. was driving home from an annual Christmas office party on the evening of December 24, when his automobile struck and killed a pedestrian by the name of Martin L. The circumstances leading to this event were as follows: The employees of the insurance office where John S. worked began to party at around 2:00 P.M. on the afternoon of the 24th. By 5:00 P.M. some people were already leaving for home, although many continued to drink and socialize. By the time John S. had finished his fourth drink, the party was beginning to break up. He then left the office building and walked to the garage where he had parked his car. It had just started to snow and traffic was very heavy at the time. He was six blocks from the garage when he ran a red light and struck Martin L., who was crossing the street. John S. immediately stopped the car. Martin L. died a few minutes later on the way to the hospital. It was later ascertained that internal hemorrhaging was the exact cause of death. John S. was arrested and charged with negligent homicide. The police medical examiner's report indicated that the defendant's estimated blood alcohol concentration was between 1.5 and 2.0% at the time of the accident. Conviction on a charge of negligent homicide is punishable by imprisonment of one to twenty-five years.

Following the description of the charges against the defendant, the biasing testimony was presented under the guise of a police psychologist and social worker's report. This testimony was either quite positive:

John S. was described by the court psychologist as a warm and sincere person who was quite friendly and co-operative during his interview, and was judged as having no psychiatric problems. The defendant is a 30-year old insurance adjuster who has been employed by the same firm for three years. His employer described him as a helpful and conscientious employee.

or quite negative:

John S. was described by the court psychologist as a rather cold and insincere person. Although he was impolite and uncooperative during his interview, he was judged as having no psychiatric problems. The defendant is a 30-year old insurance adjuster who has been employed by the same firm for three years. His employer described him as an average employee who seemed self-centered and sometimes unfriendly to his co-workers.

Immediately following this testimony was one of three possible instructions from the judge. The judge either ordered that the testimony be disregarded:

The above testimony, in response to a lawyer's request, was ruled irrelevant and immaterial by the judge for this trial, and the judge cautioned the jury to disregard this evidence.

or that the jury give it special attention:

The above testimony, in response to a lawyer's request, was ruled by the judge as warranting special attention and consideration in the disposition of this case.

In a third group, subjects were given no instructions by the judge following the testimony.

After reading this summarized trial transcript, subjects were asked to rate their degree of certainty as to the defendant's guilt. This item was in the form of a seven-point scale, ranging from "I feel that the defendant is definitely guilty" to "I feel the defendant is definitely not guilty." Each subject was then asked to give his recommended punishment for the defendant. Subjects were given a choice of from 1 to 25 years as a prison sentence.

A third question asked the subject-jurors to recommend the percentage of their suggested prison term that the defendant should serve before being eligible for parole. This question about parole was phrased as a ten-point scale ranging from "10% of sentence" to "100% of sentence." After the parole recommendation, subjects were asked to indicate their impressions of the defendant on 13 evaluative bipolar adjectives, such as moral-immoral, positive-negative, and pleasant-unpleasant. Each adjective pair was placed on a seven-point scale. The consistency of the adjectives was established by means of factor analysis, and the items were therefore summed in order to provide a total evaluative judgment of the defendant. After completing the bipolar adjectives, subjects were asked not to turn back to the trial material and were given an Information Recall Questionnaire. Subjects were asked a number of facts about the trial, such as the defendant's name, age, specific charge made, etc. They were also asked about the judge's instructions concerning the testimony of the court psychologist and social worker. The primary purpose of this questionnaire was to assure that subjects had read the case material carefully and as a manipulation check to determine if they had read the judge's instructions regarding the biasing testimony.

Since completion of the simulated trial experiment took less than the student's required hour of participation for this experiment, they were asked to complete a general opinion survey for another research project. This request was genuine, but along with the questionnaire, subjects were given a 22-item acquiescence-free version of the authoritarianism scale (Bryne & Lamberth, 1971). Subjects were not aware that these questions were in any way related to the earlier experiment. After these data were collected, the experiment was discussed with the students and its rationale described.

For the purpose of analysis only those subjects ($n = 92$) scoring in the highest ($\overline{X} = 90.6$) and lowest ($\overline{X} = 57.9$) third of the authoritarianism scale were analysed (Feldt, 1961). This resulted in a 2 by 2 by 3 factorial design with a positively or negatively described defendant, high or low authoritarian subject-jurors, and three conditions of judge's instructions.

RESULTS

A 2 by 2 by 3 factorial unweighted means analysis of variance (Winer, 1971) was computed for each of the four dependent measures. Consistent with the findings of Landy and Aronson (1969), subjects uniformly perceived the defendant in this case as being guilty as charged. These ratings of guilt were not influenced by any of the factors examined in this study.

Character of the Defendant and Authoritarianism

As expected, the character description of the defendant showed a strong main effect on recommended punishments, with the negatively described defendant receiving a more harsh sentence ($F = 9.36$, $df = 1/80$, $p < .01$). Also, consistent with earlier findings, high authoritarians recommended more severe punishments than low authoritarians ($F = 9.83$, $df = 1/80$, $p < .01$).

Instructions of the Judge

Figure 1 shows the effect of these three variables (authoritarianism of subject-jurors, the character of the defendant, and the judge's instructions) on recommended punishment. If subjects followed appropriately the judge's instructions, then it would be expected that they would render harsher penalties when told to ignore the positive character testimony concerning the defendant than when told to pay special attention to this information. The obverse should hold for the negative defendant. This interactive relationship of judge's instructions with character of the defendant was observed only for low authoritarian subjects ($F = 3.63$, $df = 2/43$, $p < .05$). This same planned comparison for high authoritarian subjects revealed that they respond only to the character of the defendant ($p < .01$),

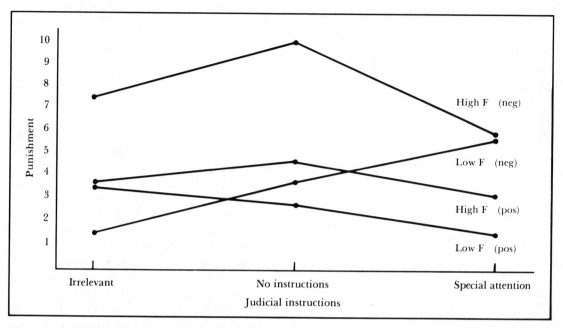

Fig. 1. Punishment (sentence in years) as a function of the judge's instructions, the juror's authoritarianism, and the character of the defendant.

regardless of the judge's instructions ($F < 1.00$). Thus, the first of the two alternative hypotheses about the effects of authoritarianism was supported.

Interaction of Defendant's Character and Authoritarianism

As in the earlier Mitchell and Byrne (in press) paper, authoritarianism was found to interact with the biasing description of the defendant ($F = 4.06$, $df = 1/80$, $p < .05$). Despite differences in the defendants type of crimes, and trial settings, the results of these two studies are strikingly similar. In both cases (see Figure 2) it is the high authoritarians presented with a negative defendant (dissimilar attitudes or negative character) who recommend the most severe punishments ($p < .01$), while those subjects in the remaining three conditions do not differ from one another.

Parole and Evaluative Judgments

Parole recommendations were also influenced by the subject-jurors' authoritarianism, in that high authoritarian subjects recommended a significantly larger percentage of the sentence be served before the defendant becomes eligible for parole ($F = 4.36$, $df = 1/80$, $p < .05$). Parole recommendations were not influenced by the character of the defendant or the judge's instructions.

The total evaluative judgment of the defendant (summed ratings of bipolar adjectives), as expected, was strongly affected by the character testimony ($F = 169.04$, $df = 1/80$, $p < .01$), but not by other factors. A correlation[4] of the evaluative response with recommended punishments by high and low authoritarian subjects revealed the

[4]In order to control for the influence of the factors investigated in this study, the correlations reported here were computed by condition and then averaged to achieve unbiased correlations for high and low authoritarian subjects.

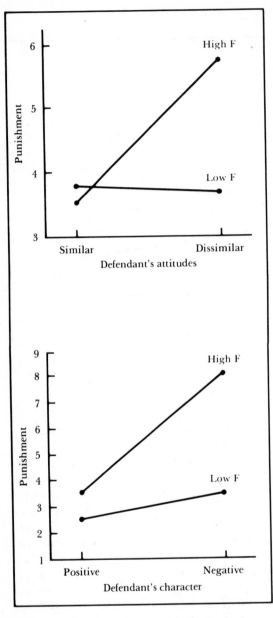

Fig. 2. Influence of juror's authoritarianism and attributes of the defendant on recommended punishments in two experiments. Similar interactions were obtained between juror authoritarianism and the positive-negative qualities of the defendant based either on his similar and dissimilar attitutdes (left panel: Mitchell & Byrne, in press) or on his character traits (right panel: present study).

same relationship reported earlier by Mitchell and Byrne (in press). Specifically, judicial decisions (recommended punishments) and evaluative judgments were related for high authoritarian subjects ($r = .38$, $p < .01$) but not for low authoritarians ($r = .06$).

DISCUSSION

The pattern of results obtained concerning the influence of judge's instructions on minimizing the effects of biasing factors in the courtroom indicates that they have little effect on high authoritarians' judicial decisions. On the other hand, low authoritarians are apparently able to ignore or give special attention to testimony in accordance with the judge's orders. The observed significant correlation between the evaluative judgments and legal decisions of high authoritarians replicated the relationship observed by Mitchell and Byrne (in press). High authoritarians not only seem to make simple "good-bad" judgments of people (Kelman & Barclay, 1963), but these judgments are inextricably bound to other decisions concerning the target person. This simple judgmental process combined with the rigidity and resistance to influence observed in high authoritarians (Mischel & Schopler, 1959) seems to lead to strongly biased decisions in the courtroom, which are not easily "unbiased" even by instructions from the judge.

These data lend little support to the relationship between authoritarianism and influenceability observed by some researchers (e.g., Crutchfield, 1955; Johnson & Steiner, 1967), but they might suggest the importance of situational factors mediating this relationship (McGuire, 1968). Under what circumstances would the judge, a clear symbol of authority, be influential in determining the decisions of high authoritarian subjects? Possibly, in live trials where the regally robed judge sits high above the jurors, surrounded by American and state flags, high authoritarian jurors would respond more readily to his instructions. Unfortunately, verbally simulated trials cannot make salient many situational influences which might be operative in actual trials. Although researchers have been barred from studying juror decision-making in actual trials (Strodtbeck, 1962), video-taped mock trials might serve as a means of exploring these situational factors.

In addition to shedding light on the problem of controlling biasing influences in the courtroom, the earlier finding of Mitchell and Byrne (in press) that only high authoritarian subjects respond strongly to prejudicial testimony has been replicated. The interactive relationship between characteristics of the defendant and subject-jurors' authoritarianism gains support and generalizability by the consistency of results across two very different trial situations. The earlier study dealt with a college student appearing before a Dean of Men's hearing for stealing an examination, while this study concerned a criminal court case of negligent homicide with an older defendant. Additionally, in the earlier study, subjects were presented with a defendant who held either similar or dissimilar attitudes in relation to the subject-jurors, while the present study manipulated the character attributes of the defendant. Despite these substantial differences, authoritarianism interacted with defendant attributes in the same fashion.

The similar effects of these different stimulus attributes of the defendant suggest that a unitary process underlies this relationship. Byrne and his associates (Byrne, 1969, 1971; Byrne & Clore, 1970) have suggested a general framework for conceptualizing the influence of a variety of stimulus characteristics on evaluative responses. In Byrne's affective-reinforcement model, evaluative judgments of another person vary as a function of the amount of positive and negative affect associated with that person. In studies of interpersonal attraction, the implicit affective response generated by such stimuli as similar or dissimilar attitudes (Byrne, 1961) and personality characteristics of the target person (Griffitt, Byrne, & Bond, 1971) have been found to have a similar influence in Byrne's interpersonal attraction situation. In the same respect, the atti-

tudes or character testimony associated with the defendant in a trial situation yield consistent effects on subject-jurors. That is, both types of stimulus information affect the evaluative and judicial decisions of high authoritarians and only the evaluative decisions of low authoritarians.

Given the findings of this study, it may be concluded that there exist two ways of controlling the apparent authoritarian proclivity to be influenced by irrelevant and biasing information during a trial. One method would be to exclude all high authoritarian citizens from participating as jurors in our legal system. This seems a highly drastic and unlikely solution and undoubtedly an unconstitutional one. A second alternative shows some promise, the exclusion of all irrelevant and biasing information from presentation to the jury. The usefulness of this approach was demonstrated empirically by Mitchell and Byrne (in press) when they found that high authoritarians did not respond differently from low authoritarians when biasing information (in their study, the defendant's attitudes) was omitted from the transcript. This method has recently been employed in an actual trial in Sandusky, Ohio. This entire trial was conducted before video-tape cameras, in the absence of a jury. The video tape was edited of all objectional testimony and irrelevant information before it was presented to the jury. It is interesting to note that the opposing lawyers and trial judge not only excluded testimony ruled irrelevant, but also changed the order of appearance of their witnesses for maximum impact. This procedure, while possibly raising new issues amenable to research, not only precludes the authoritarian bias but also eliminates entirely "the common legal trick of introducing improper testimony in the hopes that jurors will be unable to forget it" [*Time*, December 27, 1971].

REFERENCES

Adorno, T. W., Frenkel-Brunswick, E., Levinson, D. J., & Sanford, R. N. *The authoritarian personality.* New York: Harper, 1950.

Berkowitz, L., & Walker, N. Law and moral judgments. *Sociometry*, 1967, *30*, 410–422.

Boehm, V. Mr. Prejudice, Miss Sympathy, and the authoritarian personality: An application of psychological measuring techniques to the problem of jury bias. *Wisconsin Law Review*, 1968, 734–738.

Broeder, D. W. Plaintiff's family status as affecting juror behavior. *Journal of Public Law*, 1965, *14* 131–143.

Bullock, R. Significance of the racial factor in the length of prison sentences. *Journal of Criminal Law*, 1961, *52*, 411–415.

Byrne, D. Interpersonal attraction and attitude similarity. *Journal of Abnormal and Social Psychology*, 1961, *62*, 713–715.

Byrne, D. Attitudes and attraction. In L. Berkowitz (Ed.), *Advances in experimental social psychology*. Vol. 4. New York: Academic Press, 1969. Pp. 35–89.

Byrne, D. *The attraction paradigm*. New York: Academic Press, 1971.

Byrne, D., & Clore, G. L. A reinforcement model of evaluative responses. *Personality: An International Journal*, 1970, *1*, 103–128.

Byrne, D., & Lamberth, J. The effect of erotic stimuli on sex arousal, evaluative responses, and subsequent behavior. *Technical Reports of the Commission on Obscenity and Pornography*. Vol. 8. Washington, D.C.: U. S. Government Printing Office, 1971.

Crosson, R. F. An investigation into certain personality variables among capital trial jurors. *Proceedings, 76th Annual Convention, American Psychological Association*, 1968, *3*, 371–372.

Crutchfield, R. S. Conformity and character. *American Psychologist*, 1955, *10*, 191–198.

Epstein, R. Authoritarianism, displaced aggression, and social status of the target. *Journal of Personality and Social Psychology*, 1965, *2*, 585–589.

Epstein, R. Aggression toward outgroups as a function of authoritarianism and imitation of aggressive models. *Journal of Personality and Social Psychology*, 1966, *3*, 574–579.

Feldt, L. S. The use of extreme groups to test for the presence of a relationship. *Psychometrika*, 1961, *26*, 307–316.

Goldberg, F. Toward expansion of Witherspoon: Capital scruples, jury bias, and use of psychological data to raise legal presumptions. *Harvard Civil Rights—Civil Liberties Law Review*, 1970, *5*, 53–69.

Gorfein, D. Conformity behavior and the "authoritarian personality." *Journal of Social psychology*, 1961, *53*, 121–125.

Griffitt, W., Byrne, D., & Bond, M. H. Proportion of positive adjectives and personal relevance of adjectival descriptions. *Journal of Experimental Social Psychology*, 1971, *7*, 111–121.

Harvey, O. J., & Beverly, G. Some personality correlates of concept change through role-playing. *Journal of Abnormal and Social Psychology*, 1961, *63*, 125–130.

James, R. M. Status and competence of jurors. *American Journal of Sociology*, 1959, *64*, 563–570.

Johnson, H. H., & Steiner, I. D. Some effects of discrepancy level on relationships between authoritarianism and conformity. *Journal of Social Psychology*, 1967, *73*, 199–204.

Jurow, G. L. New data on the effect of a "death qualified" jury on the guilt determination process. *Harvard Law Review*, 1971, *84*, 567–611.

Kalven, H., Jr., & Zeisel, H. *The American jury*. Boston: Little, Brown, 1966.

Kelman, H. C., & Barclay, J. The F Scale as a measure of breadth of perspective. *Journal of Abnormal and Social Psychology*, 1963, *67*, 608–615.

Kolaan, B. J. Psychology and law. *American Psychologist*, 1972, *27*, 499–503.

Landy, D., & Aronson, E. The influence of the character of the criminal and his victim on the decisions of simulated jurors. *Journal of Experimental Social Psychology*, 1969, *5*, 141–152.

Lawson, R. G. Order of presentation as a factor in jury persuasion. *Kentucky Law Journal*, 1967, *56*, 524–555.

Lawson, R. G. The law of primacy in the criminal courtroom. *Journal of Social Psychology*, 1969, *77*, 121–131.

McGuire, W. J. Personality and susceptibility to social influence. In E. F. Borgatta and W. Lambert (Eds.), *Handbook of personality theory and research*. Chicago: Rand McNally, 1968. Pp. 1130–1187.

Mischel, W., & Schopler, J. Authoritarianism and reactions to "Sputnik." *Journal of Abnormal and Social Psychology*, 1959, *59*, 142–145.

Mitchell, H. E., & Byrne, D. The defendant's dilemma: Effects of jurors' attitudes and authoritarianism on judicial decisions. *Journal of Personality and Social Psychology*, in press.

Münsterberg, H. *On the witness stand*. New York: S. S. McClure, 1907.

Nadler, E. B. Yielding, authoritarianism, and authoritarian ideology regarding groups. *Journal of Abnormal and Social Psychology*, 1959, *58*, 408–410.

Nagel, S. S. *The legal process from a behavioral perspective*. Homewood: The Dorsey Press, 1969.

Roberts, A. H., & Jessor, R. Authoritarianism, punitiveness, and perceived social status. *Journal of Abnormal and Social Psychology*, 1958, *56*, 311–314.

Rubin, Z., & Moore, J. C., Jr. Assessment of subjects' suspicions. *Journal of Personality and Social Psychology*, 1971, *17*, 163–170.

Sears, D. O., & Freedman, J. L. Effects of expected

familiarity with arguments upon opinion change and selective exposure. *Journal of Personality and Social Psychology*, 1965, *2*, 420–426.

Sherwood, J. J. Authoritarianism, moral realism, and President Kennedy's death. *British Journal of Social and Clinical Psychology*, 1966, *5*, 264–269.

Steiner, I. D., & Johnson, H. H. Authoritarianism and conformity. *Sociometry*, 1963, *26*, 21–34.

Strodtbeck, F. L. Social process, the law, and jury functioning. In W. M. Evan (Ed.), *Law and sociology*. New York: The Macmillan Co., 1962. Pp. 144–164.

Strodtbeck, F. L., James, R. M., & Hawkins, C. Social status in jury deliberations. *American Sociology Review*, 1957, *8*, 95–120.

Thibaut, J. W., & Riecken, H. W. Authoritarianism, status, and communication of aggression. *Human Relations*, 1955, *8*, 95–120.

Vidmar, N. Effects of decision alternatives on the verdicts and social perceptions of simulated jurors. *Journal of Personality and Social Psychology*, 1972, *22*, 211–218. (a)

Vidmar, N. Group-induced shifts in simulated jury decisions. Paper presented at the Midwestern Psychological Association Convention, Cleveland, Ohio, May 4–6, 1972. (b)

Weld, H. P., & Danzig, E. R. A study of the way in which a verdict is reached by a jury. *American Journal of Psychology*, 1940, *53*, 518–536.

Weld, H. P., & Rolf, M. A study of the formation of opinion based upon legal evidence. *American Journal of Psychology*, 1938, *51*, 609–628.

Wells, W. D., Weinert, G., & Rubel, M. Conformity pressure and authoritarian personality. *Journal of Psychology*, 1956, *42*, 133–136.

Winer, B. J. *Statistical principles in experimental design*. New York: McGraw-Hill, 1971.

Winick, C. The psychology of juries. In H. Toch (Ed.), *Legal and criminal psychology*. New York: Holt, Rinehart and Winston, Inc., 1961. Pp. 96–120.

Winick, C., Gerver, I., & Blumberg, A. The psychology of judges. In H. Toch (Ed.), *Legal and criminal psychology*. New York: Holt, Rinehart and Winston, Inc., 1961. Pp. 121–145.

STUDY QUESTIONS

1. Mitchell and Byrne make reference to another of their studies in which they found that "high authoritarian jurors yield a strong correlation between evaluative judgments of the defendant (e.g., attractiveness and morality) and their legal-judicial decisions (guilt and recommended punishment). Low authoritarians, to the contrary, do not appear to allow their evaluative judgments to affect their legal decisions." What is your best guess at what the independent and dependent variables in that study were and how they might have been measured? How might the independent variables have been summarized in a factorial analysis of variance? (Consider the number of levels each predictor variable might have had.)

2. Mitchell and Byrne's report contains the description of the negligent homicide case used in the experiment. What further variations could be built into this material to allow the testing of additional hypotheses concerning factors influencing juror decisions?

3. What other research questions occur to you after reading Mitchell and Byrne's report? How would you design tests of hypotheses derived from these research questions?

EXERCISE

Designing Experiments

This exercise can be completed either individually or in small groups. Your goal is to design an experiment to test each of the hypotheses. Identify the independent and dependent variables and indicate how you would operationalize them. Decide on the nature of your sample and the procedures you would follow to conduct your experiment. Briefly describe your experimental design.

Hypothesis: Depending on their identity status (for example, achievement, moratorium, foreclosure, diffusion), individuals will differ in the tendency to become anxious in unstructured situations.

Hypothesis: Depending on their identity status individuals will differ in the tendency to become less trusting in situations of stress.

Hypothesis: Depending on their identity status individuals will differ in their tendency to become more authoritarian in situations of stress.

Hypothesis: Depending on their identity status individuals will differ in their tendency to give up previously espoused values when faced with opposing arguments.

Hypothesis: Depending on their identity status individuals will differ in their tendency to become group leaders in unstructured group situations.

ANNOTATED BIBLIOGRAPHY

Fugita, S. S., Agle, T. A., Newman, E., & Walfish, A. Attractiveness, self-concept, and a methodological note about gaze behavior. *Personal and Social Psychology Bulletin*, 1977, *3*, 240–243.

High- and low–self-concept men were observed interacting with either a physically attractive or unattractive female confederate. Both self-concept and the physical attractiveness of the female were related to the subject's nonverbal behavior.

Jaeger, M. E., Anthony, S., & Rosnow, R. L. Who hears what from whom and with what effect: A study of rumor. *Personal and Social Psychology Bulletin*, 1980, *6*, 473–478.

In this factorial experiment, the investigators found that subjects scoring high on an anxiety scale were more likely than less anxious subjects to repeat a rumor when the source was a peer, but not when it was an authority figure.

Kleinke, C. L., & Singer, D. A. Influence of gaze on compliance with demanding and conciliatory requests in a field setting. *Personal and Social Psychology Bulletin*, 1979, *5*, 386–390.

In this field experiment, leaflets were offered to male and female pedestrians by male and female experimenters who either gazed or did not gaze at the subject, and who used either a conciliatory tone ("Excuse me, would you like one?"), a demanding tone ("Take one!"), or no verbalization. Findings included main effects for gaze and sex of experimenter as well as several interactive effects.

Rubin, Z. Naturalistic studies of self-disclosure. *Personal and Social Psychology Bulletin*, 1976, *2*, 200–263.

Rubin describes three naturalistic experiments designed for studying self-disclosure between strangers. Conducted in an airport, at a bus station, and over the phone, these experiments allowed measurement of communication intimacy under a number of conditions. Rubin discusses both the methodological and ethical advantages and limitations of his procedures.

Tanke, E. D. Perceptions of ethicality of psychological research: Effects of experimenter status, experiment outcome, and authoritarianism. *Personal and Social Psychology Bulletin*, 1979, *5*, 164–172.

Using a factorial design, Tanke investigated the effect of experimenter status and experiment outcome on subjects classified as high and low authoritarians. She found that high authoritarians but not low authoritarians judged the experiment as more ethical when the experimenter was of high status and when the experimental hypothesis was confirmed.

ADDITIONAL SOURCES

Diener, E., & Defour, D. Does television violence enhance program popularity? *Journal of Personality and Social Psychology*, 1978, *36*, 333–340.

Feinberg, R. A. & Lombardo, J. P. Perceived locus of control and attraction as a function of locus of control orientation. *Personal and Social Psychology Bulletin*, 1978, *4*, 244–247.

Gibbons, F. X. Sexual standards and reactions to pornography: Enhancing behavioral consistency through self-focused attention. *Journal of Personality and Social Psychology*, 1978, *36*, 976–987.

Hamilton, V. L. Obedience and responsibility: a jury simulation. *Journal of Personality and Social Psychology*, 1978, *36*, 126–146.

Ickes, W., & Barnes, R. D. Boys and girls together and alienated: On enacting stereotyped sex roles in mixed-sex dyads. *Journal of Personality and Social Psychology*, 1978, *36*, 669–683.

Katzev, R., Edelsack, L., Steinmetz, G., Walkes, T., & Wright, R. The effect of reprimanding transgressions on subsequent helping behavior: Two field experiments. *Personal and Social Psychology Bulletin*, 1978, *4*, 326–329.

Latta, R. M. Relation of status incongruence to personal space. *Personal and Social Psychology Bulletin*, 1978, *4*, 143–146.

Malamuth, N. M., Shayne, E., & Pogue, B. Infant cues and stopping at the crosswalk. *Personal and Social Psychology Bulletin*, 1978, *4*, 334–336.

Snyder, M., & Uranowitz, S. W. Reconstructing the past: Some cognitive consequences of person perception. *Journal of Personality and Social Psychology*, 1978, *36*, 941–950.

Sorrentino, R. M., & Sheppard, P. H. Effects of affiliation-related motives on swimmers in individual versus group competition: A field experiment. *Journal of Personality and Social Psychology*, 1978, *36*, 704–714.

Stewart, J. E. II, & Moore, K. P. Time perception as a function of locus of control. *Personal and Social Psychology Bulletin*, 1978, *4*, 56–58.

Weyant, J. M. Effects of mood states, costs, and benefits on helping. *Journal of Personality and Social Psychology*, 1978, *36*, 1169–1176.

Zuckerman, M. Belief in a just world and altruistic behavior. *Journal of Personality and Social Psychology*, 1975, *31*, 972–976.

10

Where Do We Go from Here?

If we ended this book with Chapter 9, you would have a useful tool kit of methodological procedures and research strategies. You would know that psychologists sometimes make inferences about personality on the basis of stickers on cars, that they administer tests assessing characteristics such as interpersonal trust, that they interview men and women about their goals for the future and their relationships with others. You would also know that they observe reactions to unexpected crises in the real world, and that they use simulated jury situations to determine the effect on potential jurors of judge's instructions concerning positive and negative biasing testimony about a defendant's character. You would have received glimpses of a wide range of studies exhibiting a variety of hypotheses and techniques, and you would have completed a number of exercises de-

signed to help you develop investigations of your own. Although all these accomplishments are valuable, they do not necessarily answer such questions as "Of what use are these accomplishments?" or "Why do we need to know these things?" or, ultimately, "Where do we go from here?"

Early in this book, we encouraged you to design studies that would not be trivial but that would somehow make a contribution to the field. It is to this point that we return now. How does one make a contribution to the field? What issues should you consider when you are trying to develop the best possible study within your reach? Certainly a first step would be to choose a research problem of some theoretical, practical, or scientific interest. Next you should select methods that are optimally suited both to your research problem and to the general advancement of psychological knowledge. For more extensive guidance this chapter's selection by Carlson is, we think, useful to students wanting to use scientific methodology to contribute to the understanding of human personality.

A number of features make Carlson's article particularly valuable as a concluding statement in a text on personality research. In discussing sampling, data-collection methods, research design, and ethics, the author uses concepts by now familiar to you. In reporting the results of her bibliographic study of two personality journals, she illustrates an application of content analysis that can be adapted easily to a variety of research questions. However, particularly helpful is her clear representation of the perspective of a personologist—that is, a psychologist interested in individuals who are whole, complex psychological beings functioning in complex environments. It is her argument that psychologists often use their methodological tool kits in ways that restrict rather than advance our knowledge of the psychological processes operating within each person.

Carlson's article is also a helpful reminder that each of the existing research strategies has an important role in the development of psychological knowledge. Although Carlson implies that experimental methods, particularly as they are applied in laboratory settings, constitute too large a portion of the current research endeavor, she does not argue that the experimental approach should be abandoned altogether. Numerous variables and research problems probably lend themselves well to experimental manipulations—in and out of the laboratory—just as many variables and research problems exist for which the correlational strategy is most appropriate.

There are whole realms of psychological research in which the experimental method is clearly the method of choice. For example, psychologists interested in determining which of a number of specialized diets are most effective in combatting hypertension will get the clearest answers by conducting experiments in which subjects are randomly assigned to different dietary conditions. Experimental psychologists testing hypotheses about the effects of different schedules of reinforcements on rats generally impose the strictest of experimental controls. Social psychologists wondering whether individuals handle dilemmas differently when they are alone than when they are in groups are likely to assign subjects randomly to individual or group conditions while keeping all other factors constant. These are only a few examples of appropriate uses of experimental research. In reality, the application of experimental methods is probably limited only by ethical considerations, the availability of appropriate controls, and the kinds of variables for which causal relationships can be readily hypothesized.

One of the most common uses of the experimental method by personality researchers is as part of a program of construct validation for a particular personality measure. This use of the experimental method is mentioned in James Marcia's "case history of a construct." As you may recall, Marcia explained that to establish the scientific worth of his identity statuses, he considered it necessary to demonstrate that individuals differing in identity status behaved in predictably different ways in an experimental setting. His experimental procedures involved administering a concept-attainment task under stressful and nonstressful conditions and determining the impact of this stress manipulation on task performance and self-esteem among subjects classified as identity achievers, moratoriums, foreclosures, and diffusions.

Another important use of the experimental method by personality psychologists is in factorial designs intended to identify personality variables intervening between environmental events and behavior. In the Mitchell and Byrne article, a classic personality measure (authoritarianism) is combined with several experimental variables to increase our ability to predict specific juror behaviors. While construct-valida-tion studies and factorial experiments are not the only use to which personality psychologists have put experimental designs, it is helpful to remember that experimental strategies, like correlational strategies, have limitations. For ex-ample, some variables might be useful predictors of behavior without being amenable to experi-mental manipulation. We cannot randomly assign subjects to conditions in which they are made male or female or young or old, yet gen-der and age are probably associated with a number of important behaviors.

The use of experimental designs is also lim-ited by ethical considerations. For example, you might hypothesize that punitive parental practices will produce aggressive personalities in children. Although possible in theory, it would clearly be unethical to take a group of newborn babies and randomly assign them to two child-rearing conditions, punitive and not punitive. However, because the research question is important, investigators have used correlational designs to shed light on the problem (for exam-ple, McCord, McCord, and Howard, 1961).

Our selections in Chapter 4 make it clear just how difficult it can be to decide about whether or not a particular experimental procedure is ethical. Middlemist and his colleagues consid-ered it perfectly reasonable to measure the stressful impact of personal distance on mictura-tion by systematically varying the personal distance of a stranger in a public men's room setting. Obviously, Koocher's judgment of the acceptability of the procedure was different. Some investigators might even question the eth-ics of Marcia's stress manipulation as a way of validating a personality test.

Carlson's emphasis on the need for more correlational studies is consistent with the per-sonologist's emphasis on psychological character-istics that are stable and consistent, that provide organization to the personality, and that can be measured in ways contributing to our under-standing of the complexity of individuals.

Wrightsman's observational study is a good example of the search for consistency in human behavior, asking Do supporters of a "law-and-order" political ticket show a stronger tend-ency to obey a particular law than supporters of other political tickets? In a more complex and less unobtrusive study, Zucker and his co-workers use a natural crisis to test the generality of hypotheses previously examined in laboratory investigations. As we've mentioned before, it is very important to balance the control of the laboratory setting with the naturalness of field settings to gain a fully valid picture of personality.

Just as she is concerned about the predomi-nance of experimental over correlational designs, Carlson is critical of the predominance of labo-ratory over naturalistic settings for research. Her concern should not be interpreted as a com-plete indictment of the laboratory setting. Keep in mind that correlational studies, like experi-ments, can be conducted in laboratory settings, and that both types of setting, like both types of design, can provide valuable answers to well-conceived research questions. A number of the selections in this book are reports of correla-tional studies conducted in laboratory settings, and all of them, we believe, are good examples of what can be achieved in the laboratory with that ubiquitous subject, the college student.

For example, incorporating concepts and measures derived from Erikson's theory of psy-chosocial development, the study by Orlofsky and his colleagues represents a thoughtful at-tempt to examine the occurrence of predicted re-lationships among personality measures. Stewart and Winter report the results of an extremely rich correlational study, which provides a wealth of information about patterns of think-ing, patterns of behavior, and background char-acteristics of women who are self-defined or socially defined in their career orientations. Like the Stewart and Winter study, Rotter's research, conducted in college classrooms and fraternities, reminds us that a program of construct valida-

tion can rely heavily on correlational procedures, which can be quite ingenious in their
own right.

Although they are frequently treated as incompatible types of research strategy, experimental and correlational methods are not
completely discontinuous. We have already
noted that experimental and correlational variables can be brought together in factorial designs.
In addition, some variables can be studied either
correlationally or experimentally. In particular,
many emotional and motivational variables
(for example, anxiety, achievement, empathy,
fear of success or failure) have been studied both
as measured variables reflecting general characteristics of individuals that are relatively stable
over time and across situations, and as states
that can be influenced experimentally by environmental manipulations.

Anxiety is a good example of a variable that
has been studied both experimentally and correlationally. In Marcia's construct-validation
study, anxiety was an experimental variable,
manipulated by requiring subjects to solve
concept-attainment problems under stressful and
nonstressful conditions. In the study by Zucker
and his co-workers, anxiety was a measured
variable assessed through a brief questionnaire.
Self-reported feelings of anxiety experienced
during the New York City blackout were compared for males versus females and first- versus
later-borns.

In the past, many psychologists have argued
that a fundamental discontinuity exists between
experimental and correlational designs because
experimental designs allow one to draw conclusions about causality in the relationships among
variables and correlational designs do not. This
argument, probably always overstated, is no
longer acceptable as a reason for rejecting correlational designs in favor of experimental ones.
As we have already noted, demonstrating that X
causes Y within the psychology laboratory in
no way "proves" that Y is caused by X in
the real world. Moreover, investigators do not

cease to search for causes when they encounter
circumstances in which they cannot deliberately
create changes in an independent variable
through manipulations in—or out—of the laboratory. Astronomers cannot cause changes in
the operations of the heavenly bodies, yet we
trust many of their causal statements. Theorists
of evolution cannot go back and create changes
in what happened millions of years ago, but
most scientists accept evidence of evolutionary
process as compelling. The point is that through
careful attention to design problems and appropriate selection of methods, investigators can
accrue convincing evidence for causal relationships even under circumstances that do not
permit the manipulation of variables. Moreover,
conceptual and analytic procedures such as
multiple regression, causal modeling, and path
analysis (see, for example, Asher, 1976; Blalock,
1972; Costner, 1974) are being used more
and more frequently in complex designs to provide estimates of the causal relationships among
variables studied through correlational
procedures.

We do not claim that there is only one right
way to do research and that this one right
way can be found in Carlson's article. However,
we do believe that Carlson documents well
some important omissions from many articles in
journals reporting research on personality.
She also presents thoughtful suggestions about
ways of combatting some of the problems she
identifies in psychological research. We are not
discouraged by her assessment of the state of
the art in psychological research and we hope
you will not be either. Carlson provides both a
challenge and a prescription for all investigations of human personality.

You might wonder whether Carlson's article,
published in 1971, is outdated. Our second
chapter selection, published by Levenson and
her colleagues in 1976, shows that very little
change in personality research methods took
place in the five years following Carlson's survey. Our impression is that the problems and

suggested solutions presented in both selections continue to deserve the thoughtful attention of all those committed to achieving a fuller understanding of human personality.

On the other hand, Carlson and others have been actively involved in revitalizing the area of personality research. Within the American Psychological Association's Division on Personality and Social Psychology, a special committee on personality was formed to grapple with such issues as why and in what ways personality research had stagnated and what solutions could be sought. Partly as a result of this committee's work, the *Journal of Personality and Social Psychology* solicited specialized papers in the area of personality in 1979 and was revamped in 1980 to have an independently edited section on personality research.

Some of the identity struggles that have been going on within the field of personality research in the second half of the 1970s and into the 1980s are reflected in the sections on personality in each issue of the *Annual Review of Psychology* since 1976. We recommend that you scan these papers, not only to get a year by year overview of research in such areas as sex-role identity and self-concept, but also to gain a glimpse of the substantive issues identified by major researchers trying to specify the trends and issues of the field.

We end this text as we began it, with a reminder that the realm of personality research is in a period of transition, and that you, the student, can make a contribution to this burgeoning field. In our effort to provide examples of investigations that you can carry out as part of a semester's work, we have neglected some areas—for example, longitudinal investigations, in which the development of a group of subjects is assessed over a fairly long period of time. To expose you to a variety of methods, we have devoted less space than we might have to some of the methods that are particularly attractive to many personologists—for example, the content analysis of case materials such as letters, autobiographies, and diaries to gain insights into the personalities of single individuals. However, we hope we have provided you with an exposure to psychological methods and the issues involved in applying these to personality research broad enough to help you continue your own pursuits in this area.

Where Is the Person in Personality Research?[1]

Rae Carlson

Educational Testing Service, Princeton, New Jersey

Constraints upon inquiry in personality imposed by current research methods were examined by (a) a survey of empirical work published in two major personality journals and (b) a consideration of methodological and ethical issues raised in recent research criticism. Review of samples, research procedures, and social-psychological context in 226 empirical studies revealed that current methodological practices are incapable of approaching questions of real importance in personality and involve serious problems beyond those noted in recent research criticism. Recent proposals for methodological reforms offer only partial solutions and require further attention to the personal involvement and responsibility of investigators. This paper proposes a conceptual schema for ordering personality research strategies, a distinction between "contractual" and "collaborative" models of subject-experimenter relationships, and suggestions for increasing the relevance and responsibility of personality research.

The greatly increased volume of empirical work on personality in recent years, and the appearance of several new textbooks on personality research and theory (e.g., Maddi, 1968; Mehrabian, 1968; Mischel, 1968; Schontz, 1965), may be read as indications of flourishing inquiry in personality. Yet there is a growing concern (Adelson, 1969; Sanford 1965) that personology is, in fact, languishing; that in adopting the research values and strategies of "process" psychology, contemporary investigators have relegated the psychology of "person" to a peripheral world of the psychotherapist, the behavior modifier, and the encounter group. Moreover, the increasing concern with general issues emerging in contemporary research on research (Argyris, 1968; Kelman, 1967; Orne,

1962; Rosenthal, 1966; Schultz, 1969; Stricker, 1967) has a particularly keen significance for the field of personality study. A reexamination of the status of personality research may help to define these issues.

There is a clear consensus among contemporary personologists concerning the goals, methods, and values informing personality research. While governed by the scientific principles and ethical concerns common to all psychology, personality has a unique, central role in the field. As Baughman and Welsh (1962) observed:

> Personality bridges the two basic branches of psychology—experimental psychology, which tends toward the biological sciences, and social psychology which is closely allied to the social studies ... the concepts of personality study can tie together the views of these two areas and minimize the danger of dehumanization ... [through clear focus upon] our unit of study, individual man [pp. 16–17].

The program of personality research has been clearly restated by Maddi (1968):

> The personologist is interested in universals ... *in the commonalities among people* [as well as] ... *in the attempt to identify and classify differences among people* ... The personologist is *rather unusual in not restricting himself to behavior easily traceable to social and biological pressures of the moment* ... Of all the social and biological scientists, then, *the personologist believes most deeply in the complexity and individuality of life* ... his *emphasis* [is] *upon characteristics* ... *that show continuity in time* ... *that seem to have psychological importance* ... that have some ready relationship to the major goals and directions of the person's life ... *The personologist is interested in all rather than only some of the psychological behavior of the person* ... Finally ... personologists ... *are* ... *primarily intererested in the adult human being* ... the fruit of development—a congealed personality that exerts a pervasive influence on present and future-behavior ... [pp. 7–9; original italics].

[1] Preparation of this paper was supported by a National Institute of Mental Health Special Fellowship administered by Educational Testing Service, Princeton, N.J.

Toward achieving these goals, the personologist employs a wide range of methods: "the cross-cultural, the developmental, the clinical, the experimental, and the quantitative [Murphy, 1968, p. 19]"

The breadth and depth of the current research stemming from this tradition may be best demonstrated by a review of the current personality literature. Whom are we studying? How much are we prepared to learn about an individual? In what settings and relationships? Answers to such questions, implicit in the research methods of the field, operate to structure and to limit the possibilities of new knowledge. Assessment of a broad sample of current published research on personality may provide an indication of whether unexamined assumptions of investigators may be restricting, rather than advancing, knowledge about the organization of psychological processes within the person.

The present report, based upon such an assessment of current research, was guided by three purposes: an examination of constraints imposed by research methods, consideration of methodological and ethical issues posed in recent research criticism, and presentation of some alternative ways of solving the problems encountered.

A SURVEY OF CURRENT PERSONALITY RESEARCH

Articles appearing in the 1968 volumes of two major journals publishing substantive research on personality (*Journal of Personality* and *Journal of Personality and Social Psychology*) constituted the sample of the review. Since the concern was with the scope and structure of inquiry, rather than its content, subject matter was disregarded, and the focus placed on selected aspects of research method: composition of subject samples, general research strategy, and social-psychological aspects of the research. Major findings, based upon tabulations for 226 substantive articles (excluding a few editorials, methodological and animal studies, and monograph supplements) are summarized in Table 1.

Whom Are We Studying?

An overwhelming reliance upon undergraduate students as subjects is clear: 71% of all studies used college students, with the vast (but indeterminate) majority of these representing introductory psychology students meeting course requirements for research participation. School children, equally "captive" subjects, were a relatively minor second choice. The expansion of inquiry to include a broader sample of adults in a variety of community settings (e.g., pregnant mothers, African tribesmen, racetrack patrons) is a heartening development. However, with a few exceptions community adults were studied in such a limited and trivial fashion as to contribute very little to knowledge of personality. Males and females were represented in approximately a 2 to 1 ratio, a finding which seems to suggest some correction of the serious imbalance in sex composition of samples noted in a review of the literature nearly a decade ago (Carlson & Carlson, 1960). However, upon closer examination, this "improvement" appears a remarkably fragile basis for the extension of knowledge. For the sexes are typically studied in segregation: approximately half of the studies used subjects of only one sex, and many of the remaining studies used single-sex groups for separate parts of an investigation. Moreover, one-fifth of the studies either failed to indicate proportions of males and females in the sample or to indicate whether sex varied at all.

Investigators' remarkable lack of interest in an intuitively (and empirically) important aspect of personality appeared in several ways. Among the studies that could have tested for sex differences, less than half reported such tests. Yet in 51 studies where sex differences *were* examined, signficant effects of sex were found in 74% of the studies. Meanwhile, an implicit awareness of sex differences may be seen in a nascent trend toward using males-only in studying achievement, bargaining, etc., and to use females-only in studying altruism, cooperation, and the like. A most illuminating instance of how sex differences are treated in current research is to be found in a study by Wilson and

TABLE 1 Summary of Selected Aspects of Research Methods in 226 Personality Studies

Subject samples			Research strategy and procedures		
Sex composition	N	%	General strategy	N	%
Males only	71	31	Experimental	177	78
Females only	33	15	Field	47	20
Both (specified)	77	34	Combined	2	
Both (unspecified)	22	10			
Indeterminate	23	10	Time span of inquiry	N	%
			Single session[a]	177	78
Age-role composition	N	%	Less than 1 month	34	15
			Over 1 month	15	7
Preschool	2	—			
Elementary	16	7	Cognitive clarity	N	%
Secondary	15	7			
College—psychology	110	44	Deception	129	57
College	50	22	Debriefing specified	42	(32)[b]
Adult—general	3	—	Interpretive feedback	1	—
Adult—special	13	6			
Multiple	17	8			

[a] Includes studies with earlier pretest administered in regular classes.
[b] Percentage of deception studies.

Insko (1968). In an investigation which combines most of the current preoccupations of the field (e.g., prisoner's dilemma, stooges, evaluative ratings of others, and a "theoretical" controversy), clear-cut findings supporting the major hypothesis were reported on the basis of tables (see Table 2) in which even *clearer* sex differences failed to capture the attention of the investigators or of journal reviewers.

Given the compelling evidence of the pervasiveness and importance of sex differences in personality, both from present "internal" data and a wealth of "external" evidence (Maccoby, 1966), current research methods seem designed to avoid, rather than to confront, a central problem of personality organization.

How Do We Study Persons?

Experimental methods predominated in current research, with over half of the published studies employing manipulative procedures. Correlational studies (broadly defined) accounted for most

TABLE 2 Mean Stooge Impression

	No interval between sessions				One wk. between sessions			
	No measurement delay		Measurement delay		No measurement delay		Measurement delay	
	Male	Female	Male	Female	Male	Female	Male	Female
Competive-Cooperative	34.80	34.60	35.40	35.80	34.00	37.40	37.00	37.00
Cooperative-Competive	28.60	34.00	28.40	33.60	27.00	35.40	30.40	32.00
Difference	6.02	.60	7.00	2.20	7.00	2.00	6.60	5.00
Direction	Recency	Recency	Recency	Recency	Recency	Recency	Recency	Recency

Note.—The recency effect is significant at the .01 level. $F = 8.56$, $df = 1/64$; all other effects are nonsignificant.
Reprinted from an article by Warner Wilson and Chester Insko published in the May 1968 *Journal of Personality and Social Psychology*. Copyrighted by the American Psychological Association, Inc., 1968.

of the remaining work, although a small, but promising upsurge of observational studies in naturalistic settings should be noted. The sole study in which experimental and field methods were combined, and a basic finding established with two appropriate samples, was contributed by a team of sociologists (O'Toole & Dubin, 1968).

How Much Are We Prepared to Learn About a Person?

Extremes of a "comprehensiveness" dimension are represented by studies in which subjects left no trace of their personal participation, merely contributing isolated bits of behavior to a data pool, and a few in which subjects provided exhaustive data on a battery of tests and biographical inventories. However, the typical study represented an individual in terms of his sex (sometimes), treatment condition, performance scores, and ratings of partner or experimenter in posttest inquiry. Although the literature as a whole has elicited a wide range of potentially important information about persons, no *single* investigation either noted or utilized much information about any individual subject. Thus the task performances of subjects in current research remain uninterpretable as personality data in the absence of anchoring information.

An interesting sidelight is the new role of introspection in contemporary research. Apart from a few studies in which the subject's account of private experience constituted primary data, introspective reports are currently used *(a)* in deriving pretest scores as a basis for assignment to experimental groups or *(b)* "as a check on the effectiveness of the experimental manipulation."

The time span of contemporary inquiry is short. The vast majority of published work was based upon a single session; less than one-fifth of reported studies involved more than a 2-week period, and rarer still were the few studies involving follow-up over significant periods of time. The only examples of investigators' extended delay of gratification were two follow-up studies (over 15 and 18 months) of smoking behavior (Johnson 1968; Mann & Janis, 1968) and a 3-year followup of mental retardates (Zigler, Balla, & Butterfield, 1968).

What Is the Interpersonal Context of Research?

With a few notable exceptions, the current mode of inquiry involves highly impersonal subject-experimenter relationships, "conscripted" subjects who are expected (and expect) to conform to research requirements with little explanation and little interpretive feedback.

Deception remains a salient feature of experimental inquiry. Over half of the total sample and 73% of the experimental studies relied upon deception as a means of manipulating major variables. There are, as Stricker (1967) has pointed out, many ways of deceiving subjects; most of these—cover stories, miscommunication of purpose, confederates, false interpretations of test performances, among others—were represented in the year's research. Moreover, deception often occurred in the context of imposing rather elaborate and demeaning demands upon subjects. It is instructive to consider the subject's experience in a dissonance study (Kiesler, Pallak, Kanouse, 1968) which illustrates the potentialities of this research tradition:

A student who *(a)* volunteered to participate in a study of "regional speech differences" for $1.50, *(b)* tape-recorded a prepared speech, and was *(c)* told that his recordings would be used in a nationwide survey and in classes at the university, *(d)* sent to another building to be interviewed by a fake "assistant to the dean," *(e)* detained by a fake schedule delay, *(f)* induced to participate in another survey while waiting, *(g)* induced to reaffirm his "choice" to participate, *(h)* told that he should report to another building a half-mile away, *(i)* rescued by another stooge who provided an empty classroom, *(j)* asked to write an essay contrary to his own beliefs, *(k)* told that his essay would be published in the campus newspaper, *(l)* required to read a prepared list of arguments, *(m)* required to reaffirm his free choice to participate;

he then *(n)* wrote an essay, and was *(o)* required to "go down four flights of stairs, traverse approximately a block to a(nother) building . . . and go up three flights of stairs . . . ," *(p)* interviewed by a fake "assistant to the dean" who expressed interest in the student's opinions, *(q)* asked to fill out an attitude questionnaire, *(r)* required to provide ratings of his experience of the first task and of the first experimenter, *(s)* required to provide ratings of his experience of choice, liking for the second task, and for the second experimenter, *(t)* asked about his parents' socioeconomic status, and *(u)* "was then completely debriefed, including an explanation of the study and hypothesis involved . . . [Kiesler et al., 1968, p. 334].[2]

Debriefing was explicitly reported in only one-third of the deception studies. Moreover, debriefing took a number of quite different forms. While a few studies reported thorough, integrative interpretations of experimental manipulations, more characteristic were several other types of debriefing: *(a) Undoing* (e.g., "After the subject completed the questionnaire, Dr. . . . entered the office and debriefed him. Because all of the subjects had received a rather negative evaluation, they were delighted to learn that the evaluation was preprogrammed rather than an accurate reflection of their creative ability"—Aronson & Cope, 1968, p. 10); *(b) Rationalization* (e.g., "After completing the questionnaire, the subject was queried as to possible suspicion and the purposes of the experiment and the need for deception explained"—Helmreich & Collins, 1968, p. 78); and *(c) Silencing* (e.g., "Before leaving, the experiment revealed the nature of the study and got the subject to promise not to discuss it with anyone"—Mills & Jellison, 1968, p. 61).

While in many studies the nature of the tasks may be presumed to be obvious, and perhaps meaningful to the subjects, it is surprising that subjects' experience of research participation was not considered worthy of mention. Only 1 of the 266 studies (Steiner, 1968) noted provision for giving subjects a report of the findings of the investigation. When one considers that the vast bulk of the year's published research was made possible by the requirement of research participation as a "learning experience" in psychology courses, this lack of concern for subjects' cognitive clarity is remarkable.

One further aspect of the subject-experimenter relationship proved impossible to tabulate. Only in a small proportion of cases was it possible to determine whether the investigator or anonymous assistants had "run" the subjects or whether, in fact, the experimenter had ever seen his subjects.

Questions We Can Neither Ask Nor Answer

It is instructive to consider the range of personological questions which cannot be investigated by our current research methods. While the year's research literature provides a few isolated exceptions to many of the following generalizations, the central tendency of our current modes of inquiry is so strong as to mark a real barrier to knowledge.

We cannot study the organization of personality because we know at most only one or two "facts" about any subject. We cannot study the stability of personality, nor its development over epochs of life, because we see our subjects for an hour. We cannot study the problems or capacities of the mature individual, because we study late adolescents. We cannot study psychosexuality, because we avoid looking at distinctive qualities of masculinity and femininity as a focal problem. We cannot study how persons strive for their important goals, because we elect to induce motivational sets. We cannot study constitutional, temperamental variables because (apart from a few glances at increments in galvanic skin response under stress) we do not consider biological bases of personality. We cannot study the development and power of friendship—nor the course of true love—because we choose to manipulate interpersonal attraction.

[2]Incredibly, a professional symposium on "commitment" prior to the appearance of this study praised this investigation for the ingenuity of its experimental design.

Such a list of cognitive deficits in the collective psyche of the field might be extended at great length. Personality psychology would seem to be paying an exorbitant price in potential knowledge for the security afforded by preserving norms of convenience and methodological orthodoxy. Must these important, unanswered questions be left to literature and psychiatry? If so, what would be the use of our work?

Obviously, no single scientist, no single study, no single research tradition can possibly deal "scientifically" with anything so complex as a whole person. But the attempt can be made collectively and cumulatively. The present impoverishment of personality research is distressing because it suggests that the goal of studying whole persons has been abandoned. However, the fragmented and limited quality of current research may stem less from myopia or opportunism than from the absence of a conceptual framework for guiding inquiry in personality.

A Typology of Research Approaches

Kluckhohn and Murray (1949) remind us that every man is " . . . like *all* other men, like *some* other men, and like *no* other men [p. 35]," and in an insightful truism have also offered an implicit model for ordering the scope and methods of inquiry in personality. The typology of research approaches suggested by this model corresponds to the major traditions from which personality study has grown: *(a)* the experimental methods of laboratory psychology, *(b)* the correlational methods of differential psychology, and *(c)* the clinical methods stemming from the tradition of French psychiatry and Viennese psychoanalysis. However, the typology has considerably more than mere historical interest, and may serve to illumine the present state of personality research and point toward a conceptually based set of solutions to present problems.

"*. . . like ALL other men.*" The psychologist working from this perspective seeks universals, the discovery of general laws of human nature. The emphasis is upon psychological processes;

persons are essentially "carriers" of the variables under investigation. Research methods reflect the basic assumptions of this approach: persons are interchangeable; random assignment to treatment conditions is employed to insure control of idiosyncratic qualities which are "noise" in the generalist's inquiry. The basic assumption of the equivalence of subjects leads to further methodological implications: *(a)* experimental manipulation of independent variables as the source of subject variability, *(b)* dimensional treatment of psychological variables, *(c)* relative deemphasis upon genetic variation and constitutional bases of individuality, and *(d)* emphasis upon situational factors as major sources of variation in human nature. Among the many current examples of generalist tradition in personality research, one notes the extensive work on cognitive dissonance, the attempts to establish laws of interpersonal attraction and impression formation, the conditions under which cooperation and competition are elicited in interpersonal events.

"*. . . like SOME other men.*" This tradition studies psychological processes and their organization in different *kinds* of subjects; its aim is that of identifying group differences that make a difference. Such inquiry establishes typologies, charts the influence of moderator variables, and, substituting measurement for manipulation, tends to employ correlational methods (broadly conceived, in all their contemporary variations). Further, the differential approach tends to *(a)* seek natural occurrences of the phenomena under investigation, *(b)* emphasize discontinuities— whether of developmental level, character types, or social class—as correctives to an assumption of continuity, *(c)* emphasize both genetic variation and cultural determinism as sources of critical differences, and *(d)* emphasize intrinsic intrapersonal structures as base lines for further inquiry. Current examples of the differential approach in personality research include inquiry on the differences between internal and external controllers, different consequences of repression and sensitization as defense styles, the nature of sex differences in personality, and studies pointing to the limits of generalists' formulations—for instance, Bishop's (1967) demonstration that prediction from cognitive dissonance theory fail to fit the "anal" personality.

"... *like NO other men.*" The clinical tradition, in its concern for mapping the intricate organization of psychological processes within the unique individual is the prototype; however, the individual approach includes less comprehensive kinds of inquiry, including "ipsative" methods (Broverman, 1962), "morphogenic" methods (Allport, 1968), a concern for "personal constructs" (Kelly, 1955) and inquiry focused upon the "representative case" (Schontz, 1965). While the potency of the case method in the development of personality study should be so obvious as to require no special emphasis, the particular quality of the contemporary (American) *zeitgeist* imposes a special problem: the "clinical" tradition has come to connote a "helping" orientation totally extraneous to the method itself. (The relevance of case materials for strictly scientific inquiry is vividly demonstrated by the fact that geologists can derive from a few pounds of nonrandom moondust inferences about the structure and history of planets.)

Inquiry in the individual tradition seeks to *(a)* examine organization of psychological processes within the individual, *(b)* establish assessment methods deriving from the intrinsic structure and dynamics of the individual—and capable of representing this intrinsic structure, *(c)* identify general psychological problems emerging from the examination of individual personality, and *(d)* provide a field for testing the formulations derived from general and differential inquiry. Contemporary examples of the individual approach include White's (1966) intensive studies of three "normal" personalities over a significant period of the life span, or, in a different mode, Alfert's (1967) demonstration that ipsative analyses of data on stress reactions revealed order and coherence which had eluded the generalist's "normative" approach to the same data.

Some of the conceptual and methodological issues involved in a comparable tripartite schema are presented in Emmerich's (1968) discussion of "classical," "differential," and "ipsative" models of development. However, while Emmerich's three models are presented as competing candidates, the three approaches presented here are conceived of as complementary rather than competitive alternatives. Tentative knowledge gained from any one approach must ultimately be weighed by alternative methods. A "general law" which operates only in certain kinds of people, or which can predict little of significance in an individual's life may prove very trivial in understanding personality. Similarly, an elaborate case study which neither inspires nor tests inquiry of a more general nature is basically irrelevant to personology.

This schema offers another way of assessing the current status of personality research: How well does current inquiry represent the person in these three fundamental aspects?

The 226 articles reviewed above were reexamined in terms of the present typology, and each article assigned to one of three categories as follows:

1. General. The research method disregarded preexisting subject variables and used random assignment to treatment conditions and/or treated subjects' scores as a continuous dimension.

2. Differential. The research method made at least minimal provision for identifying group differences on the basis of preexisting subject variables. Assignment to this category was "lenient" in the sense that a problem conceived in general terms was classified as "differential" if tests for qualitative differences (e.g., sex differences) were reported.

3. Individual. The research method included extensive study of one or more individuals, and *(a)* retained individual cases as the unit of analysis or *(b)* included extensive case examples in presentation of findings.

The results of this analysis give a clear and consistent picture of the "generalist" bias in contemporary personality research, with 128 (57%) of the studies disregarding subject variables. Ninety-eight (43%) of the studies classified as "differential" examined a somewhat limited set of bases of group differences (e.g., high versus low anxiety, repressors versus sensitizers, first borns versus later-borns, males versus females); extreme groups defined on single dimensions rather than "types" were the norm. Finally, the analysis revealed that *not a single published study attempted even minimal inquiry into the organization of personality variables within the individual.*

Thus the present analysis provides a further basis for concern about the status of personality research. Conceivably, personological studies may appear from time to time in clinical and psychiatric journals not encompassed in the present review. But even if this could be demonstrated, what are the implications? Is personology to be left to the exclusive concern of the healer rather than the scientist? Should personality research be redefined as "the experimental study of personality fragments in artificial situations?" It is not so much the pretensions of the field as the neglect of legitimate and necessary pretensions which poses problems for the serious personologist.

Possible reasons for the current state of affairs, along with suggestions for enlarging the scope and relevance of personality study are considered in a later section. First, however, parallels between the methodological problems noted in personality literature and the issues raised in recent criticism of general psychological literature should be noted.

ERROR, ETHICS, AND DISCIPLINARY INTEGRITY

The pervasive effects of atmosphere, expectancies, and demand characteristics, long recognized by some psychologists (Allport, 1968; Kelly, 1955; Lewin, 1935), and recently rediscovered and developed as a research area by a newer generation, now threaten to require a wholesale reexamination of much of psychology's substance. Recently,

implications of this state of affairs have been examined in incisive comments of Adelson (1969), Argyris (1968), and Schultz (1969), among others.

Adelson (1969), in a brilliant critique of a year's worth of personality research, noted the rigidity and irrelevance of current methodology and the availability of more appropriate models of inquiry, but offered little optimism about reform. Argyris (1968) pointed to "unintended consequences of rigorous research," noting that organization theory predicts current problems: the dependency or covert hostility of subjects caught in an authoritarian relationship, the "unionization" of subjects, the unintentional programming of people to become interpersonally incompetent. Schultz (1969) provided historical perspective on the role of the subject in psychological inquiry and underscored problems noted by recent critics of research methods: distortion of data through the use of irrelevant and nonrepresentative samples, deception of the deceiver, and the ethical problems involved in investigators' systematic disregard for the dignity and welfare of subjects.

The personologist—for whom all of these issues are of the deepest concern—finds that additional problems are posed by current research conventions. Among the unintended consequences of acquiescence in these conventions is the abandonment of the field of normal personality as a primary scientific enterprise. Surely this is a territory worth defending against benign encroachments of the experimental and social psychologists whose "process" orientation is more consonant with their mission, or the "abnormal" clinical psychologists whose concern with helping persons makes their journals and textbooks more receptive to person-centered inquiry.

Another serious consequence of acquiescence in current methodology is found in the abandonment of students and of curricular responsibilities (Carlson[3]). By permitting personality courses to become "adjustment" courses for nonmajors and

[3]Carlson, R. (Chm.). Personality in the undergraduate curriculum. Symposium presented at the meeting of the American Psychological Association, San Francisco, August 1968.

"theory" courses for psychology majors, we are implicitly communicating a disbelief in the value or possibility of inquiry in personology. Thus psychologists are unintentionally cutting off sources of future scholars prepared to confront the intellectual problems of "personality" in a world where "depersonalization" has, for some years, been both a battle cry and a genuine human concern.

Further, a personologist, relatively sensitive to personality consequences of situational pressures and role demands, must be particularly concerned about the *other* edge of the double blade of current methodology. For that violation of human dignity experienced by subjects in manipulative-deceptive relationships equally demeans the psychologist who adapts to a norm of distrust,[4] and comes to confuse games with the pursuit of science.

Toward Solutions

Once the depth and pervasiveness of the problem is genuinely confronted, solutions would seem to be well within the power of those seriously committed to the integrity and survival of the discipline. Several relevant proposals have been advanced by recent critics of the general psychological scene.

Argyris' (1968) proposals include the important conceptions that subjects should be given greater control and influence, longer time perspective, and greater internal involvement in research projects. Noting that contamination of research by subjects' expectancies is inevitable, he pointed out that greater control of such contamination can be achieved by research methods which increase awareness of such expectations. Moreover, his

empirical work demonstrating the resistance to change of "behavior that is internalized, highly potent, and related to . . . feelings of intellectual and interpersonal competence . . . " strongly supports Argyris' interpretation that "the more researchers study such behavior, the less they may need to worry about such contamination [p. 195]."

Schultz (1969) posed two basic dimensions of reform: *(a)* the broadening of inquiry to include more representative noncollege samples, and *(b)* development of research methods which would reflect ethical responsibility and a contemporary image of man and of the scientific enterprise.

Toward achievement of broad-gauged sampling, Schultz gave an ambivalent endorsement to Rosenthal's (1966) suggestion that independent data-collection centers undertake execution of studies designed by academic investigators, in the belief that standardization of experimenter bias and the procurement of more representative samples would correct some of the serious deficiencies of current research. While the problem of the expense of establishing and maintaining such centers is noted by Schultz, more serious problems are also involved. From the standpoint of the present critique, this proposal would seem to exacerbate fundamental problems. By increasing the distance between the investigator and his data, and by decreasing his personal involvement and responsibility, the Rosenthal proposal would extend the investigator's license to ignore the relevance of his inquiry and to exploit or ignore dependency and counter-manipulation of subjects. Conceivably, the Rosenthal proposal could have some merit in broadening inquiry on certain impersonal problems of classical experimental psychology. But the overall effects of establishing such an elaborate hand-washing apparatus would seem to be lethal for those engaged in issues of personality and interpersonal relationships.

Toward solution of the second class of problems—ethics and relevance—Schultz gave tentative endorsement ot Kelman's (1967) proposal of role playing as a research technique and to Jourard's (1968) suggestion that mutual self-disclosure

[4]An incident illustrating the depth and duration of this problem occurred in the writer's experience of interviewing a prospective junior colleague several years ago. Asked about his own experience as a student in a West Coast university, the candidate recalled his experience of hearing about the assassination of the late President Kennedy in a psychology class, his calm assumption that this was naturally an experimental manipulation, and his continued disbelief in the reality of the tragedy for some time—on "professional" rather than human grounds.

by experimenter and subject might dispel the cloud of distrust which surrounds much current inquiry.

Undoubtedly, Kelman's (1967) suggestion for cooperative engagement of the subject's imaginative resources in role playing the confrontation of psychological problems is a notable improvement over current deceptive-manipulative methods. However, this proposal does not touch critical issues of problem finding or of real-life involvement; and one can imagine that the role-playing technique might even perpetuate (by legitimizing) the systematic irrelevance of much psychological research. As Schultz (1969) noted, the value of this method would be highly dependent upon characteristics of subjects and of subject-experimenter relationships. Fundamental personological questions (e.g., What kinds of people can invest themselves in what kinds of role playing?) entirely bypassed in this proposal would define the limits of its relevance. There is a clear (but probably small) place for the role-playing technique in investigating a wide range of theoretically significant problems; considerable thought should be given to these limits before the technique is blessed as a solution to our current malaise.

Jourard's (1968) recommendation of mutual self-disclosure poses somewhat different problems. As Schultz (1969) noted, the personality of the investigator would be a major factor—along with issues of the time and expense involved. But more serious objections should be noted. Admittedly, almost *any* methods of restoring confidence, trust, and dignity in subject-experimenter relationships could be justified at this point in time. However, the correction of a destructive relationship can, at most, create an atmosphere in which genuine research is possible; it does not constitute a research method. Moreover, there are real risks that experimenter and subject alike may be seduced by the "togetherness" aspects of interaction; that the Jourard proposal, in the hands of investigators characterologically unsuited to this mode of inquiry, might cloud the purposes of scientific inquiry as thoroughly as the manipulative-experimental techniques in current vogue. There are

a number of ways of deriving irrelevant gratifications from research, and in the absence of scientific commitment and conceptual clarity, soft hearts are probably no better than hard heads as tools of the trade.

The climate of change, of self-examination, of genuine concern for reform of psychological inquiry is unmistakable. In this context, the present critique of several current proposals stems from a concern that basic issues may be obscured by the sense of urgency toward reform. At the risk of oversimplifying several thoughtful contributions, current reform proposals appear to address two quite different issues of control and of alienation. Control of unwanted variance (whether generated by inappropriate sampling, experimenter bias, or subject expectancy) and counteracting forces toward alienation (of experimenter from subject, of experimental inquiry from real-life relevance) are the explicit goals of most current proposals, or the rationales for more fundamental ones (e.g., Argyris, 1968). However, most of the proposals fail to deal explicitly with issues of *relevance* of method to problem, or to locate clearly the *responsibility* for various reforms. Some explicit consideration of these issues seems warranted.

On the relevance of subject samples. Most of the current concern about overreliance upon undergraduate students as research subjects (cf. Schultz, 1969) reflects the generalist's concern with nonrepresentative samples which constrain the generality of laws to be established from inquiry. There exists sufficient evidence of "bias" in college samples (volunteer bias, birth-order effects, socioeconomic selectivity) to establish that undergraduate students are probably not representative of humankind.

But a more serious concern may be raised about the *misuse,* rather than the use of college students as research subjects. For students, as a group, possess many characteristics which make them highly appropriate subjects for personality research: they are curious, intelligent, motivated to explore their lives and experiences, capable of articulate introspection—and their life situations generally provide both time and meaningful settings for research participation. Yet it is precisely this set of subject characteristics which tends to be ignored (or violated) in current research conventions. When the student's intrinsic motivation is "controlled" by external requirements of research participation and by induction of motivational sets, when his introspective capacities are constrained by the formats of rating scales and checklists, when his curiosity is violated by deception and false or partial feedback, the very characteristics which recommend him as a research subject are thrown away.

Moreover, certain limitations upon the generality of student-based research are equally ignored. Clearly, students are "unfinished" personalities. Coherent changes in ego structure within and beyond college years have been demonstrated in a wide variety of studies ranging from Constantinople's (1969) charting of ego changes in questionnaire responses over the undergraduate years through White's (1966) intensive longitudinal clinical studies of students whose postcollege years revealed surprising but theoretically significant consolidations and restructurings of intrapersonal and interpersonal dynamics.

While the year's published personality research occasionally noted the selection of samples considered intrinsically relevant to the research problem (e.g., a series of obesity and eating studies published in the October 1968 *Journal of Personality and Social Psychology*), the typical study evidently used college students simply because they were there.

"Reform" proposals directed toward broadening of research samples need to be based upon thoughtful consideration of the subject characteristics of intrinsic relevance to research problems. Once such criteria are established, a range of populations might be sampled: colleagues, community adults, friends and families of students—along with a range of special populations (e.g., military personnel, prisoners, etc.) whose experience of special situations might illumine important problems rarely encountered by subjects from the general population. Moreover, a vast range of individuals whose biographies and personal documents are capable of transcending demographic constraints of usual research samples is available for inquiry in general, differential, and individual terms, for instance, Cox's (1926) or Goertzel and Goertzel's (1962) studies of gifted individuals; Baldwin's (1942) analysis of personal letters.

On the relevance of research strategies. Three considerations may summarize the status of the field: (a) over three-fourths of the personality literature surveyed used "experimental" methods; (b) these experimental designs relied upon "remote control" of variables which, as Schontz (1965) has noted, are especially vulnerable to ambiguity and error; (c) within general psychology, there is an increasing conviction that strictly "experimental" methods are incapable of dealing with central aspects of human psychology (Deese, 1969; Walker, 1969).

One clear recommendation for personality study emerges from a serious reading of general psychological research criticism: until "experimental" methods are developed which can (a) accommodate present knowledge and (b) offer relevant new knowledge not attainable through development of other scientific tools, "experimental" studies of personality should be clearly deemphasized. This is not so radical a proposal as might appear, for it simply asks "time out" for untangling a basic confusion in the field. One can study persons in experimental situations—but one cannot "study personality experimentally." As Sarason (1969), among others, has observed: "An experimental approach is useful in analyzing reactions of *particular people in special situations* [p.v; italics added]." Only as experimental inquiry derives from concern for preexisting subject variables, and provides experimental treatments theoretically focused upon such subject characteristics can experimental methods hope to illumine personality structure or dynamics.

Meanwhile, the most serious thought should be given to alternative strategies of inquiry. Tyler (1959), in a paper which should be reexamined by all personality researchers, has presented a compelling case for the abandonment of dimensional approaches to individuality on the pragmatic grounds that this traditional approach has failed to improve upon predictabilities. As an alternative, Tyler recommended construction of personality inquiry in terms of "choice" and "organization"—along with a search for measurement approaches capable of representing individuality. Problems and possibility for developing approaches to reliability and validity in research on choice were presented in a further paper (Tyler, 1961), which incidentally serves as a model of an investigator's serious involvement in the intrinsic problems of research.

A wide variety of alternative research strategies has become available in recent years: a range of "nonreactive" measures (Webb, Campbell, Schwartz, & Sechrest, 1966), methods of naturalistic observation (Barker, 1963; Raush, 1967), methods for investigating the single case (Davidson & Costello, 1969) to name a few. Meanwhile, psychologists would do well to become acquainted with the work of contemporary anthropologists who have developed concepts and methods of great relevance to personality study.[5]

On the scope of personality study. Over 30 years ago, Murray (1938) noted that "the reason why the results of so many researches in personality have been misleading or trivial is that experimenters have failed to obtain enough pertinent information about their subjects. Lacking these facts, accurate generalizations are impossible [p. ix]." This comment could stand as a summary of current work—with the important amendment that the accumulation of more "facts" (including much unassimilated data collected through *Explorations in Personality*) has not provided, nor is likely to provide, the basic generalizations needed in this field.

Beyond noting the extraordinarily narrow and impoverished scope of current personality research, what suggestions for broadening and deepening inquiry might be advanced? At a very general level, this problem involves setting the collective level of aspiration of the entire field to include a shared responsibility that personality be investigated in its basic aspects ("like all other men, like some other men, like no other men"). Within the context of any single investigation, this problem requires that the individual researcher pay the most serious attention to the need for obtaining information which is (a) potentially available, and (b) necessary to full understanding of the intrinsic problem—whether or not such information is explicitly demanded by his immediate research design.[6] Glaring examples of current failure to consider appropriate breadth of scope may be drawn from experimental research in which (a) subjects' phenomenological reports are routinely sought (via checklists, ratings, and other means) and equally routinely nonanalyzed and nonreported; and (b) even more serious misuse of subjects' reported experience to exclude individuals who do not readily accommodate to the Procrustean theoretical bed via "dropping" or "reassigning" recalcitrant subjects (as in dissonance research—cf. Chapanis & Chapanis, 1964) or via deliberate nonsampling of subjects known to fail to conform to theoretical expectations (e.g., Katz, 1967).

More positively, the investigator should continually reconsider that the point of inquiry is to understand the phenomena under investigation. Inevitably, this requires attention to the intrapersonal context of research performances—here research subjects' willingness to provide this context could be developed much more fully and fruitfully than we are inclined to do (cf. Lewin, 1935).

---

[5]Interestingly, the insularity of the psychologist seems to be increasing in recent years. While anthropologists have consistently "borrowed" psychological concepts and methods, psychologists' awareness of anthropological inquiry often seems to have been arrested at the level of Malinowski and early Mead, and our "borrowing" largely limited to fields of mathematics and physics.

[6]A colleague has offered an instructive example from his own work: in a study (Levy, 1969) which involved asking 2800 school children about their preferences for Card IV versus Card VII of the Rorschach, he failed to inquire, Why? (N. Levy, personal communication, September 1969.)

More specific recommendations for extending the scope of inquiry in selected aspects may also be noted:

1. Critically important problems concerning the personality development and change clearly require longitudinal study. Why are longitudinal studies so rare? The traditional reasons are of two sorts: (a) longitudinal studies require such massive commitments of time and research technology as to demand large-scale organization support; and (b) obsolescence of research concepts and methods over the life span of a longitudinal study pose problems.

However, a second look at the underlying assumptions is in order. If "longitudinal study" is identified with such large-scale endeavors as the Fels studies (cf. Kagan & Moss, 1962) or the Berkeley Growth Study (Jones & Bayley, 1941) the first of these traditional deterrents is obviously relevant; but the Fels and Berkeley studies offer demonstrations that longitudinal data collected by imaginative and responsible investigators are remarkably fruitful fields for "up-dated" analyses which keep pace with advances in the field. However, more modest studies are urgently needed in the personality field and are quite feasible. Short-term (e.g., 5-year) investigations of selected aspects of personality would immensely enrich inquiry, and need not involve massive and comprehensive sampling and instrumentation, as seen in such examples as Escalona and Heider's (1959) predictions of nursery school behavior from observations in infancy, E. L. Kelly's (1955) 20-year study of marriage partners, or Carlson's (1965) 6-year follow-up study of sex differences in the basis of self-esteem. (Incidentally, the last example illustrates the feasibility of longitudinal investigation conducted without any financial or formal institutional support whatsoever.) Provision for longitudinal follow-up studies could be readily built into a wide range of personality studies with very little additional effort—and with extraordinarily rich potentialities for advancement of knowledge.

2. Somewhat paradoxically, personality research might be strengthened and enriched by becoming an incidental by-product (rather than the focus) of naturally occurring data-collection situations. This rather obscure point may, perhaps, be illustrated with the writer's personal experiences in teaching upper division personality courses: In developing primary instructional purposes, I have often asked students to produce brief, introspective (and anonymous) accounts of selected personality constructs for use in class projects exploring methods of personality assessment. Such materials have often yielded "incidental" data of considerable relevance and richness for later testing of theoretical formulations which were not envisaged at the time of original data collection (cf. Carlson, 1971).

The relevance of such "incidental" data collection to psychology courses—where the vast bulk of personality research is conducted—is obvious (and might also serve important additional purposes of increasing the relevance of psychology instruction to students' purposes of exploring their own lives, and of incidental "recruitment" of potential scholars through the experience of disciplined inquiry or personological questions). However, in principle, this suggestion would apply equally to many other data-gathering settings, and fundamentally involves the use of informal "archival records" (whether freshman English themes, college-application essays, contents of employees' suggestion boxes, comments of subjects in instructional-methods-evaluation studies, etc.) as unobtrusive measures of personality functioning in natural situations.

3. Finally, as a general consideration relevant to many kinds of research problems, it is safe to assume that most subjects are willing to tell us much more than our current research designs ask about their experiences and the personal meanings of these experiences. Psychology is probably much poorer for its disinclination to listen to such potentially important messages; hopefully, the recent demise of naive behaviorism will liberate us to take seriously human construction of experience

as more than merely countable "responses" or "verbal reports."

On the relevance of social-psychological context. Two models of subject-investigator relationships may be discerned in current psychological inquiry: (a) a contractual relationship in which the subject is an "employee," and (b) a collaborative relationship in which the subject is a "colleague." Because the contractual model appears to be the increasingly dominant one (and even "reform" proposals urging the collaborative mode contain strongly contractual features), some of its implications need to be examined.

The contractual relationship seems to have developed in the service of scientific concerns and to reflect some basic values and assumptions about human nature. Thus, paying subjects for their services—whether in terms of money or course credit, or both—is seen as minimizing volunteer bias, minimizing the dependency of subjects, offering a more meaningful model for the participation of noncollege samples, avoiding troublesome problems of overdetermined motives for research participation—and as expressing concerns for equity, for fairness and regularity in defining rights and roles of subjects. Undoubtedly a contractual model is capable of correcting certain abuses of research relationships and offers a relevant model for some kinds of inquiry. However, important consequences of the use of this model should be examined. The "contract" encourages investigators' denial of the intrinsically "volunteer" quality of participation in personality research. Moreover, by maintaining orderliness of one set of contractual obligations, investigators are enabled to deny the legitimacy of other fundamental obligations which are not written into the contract. (Two examples may illustrate this point: (a) scrupulous observation of obligations as an "experimenter" enables the academic researcher to ignore his equally relevant obligations as a "teacher" to provide maximum cognitive clarity to student-subjects; (b) the concept of "debriefing"—a military metaphor of extremely dubious relevance to psychological inquiry—implies that it is possible to

undo an experimental set, and encourages the investigator to ignore his responsibility for consequences to the subject which were not intended.) Further, a host of troubles have been introduced into the research enterprise as subjects, increasingly cynical about psychological inquiry and frankly motivated to pick up extra money, have tended to give only perfunctory attention to research tasks.

Fundamentally, the contractual model imposes its own character upon research; it can only be appropriate in the investigation of contractual relationships, and even there may lead to immense confounding of the research findings by the effects of research context. In the study of personality, there are very few problems or occasions for which a contractual model is capable of providing valid information about persons' spontaneous ways of organizing experience. As Loevinger (1966) has pointed out, a "contractual" interpersonal style is characteristic of particular stages of ego development, and thus important differences among individuals are necessarily obscured when this interpersonal mode is also built into the context of inquiry.

The alternative—a collaborative model—has its own problems and its own defining characteristics. Basically, the collaborative model does not insist upon control or standardization of motivation for research participation, but assumes that (a) subjects and settings are chosen for their intrinsic relevance to the problem at hand; and (b) the basic motive for research participation must be the subject's intrinsic involvement in exploring his own experience. (This motivation may take many equally appropriate forms: that of the patient wishing to be helped, the student wishing to understand and master his life experience, the excluded or alienated person who wants to assert and explore his individuality, the "intelligent layman" who wants to express and understand his values and concerns in an intellectual framework.) The collaborative model does *not* rest upon narrow or egalitarian assumptions of undifferentiated "togetherness" but assumes that subject and investigator have their different kinds of expertise which are united by a common belief in the possibility and value of clarification of experience through research participation. Unquestionably, a collaborative model is more demanding and more rewarding to subject and experimenter alike. It demands more candor and more thought on the part of the investigator in posing research problems, in engaging appropriate subjects, and in interpreting the nature of the experience; it demands more involvement from the subject, and offers the important reward of having his experience taken seriously. From the standpoint of personality research, these conditions are likely to provide more genuine understanding of human personality organization and development.[7]

So much serious exploration of the ethical implications of research methodology has appeared in recent literature that very little needs to be added on this score. Our loss of innocence now requires that the psychologist give very serious attention to his own part in the research enterprise, accepting the responsibility for his own choices and for the consequences of these choices. While several specific research recommendations might follow from the recent Enlightenment, the most general one would be the commandment: Do not administer to any subject a research treatment you have not first "taken" yourself.

Although this proposal tends to elicit initial incredulity and irritation from professional colleagues, it is a completely serious recommendation; one which could enable psychologists to examine and discard tendencies to impose unnecessary and brutally exhaustive testing programs or elaborate and unnecessary manipulation of their subjects— and, more importantly engage the thoughtful participation of the psychologist as a person toward enriching the relevance of his inquiry. Obviously, this recommendation would eliminate deception as a technique of inquiry. However, there is considerable reason (Kelman, 1967; Stricker, 1967;

Stricker, Messick, & Jackson, 1967) to believe that this would be a very minor loss as contrasted with the increased veridicality and responsibility of nondeceptive research.

Toward disciplinary responsibility. Clearly, the investigator must be permitted and encouraged to define and explore problems in terms of their intrinsic merit. However, a climate of scientific freedom is not equivalent to a norm of *laissez-faire.* Since scientific inquiry is currently conducted through an elaborate set of institutional apparatus, there are clear responsibilities at various levels of this network. Insofar as the individual investigator neglects social responsibility and ethical concerns, the agencies of public policy must fill that vacuum. Recent Public Health Service directives concerning the welfare of human subjects represent a benign exercise of this responsibility; more restrictive and irrelevant constraints upon psychological inquiry should be anticipated if psychologists fail to consider fully their own responsibilities in the conduct of research.

Among several ways in which the discipline might cooperate toward development of more responsible and meaningful inquiry, the following suggestions are offered:

1. Psychology departments have a major concern for the integrity of instructional purposes upon which requirements for research participation are based. Thus, explicit plans for valid interpretations of problems, methods, and findings (a) to individual subjects, and (b) to class groups from which subjects are recruited—should be required of investigators who use departmental research-participation requirements as a means of obtaining subjects.

2. Psychological journals inevitably play a major part in determining the content and methods of scientific inquiry, and thus bear a major responsibility for the quality of research. (This responsibility is particularly clear in the case of journals of the American Psychological Association which are directly supported by and responsible to the entire discipline.) Among the obvious ways in which our journals might exercise this

[7]An example of such collaborative research is provided by Sanford (1969).

responsibility, three specific suggestions are noted: (a) Intrinsic relevance and responsibility of inquiry could be fostered by the adoption of Loevinger's (1968) two-fold suggestion that published studies should be based upon samples clearly relevant to the problem and upon replicated findings. (b) Explicit attention to well replicated findings as "control" variables should be required for publication. An obvious example is the suggestion of several investigators (Carlson & Carlson, 1960; Garai & Scheinfeld, 1968) that sex differences be considered in all published studies employing mixed-sex samples. *Developmental Psychology,* presently unique in making this an explicit criterion, provides a model of editorial responsibility in this sphere. (c) Since journals, unlike individual investigators, have unique responsibility and power to consider the total import of inquiry in any field, considerations of balance and emphasis fall within the domain of journal editors. (An example from recent history is the *Journal of Social Psychology's* giving explicit priority to cross-cultural research.) From the standpoint of the present critique, those journals primarily concerned with personality research should exercise their responsibility toward correcting imbalance in current research by giving priority to investigations of personality organization within individuals, and to inquiry on qualitative, typological bases of personality organization since the present survey of personality literature clearly shows these facets neglected in favor of general experimental studies.

Where Is the Person in Personality Research?

That the person is not really studied in current personality research is clearly shown in the survey of the literature. But is it possible that the product of this inquiry, in its basic denial of the importance of personality, may be a faithful projection of the real lives and the real world of personality researchers? This is a chilling thought—but one which deserves very serious examination.

Consider the passage with which Adelson

(1969) ends the methodological section of his review of personality research:

> We like to pretend that our choice of methods is dictated by scientific considerations alone. In fact, the exigencies of the academic marketplace play an important and perhaps decisive role. The methodological problems we have noted . . . reflect the pressure for quick publication. *There is reason to doubt that there will be rapid reforms in methodology until there is some reform of the university* [p. 222, italics added].

It would be difficult to find a clearer statement of real despair: Adelson is suggesting that personality researchers really are such willing or powerless captives of field forces of academic and professional status definitions that they must await liberation at the hands of some external force which will alter the environment.

Conceivably, studies of the "sociology of knowledge" might add to our awareness of—and liberation from—unexamined constraints upon inquiry. However, such studies are unlikely to tell us much more than we already know: that scholars are attracted to research problems through the influence of potent research models and teachers; that their training, support, publication, and visibility are contingent upon the "cumulative" character of potential contributions; that innovative methods or findings are unlikely to achieve an impact until the field is prepared to assimilate them. From the standpoint of the present critique, it might be more valuable to develop inquiry in the "personology of knowledge," examining the personality characteristics which determine an investigator's resonance to and involvement in various substantive problems, his openness to innovations in content and method, his independence of external supports in pursuit of inquiry, and his capacity to transmit a sense of personal involvement in disciplined inquiry to his colleagues and students.

Pending such inquiry, it may be that the current trends may continue. However, even within these constraints, a more optimistic prognosis could be supported by a range of literature suggesting that significant personal change can result from the confrontation of the discrepancy between one's behavior and one's values; that such changes involve the engagement of one's basic "ideoaffective postures" (Tomkins, 1965); and that such changes may be facilitated in times of widespread questioning and change. That we live in such a time of social change scarcely needs documentation; the present critique is offered as part of the dicipline's clear confrontation of its value-behavior discrepancies, and urges the engagement of our basic cognitive and affective commitments toward more relevant and responsible inquiry.

The original question—Where is the person in personality research?—may have two different answers. If the fully functioning person is not portrayed in our current personality literature, we may simply be looking in the wrong place. There are serious investigators of personality—perhaps increasingly found outside psychology—whose inquiry and understanding will continue to appear in the books and papers which illumine the field. But this is no radical departure from the past. If White, Erikson, Tomkins, or Keniston—to mention a few prominent personologists—are not indexed in the volumes of our current personality journals, neither were Freud, Jung, Angyal, or Piaget. We might simply retitle our journals to reflect their functions somewhat more accurately, and proceed as before.

A second answer is this: The person is there—in our personality laboratories, classrooms, and in the community—waiting to be engaged in serious studies of personality once those of us who investigate personality become able to invest *ourselves* in this task.

REFERENCES

Adelson, J. Personality. In P. H. Mussen & M. R. Rosenzweig (Eds.), *Annual review of psychology.* Palo Alto, Calif.: Annual Reviews, 1969.

Alfert, E. An ideographic analysis of personality differences between reactors to a vicariously experienced threat and reactors to a direct threat. *Journal of Experimental Research in Personality,* 1967, *2*, 200–207.

Allport, G. *The person in psychology: Selected essays.* Boston: Beacon, 1968.

Argyris, C. Some unintended consequences of rigorous research. *Psychological Bulletin*, 1968, *70*, 185–197.

Aronson, E., & Cope, V. My enemy's enemy is my friend. *Journal of Personality and Social Psychology,* 1968, *8*, 8–12.

Baldwin, A. L. Personal structure analysis: A statistical method for investigating the single personality. *Journal of Abnormal and Social Psychology.* 1942, *37*, 163–183.

Barker, R. G. (Ed.) *The stream of behavior: Exploration of its structure and content.* New York: Appleton-Century-Crofts, 1963.

Baughman, E. E., & Welsh, G. S. *Personality: A behavioral science.* Englewood Cliffs, N. J.: Prentice-Hall, 1962.

Bishop, F. V. The anal character: A rebel in the dissonance family. *Journal of Personality and Social Psychology,* 1967, *6*, 23–36.

Broverman, D. M. Normative and ipsative measurement in psychology. *Psychological Review,* 1962, *69*, 295–305.

Carlson, E. R., & Carlson, R. Male and female subjects in personality research. *Journal of Abnormal and Social Psychology,* 1960, *61*, 482–483.

Carlson, R. Stability and change in the adolescent's self-image. *Child Development,* 1965, *36*, 659–666.

Carlson, R. Sex differences in ego functioning: Exploratory studies of agency and communion. *Journal of Consulting and Clinical Psychology,* 1971, in press.

Chapanis, N. P., & Chapanis, A. Cognitive dissonance: Five years later. *Psychological Bulletin,* 1964, *61*, 1–22.

Constantinople, A. An Eriksonian measure of personality development in college students. *Developmental Psychology,* 1969, *1*, 357–372.

Cox, C. M. *Genetic studies of genius.* Stanford: Stanford University Press, 1926.

Davidson, P. O., & Costello, C. G. *N—1: Experimental studies of single cases.* New York: Van Nostrand Reinhold, 1969.

Deese, J. Behavior and fact. *American Psychologist,* 1969, *24*, 515–522.

Emmerich, W. Personality development and concepts of structure. *Child Development* 1968, *39*, 671–690.

Escalona, S., & Heider, G. *Prediction and outcome: A study in child development.* New York: Basic Books, 1959.

Garai, J. E., & Scheinfeld, A. Sex differences in mental and behavioral traits. *Genetic Psychology Monographs,* 1968, *77,* 169–299.

Goertzel., V., & Goertzel, M. G. *Cradles of eminence.* Boston: Little, Brown, 1962.

Helmreich, R., & Collins, B. E. Studies in forced compliance: Commitment and magnitude of inducement to comply as determinants of opinion change. *Journal of Personality and Social Psychology,* 1968, *10,* 75–81.

Johnson, R. E. Smoking and the reduction of cognitive dissonance. *Journal of Personality and Social Psychology,* 1968, *9,* 260–265.

Jones, H. E., & Bayley, N. The Berkeley growth study. *Child Development,* 1941, *12,* 167–173.

Jourard, S. M. *Disclosing man to himself.* Princeton, N. J.: Van Nostrand, 1968.

Kagan, J., & Moss, H. *Birth to maturity.* New York: Wiley, 1962.

Katz, I. The socialization of academic motivation in minority group children. *Nebraska Symposium on Motivation,* 1967, *15,* 133–191.

Kelly, E. L. Consistency of the adult personality. *American Psychologist,* 1955, *10,* 659–681.

Kelly, G. A. *The psychology of personal constructs.* New York: Norton, 1955.

Kelman, H. The problem of deception in social psychological experiments. *Psychological Bulletin,* 1967, *67,* 1–11.

Kiesler, C. A., Pallak, M. S., & Kanouse, D. E. Interactive effects of commitment and dissonance. *Journal of Personality and Social Psychology,* 1968, *8,* 331–338.

Kluckhohn, C., & Murray, H. A. *Personality in nature, society and culture.* (1st ed.) New York: Knopf, 1949.

Levy, N. Affective preference for card IV or VII of the Rorschach as related to sex and age. *Perceptual and Motor Skills,* 1969, *28,* 741–742.

Lewin, K. *Dynamic theory of personality.* New York: McGraw-Hill, 1935.

Loevinger, J. The meaning and measurement of ego development. *American Psychologist,* 1966, *21,* 195–206.

Loevinger, J. The "information explosion." *American Psychologist,* 1968, *23,* 455.

Maccoby, E. (Ed.) *The development of sex differences.* Stanford: Stanford University Press, 1966.

Maddi, S. *Personality theories: A comparative analysis.* Homewood, Ill.: Dorsey, 1968.

Mann, L., & Janis, I. L. A follow-up study on the long-term effects of emotional role playing. *Journal of Personality and Social Psychology,* 1968, *8,* 339–342.

Mehrabian, A. *An analysis of personality theories.* Englewood Cliffs, N. J.: Prentice-Hall, 1968.

Mills, J., & Jellison, J. M. Avoidance of discrepant information prior to commitment. *Journal of Personality and Social Psychology,* 1968, *8,* 59–62.

Mischel, W. *Personality and assessment.* New York: Wiley, 1968.

Murphy, G. Psychological views of personality and contributions to its study. In E. Norbeck, D. Price-Williams, & W. McCord (Eds.), *The study of personality.* New York: Holt, Rinehart & Winston, 1968.

Murray, H. A. *Explorations in personality.* New York: Oxford, 1938.

Orne, M. T. On the social psychology of the psychology experiment: With particular reference to demand characteristics and their implications. *American Psychologist,* 1962, *17,* 776–783.

O'Toole, R., & Dubin, R. Baby feeding and body sway: An experiment in George Herbert Mead's "Taking the role of the other." *Journal of Personality and Social Psychology,* 1968, *10,* 59–65.

Raush, H. Naturalistic aspects of the clinical research method. *Human Development,* 1967, *10,* 155–169.

Rosenthal, R. *Experimenter effects in behavioral research.* New York: Appleton-Century-Crofts, 1966.

Sanford, N. Will psychologists study human problems? *American Psychologist,* 1965, *20,* 192–202.

Sanford, N. Research with students as action and education. *American Psychologist,* 1969, *24,* 544–546.

Sarason, I. *Contemporary research in personality.* Princeton, N.J.: Van Nostrand, 1969.

Schontz, F. C. *Research methods in personality.* New York: Appleton-Century-Crofts, 1965.

Schultz, D. P. The human subject in psychological research. *Psychological Bulletin,* 1969, *72,* 214–228.

Steiner, I. D. Reactions to adverse and favorable evaluations of one's self. *Journal of Personality,* 1968, *36,* 553–562.

Stricker, L. J. The true deceiver. *Psychological Bulletin,* 1967, *68,* 13–20.

Stricker, L. J., Messick, S., & Jackson, D. N. *Evaluating deception in psychological research.* (Research Bulletin 68–59) Princeton, N.J.: Educational Testing Service, 1968.

Tomkins, S. S. Affect and the psychology of knowledge. In S. S. Tomkins & C. E. Izard (Eds.), *Affect, cognition, and personality: Empirical studies*. New York: Springer, 1965.

Tyler, L. Toward a workable psychology of individuality. *American Psychologist*, 1959, *14*, 75–81.

Tyler, L. E. Research explorations in the realm of choice. *Journal of Counseling Psychology*, 1961, *8*, 195–201.

Walker, E. L. Experimental psychology and social responsibility. *American Psychologist*, 1969, *24*, 862–868.

Webb, E. W., Campbell, D. T., Schwartz, R. D., & Sechrest, L. *Unobtrusive measures: Nonreactive research in the social sciences*. Chicago: Rand McNally, 1966.

White, R. E. *Lives in progress*. (2nd ed.) New York: Holt, Rinehart & Winston, 1966.

Wilson, W., & Insko, C. Recency effects in face-to-face interaction. *Journal of Personality and Social Psychology*, 1968, *9*, 21–23.

Zigler, E., Balla, D., & Butterfield, E. C. A longitudinal investigation of the relationships between preinstitutional social deprivation and social motivation in institutionalized retardates. *Journal of Personality and Social Psychology*, 1968, *10*, 437–445.

STUDY QUESTIONS

1. In her 1971 article, Carlson anticipates some of the issues raised in the American Psychological Association's *Manual for Ethical Principles in the Conduct of Research with Human Participants (1973)*, discussed in Chapter 4 of this book. Look back at Chapter 4 and review the ethical principles covered there. Which of these principles seem not to have been considered fully in the articles discussed by Carlson?

2. Examine the selections in this book in light of the issues raised by Carlson. Do any of the selections exhibit one or more of the methodological or ethical characteristics criticized by Carlson in the articles she reviews? Could any reasonable steps have been taken by the authors to make their investigations more responsive to the interests of personologists?

3. When doing library research as part of your own project development, evaluate each article you read in terms of the issues raised by Carlson. Consider the extent to which each article avoids or fails to avoid what Carlson sees as ethical and methodological pitfalls.

4. Evaluate Carlson's article. Are all the issues she discusses equally important? Are some points more convincing than others? What would be the implications of a situation in which all personologists tried to adhere to all Carlson's suggested solutions? Are there any points on which you would take issue with Carlson? Are there others which you want to take very seriously when designing your own research?

Research Methods in Personality Five Years After Carlson's Survey

Hanna Levenson, Morris J. Gray
and Arnette Ingram
Texas A&M University

Abstract. This study examined the degree to which research published in 1973 avoided the methodological and ethical problems found by Carlson in 1968. Findings are reported on 304 individual studies published in the 1973 volumes of *Journal of Personality* and *Journal of Personality and Social Psychology*. Contrary to expectation, research published in 1973 as compared with that from 1968 (a) included less information on sex differences, (b) focused as heavily on undergraduate samples, (c) used fewer interactionist designs, (d) employed more one-shot sessions, and (e) involved as much deception. The one area of improvement is that increases in the incidence of debriefing were observed. Differences in findings between the two journals are delineated, and suggestions for improving research procedures are outlined.

Carlson (1971) surveyed articles appearing in the 1968 volumes of the *Journal of Personality (JP)* and the *Journal of Personality and Social Psychology (JPSP)* in order to ascertain the method and focus of personality research. Her results indicated that there was an overwhelming reliance on the use of male undergraduates for subjects, and among those studies which could have tested for sex differences, less than half reported such findings. In addition, she observed that experimental methods were predominantly used in "one-shot" studies employing deception.

The first author of this present paper had assigned Carlson's article to be read and discussed in a graduate seminar on personality research. The class members had already been exposed to

The authors would like to thank the following people who served as raters: Bill Brown, Randy Godsey, Marcy Harper, Carol Kay, Greg King, Steve Logsdon, Doug Mould, and Judy Sears. An earlier version of this paper was presented at the 1975 American Psychological Association Convention in Chicago.

Entire article from *Personal and Social Psychology Bulletin,* 1976, *2,* 158–161. Copyright 1976 by the Society for Personality and Social Psychology. Reprinted by permission.

several articles on other procedural and ethical problems similar to those raised by Carlson which were published at approximately the same time. They observed that studies published in the 1968 journals reviewed by Carlson were probably conducted at least three years earlier and therefore might not reflect the concurrent rise in awareness of methodological issues. Many class members believed that research conducted later (and published in the early 1970s) would show a trend away from the use of restricted samples and inadequate methodologies.

In order to test this prediction, members of the personality seminar undertook a replication of Carlson's work, examining research published five years after her survey. The primary goal of such a review was to ascertain the degree to which current research avoided the methodological and ethical problems stressed by many psychologists and dramatically stated by Carlson. Additionally, the present paper was designed to include more specific information concerning the operational definitions of the classification categories than was provided in Carlson's article.

METHOD

Articles. The survey was conducted using the same journals surveyed by Carlson (*JP* and *JPSP*) for the year 1973. These journals were reviewed in order to permit direct comparisons to Carlson's work. Consistent with Carlson's method, the subject matter of the article was disregarded. All studies using human subjects were categorized on the basis of (a) sex composition of the sample; (b) age composition; (c) research strategy; (d) time span of the study; and (2) information provided to the subjects. Findings are reported on 304 individual studies contained in 243 articles.

Procedure. The 10 graduate students in the personality seminar served as raters. Each of the 304 studies was coded independently by two students according to refinements added to Carlson's coding system. An interjudge agreement of 99%

was obtained. All tests of significance were made through the use of a $\bar{z}$ ratio for uncorrelated proportions (Guilford & Fruchter, 1973).

RESULTS AND DISCUSSION

Sex composition. The percentage of studies using only male subjects decreased from 1968 (31%) to 1973 (22%) in the two journals surveyed ($p < .05$). The frequency of studies using only females remained about the same (15% vs. 17%). Unfortunately the decrease in the percentage of male single-sex studies appears to be offset by a marked increase from 1968 in the percentage of studies which included both sexes, but which did not test for such differences (11% vs. 24%, $p < .05$). While 1973 investigators appear to have collected data on males *and* females they did not analyze for sex differences which may have moderated the observed relationship between independent and dependent variables.

Age composition. We hypothesized that a lower percentage of 1973 studies compared to those published in 1968 would rely on undergraduate students. However, the present survey found that undergraduates were used in 72% of the studies, an increase of 6% over the last five years. Furthermore, the great majority of these college students, 60%, were being recruited from psychology classes.

There has been little change between the present survey and that of Carlson when the total percentage of all the non-college categories are compared. The present study found only 3% of the studies using general adults while Carlson reported none. Three percent of the studies in the present survey used preschool subjects; none was reported by Carlson. There were no significant differences in percentages between *JP* and *JPSP*. From these data, it is apparent that the non-college population continues to be overlooked in lieu of an expedient alternative, the captive and convenient (psychology) undergraduate.

Research strategy. It was considered quite important to ascertain if there had been any changes in the research strategies employed by authors of articles published in 1973. Since Carlson and others who have surveyed the research literature have categorized each article based on the method most frequently used in that article, all of the 1973 studies surveyed for this paper were initially classified into one of three categories. Results indicated that there were 71% generalist (manipulation of variables) studies and 29% differential (focus on preexisting variables) studies, with no studies using individual cases as the unit of analysis. Contrary to expectation, these data indicate a marked increase in the number of generalist studies from the 57% Carlson observed in 1968 ($p < .01.$), while the number of individual case studies remained at zero.

There is a significant difference between the 1973 journals with more manipulation studies in *JPSP* (74%) than in *JP* (60%, $p < .05$). Data presented in a recent article (Helmreich, 1975) indicate that most of the generalist studies in *JPSP* are probably of the classical, laboratory manipulation variety. Helmreich found that the percentage of laboratory experiments reported in *JPSP* had increased in 1974 to 84%.

We wished to test the hypothesis that there was an increase in studies which examined interactions between situations and personality. The initial tripartite classification of generalist, differential, and individual, however, did not represent the research designs adequately to examine this hypothesis, since it did not allow for a combination of the experimental and correlational methods within the same design. Therefore, all the 1968 and 1973 studies were recategorized according to four categories: the experimental category contained those studies in which independent variables were manipulated; correlational studies represented research emphasizing group differences and relating scores on various measures; a mixed category was provided to classify research which was designed to examine interactions between situations and personality; and an observation category was included for data collected through unobtrusive measures (e.g., archival research).

Results from the present survey indicate that, contrary to expectation, a significantly higher proportion of the 1968 studies used an interactionist approach (29%) as compared to those published in 1973 (23%, $p <.05$). While there were no significant differences between *JPSP* and *JP* in 1968 in the type of research strategies employed, by 1973 methodological differences reflect the particular emphasis of each journal. In 57% of the *JPSP* studies, variables were manipulated without consideration of individual differences, while only one-quarter of the studies in *JP* were so classified. ($p < .01$).

Time span. The three categories in this section indicate whether the study was completed in one session (including studies with an earlier pretest), more than one session but less than one month, or more than one month (longitudinal). Results indicate that, contrary to the hypothesis, the percentage of studies using only one session increased from 78% in 1968 to 89% ($p < .01$). Studies using more than one session but less than one month and studies taking more than one month each decreased by approximately half of what Carlson found. Journal differences are apparent in this category as *JP* had 10% fewer studies using only one session ($p < .05$).

Information. Three areas were investigated in this section: (a) deception, (b) debriefing, and (c) feedback. Studies were classified as deceptive only when subjects were purposively given or led to believe inaccurate information, e.g., cover stories, false feedback, use of confederates. Studies in which subjects were given no or partial information were not included in the deception category. Thus, a conservative estimate of deception was used. Debriefing was scored only for those studies which explicitly state that the subjects were informed regarding any deceptions used. A feedback category was used to classify studies in which mention was made of the investigator's intent to provide subjects with the results and/or conclusions of the experiment.

Failing to support the hypothesis, results indicate that approximately the same percentage of studies used deception in 1973 as compared to 1968 (59% vs. 57%). The more striking difference is the one between the two journals. Whereas deception was used in 62% of the published studies in *JPSP* deception occurred in only 42% of the studies in *JP* ($p < .01$). Such a difference is probably related to the fact that social psychological studies often involve the use of disguised situational manipulations.

Reported debriefing increased from 32% to 43% for those studies using deception. However, a striking difference between journals is also noted in this category. In *JP* 64% of the studies in which deception was used reported debriefing, while only 40% of the *JPSP* studies reported debriefing ($p < .05$). In the survey of 1973 research, *three* studies out of 304 reported making arrangements for feedback. This is a slight increase from 1968, but it is hardly a high number.

CONCLUSION

Based on our 1973 survey, we have three recommendations designed to improve current research methods. First, we suggest that journal editors issue more explicit requirements for manuscripts and that they publish articles which fulfill those requirements. Secondly, we can develop and implement new guidelines and courses for our graduate students which might foster the adoption of more adequate research methods. The third suggestion is that surveys such as this one be repeated over time so that we can document research trends in order to identify some of the factors associated with changes. As pointed out by Carlson, such self-studies might help us liberate ourselves from unexamined constraints upon inquiry.

REFERENCES

Carlson, R. Where is the person in personality research. *Psychological Bulletin*, 1971, *75*, 203–219.

Guilford, J. P., & Fruchter, B. *Fundamental statistics in psychology and education*. New York: McGraw-Hill, 1973

Helmreich, R. Applied social psychology: the unfulfilled promise. *Personality and Social Psychology Bulletin*, 1975, *1*, 548–560.

STUDY QUESTIONS

1. Note that the research report by Levenson and her colleagues is somewhat different in structure and style from Carlson's more conceptual paper. What are the major differences of the structure and style? What are the advantages and disadvantages of each type of paper—that is, what information is gained and what is lost in an article intended as a research report rather than as more of a position paper?

2. Do the data presented in this report lead you to think that investigators are giving more attention to ethical issues?

3. Can you think of any additional methodological or ethical questions not covered in this chapter's selections that could be studied by the type of content analysis survey used by Carlson and Levenson and her co-workers?

4. In what ways could you use the findings of Carlson's and Levenson's studies to help you in developing empirical investigations?

ADDITIONAL SOURCES

Canavan-Gumpert, D., Garner, K., & Gumpert, P. The success-fearing personality. Lexington, Mass. Lexington Books, division of D.C. Heath, & Co. 1978.

Edney, J. J. Territoriality and control: A field experiment. *Journal of Personality and Social Psychology*, 1975, *31*, 1108–1115.

Goldman, E. K. Need achievement as a motivational basis for the risky shift. *Journal of Personality*, 1975, *43*, 346–356.

Losco, J., & Epstein, S. Humor preference as a subtle measure of attitudes toward the same and opposite sex. *Journal of Personality*, 1975, *43*, 321–334.

Ludwig, L. D. Elation-depression and skill as determinants of desire for excitement. *Journal of Personality* 1975, *43*, 1–22.

McArthur, L. Z., & Burstein, B. Field dependent eating and perception as a function of weight and sex. *Journal of Personality* 1975, *43*, 402–420.

McClelland, D. C., & Teague, G. Predicting risk preferences among power related tasks. *Journal of Personality* 1975, *43*, 266–285.

Moriarty, T. Crime, committment and the responsive bystander.. Two field experiments. *Journal of Personality and Social Psychology*, 1975, *31*, 370–376.

Speisman, J. C., Lazarus, R. S. Davison, L., & Mordkoff, A. M. Experimental analysis of a film used as a threatening stimulus. *Journal of Consulting Psychology*, 1964, *28*, 23–33.

Sundstrom, E. An experimental study of crowding: Effects of room size, intrusion, and goal blocking on nonverbal behavior, self-disclosure, and self-reported stress. *Journal of Personality and Social Psychology*, 1975, *32*, 645–654.

Appendix A
Statistics
Michael Sokol[1]

The purpose of this appendix is to help you understand and apply several types of statistical analysis to your psychological data. Statistical techniques are neither mysterious nor awesome. They are simply tools that can provide a special kind of knowledge about the relationships among the variables you are studying. They will help you to decide whether differences exist between groups of subjects from whom the same type of data was collected and to determine whether subjects' scores on a measure change as a result of an experimental treatment. For example, statistics would permit you to determine whether a relationship exists between need for achievement and the amount of money people make, or whether a difference exists between men and women in the amount of aggression they show in a particular situation. Without statistics, you can guess and speculate. With statistics, you can make inferences with a reasonable degree of certainty. Statistics give you a way of extracting information from randomness and serve as a powerful tool of science.

In this appendix, we illustrate the use of statistics through the analysis of an imaginary

set of data. Information from 24 subjects was used to make up this compilation, known as a *data set*. The data collected from the 24 subjects included sex, height, weight, and two sets of scores on Rotter's measure of internal/external locus of control. Subjects took the locus-of-control test both before and after they participated in a basketball game. Moreover, during the game an observer noted the number of aggressive actions performed by each subject.

ORGANIZING THE DATA

The first task is to organize the collected data. You would have difficulty beginning to test a research hypothesis if you had nothing in front of you except a calculator, a pile of test forms and separate record sheets showing each subject's height, weight, and sex. First, then, you need to organize the information you have gathered from all your subjects to allow you easy access to it. It would be very inefficient if you had to go back to all those test forms and record sheets every time you had a question about the data you had collected. Abstracting,

[1]Written especially for this volume.

centralizing, and organizing all your data is your first step.

One useful approach is to organize the data for computer analysis. Then, if you decide to use a computer for your statistical analyses, the data will be already organized in the appropriate way. But even if you decide to do your calculations by hand, organizing the data this way will be useful. The first step in this procedure is to make a *code book* (see Table A-1), especially if you intend to use a digital computer. A code book serves as a written record of your data, and should consist of the following items: (1) a record of where the data are (that is, which column on the graph paper represents what information [See Figure A-1]); (2) the name of each variable (in our example, sex, weight, and so on); and (3) the numbers you will use to represent the different kinds of information (for example, males = 1, females = 2).

TABLE A-1.
Code Book

Column	Variable	Coding of Variable
1–2	Subject's number	Subject's experiment number (01 thru 24)
3		Blank column
4	Subject's sex	Sex of subject (1 = male/2 = female)
5		Blank column
6–7	Subject's height	Height of subject in inches
8		Blank column
9–11	Subject's weight	Weight of subject in pounds
12		Blank column
13–14	Pre-I/E	Subject's pre-test internal/external locus-of-control score
15		Blank column
16–17	Post-I/E	Subject's post-test internal/external locus-of-control score
18		Blank column
19	Aggressive acts	Number of aggressive acts committed by subject during the experimental session

Finally, on a sheet of paper organize your data to correspond with the code book. This organization, called a *data layout*, can be done most easily on graph paper, as shown in Figure A-1.

Once you have completed your *data layout* and checked to make sure none of the numbers were accidently changed when you transferred them from the original recording forms to the layout sheets, you are ready to begin your first statistical analysis.

DESCRIPTIVE STATISTICS

The first group of statistics we cover are called *descriptive statistics*. These statistics are used to summarize the data to make them easy to understand. In Figure A-1, you can find the heights of all our subjects by examining columns 6 and 7, but inspecting the numbers in these columns does not give you a conceptual grasp of the subjects' heights. The first step toward forming a conceptual picture of subjects' heights as a group would be to find the minimum and maximum heights; in our data these are 59 and 78 inches. From this information, by subtracting 59 inches from 78 inches, we find the *range* of heights, which is 19 inches. The range gives us a rough estimate of the variability of our scores and is greatly affected by extreme values in the data. It tells us very roughly what the spread of our data is, and in this case we could say that the range of heights in our sample is quite wide. However, by knowing the range we are unable to tell if the heights are evenly distributed from 59 to 78 inches or if most of the heights are concentrated at one end of the distribution.

One way to gain information on the data distribution would be to organize the data into a *frequency distribution*. To perform this technique we must first arrange the heights by magnitude into an *array* (Figure A-2), with heights going from shortest to tallest: 59 59 59 60 61 62 62 62 62 63 63 64 64 65 65 66 66 68 68 70 72 74 74 78. Next, we divide the range of

IBM

PROGRAM	
PROGRAMMER	DATE

COMM.	STATEMENT NUMBER				CONT.	7 8	9 10 11 12	13 14	16 17	19
0	1				1	66	160	23	20	7
0	2				1	72	180	20	17	2
0	3				1	62	150	19	19	3
0	4				1	65	155	15	10	4
0	5				1	66	160	20	19	5
0	6				1	59	115	22	18	1
0	7				1	74	190	15	17	4
0	8				1	74	185	12	12	3
0	9				1	70	180	03	04	5
1	0				1	63	140	04	07	2
1	1				1	64	150	17	15	5
1	2				1	78	210	20	15	2
1	3				2	62	130	09	08	1
1	4				2	63	135	14	15	2
1	5				2	64	140	03	05	4
1	6				2	59	115	16	12	3
1	7				2	59	115	12	08	4
1	8				2	60	110	12	09	3
1	9				2	62	105	08	05	5
2	0				2	65	115	22	17	1
2	1				2	68	120	20	18	4
2	2				2	66	120	04	05	2
2	3				2	62	130	13	10	3
2	4				2	61	115	11	08	1

*A standard card form, IBM electro 888157, is available for punching statements from this form

Figure A-1. Data set for an imaginary group of subjects

scores into clumps, or *class intervals*. It is the function of a frequency distribution to "collapse" single pieces of data into class intervals. It is up to us to decide how large we want our class intervals to be; the number can range from 2 units of measurement on up, depending on the range of our data. In our imaginary set of data on height, clumps of 3 inches seem appropriate. This decision on clump size results in a frequency distribution composed of seven separate class intervals.

In examining this particular frequency distribution, we see that the scores are *skewed* to the right—that is, there is a greater frequency of short people than tall people. The distribution might also have looked like the one in Figure A-3. If so, we would have said it was a *bell-shaped*, or *normal*, *distribution*, with the majority of heights falling in the middle and a few falling at each end of the distribution.

Measures of Central Tendency

The frequency distribution helps us to form a visual picture of our data. However, we would find it difficult to summarize and describe our findings by using the frequency alone. Such a distribution tells us little, for example, about any kind of "average" subject with respect to the measure. For this kind of information, we turn to measures of *central tendency*—that is, measures that provide us with a "best guess" as to where a randomly selected subject would fall.

The first and easiest measure of central tendency is the *mode*. The mode is the number that occurs most frequently in a distribution. In the height data we have been using, the mode would be 62 inches, as that particular height occurs more often than any other. If we knew only the mode of this distribution and were asked to guess the height of any member of the distribution, our best guess would be the mode, or 62 inches.

If we wanted to split the subjects into tall and short groups with an even number of subjects in each group, we would have to find the *median*. The median is the numerical value of the case lying exactly on the 50th percentile of an array. That is, the median is the point along an array at which half the scores will lie above and half below. To find the median in our sample of heights, we would take the following steps:

1. Arrange all the heights by magnitude (size): 59 59 59 60 61 62 62 62 62 63 63 64 64 65 65 66 66 68 68 70 72 74 74 78
2. Count the heights and divide by 2 in order to find half the number of scores: 24 ÷ 2 = 12
3. Count up from the lowest score until reaching the point needed to make half the scores.

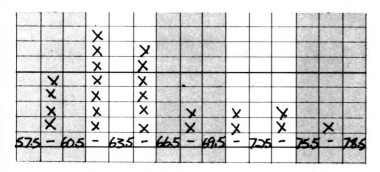

Figure A-2. Data array for subjects' heights

4. Since we have an even number of scores in this particular set, we add the two scores that are closest to the point reached and divide by the number 2:

$$\frac{64 + 64}{2} = \frac{128}{2} = 64.0$$

Thus, for our height data, the median calculates out as 64.0. However, in this particular data set, there are two 64s, with 11 rather than 12 numbers falling above and below the median. We still choose 64 as our "best bet" for the median score. If the median had fallen between 64 and 65, it would calculate out at 64.5 and exactly half (12) scores would be above and below it.

If we had an odd number of scores, the number that we counted up to would be the median. Suppose we wanted to find the median height for a sample of seven people with the following heights: 61, 63, 64, 72, 75, 78, and 78. Half the number of scores in this case is 3.5 (7 ÷ 2 = 3.5). Because there are an odd number of scores, we round this number off to the next highest number, 4. If we count 4 spaces up from the lowest score, we find our median, 72.

The median gives us a value of central tendency that is affected not by the magnitude of scores but rather by the number of scores. It is an average of position. This means that the median is not affected by outlying or extreme scores at all. For example, if one of our subjects were 8 feet tall, this fact would not affect the median; nor would a subject 3 feet tall affect the median. For this reason, the median is probably less biased than the measure we cover next: the arithmetic average, or the mean of a set of scores.

Probably the most commonly used measure of central tendency is the *mean*, or, as it is often called, the arithmetic average. The mean height for our data is 65.25. That is, the arithmetic midpoint of our data on height is 65.25. We compute the mean by adding up the measurements and dividing by the number of measurements. The mean has the advantage of being both easy to understand and easy to calculate. The mean is more reliable than the mode or median because it takes into account all the measurements. That is, it tends to change less from one sample to another sample than either the mode or the median. Also, since the mean is an average of scores rather than of position, it can be used in more complicated statistical analysis than the other measures of central tendency.

Measures of Variance

Now that we have an idea of the central tendency of our data, we want to determine how the data are spread out, or how the they vary from the central tendency. We have already looked at two ways of gaining information about how data vary—that is, by computing the range (subtracting the minimum value from the maximum value) and by looking at the frequency distribution. We noted that the range is limited in that it is affected greatly by the extremes

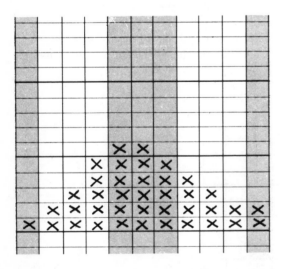

Figure A-3. Illustration of a normal distribution

of the data. The frequency distribution also has a particular type of limitation: it cannot be represented by a single number.

A statistic that is less affected by extreme values and that does describe the spread of the data in a single number is the *variance*. To find the variance for our data on height, we would follow the steps outlined in Table A-2.

When we calculate the variance, we square each score's deviation from the mean, making the variance statistic come out in squared units; in our study, the variance is given in squared inches. To get a better understanding of the variance of our data, we take the square root of the variance, which results in the statistic called the *standard deviation*. The standard deviation

represents the variance of the data in the original measurement units, which in our example is inches. For our sample of heights, the standard deviation is equal to the square root of 25.768 square inches, or 5.07 inches. This means that the average deviation of the scores for height from the mean height is 5.07 inches. If you know a few more things about the properties of the standard deviation, this information is even more meaningful. For example, when you move 1 standard deviation up and down from the mean, you include 68% of the data; when you move up and down 2 standard deviations from the mean, you include 95% of your data. Finally, when you move 3 standard deviations up and down from the mean you include 99% of all your data. These properties of data distributed in a normal curve are illustrated in Figure A-4.

TABLE A-2.
Calculating the variance and standard deviation on our sample data for height

Ht.	$\bar{x}$		d	d^2	
68	− 65.25	=	2.75	7.56	1. Calculate the mean ($\bar{x}$) of all scores.
72	− 65.25	=	6.75	45.56	2. Subtract the mean
62	− 65.25	=	−3.25	10.56	from each of the
65	− 65.25	=	−.25	.062	scores to get the
66	− 65.25	=	.75	.562	deviation from the
59	− 65.25	=	−6.25	39.06	mean (d).
74	− 65.25	=	8.75	76.56	3. Square each score's
74	− 65.25	=	8.75	76.56	deviation from the
70	− 65.25	=	4.75	22.56	mean (d^2).
63	− 65.25	=	−2.25	5.06	4. Sum the squared
64	− 65.25	=	−1.25	1.56	deviations.
78	− 65.25	=	12.75	162.56	5. Divide the sum of
62	− 65.25	=	−3.25	10.56	the squared
63	− 65.25	=	−2.25	5.06	deviations by the
64	− 65.25	=	−1.25	1.56	number of scores.
59	− 65.25	=	−6.25	39.06	
59	65.25	=	−6.25	39.06	$\text{variance} = \dfrac{\Sigma d^2}{N}$
60	− 65.25	=	−5.25	27.56	$\text{variance} = \dfrac{618.448}{24}$
62	− 65.25	=	−3.25	10.56	$\text{variance} = 25.768$
65	− 65.25	=	−.25	.062	
68	− 65.25	=	2.75	7.56	
66	− 65.25	=	.75	.562	
62	− 65.25	=	−3.25	10.56	
61	− 65.25	=	−4.25	18.06	

$\Sigma = 1566$ $\quad\quad \Sigma d^2 = 618.448$

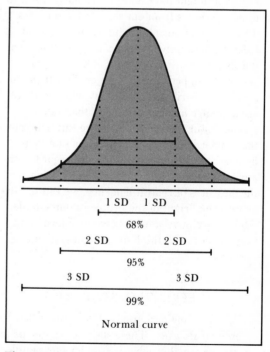

Figure A-4. A normal distribution illustrating the percentages of scores distributed in standard deviations around the mean.

In general, then, we can say that if we measured the heights of all the people in the population of interest to us, 68% of them would fall between 60.18 inches and 70.32 inches. This span represents the mean (65.25 inches) plus and minus the standard deviation (5.07). Ninety-five percent of this population would have a height somewhere between 55.11 and 75.39 inches (the mean plus and minus 2 standard deviations), and 99% of the heights would fall between 50.04 and 80.46 inches.

From the variance and standard deviation, then, we can determine whether the heights of our subjects are closely bunched (when the variance and standard deviation are small) or quite different from each other (when the variance and standard deviation are large). The variance and the standard deviation are also used as part of other more complicated statistical computations.

As you might have noticed, we have begun to draw inferences from our descriptive statistics. That is, we are using the information gained from the descriptive statistics to determine what our data mean. For example, if our data are skewed (clumped) to the right or the left in our frequency distribution, we know whether there are a greater number of shorter than taller people in our sample. That is, we can tell from the standard deviation whether our sample is homogeneous or heterogenous with regard to the attribute being measured. Finally, by using the measures of central tendency, we can tell in general the height of the people in our sample. Thus, descriptive statistics give us information that enables us to think meaningfully about our data.

INFERENTIAL STATISTICS

We turn now to a group of statistics called *inferential statistics*. These statistics enable us to determine whether what is true for our sample of men and women is also true for the larger population from which the sample was drawn.

Let's continue to work with the example of height. If we wanted to know whether American men were different in height from American women, we could do one of two things. If it were feasible, we could measure all the men and women in America and determine the average heights for men and for women. Then it would be easy to see if a difference existed. Alternatively, we could take a small random sample of men and a small random sample of women and compare the two samples, using a statistical test.

Clearly, measuring all the men and women in America would be impossible; thus, we choose to measure a random sample. Looking at the random sample we have already collected of 12 men and 12 women, we first compute the mean for each group. Table A-3 shows these calculations.

We find that a difference of 5.33 inches exists between the mean for male heights (67.91 inches) and the mean for female heights (62.58 inches).

The t Test

The question now is How significant is this difference? Even if we had selected two samples of men, we would expect the sample means to differ at least a little because of natural variability occurring in the population. That is, because our samples would not contain men with exactly the same heights, the means of the two samples would be likely to differ by a certain number of inches, just by chance. So, how do we know if there is a *significant* difference between men and women without measuring each and every one of them? The answer can be found by using a statistic called a *t test*.

The word *significant* in statistics does not mean important or of consequence. It is used to indicate a difference between two groups that is not due to chance. In the culture of science, we have come to call a difference between two groups significant if it would occur only 1 in 20 times by chance. That is, if we took 20 samples

TABLE A-3.
Computation of mean heights for males and females from data set

Male	Female
68	62
72	63
62	64
65	59
66	59
59	60
74	62
74	65
70	68
63	66
64	62
78	61

$$\Sigma = 815 \qquad \Sigma = 751$$

$$\bar{x}_m = \frac{815}{12} = 67.91 \qquad \bar{x}_f = \frac{751}{12} = 62.58$$

of men and women and measured each sample on height, we would expect to get significant results once, even if no true difference existed between the average heights of men and women.

Testing for significance is a procedure to decide if the difference obtained on the variable under consideration represents a true difference between the populations sampled or if the difference occurs because of sampling error. When we find, using a statistical table,[2] that a difference is significant at the .05 level (p < .05), we know that a difference of this size would have occurred by "chance", or sampling error, only five times out of a hundred. Conventionally, differences significant at the .05 and .01 levels (p < .05 and p < .01) are considered large enough to be interpreted as providing support for one's research hypothesis. A provocative discussion of issues surrounding levels of significance can be found in the book edited by Morrison and Henkel (1970).

[2]It is possible to buy paperback books of statistical tables in most university bookstores. Most basic statistics texts include an appendix containing statistical tables for common statistics as t tests and chi squares.

Table A-4 shows the computation of a t test for two independent samples using the data on the heights of our male and female subjects.

Once we calculate the value of t, we must determine whether or not it indicates a significant difference between our two samples. To do this, we must find the *degrees of freedom*[3] for the two samples and then look up the statistical-table value of t for the appropriate degrees of freedom and the *level of significance* desired. The way to find the appropriate number of degrees of freedom for the simple t test of independent groups is to add the number of subjects in one sample to the number of subjects in the other sample and subtract 2 (degrees of freedom = $N1 + N2 - 2$). After we find the degrees of freedom and decide on the appropriate level of significance (for most tables .05 or .01), we can then see if the obtained value for t is greater than the tabled value.

If the obtained t value is greater than the tabled value, then we can say that a significant difference exists between our two groups. Where the t value is smaller than the tabled value, then we cannot say there is a significant difference. For the case at hand, we find that the degrees of freedom for our t test is 12 + 12 − 2 = 22.

When we look in our table of t values at df = 22, we find that our obtained t value must be greater than 2.074 to be significant at the .05 level and greater than 2.819 to be significant at the .01 level. This means that if our obtained t value is greater than 2.074 and not greater than 2.819, we would expect a difference between the samples of the size obtained here to

[3]Degrees of freedom is a complex statistical concept. Different guidelines for computing degrees of freedom are associated with different statistical tests. When using statistical tables to determine if a particular calculated statistic reaches significance, one must know the degrees of freedom associated with the test. Most statistics texts contain guidelines for computing degrees of freedom. For a classic discussion of degrees of freedom, read H. M. Walker, Degrees of freedom, *Journal of Educational Psychology*, 1940, *31*, 253—260.

TABLE A-4
Calculation of t test for two independent samples with data on heights of males and females

Male heights	$\bar{x}_m$	d	d²	Female heights	$\bar{x}_f$	d	d²
68	− 67.91 =	.09	.008	62	− 62.58 =	−.58	.336
72	− 67.91 =	4.09	16.728	63	− 62.58 =	.42	.176
62	− 67.91 =	−5.91	34.928	64	− 62.58 =	1.42	2.016
65	− 67.91 =	−2.91	8.468	59	− 62.58 =	−3.58	12.816
66	− 67.91 =	−1.91	3.648	59	− 62.58 =	−3.58	12.816
59	− 67.91 =	−8.91	79.388	60	− 62.58 =	−2.58	6.656
74	− 67.91 =	6.09	37.088	62	− 62.58 =	−.58	.336
74	− 67.91 =	6.09	37.088	65	− 62.58 =	2.42	5.856
70	− 67.91 =	2.09	4.368	68	− 62.58 =	5.42	29.376
63	− 67.91 =	−4.91	24.108	66	− 62.58 =	3.42	11.696
64	− 67.91 =	−3.91	15.288	62	− 62.58 =	−.58	.336
78	− 67.91 =	10.09	101.808	61	− 62.58 =	−1.58	2.496

$\Sigma m = 815$ $\Sigma f = 751$

$\bar{x}_m = \dfrac{815}{12} = 67.91$ $\bar{x}_f = \dfrac{751}{12} = 62.58$

$\Sigma d^2_m = 362.916$ $\Sigma d^2_f = 84.912$

Steps:

1. Find the mean (x) for each sample.

2. Find the deviation (d) of each score from the mean of its respective sample.

3. Square each of the two sets of deviations (d^2).

4. Sum the squared deviations (Σd^2).

5. Subtract one mean from the other mean ($\bar{x}_m - \bar{x}_f$).

6. Divide the difference by the square root of the sum of the squared deviations, divided by the number of subjects minus 1 $\dfrac{(\Sigma d^2_m + \Sigma d^2_f)}{N(N-1)}$.

$$t = \frac{\bar{x}_m - \bar{x}_f}{\sqrt{\dfrac{\Sigma d^2_m + \Sigma d^2_f}{N(N-1)}}}$$

$$t = \frac{67.91 - 62.58}{\sqrt{\dfrac{362.916 + 72.096}{(12)(12 - 1)}}}$$

$$t = \frac{5.33}{\sqrt{\dfrac{435.012}{132}}}$$

$$t = \frac{5.33}{\sqrt{3.39}}$$

$$t = \frac{5.33}{1.84}$$

$$t = 2.90$$

occur by chance 1 out of 20 times. If the t value was greater than 2.819, we would expect it to occur by chance only 1 out of 100 times. In the case of our height data, our obtained t value is 2.90. Since this figure is greater than the tabled value 2.819, we can say that at the .01 level of significance a significant difference exists between American men and women on height. Thus, by looking at mean scores for height we can conclude that in general men are taller than women.

The Correlated t Test

In psychological research, and in personality research in particular, the samples we want to compare are often *related* to each other. The clearest example of this situation is when we measure subjects before and after an experimental treatment so that they "serve as their own controls". Another good example is when research is done on twins or siblings where half of a pair of twins or siblings is exposed to an experimental treatment and the other half is not. Since in these circumstances the subjects are closely matched (or identical, being the same people) on background variables, we apply a different formula for obtaining our t value, one that takes into account the fact that the samples are closely matched. This computation is called the *correlated*, or *paired*, t test. As an example, if we took sets of identical twins and split them up so that each boy or girl were in a separate sample from his or her twin and then compared them on height, we would expect little if any difference. Then, if we assigned one sample to a special diet that we thought would increase height and left the other sample on a normal balanced diet, we could come back in a year's time and measure our two samples again. If the subjects on the special diet were just a little bit taller, we might be able to say that they were significantly taller, because we expected them to be the same since they are identical twins.

Returning to our sample data set, we collected data on locus of control both before and after our subjects participated in a basketball game. If we wanted to determine whether scores changed significantly between the before-game and after-game periods, we would perform the following correlated, or paired, t test. The computation for this test is given in Table A-5.

Having calculated the t value, we must determine whether or not it is greater than the tabled t value. To do this, we use the same technique we used for the simple t test, except that the formula for degrees of freedom is different. In the case of a paired or correlated t test, we calculate the degrees of freedom by subtracting 1 from the number of paired observations (Np) (degrees of freedom $= Np - 1$). In the case at hand, we have 24 pairs of observations, so

our degrees of freedom are 23 ($df = 24 - 1 = 23$). When we look up the tabled value for t at 23 degrees of freedom, we find that for our obtained t value to be significant at the .05 level, it must be greater than 2.069. For our obtained t value to be significant at the .01 level, it must be greater than 2.087. Since our obtained t value is 3.436, we can say that a statistically significant difference exists at the .01 level in internal/external locus of control after our subjects played basketball. This means that we would expect a difference of the size we found to occur by random chance only 1 in 100 times. By looking at the mean difference between our pre- and postgame measurement of locus of control, we can say that a significant increase occurred in internal locus of control.

TABLE A-5.
Calculation of correlated t test for two sets of locus-of-control scores

Pre-I/E		Post-I/E	$(d - \bar{x}d)$	D	D^2
23	—	20	$3 - 1.708$	1.292	1.669
20	—	17	$3 - 1.708$	1.292	1.669
19	—	19	$0 - 1.708$	-1.708	2.917
15	—	10	$5 - 1.708$	3.292	10.837
20	—	19	$1 - 1.708$	$-.708$	.501
22	—	18	$4 - 1.708$	2.292	5.253
15	—	17	$-2 - 1.708$	-3.708	13.749
12	—	12	$0 - 1.708$	-1.708	2.917
03	—	04	$-1 - 1.708$	-2.708	7.333
04	—	07	$-3 - 1.708$	-4.708	22.165
17	—	15	$2 - 1.708$	.292	.085
20	—	15	$5 - 1.708$	3.292	10.837
09	—	08	$1 - 1.708$	$-.708$	.501
14	—	15	$-1 - 1.708$	-2.708	7.333
03	—	05	$-2 - 1.708$	-3.708	13.749
16	—	12	$4 - 1.708$	2.292	5.253
12	—	08	$4 - 1.708$	2.292	5.253
12	—	09	$3 - 1.708$	1.292	1.669
08	—	05	$3 - 1.708$	1.292	1.669
22	—	17	$5 - 1.708$	3.292	10.837
20	—	18	$2 - 1.708$	.292	.085
04	—	05	$-1 - 1.708$	-2.708	7.333
13	—	10	$3 - 1.708$	1.292	1.669
11	—	08	$3 - 1.708$	1.292	1.669

$$\Sigma d = 41 \qquad \Sigma D^2 = 136.952$$

$$\bar{x}d = \frac{41}{24} = 1.708$$

1. Match each subject with the appropriate control or alternative-treatment subject.
2. Subtract one set of scores from the other.
3. Sum the differences (Σd) and find their mean ($\bar{x}d$).
4. Subtract the mean ($\bar{x}d$) from each individual difference (d). The result is D.
5. Square the difference (D) to get (D^2).
6. Sum D^2 to get ΣD^2.
7. Divide the mean deviation score ($\bar{x}d$) by the square root of the summed squared differences (ΣD^2) divided by the number of paired (Np) scores multiplied by the number of paired scores minus 1.

$$t = \frac{\bar{x}d}{\sqrt{\frac{\Sigma D^2}{(Np)(Np-1)}}}$$

$$t = \frac{1.708}{\sqrt{\frac{136.952}{(24)(24-1)}}}$$

$$t = \frac{1.708}{\sqrt{\frac{136.952}{552}}}$$

$$t = \frac{1.708}{\sqrt{.248}}$$

$$t = \frac{1.708}{.497}$$

$$t = 3.436$$

The Pearson Product Moment Correlation Coefficient

Next we come to the *Pearson product moment correlation coefficient*. The correlation coefficient is a single number that summarizes the degree of relatedness between two sets of variables. Returning to our sample set of data, we could correlate a number of different pairs of variables—for example, height and pregame I/E scores, weight and postgame I/E scores, or pre- and postgame I/E scores—to see how they relate to each other.

For illustrative purposes, here we correlate the subjects' height and weight. When we compute a correlation coefficient between height and weight, we end up with a number summarizing both the way one variable is related to the other and the strength of that relationship. This number does *not* tell us that height *causes* weight or weight causes height; it merely indicates how variation or change in one goes along with variation in the other. That is, if scores on one variable fluctuate, the correlation coefficient indicates in what direction and to what degree scores on the other variable will tend to change also.

A correlation coefficient can indicate a relationship in only two directions: (1) a positive direction, where if one variable increases, the correlation indicates that the other one will also increase, and (2) a negative direction, where if one variable increases the correlation coefficient indicates that the other will decrease. The direction of a correlation is indicated by a positive sign (+) or a negative sign (−). The magnitude of a relation is expressed numerically, ranging from +1.00 to −1.00. A perfect positive correlation (+1.00) would mean that for every unit one of the variables would go up, the other variable in the correlation would also go up a fixed amount. If height and weight were perfectly correlated, every inch of height would be matched by a constant increase in weight—say, 2 pounds. This relationship is graphically represented as in Figure A-5. If a

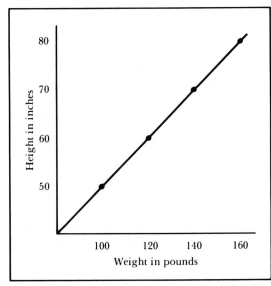

Figure A-5. A perfect positive correlation of height and weight

perfect negative correlation (−1.00) existed between height and weight, for every inch that height increased, there would be a consistent drop in weight—say, 2 pounds. This relationship could be represented graphically as in Figure A-6.

A complete absence of any relationship between height and weight would yield a zero correlation (0.00) between height and weight. This lack of relationship could be the result of three possible configurations of the two variables. One way, shown in Figure A-7, is where weight remains constant regardless of how height varies.

Another possibility, represented in Figure A-8, is where height remains constant regardless of how weight varies.

Finally, a purely random relationship might result in a perfect zero correlation. This possibility is shown graphically in Figure A-9.

Very rarely does a researcher find either a perfect positive, negative, or zero correlation. Rather, investigators find correlations that

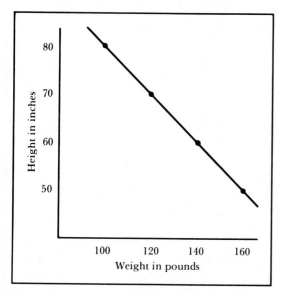

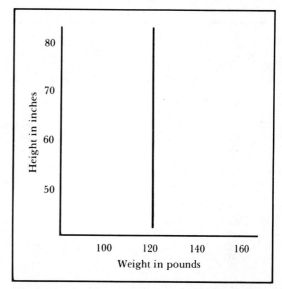

Figure A-6. A perfect negative correlation of height and weight.

Figure A-7. A zero correlation between height and weight where weight remains constant.

fall somewhere between the extremes of −1.00, 0.00, and +1.00.

See Table A-6 for the calculations for the Pearson product moment correlation coefficient between the heights and weights in our imaginary sample of subjects.

Now that we have computed the correlation coefficient between height and weight and have calculated the appropriate degrees of freedom, we can look up the tabled value of the correlation coefficient for 22 degrees of freedom.

Since our obtained value of .87 is greater than the tabled value of .404, we can say that a statistically significant positive linear relationship exists between height and weight. Moreover, we would expect a correlation of this magnitude to occur by random chance only 1 out of 20 times. Indeed, since a value of .87 is also greater than the tabled value of .515, we can say that a significant linear relationship exists that would occur by chance only 1 out of 100 times. Of course, we would mention the latter significance level only, because the .01 level

is "higher" than the .05 level, indicating a somewhat stronger relationship.

If our correlation were not significant at the .05 or .01 level, we would be unable to claim that the linear relationship differed from zero to a greater degree than we could expect from random chance.

The Coefficient of Determination

Once we have a correlation coefficient and have determined that it is significant, we can square the correlation coefficient and come up with a statistic called the *coefficient of determination*. This number tells us how much of the variance is shared by each variable. In a perfect positive (+1.00) or negative (−1.00) correlation, this number would be 1.00, meaning that 100% of the variance of each variable could be predicted from knowing the other variable. That is, if one variable changed, we would know the corresponding change in the other. For example, if height and weight were perfectly correlated and we knew that for every

TABLE A-6.
Calculation of Pearson Product Moment Correlation Coefficient between Heights and Weights of Imaginary Subjects

Height (h)	Weight(w)	$(H - \bar{x}h) = dh$	$(w - \bar{x}w) = dw$	dh^2	dw^2	$[(dh)\,(dw)] = D$
68	160	2.75	17.3	7.56	299.29	47.57
72	180	6.75	37.3	45.56	1391.29	251.77
62	150	−3.25	7.3	10.56	53.29	−23.72
65	155	−.25	12.3	.06	151.29	−3.07
66	160	.75	17.3	.56	299.29	12.97
59	115	−6.25	−27.7	39.06	767.29	173.13
74	190	8.75	47.3	76.56	2237.29	413.87
74	185	8.75	42.3	76.56	1789.29	370.12
70	180	4.75	37.3	22.56	1391.29	177.17
63	140	−2.25	−2.7	5.06	7.29	6.07
64	150	−1.25	7.3	1.56	53.29	−9.12
78	210	12.75	67.3	162.56	4529.29	858.07
62	130	−3.25	−12.7	10.56	161.29	41.27
63	135	−2.25	−7.7	5.06	59.29	17.32
64	140	−1.25	−2.7	1.56	7.29	3.37
59	115	−6.25	−27.7	39.06	767.29	173.12
59	115	−6.25	−27.7	39.06	767.29	173.12
60	110	−5.25	−32.7	27.56	1069.29	171.67
62	105	−3.25	−37.7	10.56	1421.29	122.52
65	115	−.25	−27.7	.06	767.29	6.92
68	120	2.75	−22.7	7.56	515.29	−62.42
66	120	.75	−22.7	.56	515.29	−17.02
62	130	−3.25	−12.7	10.56	161.29	41.27
61	115	−4.25	−27.7	18.06	767.29	117.72
$\Sigma h = 1566$	$\Sigma w = 3425$			$\Sigma dn^2 = 618.44$	$\Sigma dw^2 = 19948.96$	$\Sigma D = 3063.69$

Figure A-8. A zero correlation between height and weight where height remains constant.

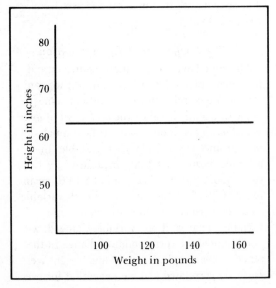

Figure A-9. A zero correlation resulting from a random relationship between height and weight.

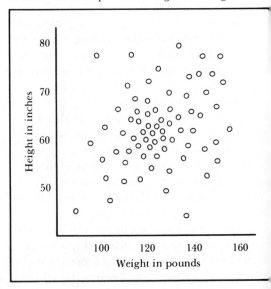

Table A-6 (continued)

$$\bar{x}h = \frac{1566}{24} = 65.25$$

$$\bar{x}w = \frac{3425}{24} = 142.70$$

$$sdh = \sqrt{\frac{\Sigma dh^2}{N}} = \sqrt{\frac{618.44}{24}} = 5.076$$

$$sdw = \sqrt{\frac{\Sigma dw^2}{N}} = \sqrt{\frac{19948.96}{24}} = 28.830$$

$$rhw = \frac{\Sigma D}{(N)\,(sdh)\,(sdw)}$$

$$rhw = \frac{3063.69}{(24)\,(5.076)\,(28.83)}$$

$$rhw = \frac{3063.69}{3512.185}$$

$$rhw = .87 \longrightarrow \text{degrees of freedom} = 24 - 2 = 22$$

(*Note: sdh* = standard deviation of height; *sdw* = standard deviation of weight; *rhw* = correlation between height and weight.)
1. Organize your two sets of variables so that all of a subject's scores for both variables fall along the same row.
2. Find the mean ($\bar{x}$) for each variable.
3. Find the deviation (d) of each individual score from the mean ($\bar{x}$) of its set of scores.
4. Square the deviations (d^2) and sum them (Σd^2).
5. Multiply the deviation from the mean of one set of variables (d_h) by the deviation from the mean of the other variables (d_w) for each subject. That result is called the gross product (D); the sum of the gross products is ΣD.
6. Compute the standard deviation (sd) for both variables.
7. Take the sum of the cross products (ΣD) and divide it by the number of pairs of subjects (N) multiplied by the standard deviation (sd) of both sets of scores.
8. To compute the appropriate degrees of freedom for a correlation coefficient, subtract 2 from the number of pairs of scores.

inch of people's height they would weigh 2 pounds, we would also know that a person who was 64 inches high would weigh 128 pounds. If this person grew 2 inches, achieving a height of 66 inches, then he or she would also gain 4 pounds.

For the correlation of .87 that we obtained between height and weight, the coefficient of determination is found by squaring .87, which results in a figure of .75. This means that height and weight share 75% of their variance with each other—that is, 75% of the variance in height can be accounted for by the variance

in weight. This number gives us a single number that summarizes the relationship between sets of variables in a sample. It is *not* the percentage one variable will change if the other variable changes.

Significance versus Importance

There is one last question you should ask yourself: Is the correlation you have found not only significant but important? If you have a large enough sample, a correlation as small as .062 can be significant though it accounts for only .003 percent of the variance. If we were looking at how internal/external scores related to basketball performance, this account of variance would be relatively unimportant. However, if we were looking at how certain foods might be related to increases in the likelihood of cancer, accounting for even this small a piece of the variance might be important.

Appendix B
The Form and Content of Research Reports

I. The Structure of the Paper

First-sheet format

TITLE OF PAPER IN CAPITAL LETTERS
a concise and informative title
(centered on one or more lines)

ABSTRACT

(The abstract should be no longer than two-thirds of a page double spaced, and preferably shorter. The abstract may contain more than one paragraph if clarity is improved thereby. Leave wide margins so your instructor has room to comment on your work).

Second-sheet format (this sheet is considered Page 1 but is not numbered).

TITLE OF PAPER IN CAPITAL LETTERS
(as on previous page)

Your name(s) centered on page

Your university (or other) affiliation

The introduction, or problem, section begins in paragraph form, but is not titled. Subheadings should be used on subsequent pages to delineate sections of your report. Use an initial capital letter and underline as specified below. Center headings or type at the margin, as indicated below. Sections follow one another without extra spacing. The reference page is the exception; it always begins a new page, regardless of where on a page the discussion section ends.

Method
(centered)

Subjects. (Type head at the margin. Text begins indented on a new line.)

Procedure.

Other Subheadings (as appropriate to your paper)

Results

Discussion

References (begins new page, last numbered
page)

Table 1, 2, 3, and so on (each on a separate unnumbered sheet).

Figure 1, 2, 3, and so on (each on a separate unnumbered sheet).

APPENDIX 1 . . . *n* (as needed for raw data,
copies of questionnaires, and
so on)

II. The Content of a Research Report, by Sections

Abstract. The abstract is like a miniature version of your paper. Although it appears at the beginning, it usually is written last, since it is a *summary* of the whole report. An abstract should give the reader a clear idea of what your study was about. It should explain the purpose of the study but should not refer to past work except in very general terms (for example, "previous studies found . . . "). The abstract gives the basic *design* and summarizes the *procedure* in general terms (for example, "aggression was assessed by time-sampling of live behavior"). It also gives the major *results*. It may hint at the interpretation in the *discussion*, but is usually too brief to include more than a sentence or two on the meaning (for instance, "The results were interpreted as supporting a structural theory of infant social development"). Like the rest of the paper (except for references to tables and figures), the abstract is written in the past tense.

Introduction, or problem section. This section describes the context of the study. It begins with general considerations—the history of the problem and any theoretical formulations behind it—and ideally should narrow down to an operational statement of the specific hypothesis under investigation.

This section should show how the study has developed out of a theoretical or practical problem and should build a case for your present hypothesis from a consideration of previous research. All the previous findings and points of view that you noted in this section should be cited explicitly in APA style (described later in this appendix). That is, the section should endeavor to show how the present research is a valid next step in investigating the problem under consideration. This is the only section without a heading.

Method. This section presents the details of how your study or experiment was conducted. Ideally it should contain enough information to enable another researcher to reconstruct your procedure and repeat the investigation from your description. Because much detailed information is usually contained in the methods section, this section is generally subdivided into subsections, usually design, subjects, stimuli, and procedure, although fewer sections are often used and different subheadings sometimes are more appropriate.

1. Design

    The *independent* and *dependent variables* should be operationally defined—that is, the steps involved in their manipulation and/or measurement should be specified. The design should be described, including the method of assigning subjects to conditions and the control procedures used. Frequently, this section is deleted if it is more convenient to discuss these matters under "stimuli" or "procedure." Statements or explanations already made in the introductory section should not be repeated here.

2. Subjects

    The number of subjects used as well as the sample characteristics such as age and sex and experimenters should be stated. The method of obtaining subjects should be reported as well.

3. Stimuli

    Any stimulus material used should be described in sufficient detail to enable a reader to duplicate equivalent stimuli. (Do not use this heading if it is not appropriate to your study. Alternative headings such as "Training Group," "Observational Settings," or "Self-Concept Interview" might be more appropriate to your particular investigation.)

4. Procedure

    This subsection provides a step-by-step description of how the investigation was conducted. Instructions should be presented verbatim, and the method of presenting any stimuli and recording the response should be described.

Results. Here the results are presented in simple, clear, and concise form. Enough information should be presented to support the statements in the discussion, but not so much that the reader is overwhelmed. The highlights of the tables, figures, and reports on statistical significance should be summarized in a narrative statement, with explicit reference to each table and figure, numbered in the order of their appearance. Make no attempt to interpret your results in this section. Your data analyses do not belong here, only the results of them. In most psychology manuscripts, figures and tables are found on separate pages at the end of the report. Only in published journal articles are the tables and figures inserted in the text.

Discussion. This section begins with descriptive statements drawn from the previous two sections, and refers back to the problem section to consider the theoretical or practical implications of these statements. The previous research cited and issues raised in the introduction are discussed and suggestions and reasons for future research are made.

If the study turned out as expected, you should consider such questions as How general is the result? What studies might be done to test its limits of generality? Are there alternative interpretations for the results? Are all the results of equal interest, plausibility, and theoretical significance? How might the more significant interpretations be tested?

If the study didn't turn out as expected, why do you think it didn't? Can you cite any observations you made while gathering the data that might support your conjecture? Are there other data you might have gathered? Would a different experimental design have given you the required information? What other studies might be done that would shed light on possible explanations for your results? Are there other ways of looking at your data that would give you relevant information? Support your interpretations (whether your hypothesis was supported or not) by reference to other studies that add plausibility to your interpretation. For example, if you are speculating that your study did not turn out because subjects were "too high in IQ" or of the "wrong social class," cite studies that show that these variables might make a difference in the problem under consideration. Not every investigation will afford an equal opportunity for exploring the questions suggested here, and they should not be dealt with slavishly and mechanically. However, when the occasion is suitable, consideration of these questions can often be fruitful.

References (for a more detailed description, see American Psychological Association [1974]).

1. Reference Section

References begin on a new page following the discussion section. This page is titled References and is frequently confused with what is commonly known as a bibliography page. According to APA style, *only* those works cited in the body of the paper are included the reference section. Every work mentioned in the text *must* appear in this section.

Following are excerpts from the *APA Publication Manual* giving some of the most commonly used forms (refer directly to the APA manual for cases not represented):

Archer, P. W. The tactile perception of roughness. *Americal Journal of Psychology*, 1950, *63*, 365–373. [Pagination by volume.]

Cardinal, M. H. Anxiety among displaced children. *Bulletin of the World Federation for Mental Health*, 1950, 2(4), 27–35. [Pagination by issue.]

Jefferds, C. V., Jr. *The psychology of industrial unrest*. New York: McGraw-Hill, 1960.

Wood, A. The reinforcement of anxiety. In J. T. Kelly (Ed.), *Theories of psychopathology*. Springfield, Ill.: Charles C. Thomas, 1965.

References are listed on the page in alphabetical order by author's last name. If more than one work by the same author is cited, list the works in order of publication, oldest first and most recent last.

2. References in text

Footnotes are used very rarely in psychology papers and then only for providing tangential information or an "aside." Following APA style, references are cited directly in the text. Refer to the APA manual for cases not represented in the following examples:

"A recent study (Jones, 1971) has shown . . ."

"According to Jones (1972) . . ."

"Another investigation (Jones & Smith, 1969) arrived at the same results as Brown, White, & Miller (1962) . . ."

"A number of studies (Allen, 1972; Brown, 1970; Jones & Smith, 1969) have shown . . ."

When a study by more than one author is cited "and" is written out when the reference is part of the body of the text—"Jones and Smith (1969) found"—but an ampersand (&) is used when the citation is within parentheses. The ampersand is also used on the reference page.

3. Quotations in text

Quotations in the text should be given exactly as they appeared in the source. The original wording, punctuation, spelling, and italics must be preserved even if they are erroneous. The citation of the source of the direct quotation should always include the page or pages as well as the publication. Give the citation in parentheses following the last word of the quoted material. The citation precedes the final punctuation and is within quotation marks when quotation marks are used. Example:

Grasse (1949) considers his test simply as a more sensitive index of "impairment in both the concrete and abstract spheres (p. 13)."

Figures and Tables (details in American Psychological Association [1974]). Figures (usually graphs) and tables are numbered separately and placed at the end of the paper. Place each one on a separate page with title and labels styled in accordance with the specifications in the APA manual. Be sure to mention tables and figures in the results section of your paper and to describe what they show.

Appendix. Attach to the body of your report your data sheets and all calculations you made in working on your tables, graphs, and tests of significance.

III. Nonsexist Language

An author must use care in choosing words to ensure accuracy, clarity, and freedom from bias. In the case of sexism, long-established cultural practices can exert a powerful influence over even the most conscientious author. To counteract sexual bias, choose nouns, pronouns, and adjectives that eliminate, or at least minimize, the possibility of ambiguity in sex identity or sex role. By definition, scientific writing should be free from any implied or irrelevant evaluation of the sexes. The following guidelines were adapted from the APA manual change sheet, "Guidelines for Non-Sexist Language in APA Journals." See the 1977 edition of the APA manual for a more complete discussion.

The universal male pronouns are often irrelevant and can be eliminated. If you can't think of a way of eliminating the use of male pronoun, use *his or her* in place of just *his*. Also, replace *man* with *humankind* and *people* with *humanity* or *human beings*.

Original	*Improved*
The *client* is usually the best judge of the value of *his* counseling.	The *client* is usually the best judge of the value of counseling.
Man's search for knowledge has led *him* into ways of learning that bear examination.	*The search* for knowledge has led *us* into ways of learning that bear examination.

Appendix C

INTRODUCTION TO APPENDIX C

This appendix is a summary of Edwin A. Rugg's investigation of judgments about the ethics of different research designs. In this study he used the Social Research Practices Opinion Survey, which is an exercise in Chapter 4. We hope that this brief description of his sample, method, design, and results stimulates further thinking about ethical issues in general, and about the types of empirical investigations of ethical issues that contribute to our understanding of issues. You might want to compare your own or your class's responses from the opinion survey, if these are available, with Rugg's general findings outlined in his abstract.

Social Research Practices Opinion Survey: Summary of Results
Edwin A. Rugg

The survey entailed evaluations of social research practices that involved the use of deception. The use of experimental deception in research has provoked controversy among social scientists and was described as a serious ethical problem in the American Psychological Associations's newly revised code of ethics for research with human participants. Although ethical questions pertaining to deception have been explored in depth, particularly in the revised code, the gravity of the use of deception is less clear. As a result, researchers were advised to seek the opinions of colleague, subject, and public groups on the issues of the use of deception.

The aims of this research study were (a) to identify some of the conditions in which the use of deception is perceived to pose a serious threat to the welfare and rights of research participants, and (b) to compare the opinions of colleague, subject, and public groups regarding the negative effects of deceptive practices. Procedural descriptions evaluated in this study were written to conform to one of two types of informed consent (limited vs none), one of two levels of stress (stressful vs nonstressful), and

From *Ethical Judgments of Social Research Involving Experimental Deception* by E. A. Rugg. Unpublished doctoral dissertation, George Peabody College for Teachers, 1975. Reproduced by permission of the author.

one of two postexperimental debriefing conditions (debriefing conducted vs debriefing not conducted). Respondent groups included research ethics committee members (N = 123), social psychologists (N = 224), clinical and counseling psychologists (N = 186), academicians in the social sciences and humanities (N = 192), an informed citizens group (Nashville League of Women Voters members, N = 148), law professors (N = 85), and undergraduate students (N = 137). Each respondent's ratings were summed to make 4 3-item scores (corresponding to the 4 stress × consent conditions) for the ethics, harm, and opposition ratings (total of 12 3-item scores per respondent). Ethics, harm, and opposition scores were analyzed in three separate analyses of variance of a 7 × 2 × 2 × 2 design (groups × debriefing × stress × consent) with repeated measure on the last two factors.

The following conclusions were indicated by the results:

a) All uses of experimental deception were not perceived by respondents as posing a serious threat to the rights and welfare of research participants. Several of the procedures involving deception were rated as highly ethical, harmless, and unobjectionable; others were rated quite to the contrary.

b) The presence or absence of stress in the procedural description appeared to be the most salient factor for purposes of distinguishing between acceptable and unacceptable social research practices. Whereas 66% of all responses were moderately to strongly opposed to stressful procedures, only 17% were similarly disposed toward nonstressful ones.

c) The importance of conducting postexperimental debriefing after the use of deception appeared greater in situations in which research participation was solicited (limited informed consent) than in disguised field experimentation in which participants are unaware of their research participation (no consent). In fact, in nonstressful research practices involving no informed consent, there was a tendency for practices involving debriefing to be rated as more harmful than those which contained no debriefing. Debriefing appeared to influence ratings of nonstressful research practices very little, particularly for groups outside of the social science.

d) Ethics committee members were typically the most stringent evaluators of research practices, closely followed by social psychologists and League of Women Voters respondents. Undergraduate students were least stringent and differed markedly from all other groups, followed by the law professor respondents. Whereas ethics committee members shared a common level of concern with most other groups over stressful research practices, they stood out as more critical of nonstressful procedures than all other groups. The level of ethical concern voiced by social psychologists, the typical users of experimental deception, was high in relation to that of other groups sampled, suggesting the existence of a strong self-regulation posture among social researchers regarding the use of deception.

Appendix D

INTRODUCTION TO APPENDIX D

Identity is a strong theme in this book, and we have made more than passing reference to James Marcia's work on ego identity. This appendix is the interview Marcia described in the Chapter 2 article and examples of his scoring guidelines. Although we did not include his entire scoring manual, the material provided is a concrete example of a system of content analysis. If you decide to use Marcia's interview for a study of your own, you may want to expand his scoring guidelines. You might also decide to use the guidelines as a foundation to determine criteria for scoring such materials as the autobiographical essays recommended in exercises in Chapters 2 and 6.

Identity Status Interview[1]
James E. Marcia

Introduction

What year are you in?
Where are you from? Living at home?
How did you happen to come to (name of school)?
Did your father go to college? Where? What does he do now?
Did you mother go to college? Where? What does she do now?

Occupation

You said you were majoring in _____;
    what do you plan to do with it?
When did you come to decide on _____;
    did you ever consider anything else?
What seems attractive about _____?
Most parents have plans for their children, things they'd like them to go into or do—did yours have any plans like that for you?
How do your folks feel about your plans now?
How willing do you think you'd be to change this if something better came along? (If S responds: "What do you mean by

[1]Abstracted from *Studies in Ego Identity* by J. E. Marcia, Simon Fraser University, 1976. Reproduced by permission of the author.

237

better?" Well, what might be better in your terms?)

Religion

Do you have any particular religious affiliation or preference?

How about your folks?

Ever very active in church? How about now? Get into many religious discussions?

How do your parents feel about your beliefs now?

Are yours any different from theirs?

Was there any time when you came to doubt any of your religious beliefs?

When? How did it happen? How did you

resolve your questions? How are things for you now?

Politics

Do you have any particular political preferences?

How about your parents?

Ever take any kind of political action—join groups, write letters, participate in demonstrations—anything at all like that?

Any issues you feel pretty strongly about?

Any particular time when you decided on your political beliefs?

What did you think of the past elections?

Sample Scoring Criteria: Occupation Questions[2]

The main objective of rating each interview is to place the individual in one of four "identity statuses:" Identity Achievement, Moratorium, Foreclosure, and Identity Diffusion. Each status represents how an older adolescent might cope with a particular identity crisis. When facing an identity crisis, the individual must decide on and commit to an occupation as well as decide on an ideology—what one believes in. In a more formal sense, the achievement of ego identity involves the synthesis of childhood identifications in the individual's own terms, so that a reciprocal relationship is established with society and a feeling of continuity between present and past is maintained. Elaborating further, childhood can be viewed as a period when society provides the materially and emotionally nutritive milieu for survival of the almost wholly dependent child. Adulthood involves a shift in responsibility, so that the individual is expected to contribute to the previously nurturant environment in a more mutual relationship. Adolescence, in

particular, late adolescence, is the period when this shift takes place. The achievement of an ego identity at this time represents the reformulation of all that the individual was into the core of what he or she is to become.

The two referents for determining Identity Status are "crisis" and "commitment" in the areas of occupation and ideology (religion and politics). The term *crisis* was chosen for its meaning of struggle, or more accurately, a period of decision. Commitment refers to a certain unwaveringness of choice, a reluctance to abandon a chosen path. Although these two referents are separately assessed, some overlap occurs. For example, when a subject says that he decided to go into industrial management in his junior year as a result of scanning the college catalogue, one does not get a sense of either an active selection among personally meaningful alternatives (crisis) or an unswerving investment in a course of action (commitment).

Instructions for rating. The following descriptions show crisis and commitment combined to yield an identity status, and give short sketches of how each type of identity status might appear in the occupation area.

[2]Abstracted from *Studies in Ego Identity* by J. E. Marcia, Simon Fraser University, 1976. Reproduced by permission of the author.

1. *Identity Achievement*

Criteria: The individual has passed through a decision period or crisis and appears committed to an occupation.

Sketch: Occupation—the individual has seriously considered occupations or deviated from what parents had planned. The individual is reluctant to switch fields and is "*a teacher*," "*an engineer*," and so on. (Being *a* something is different from "taking courses in education".) The ultimate choice may be a variation of parental wishes, and the crisis has been resolved.

1. Has tried business—focused on general medical profession—tried dentistry, tried pharmacy—now in optometry. Likes it because it's in the area of helping people medically and has variety. (Willing to change?) "I really like what I'm doing. I have too much investment in it now to do anything else."

2. Came from farm background and likes farming, but being a farmer not too interesting or feasible. Decided to go into agricultural economics, which is sort of an over-all business manager for farmers. Somewhat defensive about farming as a viable career.

3. When first went to college, felt no sense of purpose. Left and joined the army. Came back with renewed interest. Finds present choice interesting and would be willing to change only routine functions, not the general area.

4. Father was a farmer and pushed for that; mother and townspeople wanted a minister; decided to become a veterinarian. "I would rather have my DVM than a Ph. D. in anything."

General Comment: The individual seems generally able to "make it." Particularly, sudden shifts in environment or unexpected burdens of responsibility would not be overwhelming. Solid interpersonal commitments—for example, marriage, engagement—are forming.

2. *Moratorium*

Criteria: The individual is presently in a crisis period—trying to make decisions. Commitments are likely to be vague and general. An important quality is an active struggle among alternatives.

Sketch: Occupation—The individual is dealing with issues described as "adolescent." One concern is with choosing a career, not with preparing for it. Parents' plans are still important, and a compromise of them, society's demands, and personal capabilities must be achieved. The individual is vitally concerned and somewhat preoccupied, not bewildered, with resolving what seem to be unresolvable questions.

1. "Other people think I'm jolly and free-lancing. Inside, I'm a big knot. I'd just like some peace and quiet." "The future seems better than the past, though." "I'm not so concerned about what people think, and I can control my temper better." Majoring in speech, wants to work for degree in psychology and sociology while in army. In general, wants to do something to help people.

2. Has considered rabbinate, law, and teaching. Present major is philosophy and religion. Thinks now it should be teaching, but struggling with parents' demands to choose a career more financially rewarding.

3. Chemistry—physics—biology major. Considers teaching high school and then going into industry. Also, occasionally still considers ministry. Seems to be an idealistic vs. economic conflict. "I can go into teaching, industrial chemistry, the ministry. I can see myself in any of those three fields."

General Comments: Some subjects' occupational choices may reflect elements of Identity Achievement, Moratorium, and Foreclosure although these cases are rare. When one status does not predominate, a score of Moratorium is given. At worst, a Moratorium is paralyzed, unable to act decisively in any direction—not because of a lack of commitment, but because of equal and opposite commitment.

3. *Foreclosure*

Criteria: The individual does not seem to have passed through any real decision period, but, nevertheless, appears committed to an occupation. In this case, the choices very likely coincide with those of parents or parent surrogates.

Sketch: Occupation—The individual has difficulty distinguising between personal goals and parents' goals. There was no decision period or only a brief, inconsequential one. Childhood influences and others' intentions for that person heavily affect what the individual is becoming. In addition, all of this seems ego-syntonic. Childhood identification figures ("like my father," "like my mother,") keep cropping up in the interview.

1. "I'm not in any mood to leave home. I'm not tied to my mother's apronstrings, but all my friends are home." Wants to go into a large corporation where "they'll run me through training and tell me how they want things done." Is also considering being a firefighter like father was. Went home every weekend throughout college and maintained membership in social groups there (for example, Kiwanis, volunteer fire department).

2. "I plan to go back and help dad farm." Took agriculture at college because "that's all I knew." Although considered other fields, "farming was always at the top of the list." I was brought up like my family was—I was with them so long I just stayed that way."

General Comment: Because of commitment and apparent self-assuredness, the individual could be considered Identity Achievement, but a certain rigidity and the absence of decision periods distinguish the types. One feels that if it were a situation where parental values were non-functional, the individual would soon be at a loss. In many instances, only a situation of severe ego stress is the differentiation from Identity Achievement. Plans may include returning to hometown and continuing life there.

4. *Identity Diffusion*

Criteria: The individual has either experienced no crisis or has passed through a crisis—in either case, there is little commitment, if any.

There appear to be two types of Diffusion. One is a pre-crisis lack of commitment. The individual might have been a Foreclosure if strong enough parental values had been established. However, it is likely that the parental attitude was one of "It's up to you; we don't care what you do." Under the guise of democratic child-rearing, the parents have provided no consistent structure to guide the growing individual or given an image to use for comparison. Because the individual never really *was* anything, it is almost impossible to envision becoming anything. The problems that are so immediate and self-consuming for the Moratorium never really occur to this "pre-crisis Diffuse" person.

The second type is the "post-crisis Diffuse" who seems committed to a lack of commitment. This individual actively seeks to avoid entangling alliances; motto: "Play the field." No area of potential gratification is really relinquished; all things are possible, and must be kept that way. The main element that both pre- and post-crisis Diffuse persons have in common is a lack of commitment.

Sketch: Occupation—The individual has neither decided on one occupational choice, nor has much real concern about it (as contrasted with the Moratorium). There is sometimes little conception of what a person in the stated preferred occupation does in a day-to-day routine. The occupation would be readily disposed of should opportunities arise elsewhere. There is sometimes an "external" orientation, so that what happens to the individual is seen as a result of luck or fate.

1. Has considered priesthood, law, and teaching math. Seems to be "bouncing around" from one thing to another. Language is strange and answers are oblique. Assumes roles of others and during the interview speaks in admonishing tones as they would speak to subject.

Although there is some closure on choice of teaching, the whole interview is bizarre. When asked about leaving seminary: "It was shown to me not to be my vocation. Some people have desire, some don't. I didn't."

2. Going into optometry—likes it because there's not too much work, make money at it, and doesn't take too long to study for it. If something better came along, "I'd change quite easily."

3. Claims greater maturity after having flunked out of school and gone to service. Major in marketing, interested in business and in being a golf pro. Main interest in life is playing golf. Emphasis not on what Father *wants*, but on what Father *gives*. "Very apt" to give up occupational choice for something better.

4. Major is engineering. In response to "willingness to change?":"Oh, I can change. I want to travel, want to try a lot of things, don't want to get stuck behind a drawing board. Want a degree mainly as an 'in' to production or something else. Don't want to get tied down."

General Comments: At worst, a Diffuse individual exhibits the disorganized thought processes, disturbed object relations, and loosened ego boundaries associated with schizophrenia.

Appendix E

INTRODUCTION TO APPENDIX E

Marcia developed more than one assessment device to measure ego identity. This appendix is his incomplete sentences task as well as scoring guidelines. As you compare the scoring systems for the two types of ego identity measure, you will notice some interesting differences. The guidelines for the interview measure, with their focus on the intersection of crisis and commitment, are designed to permit *categorization* of respondents into four identity statuses. If you score an interview or autobiographical essay using these criteria, you will be describing the respondent as one who demonstrates achievement, moratorium, foreclosure, or diffusion.

By contrast, an ordinal scale is built into the scoring guidelines for the incomplete sentences task. In this scoring system, responses to every sentence stem are scored for high (3 points), middle (2 points) or low (1 point) identity commitment. Scores for all items are then summed to provide an overall identity score. If both Marcia's measures provide valid data concerning ego identity, then respondents categorized as identity achievers on his interview measure should receive high scores on the sentence completion task. You might want to design a study to test this prediction empirically.

Ego Identity Sentence Completion Task and Sample Scoring Criteria
James E. Marcia

A. The Incomplete Sentences
  1. For me, success would be _____.
  2. When I consider my goals in the light of my family's goals _____.
  3. I'm at my best when _____.

  4. Sticking to one occupational choice _____.
  5. When I let myself go, I _____.
  6. I chose to come to this college after _____.
  7. I know that I can always depend on _____.
  8. (choose one) a. I am _____.
                   b. I am not _____.

Abstracted from *Studies in Ego Identity* by J. E. Marcia, Simon Fraser University, 1976. Reproduced by permission of the author.

9. It seems I've always _____.
10. I wish I could make up my mind about _____.
11. Getting involved in political activity _____.
12. What happens to me depends on _____.
13. As compared with four years ago, I _____.
14. I belong to _____.
15. To change my mind about my feelings toward religion _____.
16. If one commits oneself _____.
17. Ten years from now , I _____.
18. It makes me feel good when _____.

B. General Scoring Guidelines
   1. Any answer indicating a commitment to one of the four major areas (occupation, religion, politics, and sexual identity) is, *a priori*, higher than a *1*.
   2. Any blatantly pathological or self-derogatory statements and those containing mutually exclusive clauses are scored *1*.
   3. All blanks are scored *1*.
   4. Trivia and inappropriate humor are given a *1*—except where noted in the specific question criteria.
   5. When the individual sees self as having overcome, or as capable of overcoming, barriers to achievement of personal goals, generally score *3*.

C. Sample Scoring Criteria: Items 1–3
   Item 1. For me, success would be _____.
   Score of *3*—In line with occupational choice.
   Example—"realizing my ambition to be a practicing veterinarian."
   "to obtain a degree in optometry, have a profitable practice, a home, and a family."
   "the achievement of a large amount of competence in my main career, namely engineering."
   "being a brilliant and recognized authority in my academic field."

Score of *2*—Any goal involving action on the part of the individual—an emphasis on attaining—that is, doing or getting as opposed to having or being given to.
Example—"fulfilling my state in life in the career I am following."
"in what I do, not in how much money I earn." (philosophy)
"attainment of the Ph.D. degree and its associated prestige and status." (specific)
"knowing, loving, and serving God daily more and more with my wife, family, and friends."
"a good job and a family and enough money to support them."

Score of *1*—General security and happiness—the idea that success would be "nice" but no specification of what its components might be. Or mutually exclusive clauses.
Example—"would be in the form of pleasure."
"desirous."
"to be superior and to be accepted by others." (for most of us, mutually exclusive)
"an inner feeling of self-satisfaction."
Item 2. When I consider my goals in the light of my family's goals _____.
Score of *3*—Either directly opposite to family goals with evidence of some commitment, or a difference from family's goals with commitment. Not enough to say: "They're different." Ideally, a *3* here would reflect a continuity—family goals transformed by the individual into his own style.
Example—"they do not tend to approve of my goals and thinking."
"they are of a higher nature than my family's."
"I realize that the ultimate goal is similar, although the pathway is different."
Score of *2*—Some goals the same, some different, but very little evidence of firm

commitment. Or indeterminate statements, such that one cannot assess whether or not a difference exists.

Example—"I find them somewhat the same."

"not much difference, but a little."

"I wonder if I'm aiming too high."

"there is no comparison." (indeterminate)

"I am happy and so are they." (indeterminate)

Score of *1*—Direct harmony, exactly the same.

Example—"they are basically the same."

"we end up agreeing on my family's goals."

"they are consistent."

Item 3. I'm at my best when _____.

Score of *3*—Self-initiated action (that is, doing something), or competition, or little dependence on environment, or activity in line of occupational choice.

Example—"I'm on my own and have sole responsibility to get a given job done."

"I'm doing work I enjoy."

"I'm talking about music." (career)

"I'm competing with others in the classroom or under conditions conducive to pressure."

Score of *2*—When the environment shifts to suit the individual, or when there is absolutely no pressure at all.

Example—"my mind is clear of all worries, even trivial ones."

"I'm happy."

"I'm with my family and being alone."

"under a small amount of tension."

"I'm in familiar surroundings." (dependent on environment)

Score of *1*—Either seldom "at my best" or completely dependent on external factors.

Example—"I've had something to drink."

"other people are helping me."

"someone tells me what should be done."

Appendix F

INTRODUCTION TO APPENDIX F

It should be clear by now that any particular construct in personality—such as ego identity—can be measured in a number of different ways. This appendix is an objective test of ego identity, developed by Dale Simmons. Compare the items in Simmons' test with the items and scoring guidelines for the Marcia interview and sentence completion task. Do you think all three assessment devices are really measuring the same construct? Do you think one device could be more successful than the others at capturing ego identity as described by Erikson? How would you proceed to design a study assessing the reliability or validity or both of any or all these measures?

Objective Test for Ego Identity
Dale Simmons

Scoring Key

All of the following items which are X'd are scored one (1) +. The total possible score is 24.

1	B	7	A	13	A	19	B
2	A	8	A	14	B	20	A
3	A	9	B	15	A	21	B
4	B	10	A	16	B	22	B
5	A	11	B	17	B	23	A
6	B	12	A	18	A	24	B

From: *Identity Achievement Scale,* by D. D. Simmons. Reproduced by permission of the author.

Personal Preferences for Completing Sentences   NAME _____

Below you will find a number of incomplete sentences followed by two possible completions. Select the completion which best fits the answer you would give, were you trying to *express your true feelings*. Mark your answer by putting an *X* through the letter of the completion you prefer.

1. When I let myself go, I
   A. sometimes say things I later regret.
   B. have a good time and do not worry about others' thoughts and standards.

2. If one commits oneself
   A. he should follow through.
   B. he should have made certain beforehand he was correct.

3. For me, success would be
   A. the achievement of a large amount of competence in my main career.
   B. a good job with a family and enough money to support them.

4. Sticking to one occupational choice
   A. does not enchant me, but will probably be necessary.
   B. is sometimes difficult.

5. It makes me feel good when
   A. I look back on the progress I have made in life.
   B. I can be with my friends and know they approve of me.

6. To change my mind about my feelings toward religion
   A. I would have to know something about religious beliefs.
   B. would require a terrific amount of convincing by some authority.

7. I'm at my best when
   A. I'm on my own and have sole responsibility to get a given job done.
   B. my mind is clear of all worries, even trivial ones.

8. When I let myself go I
   A. don't change much from my regular self.
   B. think I talk too much about myself.

9. I am
   A. not as grateful as I should be.
   B. not hard to get along with.

10. Getting involved in political activity
    A. is as futile as necessary.
    B. doesn't appeal to me.

11. When I consider my goals in the light of my family's goals
    A. they are basically the same.
    B. I feel that they are missing a lot.

12. If one commits oneself
    A. one must know oneself.
    B. then he's liable to miss a lot of opportunities.

13. For me, success would be
    A. in what I do, not in how much money I earn.
    B. to be accepted by others.

14. If I had my choice
    A. I would live in a warm climate such as Southern California or Hawaii.
    B. I would do things as I have.

15. It seems I've always
    A. wanted to go to college.
    B. held back from reacting to certain things.

16. Sticking to one occupational choice
    A. does not enchant me, but it will probably be necessary.
    B. suits me fine.

17. It makes me feel good when
    A. I can be with my friends and know they approve of me.
    B. I think of all the good things that can happen in a lifetime.

18. When I let myself go I
    A. have a good time and do not worry about others' thoughts and standards.
    B. never know exactly what I will say or do.

19. To change my mind about my feelings toward religion
   A. is not hard to do, but I keep going back to the religion I started with.
   B. would require a terrific amount of convincing by some authority.

20. The difference between me as I am and as I'd like to be
   A. is very likely to be dissolved in time.
   B. is that I have potential, but lack a certain amount of drive.

21. I know that I can always depend on
   A. the good will of others, if I treat them right.
   B. my mind and diligence to surmount my barrier.

22. If one commits oneself
   A. one must know oneself.
   B. he should finish the task.

23. For me, success would be
   A. being a recognized authority in my chosen field.
   B. to be accepted by others.

24. When I let myself go I
   A. never know exactly what I will say or do.
   B. am most apt to do well.

References

Abelson, H., Cohen, R., Heaton, E., & Suder, C. Public attitudes toward and experience with erotic material. *Technical reports of the Commission on Obscenity and Pornography* (Vol. 6). Washington, D.C.: U.S. Government Printing Office, 1971.

Adorno, T. W., Frenkel-Brunswik, E., Levinson, D. J., & Sanford, R. N. *The authoritarian personality.* New York: Harper & Row, 1950.

Allport, G. W. *Letters from Jenny.* New York: Harcourt Brace Jovanovich, 1965.

Allport, G. W., Bruner, J. S., & Jandorf, E. M. Personality under social catastrophe: Ninety life-histories of the Nazi revolution. *Character and Personality,* 1941, *10,* 1–22.

American Psychological Association, *Publication Manual,* 2nd ed. Washington, D.C.: American Psychological Association, 1974.

American Psychological Association. Testing and public policy. *American Psychologist* (Special Issue), Nov. 1965, *20.*

Anastasi, A. *Psychological testing* (4th ed.). New York: Macmillan, 1976.

Andrews, T. G., & Muhlhan, G. Analysis of congruent idea patterns as a study in personality. *Character and Personality,* 1943, *12,* 101–110.

Asher, H. B. *Causal modeling.* Beverly Hills, Calif.: Sage, 1976.

Atkinson, J. W. (Ed.). *Motives in fantasy, action, and society,* New York: Van Nostrand Reinhold, 1958.

Barber, T. X., & Silver, M. J. Fact, fiction, and the experimenter effect. *Psychological Bulletin Monographs,* 1968, *70,* 1–29.

Barker, R. G. (Ed.). *The stream of behavior.* New York: Appleton-Century-Crofts, 1963.

Barker, R. G. Explorations in ecological psychology. *American Psychologist,* 1965, *20,* 1–14.

Barker, R. G., & Barker, L. S. Social actions in the behavior streams of American and English children. In R. G. Barker (Ed.), *The stream of behavior.* New York: Appleton-Century-Crofts, 1963, 127–159.

Barker, R. G., & Gump, P. V. *Big school, small school.* Palo Alto, Calif.: Stanford University Press, 1964.

Barker, R. G., & Wright, H. F. *Midwest and its children.* Evanston, Ill.: Row, Peterson, 1955.

Baron, R. M., Cowan, G., Ganz, R. L., & McDonald, M. Interaction of locus of control and type of performance feedback: Considerations of external validity. *Journal of Personality and Social Psychology,* 1974, *30,* 285–292.

Baumrind, D. Principles of ethical conduct in the treatment of subjects: Reaction to the draft of the Committee on Ethical Standards in Psychological Research. *American Psychologist,* 1971, *26,* 887–896.

Baumrind, D. Reactions to the May 1972 draft report of the ad hoc Committee on Ethical Standards on Psychological Research. *American Psychologist,* 1972, *27,* 1083–1086.

Bem, S. L. The measurement of psychological androgyny. *Journal of Consulting and Clinical Psychology,* 1974, *42,* 155–162.

Berkowitz, L., & LePage, A. Weapons as aggression-eliciting stimuli. *Journal of Personality and Social Psychology,* 1967, *7,* 202–207.

Berscheid, E., Baron, R. S., Dermer, M., & Libman, M. Anticipating informed consent: An empirical approach. *American Psychologist,* 1973, *28,* 913–925.

Blalock, H. M., Jr. *Causal inferences in nonexperimental research.* New York: W.W. Norton, 1972.

Block, J. *The Q-sort method in personality assessment*

and psychiatric research. Springfield, Ill.: Thomas, 1961.

Blos, P. *The adolescent personality.* New York: Appleton-Century-Crofts, 1941.

Bowman, P. C., & Auerbach, S. M. Measuring sex-role attitudes: The problem of the well-meaning liberal male. *Personality and Social Psychology Bulletin,* 1978, *4,* 265-271.

Bullen, B. A., Reed, R. B., & Mayer, J. Physical activity of obese and nonobese adolescent girls appraised by motion picture sampling. *American Journal of Clinical Nutrition,* 1964, *14,* 211-223.

Buros, O. K. *Personality tests and reviews.* Highland Park, N.J.: Gryphon Press, 1970.

Buros, O. K. (Ed.). *The seventh mental measurements yearbook* (Vols. 1 & 2). Highland Park, N.J.: Gryphon Press, 1972.

Byrne, D., Fisher, J. D., Lamberth, J., & Mitchell, H. E. Evaluations of erotica: Facts or feelings? *Journal of Personality and Social Psychology,* 1974, *29,* 111-116.

Campbell, D. P. *Handbook for the Strong Vocational Interest Blank.* Palo Alto, Calif.: Stanford University Press, 1971.

Campbell, D. T., & Fiske, D. W. Convergent and discriminant validation by the multitrait-multimethod matrix. *Psychological Bulletin,* 1959, *56,* 81-105.

Carlson, J., Cook, S. W., & Stromberg, E. L. Sex differences in conversation. *Journal of Applied Psychology,* 1936, *20,* 727-735.

Carlson, R. Where is the person in personality research? *Psychological Bulletin,* 1971, *75,* 203-219.

Cattell, R. B. *Personality, a systematic theoretical and factual study.* New York: McGraw-Hill, 1950.

Cattell, R. B. *The scientific analysis of personality.* Baltimore: Penguin, 1965.

Child, I. L., Potter, E. H. & Levine, E. M. Children's textbooks and personality development: An exploration in the social psychology of education. *Psychological Monographs,* 1946, *60* (3), 1-7; 43-53.

Cialdini, R. B., & Schroeder, D. A. Increasing compliance by legitimizing paltry contributions: When even a penny helps. *Journal of Personality and Social Psychology.* 1976, *34,* 599-604.

Climo, L. H. Acting out of character: Window on the identity crisis. *Journal of Youth and Adolescence,* 1975, *4,* 93-107.

Committee on Ethical Standards in Psychological Research. *Ethical principles in the conduct of research with human participants.* Washington, D.C.: American Psychological Association, 1973.

Costner, H. L. *Sociological methodology: 1973-1974.* San Francisco: Jossey-Bass, 1974.

Cox, D. E., & Sipprelle, C. N. Coercion in participation as a research subject. *American Psychologist,* 1971, *26,* 726-728.

Cronbach, L. J. *Essentials of psychological testing* (3rd ed.). New York: Harper & Row, 1970.

Cronbach, L. J., & Meehl, P. E. Construct validity in psychological tests. *Psychological Bulletin,* 1955, *52,* 281-302.

Crowne, D. P., & Marlowe, D. *The approval motive: Studies in evaluative dependence.* New York: Wiley, 1964.

Darley, J. M., & Latané, B. Bystander intervention in emergencies: Diffusion of responsibility. *Journal of Personality and Social Psychology,* 1968, *8,* 377-383.

Dawe, H. C. An analysis of two hundred quarrels of preschool children. *Child Development,* 1934, *5,* 139-157.

de Charms, R., & Moeller, G. H. Values expressed in American children's readers: 1800-1950. *Journal of Abnormal and Social Psychology,* 1962, *64,* 136-147.

Diener, E. & Crandall, R. *Ethics in social and behavioral research.* Chicago: University of Chicago Press, 1978.

Diener, E., Fraser, S. C., Beaman, A. L., & Kelem, R. T. Effects of deindividuation variables on stealing among Halloween Trick-or-Treaters. *Journal of Personality and Social Psychology,* 1976, *33,* 178-183.

Donley, R. E., & Winter, D. G. Measuring the motives of public officials at a distance: An exploratory study of American Presidents. *Behavioral Science,* 1970, *15,* 227-236.

Eaton, W. O., & Clore, G. L. Interracial imitation at a summer camp. *Journal of Personality and Social Psychology,* 1975, *32,* 1099-1105.

Eberts, E. H., & Lepper, M. R. Individual consistency in the proxemic behavior of preschool children. *Journal of Personality and Social Psychology,* 1975, *32,* 841-849.

Edney, J. J. Territoriality and control: A field experiment. *Journal of Personality and Social Psychology,* 1975, *31,* 1108-1115.

Ekehammar, B. Interactionism in personality from a historical perspective. *Psychological Bulletin,* 1974, *81,* 1026-1048.

Ekman, P. Communication through nonverbal behavior: A source of information about an interpersonal relationship. In S. S. Tomkins & C. E. Izard (Eds.), *Affect, cognition, and personality.* New York: Springer, 1965.

Endler, N. S., & Magnusson, D. Toward an interactional psychology of personality. *Psychological Bulletin,* 1976, *83,* 956-974.

Erikson, E. E. *Gandhi's truth*. New York: Norton, 1969.

Epstein, S. Traits are alive and well. In D. Magnussen & N. S. Endler (Eds.). *Personality at the crossroads: Current issues in interactional psychology*. Hillsdale, N.J.: Erlbaum, 1976.

Exline, R. V. Explorations in the process of person perception: Visual interaction in relation to competition, sex, and need for affiliation. *Journal of Personality*, 1963, *31*, 1–20.

Eysenck, H. J. *The structure of human personality*. New York: Wiley, 1953.

Feldman, R. E. Response to compatriot and foreigner who seek assistance. *Journal of Personality and Social Psychology*, 1968, *10*, 202–214.

Feshback, S., & Singer, R. D. *Television and aggression*. San Francisco: Jossey-Bass, 1971.

Fisher, J. D., & Byrne, D. Too close for comfort. Sex differences in response to invasions of personal space. *Journal of Personality and Social Psychology*, 1975, *32*, 15–21.

Freud, A., & Dann, S. An experiment in group upbringing. *The psychoanalytic study of the child*. New York: International University Press, 1951.

Freud, S., & Bullitt, W.C. *Thomas Woodrow Wilson: A psychological study*. Boston: Houghton Mifflin, 1967.

Gaertner, S., & Bickman, L. Effects of race on the elicitation of helping behavior: The wrong number technique. *Journal of Personality and Social Psychology*, 1971, *20*, 218–222.

Gallois, C., & Markel, N. N. Turn-taking: Social personality and conversational style. *Journal of Personality and Social Psychology*, 1975, *31*, 1134–1140.

Gardner, L. E. A relatively painless method of introduction to the psychological literature search. *Teaching of Psychology*, 1977, *4*, 89–91.

Gelfond, P. *Children and puddles*. Unpublished study, Boston University.

Gergen, K. J. The codification of research ethics: Views of a doubting Thomas. *American Psychologist*, 1973, *28*, 907–912.

Goethals, G. W., & Klos, D. S. *Experiencing youth: First-person accounts*. Boston: Little, Brown, 1976.

Gough, H. G., & Heilbrun, A. B. *Joint manual for the adjective check list and the need scales for the ACL*. Palo Alto: Consulting Psychologists Press, 1965.

Greene, L. R. Effects of field dependence on affective reactions and compliance in dyadic interactions. *Journal of Personality and Social Psychology*, 1976, *34*, 569–577.

Gregory, T. L. *Adolescence in literature*, New York: Longman, 1978.

Gross, M. *The brain watchers*. New York: Random House, 1962.

Guilford, J. P. *Personality*. New York: McGraw-Hill, 1959.

Haan, N. Changes in young adults after Peace Corps experiences: Political-social views, moral reasoning, and perceptions of self and parents. *Journal of Youth and Adolescence*, 1974, *3*, 177–193.

Helmreich, R. Applied social psychology: The unfulfilled promise. *Personality and Social Psychology Bulletin*, 1975, *1*, 548–560.

Henle, M., & Hubbell, M. B. "Egocentricity" in adult conversation. *Journal of Social Psychology*, 1938, *9*, 227–234.

Holmes, D. S., & Bennett, D. H. Experiments to answer questions raised by the use of deception in psychological research: I. Role playing as an alternative to deception; II. Effectiveness of debriefing after a deception; III. Effect of informed consent on deception. *Journal of Personality and Social Psychology*, 1974, *29*, 358–367.

Horner, M. The motive to avoid success and changing aspirations of college women. In J. H. Bardwick (Ed.), *Readings on the psychology of women*. New York: Harper & Row, 1972. (Reprinted from *Women on campus: 1970, A symposium*. Ann Arbor, Mich.: Center for the Continuing Education of Women.)

Huck, S. W., Cormier, W. H., & Bounds, Jr, W. G. *Reading statistics and research*. New York: Harper & Row, 1974.

Kahn, R. L., & Cannell, C. F. *The dynamics of interviewing: Theory, technique, and cases*. New York: Wiley, 1957.

Katz, I., Cohen, S., & Glass, D. Some determinants of cross-racial helping behavior. *Journal of Personality and Social Psychology*, 1975, *32*, 964–970.

Keesing, H. A. *The pop message: A trend analysis of the psychological content of two decades of music*. Paper presented at the 45th Annual Meeting of the Eastern Psychological Association, Philadelphia, Pennsylvania, 1974.

Keniston, K. Inborn: An American. In R. W. White (Ed.), *The study of lives*. New York: Atherton, 1963.

Kerlinger, F. N. Draft report of the American Psychological Association Committee on Ethical Standards in Psychological Research: A critical reaction. *American Psychologist*, 1972, *27*, 894–896.

Kerlinger, F. N. *Foundations of behavioral research*. New York: Holt, Rinehart & Winston, 1973.

Kohlberg, L. *Moral judgement interview and procedures for scoring.* Unpublished manuscript, Harvard University, 1977.

Kohlberg, L., & Gilligan, C. The adolescent as a philosopher: The discovery of the self in a postconventional world. *Daedalus,* 1971, *100,* 1051–1086.

Koocher, G. P. Bathroom behavior and human dignity. *Journal of Personality and Social Psychology,* 1977, *35,* 120–121.

Kutner, B., Wilkins, C., & Yarrow, P. R. Verbal attitudes and overt behavior involving racial prejudice. *Journal of Abnormal and Social Psychology,* 1952, *47,* 649–652.

LeUnes, A. D. The developmental psychology library search: Can a nonsense assignment make sense? *Teaching of Psychology,* 1977, *4,* 86.

Levenson, H., Gray, M. J., & Ingram, A. Research methods in personality five years after Carlson's survey. *Personality and Social Psychology Bulletin,* 1976, *2,* 158–161.

Leventhal, H., & Sharp, E. Facial expressions as indicators of distress. In S. S. Tomkins & C. E. Izard (Eds.), *Affect, cognition, and personality.* New York: Springer, 1965, 296–318.

Levin, G. R. *A self-directing guide to the study of child psychology.* Monterey, Calif.: Brooks/Cole, 1973.

Lewin, H. S. Hitler Youth and the Boy Scouts of America: A comparison of aims. *Human Relations,* 1947, *1,* 206–227.

Loevinger, J., & Wessler, R. *Measuring ego development (Vol. 1), Construction and use of a sentence-completion test.* San Francisco: Jossey-Bass, 1970.

Loevinger, J., Wessler, R., & Redmore, C. *Measuring ego development (Vol. 2), Scoring manual for women and girls.* San Francisco: Jossey-Bass, 1970.

Maas, H. S. The role of members in clubs of lower-class and middle-class adolescents. *Child Development,* 1954, *25,* 241–251.

Marcia, J. E. Ego identity scale (ISB), Unpublished scoring manual.

Marcia, J. E. Determination and construct validity of ego identity status. Unpublished doctoral dissertation, Ohio State University, 1964.

Marcia, J. E. Case history of a construct: Ego identity status. In E. Vinacke (Ed.), *Readings in general psychology.* New York: American, 1968.

Marcia, J. E. *Identity status interview.* Unpublished manuscript, 1976.

Marlowe, D., & Crowne, D. P. Social desirability and response to perceived situational demands. *Journal of Consulting Psychology,* 1961, *25,* 109–115.

Marsden, G. Content-analysis studies of therapeutic interviews: 1954 to 1964. *Psychological Bulletin,* 1965, *63,* 298–321.

May, R. Sex differences in fantasy patterns. *Journal of Projective Techniques,* 1966, *30,* 252–259.

Mazlish, B. *In search of Nixon: A psychohistorical inquiry.* New York: Basic Books, 1972.

McClelland, D. C. Some social consequences of achievement motivation. In M. R. Jones (Ed.), *Nebraska symposium on motivation* (Vol. 3). Lincoln, Neb.: University of Nebraska Press, 1955. (a)

McClelland, D. C. *Studies in motivation.* New York: Appleton-Century-Crofts, 1955. (b)

McClelland, D. C. *The achieving society.* New York: Van Nostrand Reinhold, 1961.

McClelland, D. C., Atkinson, J. W., Clark, R. A., & Lowell, E. L. *The achievement motive.* New York: Appleton-Century-Crofts, 1953.

McCord, W., McCord, J., & Howard, A. Familial correlates of aggression in non-delinquent male children. *Journal of Abnormal and Social Psychology,* 1961, *62,* 79–93.

McCurdy, H. G. A study of the novels of Charlotte and Emily Bronte as expressions of their personalities. *Journal of Personality,* 1947, *16,* 109–156.

McGuire, W. J. The yin and yang of progress in social psychology: Seven Koan. *Journal of Personality and Social Psychology,* 1973, *26,* 446–456.

McGurk, H., & Lewis, M. Birth order: A phenomenon in search of an explanation. *Developmental Psychology,* 1972, *7,* 366.

Medley, D. M., & Smith, L. H. *Instructions for recording behavior with Oscar R.* Unpublished manuscript, City University of New York, 1964.

Menges, R. J. Openness and honesty versus coercion and deception in psychological research. *American Psychologist,* 1973, *28,* 1030–1034.

Middlemist, R. D., Knowles, E. S., & Matter, C. F. Personal space invasions in the lavatory: Suggestive evidence for arousal. *Journal of Personality and Social Psychology,* 1976, *33,* 541–546.

Middlemist, R. D., Knowles, E. S., & Matter, C. F. What to do and what to report: A reply to Koocher. *Journal of Personality and Social Psychology,* 1977. *35,* 122–124.

Milgram, S. Behavioral study of obedience. *Journal of Abnormal and Social Psychology,* 1963, *67,* 371–378.

Miller, A. G. Role playing: An alternative to deception? A review of the evidence. *American Psychologist,* 1972, *27,* 623–636.

Mills, J. A procedure for explaining experiments following deception. *Personality and Social Psychology Bulletin,* 1976, *2,* 3–13.

Mirels, H. L. Dimensions of internal versus external control. *Journal of Consulting and Clinical Psychology*, 1970, *34*, 226-228.

Mischel, W. *Personality and assessment.* New York: Wiley, 1968.

Mischel, W. Toward a cognitive social learning reconceptualization of personality. *Psychological Review*, 1973, *80*, 252-283.

Mischel, W. *Introduction to personality* (2nd ed.). New York: Holt, Rinehart & Winston, 1976.

Mitchell, H. E., & Byrne, D. *Minimizing the influence of irrelevant factors in the courtroom: The defendant's character, judge's instructions and authoritarianism.* Paper presented at the meeting of the Midwestern Psychological Association, Cleveland, Ohio, May, 1972.

Morrison, D. E., & Henkel, R. E. (Eds.). *The significance test controversy: A reader.* Chicago: Aldine, 1970.

Murray, H. A. *Explorations in personality.* Fairlawn, N. J.: Oxford University Press, 1938.

Nye, R. D. *Three psychologies: Perspectives from Freud, Skinner, and Rogers* (2nd ed.). Monterey, Calif.: Brooks/Cole, 1981.

Orlofsky, J. E., Marcia, J. E., & Lesser, I. M. Ego identity status and the intimacy versus isolation crisis of young adulthood. *Journal of Personality and Social Psychology*, 1973, *27*, 211-219.

Orne, M. T. On the social psychology of the psychological experiment: With particular reference to demand characteristics and their implications. *American Psychologist*, 1962, *17*, 776-783.

Pervin, L. A. *Personality: Theory, research, and assessment.* New York: Wiley, 1975.

Resnick, J. H., & Schwartz, T. Ethical standards as an independent variable in psychological research. *American Psychologist*, 1973, *28*, 134-139.

Robinson, J. P., & Shaver, P. R. *Measures of social psychological attitudes.* Ann Arbor, Mich.: University of Michigan, Survey Research Center, Institute for Social Research, 1973.

Rogers, C. R., & Dymond, R. F. *Psychotherapy and personality change.* Chicago: University of Chicago Press, 1954.

Rokeach, M. *The open and closed mind.* New York: Basic Books, 1960.

Rosenthal, R. *Experimenter effects in behavioral research* (enlarged ed.). New York: Irvington, 1976.

Rotter, J. B. *Social learning and clinical psychology.* New York. Prentice-Hall, 1954.

Rotter, J. B. Generalized expectancies for internal versus external control of reinforcement. *Psychological Monographs*, 1966, *80* (whole no. 609).

Rotter, J. B. Interpersonal trust, trustworthiness, and gullibility. *American Psychologist*, 1980, *35*, 1-7.

Ruebhausen, O. M., & Brim, O. G., Jr. Privacy and behavioral research. *American Psychologist*, 1966, *21*, 423-437.

Rugg, E. A. *Ethical judgments of social research involving experimental deception.* Doctoral dissertation, George Peabody College for Teachers, 1975.

Rummell, J. F. *An introduction to research procedures in education.* New York: Harper & Row, 1964.

Sahakian, W. S. (Ed.). *Psychology of personality: Readings in theory,* 2nd ed. Chicago: Rand McNally College Publishing, 1974.

Sales, S. M. Economic threat as a determinant of conversion rates in authoritarian and nonauthoritarian churches. *Journal of Personality and Social Psychology*, 1972, *23*, 420-428.

Schachter, S. *The psychology of affiliation.* Palo Alto, Calif.: Stanford University Press, 1959.

Schappe, R. H. The volunteer and the coerced subject. *American Psychologist*, 1972, *27*, 508-509.

Sellitz, C., Wrightsman, L. S., & Cook, S. W. *Research methods in social relations.* New York: Holt, Rinehart & Winston, 1976.

Selman, R. L., & Byrne, D. *Manual for scoring social role-taking stages in moral dilemmas.* Unpublished manuscript, Harvard University, 1972.

Sheridan, C. L. *Fundamentals of experimental psychology.* New York: Holt, Rinehart & Winston, 1976.

Siegel, S. *Nonparametric statistics for the behavioral sciences.* New York: McGraw-Hill, 1956.

Sigusch, V., Schmidt, G., Reinfeld, A., & Wiedemann-Sutor, I. Psychosexual stimulation: Sex differences. *Journal of Sex Research*, 1970, *6*, 10-24.

Simmons, D. D. Development of an objective measure of identity achievement status. *Journal of Projective Techniques and Personality Assessment*, 1970, *34*, 241-244.

Simonton, D. K. Sociocultural context of individual creativity: A transhistorical time-series analysis. *Journal of Personality and Social Psychology*, 1975, *32*, 1119-1133.

Skinner, B. F. *Science and human behavior.* New York: Macmillan, 1953.

Smith, M. B. Some perspectives on ethical/political issues in social science research. *Personality and Social Psychology Bulletin*, 1976, *2*, 445-453.

Steiner, I. D. The evils of research: Or what my mother didn't tell me about the sins of academia. *American Psychologist*, 1972, *27*, 766-768.

Stephenson, W. *The study of behavior: Q-technique and its methodology.* Chicago: University of Chicago Press, 1953.

Sternglanz, S. H., & Serbin, L. A. Sex role stereotyping in children's television programs. *Developmental Psychology*, 1974, *10*, 710-715.

Stewart, A. J., & Winter, D. G. Self-definition and

social definition in women. *Journal of Personality*, 1974, *42*, 238–259.

Stewart, A. J., Winter, D. G., & Jones, A. D. Coding categories for the study of child-rearing from historical sources. *Journal of Interdisciplinary History*, 1975, *4*, 687–701.

Strong, Jr., E. K., *Vocational interests of men and women*. Palo Alto, Calif.: Stanford University Press, 1943.

Sullivan, D. S., & Deiker, T. E. Subject-experimenter perceptions of ethical issues in human research. *American Psychologist*, 1973, *28*, 587–591.

Taylor, J. A. Drive theory and manifest anxiety. *Psychological Bulletin*, 1956, *53*, 303–320.

Tesch, F. E. Debriefing research participants: Though this be method there is madness to it. *Journal of Personality and Social Psychology*, 1977, *35*, 217–224.

Thompson, W. R., & Nishimura, R. Some determinants of friendship. *Journal of Personality*, 1952, *20*, 305–314.

Tozzer, A. M. Biography and biology. In C. Kluckhohn & H. A. Murray (Eds.), *Personality in nature, society, and culture*. New York: Knopf, 1948.

Troll, L. E. *The salience of members of three-generation families for one another*. Paper presented at the American Psychological Association meeting, Honolulu, 1972.

Troll, L. E. *Generational change in women's cognitive and achievement orientation*. Paper presented at the Symposium on the Future of Aging Women, International Gerontological Society, Jerusalem, 1975.

Turner, C. W., Layton, J. F., & Simons, L. S. Naturalistic studies of aggressive behavior: Aggressive stimuli, victim visibility, and horn honking. *Journal of Personality and Social Psychology*, 1975, *31*, 1098–1107.

Walker, H. M. Degrees of freedom. *Journal of Educational Psychology*, 1940, *31*, 253–260.

Webb, E. J., Campbell, D. T., Schwartz, R. D., & Sechrest, L. *Unobtrusive measures: Nonreactive research in the social sciences*. Chicago: Rand McNally, 1966.

Weitzman, L. J., Eifler, D., Hokada, E., & Ross, C. Sex-role socialization in picture books for preschool children. *American Journal of Sociology*, 1972, *77*, 1125–1150.

Wells, W. D., & Lo Sciuto, L. A. Direct observation of purchasing behavior. *Journal of Marketing Research*, 1966, *3*, 227–233.

Weston, P. J., & Mednick, M. T. Race, social class,

and the motive to avoid success in women. *Journal of Cross-Cultural Psychology*, 1970, *1*, 284–291.

White, K. M. Conceptual style and conceptual ability from kindergarten through eighth grade. *Child Development*, 1971, *42*, 1652–1656.

White, R. K. "Black Boy": A value analysis. *Journal of Abnormal and Social Psychology*, 1947, *42*, 440–461.

Whiting, J. W. M., & Child, I. L. *Child training and personality*. New Haven, Conn.: Yale University Press, 1953.

Whyte, Jr., W. H. *The organization man*. New York: Simon & Schuster, 1956.

Wiggins, J. S. *Personality and prediction: Principles of personality assessment*. Reading, Mass.: Addison-Wesley, 1973.

Wilson, D. W., & Donnerstein, E. Legal and ethical aspects of nonreactive social psychological research. *American Psychologist*, 1976, *31*, 765–773.

Wilson, G. T. Case reports and studies: Innovations in the modification of phobic behaviors in two clinical cases. *Behavior Therapy*, 1973, *4*, 426–430.

Winter, D. G. The need for power. In D. C. McClelland & R. S. Steele (Eds.), *Human motivation: A book of readings*. Morristown, N.J.: General Learning Press, 1973. (a)

Winter, D. G. *The power motive*. New York: Free Press, 1973. (b)

Winter, D. G. What makes the candidates run? *Psychology Today*, 1976, *10*(2), 45–49; 92.

Winter, D. G., & Stewart, A. J. Content analysis as a technique for assessing political leaders. In T. Milbrun & M. Hermann (Eds.), *The psychological examination of political leaders*. New York: Free Press, 1977.

Witkin, H. A., Dyk, R. B., Faterson, H. F., Goodenough, D. R., & Karp, S. A. *Psychological differentiation*. New York: Wiley, 1962.

Witkin, H. A., Goodenough, D. R., & Oltman, P. K. Psychological differentiation: Current status. *Journal of Personality and Social Psychology*, 1979, *37*, 1127–1145.

Witkin, H. A., Oltman, P. K., Raskin, E., & Karp, S. A. *Manual for the Embedded Figures Test*. Palo Alto, Calif.: Consulting Psychologists Press, 1971.

Wrightsman, L. S. Wallace supporters and adherence to law and order. *Journal of Personality and Social Psychology*, 1969, *13*, 17–22.

Zucker, R. A., Manosevitz, M., & Lanyon, R. I. Birth order, anxiety, and affiliation during a crisis. *Journal of Personality and Social Psychology*, 1968, *8*, 354–359.

Name Index

Subject Index